This book belongs to

Name: _____

www.math-knots.com

Cover Design by :
Gowri Vemuri

First Edition :
December , 2023

Author :
Gowri Vemuri

Edited by :
Raksha Pothapragada

Questions: mathknots.help@gmail.com

NOTE : CCSSO or NCTM or VDOE is neither affiliated nor sponsors or endorses this product.

Dedication

This book is dedicated to:

My Mom, who is my best critic, guide and supporter.

To what I am today, and what I am going to become tomorrow,

is all because of your blessings, unconditional affection and support.

This book is dedicated to the

strongest women of my life ,

my dearest mom

and

to all those moms in this universe.

G.V.

8 www.math-knots.com | www.a4ace.com

Grade 7
Volume 1
Notes

Integers notes

Integers are a group , or set of numbers that consist of "whole numbers and their opposites"

1. Natural numbers and whole numbers are subset of integers.

2. The set does not include fractions or decimals.

3. The set includes positive and negative numbers.

4. Integers include : $-\infty$..... , -5 , -4 , -3 , -2 , -1 , 0 , 1 , 2 , 3 , 4 , 5 ...... $+\infty$

5. Integers greater than zero are called positive integers.

6. Integers less than zero are called negative integers.

7. Zero is neither negative nor positive.

8. Negative integers are the numbers to the left of 0.
    Example : -5 , -4 , -3

9. Negative numbers have a negative (-) sigh in front of the number.

10. Positive integers are the numbers to the right of 0.

11. Positive numbers do not require the + sign in front.

12. If a number has no sign , it is a positive number.
    Example : 2 , 3 , 4 , 10 , 20

13. Negative numbers are frequently used in measurements.
    Example : To measure temperatures , depth etc
    4^0 C below zero degree celsius is represented as -4^0
    100 ft below sea level is represented as -100 ft.

14. Arrows on a number line represent the numbers continuing for ever.

15. Positive numbers are represented on the right side of zero on the number line.

16. Negative numbers are represented on the left side of zero on the number line.

17. Number are placed at equal intervals on the number line. Not necessarily one unit.

www.math-knots.com | www.a4ace.com

Integers can be represented on a number line as below

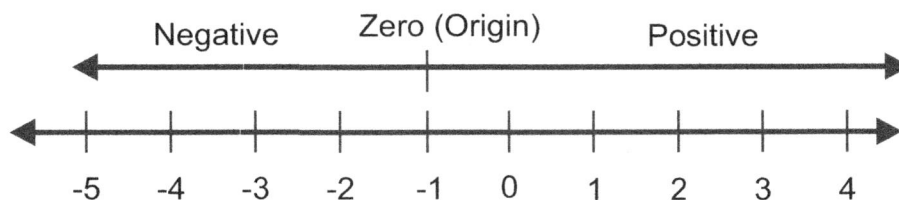

Negative   Zero (Origin)   Positive

-5   -4   -3   -2   -1   0   1   2   3   4

Absolute value :

The number line can be used to find the absolute value. The absolute value of an integer is the distance the number is from zero on the number line.

The absolute value of 2 is 2. Using the number line , 2 is a distance of 2 to the right of zero. The absolute value of -2 is also 2. Again using the number line , the distance from -2 to zero is 2. A measure of distance is always positive.

The symbol for absolute value of any number , x , is | x |.

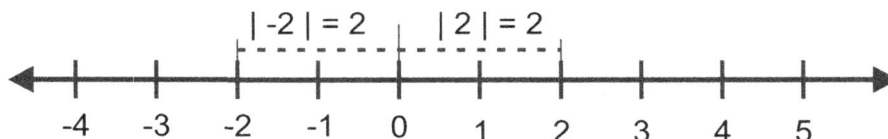

$|-2| = 2$ $|2| = 2$

-4   -3   -2   -1   0   1   2   3   4   5

Opposite integers :

The opposite of an integer is the number that is at the same distance from zero in the opposite direction. Every integer has an opposite value, but the opposite of zero is itself.

The opposite of -4 is 4 because it is located the same distance from zero as 4 is , but in opposite direction.

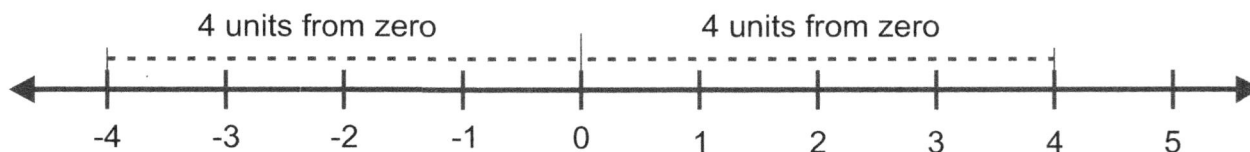

4 units from zero   4 units from zero

-4   -3   -2   -1   0   1   2   3   4   5

                   www.math-knots.com | www.a4ace.com

Integers notes

Integers are a group , or set of numbers that consist of "whole numbers and their opposites"

1. Natural numbers and whole numbers are subset of integers.

2. The set does not include fractions or decimals.

3. The set includes positive and negative numbers.

4. Integers include : $-\infty$..... , -5 , -4 , -3 , -2 , -1 , 0 , 1 , 2 , 3 , 4 , 5 ...... $+\infty$

5. Integers greater than zero are called positive integers.

6. Integers less than zero are called negative integers.

7. Zero is neither negative nor positive.

8. Negative integers are the numbers to the left of 0.
    Example : -5 , -4 , -3

9. Negative numbers have a negative (-) sigh in front of the number.

10. Positive integers are the numbers to the right of 0.

11. Positive numbers do not require the + sign in front.

12. If a number has no sign , it is a positive number.
    Example : 2 , 3 , 4 , 10 , 20

13. Negative numbers are frequently used in measurements.
    Example :   To measure temperatures , depth etc
                 4^0 C below zero degree celsius is represented as -4^0
                 100 ft below sea level is represented as -100 ft.

14. Arrows on a number line represent the numbers continuing for ever.

15. Positive numbers are represented on the right side of zero on the number line.

16. Negative numbers are represented on the left side of zero on the number line.

17. Number are placed at equal intervals on the number line. Not necessarily one unit.

Integers can be represented on a number line as below

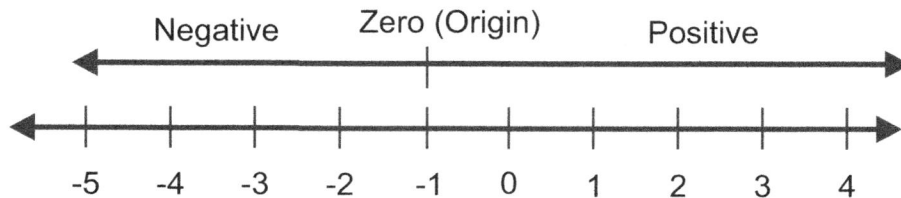

Absolute value :

The number line can be used to find the absolute value. The absolute value of an integer is the distance the number is from zero on the number line.

The absolute value of 2 is 2. Using the number line , 2 is a distance of 2 to the right of zero.The absolute value of -2 is also 2. Again using the number line , the distance from -2 to zero is 2. A measure of distance is always positive.

The symbol for absolute value of any number , x , is | x |.

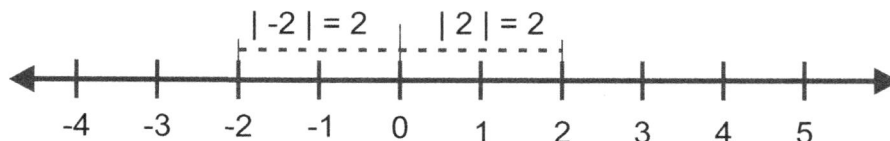

Opposite integers :

The opposite of an integer is the number that is at the same distance from zero in the opposite direction. Every integer has an opposite value, but the opposite of zero is itself.

The opposite of -4 is 4 because it is located the same distance from zero as 4 is , but in opposite direction.

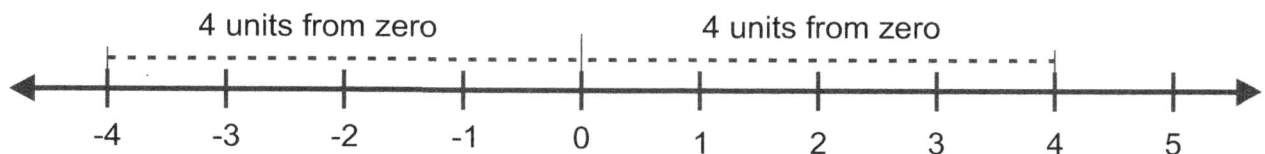

Adding integers using a number line :

The number line is visual representation to understand the addition of positive and negative numbers. Start with the one value on the number line, then add the second value. If the second value (that is added) is positive, we move to the right that many spaces.

If the second value (that is added) is negative, we move to the left that many spaces.
The value where we land on the number line is the solution for the addition of two integers.

Example 1 : (-4) + (5) = 1
Start at the first number, -4, and travel 5 units to the right.

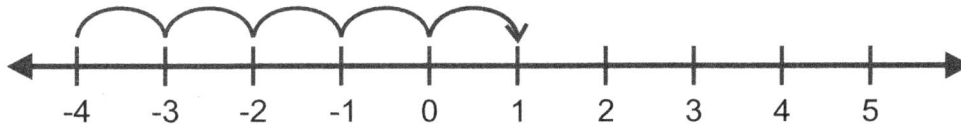

Example 2 : (5) + (-7) = -2
Start at the first number, 5, and travel 7 units to the left.

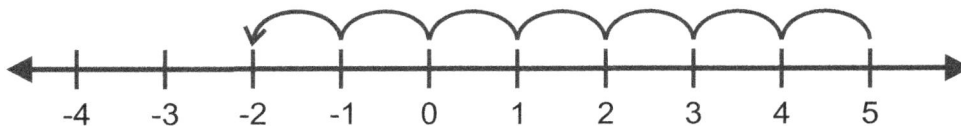

Adding integers using the rules :

Rules for adding integers :

If the signs are the same, add their absolute values, and keep the common sign.

If the signs are different, find the difference between the absolute values of the two numbers, and keep the sign of the number with the greater numerical value.

To the Tune of "Row Your Boat"

Same signs add and keep
Different signs subtract
Keep the sign of the greater digits
then you'll be exact

         www.math-knots.com | www.a4ace.com

Subtacting integers using a number line :

A number line is helpful in understanding subtraction of positive and negative values. Start with the first value on the number line, then subtract the second value. If the second value (that is subtracted) is positive, we move to the left that many spaces.

If the second value (that is subtracted) is negative, we move to the right that many spaces. This is because subtraction a negative is the same as adding.
The value where we end on the number line is the answer.

Example 1 : (-2) + (5) = 3
Start at the first number, -2, and travel 5 units to the right.

Subtacting integers using the rules :

Every subtraction problem can be written as an additional problem. When we subtract two integers, just ADD THE OPPOSITE. Subtracting a positive is the same as adding a negative. Subtracting a negative is the same as adding a positive.

Multiplying Integers :

Multiplying integers is same as multiplying whole numbers, except we must keep track of the signs associated to the numbers.

To multiply signed integers, always multiply the absolute values and use these rules to determine the sign of the product value

When we multiply two integers with the same signs, the result is always a positive value.

Positive number X Positive number = Positive number

Negative number X Negative number = Positive number

When we multiply two integers with different signs, the result is always a negative value.

Positive number X Negative number = Negative number

Negative number X Positive number = Negative number

Positive X Positive :	7 X 6 = 42	negative X negative :	-7 X -6 = 42
Positive X negative :	7 X -6 = -42	negative X Positive :	-7 X 6 = -42

Dividing Integers :

Division of integers is similar to the division of whole numbers, except we must keep track of the signs associated.

To divide signed integers, we must always divide the absolute values and use the below rules to find the quotient value.

When we divide two integers with the same signs, the result is always a positive value.

Positive ÷ Positive = Positive

Negative ÷ Negative = Positive

When we divide two integers with opposite signs, the result is always a negative value.

Positive ÷ Negative = Negative

Negative ÷ Positive = Negative

Examples :

Positive ÷ Positive : $81 \div 9 = 9$ Positive   negative : $81 \div -9 = -9$

negative ÷ negative : $-81 \div -9 = 9$ negative   Positive : $-81 \div 9 = -9$

Golden Rules of Integers :

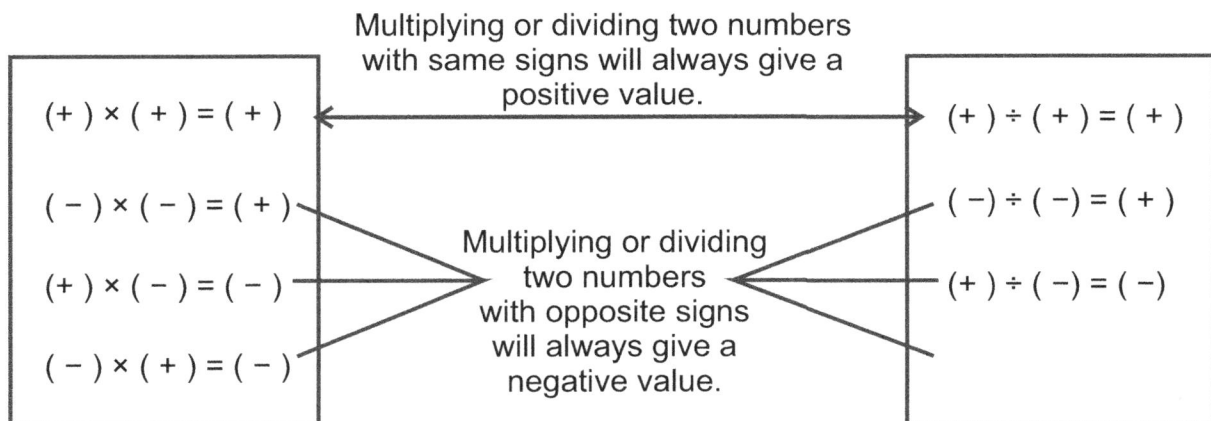

Multiplying or dividing two numbers with same signs will always give a positive value.

$(+) \times (+) = (+)$ $(+) \div (+) = (+)$

$(-) \times (-) = (+)$ $(-) \div (-) = (+)$

Multiplying or dividing two numbers with opposite signs will always give a negative value.

$(+) \times (-) = (-)$ $(+) \div (-) = (-)$

$(-) \times (+) = (-)$

Like Terms :

Two or more terms are said to be alike if they have the same variable and the same degree.
Coefficients of like terms are not necessarily be same.

An expression is in its simplest form when

1.   All like terms are combined.
2.   All parentheses are opened and simplified.

Like Terms can combined by adding or subtracting their coefficients (pay attention to the positive and negative signs of the coefficient and apply rules of adding integers)

Example 1 : -2x + 5x + 7 = 3x + 7

> Note : -2x and 5x are like terms and can be combined using rules of integers

Example 2 : -11y + 5 + 8y - 7 = -3y - 2

> Note : -11y and 8y are like terms and can be combined using rules of integers. 5 and -7 are like terms and can be combined using rules of integers

Example 3 : -12a - 5a + 8 - 3 = -17a + 5

> Note : -12a and -5a are like terms and can be combined using rules of integers. 8 and -3 are like terms and can be combined using rules of integers

Example 4 : -5b + 7 - 3b + 2a - a + 10 = -8b + a + 17

> Note : -5b and -3b are like terms and can be combined using rules of integers. 2a and -a are like terms and can be combined using rules of integers. 7 and 10 are like terms and can be combined using rules of integers.

Distributing with the negative sign :

Remember to apply the integer rules of positive and negative numbers while distributing.

Combining like terms on the opposite side of the equal sign :

When the like terms are on opposite sides, we have to combine like terms by using the inverse operation and by undoing the equation.

Example 5 : -2x + 5 = -7x

$$-2x + 5 = -7x$$
$$+7x \qquad 7x$$
$$\overline{}$$
$$-2x +7x + 5 = -7x+ 7x$$
$$5x + 5 = 0$$

Solving equations using the distributive property :

The number in front of the parentheses needs to be multiplied with every term within the parentheses. After the distribution and opening up the parentheses, combine like terms and solve.

Distributing with the negative sign :

Remember to apply the integer rules of positive and negative numbers while distributing.

+ X + = +
- X - = +
- X + = -
+ X - = -

Example 6 :
(a) $2(5x + 7) = 2(5x) + 2(7) = 10x + 14$
(b) $-7(3a + 8) = (-7)(3a) + (-7)(8) = -21a + (-56) = -21a - 56$
(c) $3(-5b - 2) = (3)(-5b) - (3)(2) = -15b - 6$
(d) $6(-4a + 5) = (6)(-4a) + (6)(5) = -24a + 30$
(e) $4(2a - 8) = (4)(2a) - (4)(8) = 8a - 32$
(f) $-5(a - 7) = (-5)(a) - (-5)(7) = -5a - (-35) = -5a + 35$
(g) $-9(-2a + 10) = (-9)(-2a) + (-9)(10) = 18a + (-90) = 18a - 90$
(h) $-8(-5a - 6) = (-8)(-5a) - (-8)(6) = 40a - (-48) = 40a + 40a$
(i) $-(a + 7) = -a - 7$
(j) $-(x - 5) = (-1)(x) - (-1)(5) = -x - (-5) = -x + 5$
(k) $-(-a - b) = (-1)(-a) - (-1)(b) = a - (-b) = a + b$
(l) $-(-a + 2b) = (-1)(-a) + (-1)(2b) = a + (-2b) = a - 2b$

                   www.math-knots.com | www.a4ace.com

Example 7 : $2x + 3 = x + 7$

$2x + 3 = x + 7$

$\underline{-x \quad - 3 \quad -x \quad -3}$

$x + 0 = 0 + 4$

$x = 4$

Inverse operation for addition is subtraction

Example 8 : $7x + 5 = -3x + 25$

$7x + 5 = -3x + 25$

$\underline{3x \quad -5 \quad 3x \quad \quad -5}$

$10x + 0 = 0 + 20$

$10x = 20$

$\dfrac{10x}{10} = \dfrac{20}{10}^{2}$

Inverse operation for addition is subtraction and vice versa

Inverse operation for multiplication is division

$\boxed{x = 2}$

Example 9 : $\dfrac{2x}{5} + 5 = 15$

$\dfrac{2x}{5} + 5 = 15$

$\underline{\quad\quad\quad -5 \quad -5 \quad}$

$\dfrac{2x}{5} + 0 = 10$

Inverse operation for addition is subtraction and vice versa

$\dfrac{2x}{5} = 10$

$5 \cdot \dfrac{2x}{5} = 5 \cdot 10$

Inverse operation for division is multiplication

$\dfrac{2x}{2} = \dfrac{50}{2}^{25}$

$\boxed{x = 25}$

Inverse operation for multiplication is division

Inequality :

An inequality is a relation between two expressions that are not equal. As a mathematical statement an inequality states one side of the equation is less than, less than or equal to or greater than or greater than equal to the other side.

If the inequality has **less than** or **greater than** symbol,
1.   The graph starts with the open circle.
2.   For less than the graphing line goes toward the left.
3.   For greater than the graphing line goes toward the right.

If the inequality has **less than or equal to** or **greater than or equal** to symbol,
1.   The graph starts with the closed circle.
2.   For less than or equal to the graphing line goes toward the left.
3.   For greater than or equal to the graphing line goes toward the right.

Inequality statement	Inequality verbal expression	Inequality graph
x > -3 or -3 < x	x is greater than -3	
x < 3 or 3 > x	x is less than 3	
x >= -1 or -1 <= x	x is greater than or equal to -1	
x <= 1 or 1 <= x	x is less than or equal to 1	

Basic inequalities :

Solving inequalities is same as solving for an equation except for one special rule.

             www.math-knots.com | www.a4ace.com

Example 10 : x + 9 > 11
Step 1 (subtract 9 from both sides) : x + 9 - 9 > 11 - 9
Step 2 (combine like terms) : x > 2

Example 11 : 2x + 5 > 10
Step 1 (subtract 5 from both sides) : 2x + 5 - 5 > 10 - 5
Step 2 (combine like terms) : 2x > 5
Step 3 (divide both sides by the coefficient of x which is 2) : $\dfrac{\cancel{2}^{1}x}{\cancel{2}_{1}} > \dfrac{5}{2}$

Step 4 (simplify both sides as needed) : $x > \dfrac{5}{2}$

Example 12 : 5x - 1 > 9
Step 1 (add 1 to both sides) : 5x - 1 + 1 > 9 + 1
Step 2 (combine like terms) : 5x > 10
Step 3 (divide both sides by the coefficient of x which is 5) : $\dfrac{\cancel{5}^{1}x}{\cancel{5}_{1}} > \dfrac{10}{5}$

Step 4 (simplify both sides as needed) : $x > 2$

Example 13 : 2x - 8 > -11
Step 1 (add 8 to both sides) : 2x - 8 + 8 > -11 + 8
Step 2 (combine like terms) : 2x > -3
Step 3 (divide both sides by the coefficient of x which is 2) : $\dfrac{\cancel{2}^{1}x}{\cancel{2}_{1}} > \dfrac{-3}{2}$

Step 4 (simplify both sides as needed) : $x > \dfrac{-3}{2}$

Example 14 : -4x + 7 > 10
Step 1 (subtract 7 from both sides) : -4x + 7 - 7 > 10 - 7
Step 2 (combine like terms) : -4x > 3
Step 3 (divide both sides by the coefficient of x which is -4) : $\dfrac{\cancel{-4}^{1}x}{\cancel{-4}_{1}} < \dfrac{3}{-4}$

When an inequality is multiplied or divided with negative number, the inequality changes to the opposite

Step 4 (simplify both sides as needed) : $x < \dfrac{3}{-4}$

$$x < \dfrac{-3}{4}$$

Example 15 : -5x - 1 < -11
Step 1 (add 1 to both sides) : -5x - 1 + 1 < -11 + 1
Step 2 (combine like terms) : -5x < -10
Step 3 (divide both sides by the coefficient of x which is -5) : $\dfrac{\cancel{-5}x}{\cancel{-5}} > \dfrac{\cancel{-10}^{\,2}}{\cancel{-5}}$

> When an inequality is multiplied or divided with negative number, the inequality changes to the opposite

Step 4 (simplify both sides as needed) : x > 2

Example 16 : -8x + 3 < -30
Step 1 (subtract 3 from both sides) : -8x + 3 - 3 < -30 - 3
Step 2 (combine like terms) : -8x < -33
Step 3 (divide both sides by the coefficient of x which is -8) : $\dfrac{\cancel{-8}x}{\cancel{-8}} > \dfrac{-33}{-8}$

Step 4 (simplify both sides as needed) : x > $\dfrac{-33}{-8}$

$$x > \dfrac{33}{8}$$

$$x > 4\dfrac{1}{8}$$

     www.math-knots.com | www.a4ace.com

Average or Mean : It is the sum of all the values divided by the number of values.

To calculate add all the values given which is called as sum. Count how many values are given
Dividing sum by count will give the average or mean value for the given data set.

Median : First arrange all the data points from smallest to largest.
If the data points are odd then median is the middle data point in the given list of values.
If the data points are even then median is the average of the two middle data points in the list.

Mode : Mode is the most repetitive data point in the given set of values.
Sometimes if two or more data points are repetitive equally then mode will have multiple values.
If no data point is repeated then mode equals to zero.

Range : First arrange all data points from smallest to largest, then subtract smallest value from
the largest which equals to range value.

Lower quartile : First arrange all the data points from smallest to largest.
If the data points are odd then median is the middle data point in the given list of values.
If the data points are even then median is the average of the two middle data points in the list.
The middle value from the smallest to the median value is the lower quartile or 1st quartile.
We follow the same process as median to find the lower quartile value.
Lower quartile value is the value under which 25% of data points are found.

Upper quartile : First arrange all the data points from smallest to largest.
If the data points are odd then median is the middle data point in the given list of values.
If the data points are even then median is the average of the two middle data points in the list.
The middle value from the greatest to the median value is the upper quartile or 3rd quartile.
We follow the same process as median to find the upper quartile value.
Upper quartile value is the value under which 75% of data points are found.

Inter quartile : It is a difference between upper quartile and lower quartile values.

       www.math-knots.com | www.a4ace.com

Complementary Angles:

Two angles that add up to 90 degrees are called as Complementary angles.

Example: $\underline{X} + \underline{Y} = 90$

$\underline{X}$ and $\underline{Y}$ are called complementary angles.

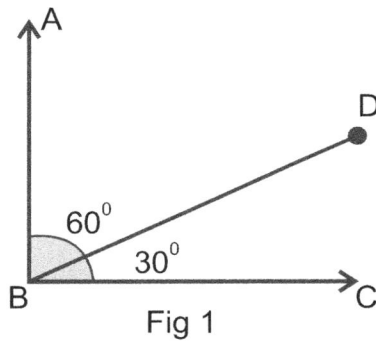

$30^0 + 60^0 = 90^0$
30^0 and 60^0 are complementary angles

Fig 1

Adjacent Angles:

Two angles that have a common side and a common vertex (corner point), and don't overlap are called adjacent angles

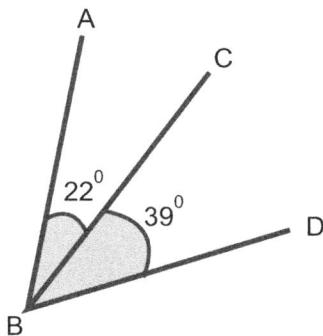

$\underline{|ABC}$ and $\underline{|CBD}$ are called as adjacent angles as they share same vertex B

         www.math-knots.com | www.a4ace.com

Supplementary Angles:

Two angles that add up to 180 degrees are called as supplementary angles.

Example: $\angle a + \angle b = 180$

$\angle a$ and $\angle b$ are called complementary angles.

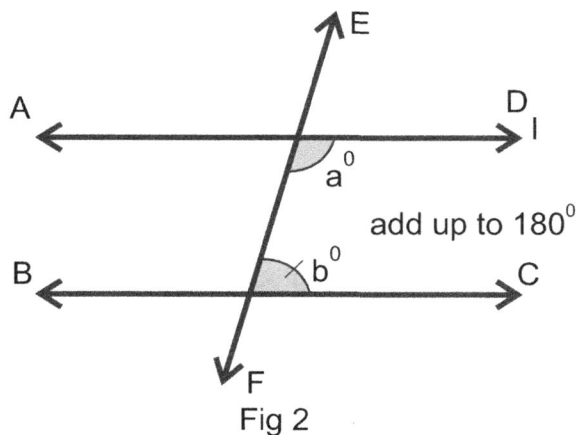
Fig 2

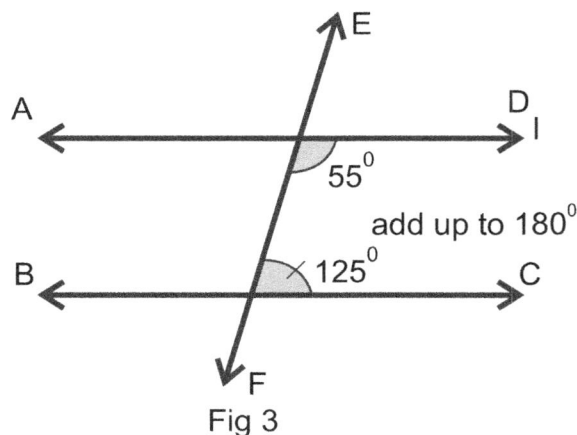
Fig 3

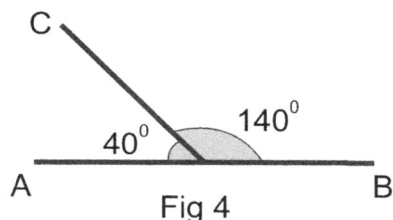
Fig 4

$\angle a + \angle b = 180 \ ; \ 55^0 + 125^0 = 180^0$

55^0 and 125^0 are called as complementary angles

$\angle a + \angle b = 180 \ ; \ 40^0 + 140^0 = 180^0$

40^0 and 140^0 are called as complementary angles

Vertical Angles:

Vertical angles are pairs of opposite angles made by intersecting lines.
If two angles are vertical, then they are congruent.

Example:

$\angle a$ and $\angle b$ are called vertical angles
$\angle a = \angle b$

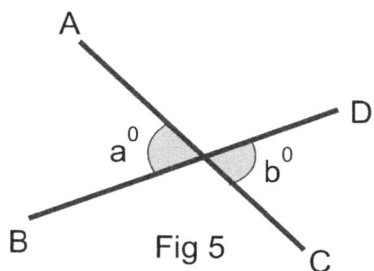
Fig 5

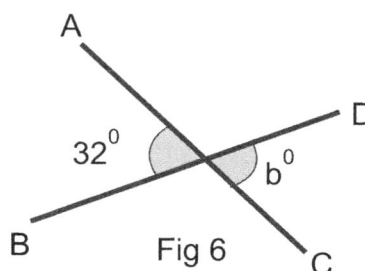
Fig 6

$\angle a$ and $\angle b$ are called vertical angles and vertical angles are equal to each other.
In Fig 6 based on the rule of the vertical angles $\angle b = 32^0$

www.math-knots.com | www.a4ace.com

Corresponding Angles

When two lines are crossed by another line (Transversal), the angles in matching corners are called as corresponding angles. A pair of angles each of which is on the same side of one of two lines cut by a transversal and on the same side of the transversal

The angles which occupy the same relative position at each intersection where a straight line crosses two others. If the two lines are parallel, the corresponding angles are equal.

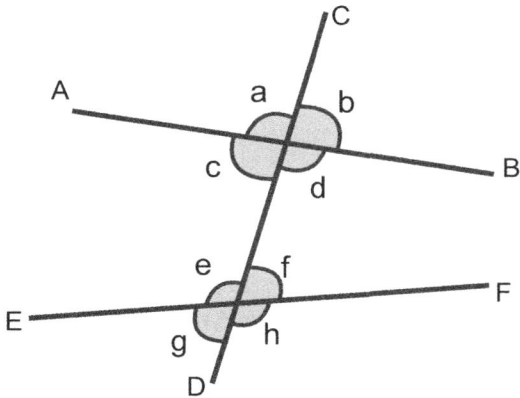

Fig 8

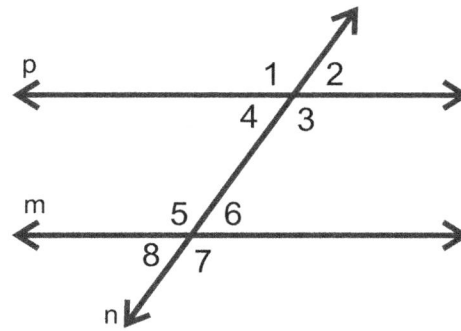

Fig 9

In Fig 8, $\overline{AB}$ and $\overline{EF}$ **are not parallel**, the corresponding angles ∟a and ∟e ; ∟c and ∟g ;∟b and∟f ;∟d and∟h are **not equal**.

In Fig 9,Lines p and m **are parallel**, the corresponding angles ∟1 and ∟5 ; ∟4 and ∟8 ; ∟2 and∟6 ;∟3 and∟7 **are equal**.

Alternate Angles

Two angles, not adjoining one another, that are formed on opposite sides of a line that intersects two other lines. If the original two lines are parallel, the alternate angles are equal.
one of a pair of angles with different vertices and on opposite sides of a transversal at its intersection with two other lines:

1. Alternate Interior Angles are a pair of angles on the inner side (inside) of each of those two intersected lines but on opposite sides of the transversal. If two parallel lines are cut by a transversal, the alternate interior angles are congruent Examples of Alternate Interior Angles In the figure shown, I is the transversal that cut the pair of lines. Angles 3 and 4 and angles 1 and 2 are alternate interior angles.

Alternate Exterior Angles are a pair of angles on the outer side (outside) of each of those two intersected lines but on opposite sides of the transversal.

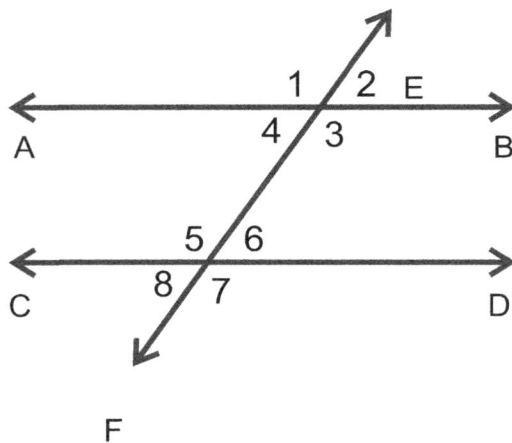

∣3 , ∣4 , ∣5 , ∣6   Interior Angles

∣1 , ∣2 , ∣7 , ∣8   Exterior Angles

∣4 , ∣5
∣3 , ∣6 } Alternate Interior Angles

∣1 , ∣8
∣2 , ∣7 } Alternate Exterior Angles

∣1 , ∣5
∣2 , ∣6
∣3 , ∣7
∣4 , ∣8 } Corresponding Angles

Fig 10

Area of a triangle

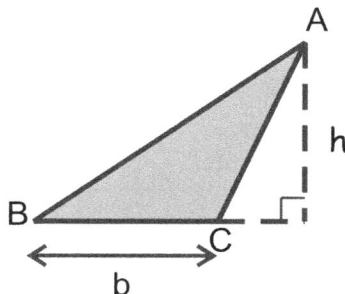

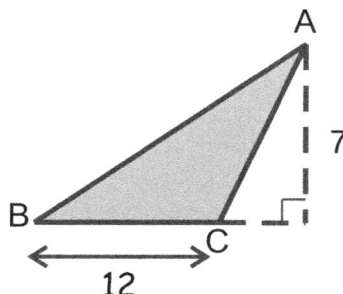

$$A = \frac{1}{2}bh$$

A = Area of the triangle
b = length of the base
h = height

$$A = \frac{1}{2}bh$$

$$A = \frac{1}{2} \times (12)(7)$$

$$= (6)(7)$$

$$= 42 \text{ sq. units}$$

Perimeter of a triangle :

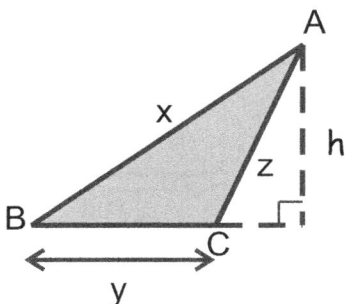

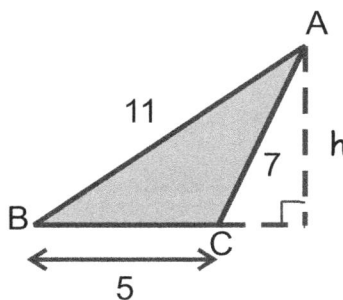

P = x + y + z
P = Perimeter
x, y, z are lengths of
the sides of the triangle

P = x + y + z
P = 11 + 5 + 7
P = 23 units

Perimeter and Area of a Square

$P = 4s$

$A = s^2$

P = Perimeter
A = Area
s = Length of the
side of the square

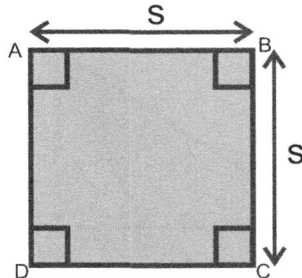

$P = 4s$

$A = s^2$

$P = 4s$
$P = 4 \times 10$
$P = 40$ units

$A = s^2$

$A = 10^2$

$A = 100$ sq.units

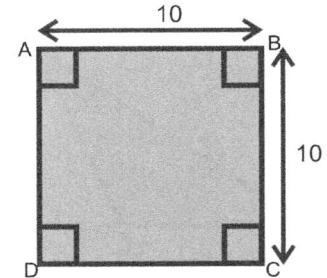

Perimeter and Area of a Rectangle

$A = l \times b$

$P = 2(l + b)$
A = Area
P = Perimeter
l = length of the rectangle
b = width of the rectangle

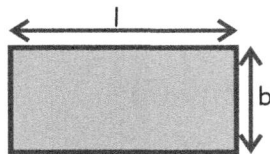

$A = 8 \times 4$
$A = 32$ sq.cm

$P = 2(8 + 4)$
$P = 2(12)$
$P = 24$ cm

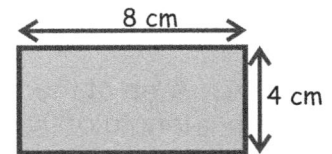

Area of a Trapezium

$A = \frac{1}{2} h(b_1 + b_2)$

A = Area
b_1, b_2 are the lengths of
parallel sides
h = Distance between
the parallel sides

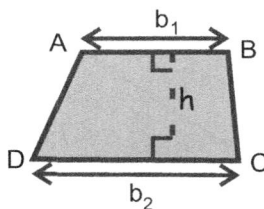

$A = \frac{1}{2} h(b_1 + b_2)$

$A = \frac{1}{2} 4(11 + 5)$

$A = 2(16)$

$A = 32$ sq.ft

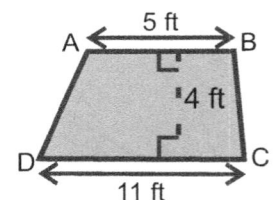

Perimeter of a Trapezium

$P = b_1 + b_2 + b_3 + b_4$
P = Perimeter
b_1, b_2 are the lengths
of parallel sides
b_3, b_4 are the lengths
of non parallel sides

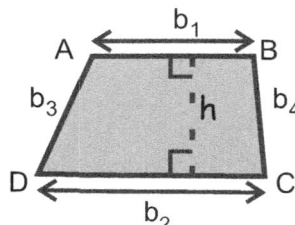

$P = b_1 + b_2 + b_3 + b_4$

$P = 5 + 11 + 7 + 6$

$P = 29$ ft

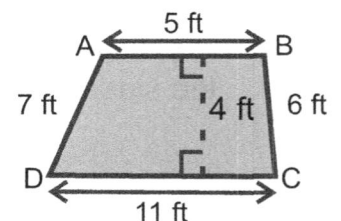

Area of a parellelogram

A = bh

A = Area

b = base

h = Height

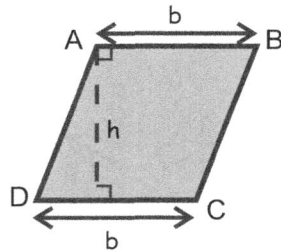

A = bh

A = 5 X 7
A = 45 sq. cm

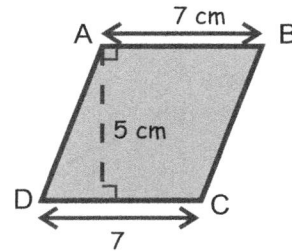

Perimeter of a parellelogram

P = a + a + b + b
  = 2(a + b)

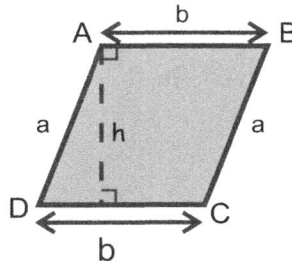

P = 6 + 6 + 7 + 7
  = 2(6 + 7)
  = 2(13)
  = 26 cm

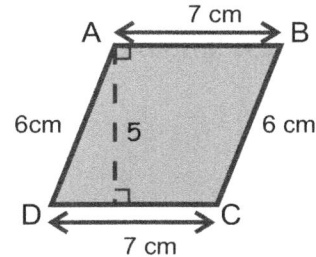

Circumference and Area of a Circle

$C = 2\Pi r$

$A = \Pi r^2$

   pi

$\Pi = 3.14$

$\Pi = \dfrac{22}{7}$

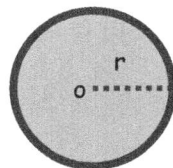

C = Circumference of the circle

A = Area of the circle
r = radius

Note : Diameter(d) = 2r

$C = 2\Pi r$

C = 2 X 3.14 X 5

C = 10 X 3.14

C = 31.4 cm
A = 3.14 X 5 X 5
A = 3.14 X 25
A = 78.5 sq.cm

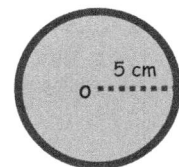

Diameter(d) = 14 cm

Radius $= \dfrac{14}{2}$

Radius = 7 cm

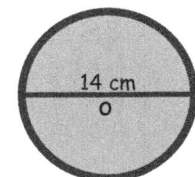

C = 2 X 3.14 X 7

C = 14 X 3.14

C = 43.86cm

A = 3.14 X 7 X 7
A = 3.14 X 49
A = 153.86 sq.cm

www.math-knots.com | www.a4ace.com

Volume of a Cube

$V = s^3$
V = Volume
s = Side length
of the cube

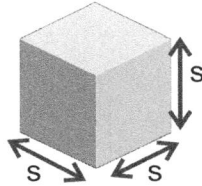

$V = s^3$
$V = 4^3$
$V = 64 \text{ ft}^3$

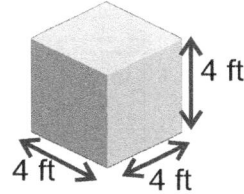

Surface area of a Cube

$T.S.A = 6s^2$
$T.S.A$ = Total surface area
s = Side length of the cube

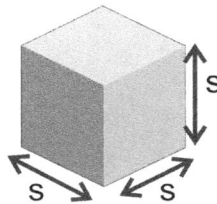

$T.S.A = 6s^2$
$T.S.A = 6 \times 4^2$
$T.S.A = 96 \text{ ft}^2$

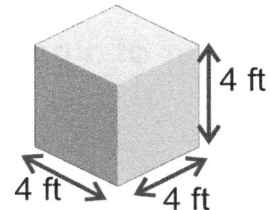

Volume of a Cuboid

$V = lwh$
V = Volume
l = Length
w = Width or breadth
h = Height

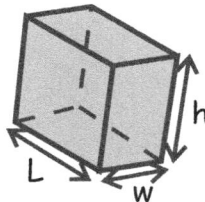

$V = lwh$
$V = 5 \times 3 \times 6$
$V = 90 \text{ ft}^3$

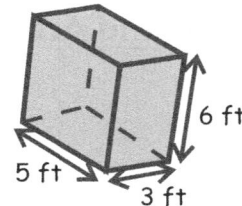

Surface area of a Cuboid

$T.S.A = 2(lw + lh + wh)$
$T.S.A$ = Total surface area
l = Length
w = Width or breadth
h = Height

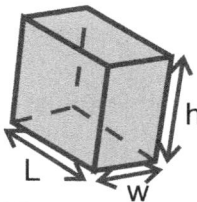

$L.S.A = 2(lh + wh)$
$L.S.A$ = Lateral surface area
l = Length
w = Width or breadth
h = Height

$T.S.A = 2(lw + lh + wh)$

$T.S.A = 2(5 \times 3 + 5 \times 6 + 3 \times 6)$

$T.S.A = 126 \text{ ft}^2$

$L.S.A = 2(lh + wh)$

$L.S.A = 2(5 \times 6 + 3 \times 6)$

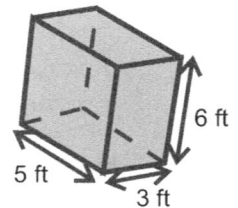

$L.S.A = 96 \text{ ft}^2$

www.math-knots.com | www.a4ace.com

Base surface area of a square Pyramid

$$B.S.A = a^2$$

$$T.S.A = a^2 + a \times \sqrt{a^2 + 4h^2}$$

B.S.A = Base surface area
T.S.A = Total surface area
T.S.A = B.S.A + L.S.A

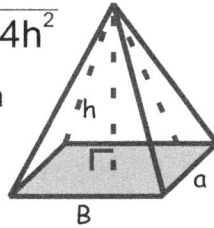

$$B.S.A = 5 \times 5$$
$$B.S.A = 25 \text{ in}^2$$

$$T.S.A = 5^2 + 5 \times \sqrt{5^2 + 4 \times 6^2}$$

$$T.S.A = 25 + 65$$

$$T.S.A = 90 \text{ in}^2$$

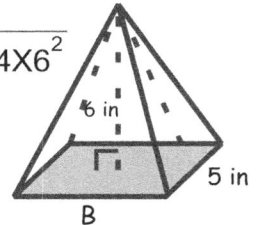

Volume of a square Pyramid

$$V = \frac{1}{3} B h$$

V = Volume
B = Base area
h = Height

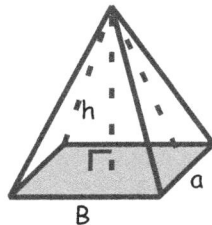

$$V = \frac{1}{3} a^2 h$$

V = Volume
a = side length
h = Height

$$V = \frac{1}{3} a^2 h$$

$$V = \frac{1}{3} \times 5^2 \times 6$$

$$V = \frac{1}{3} \times 150$$

$$V = 50 \text{ in}^3$$

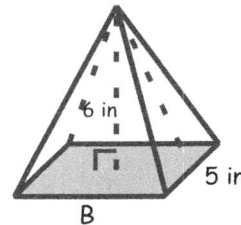

Lateral surface area of a square Pyramid

$$S.\,A = a \times \sqrt{a^2 + 4h^2}$$

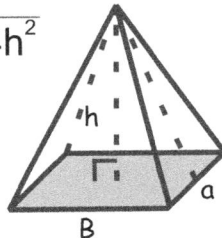

$$S.\,A = a \times \sqrt{a^2 + 4h^2}$$

$$S.A = 5 \times \sqrt{5^2 + 4 \times 6^2}$$

$$S.A = 65 \text{ in}^2$$

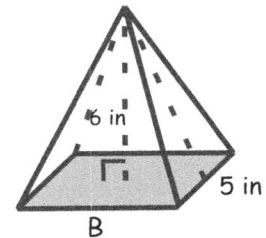

www.math-knots.com | www.a4ace.com

Abbreviations

milligram	mg	volume	V
gram	g	total Square Area	S.A
kilogram	kg	area of base	B
milliliter	mL	ounce	oz
liter	L	pound	lb
kiloliter	kL	quart	qt
millimeter	mm	gallon	gal.
centimeter	cm	inches	in.
meter	m	foot	ft
kilometer	km	yard	yd
square centimeter	cm^2	mile	mi.
cubic centimeter	cm^3	square inch	sq in.
		square foot	sq ft
		cubic inch	cu in.
		cubic foot	cu ft

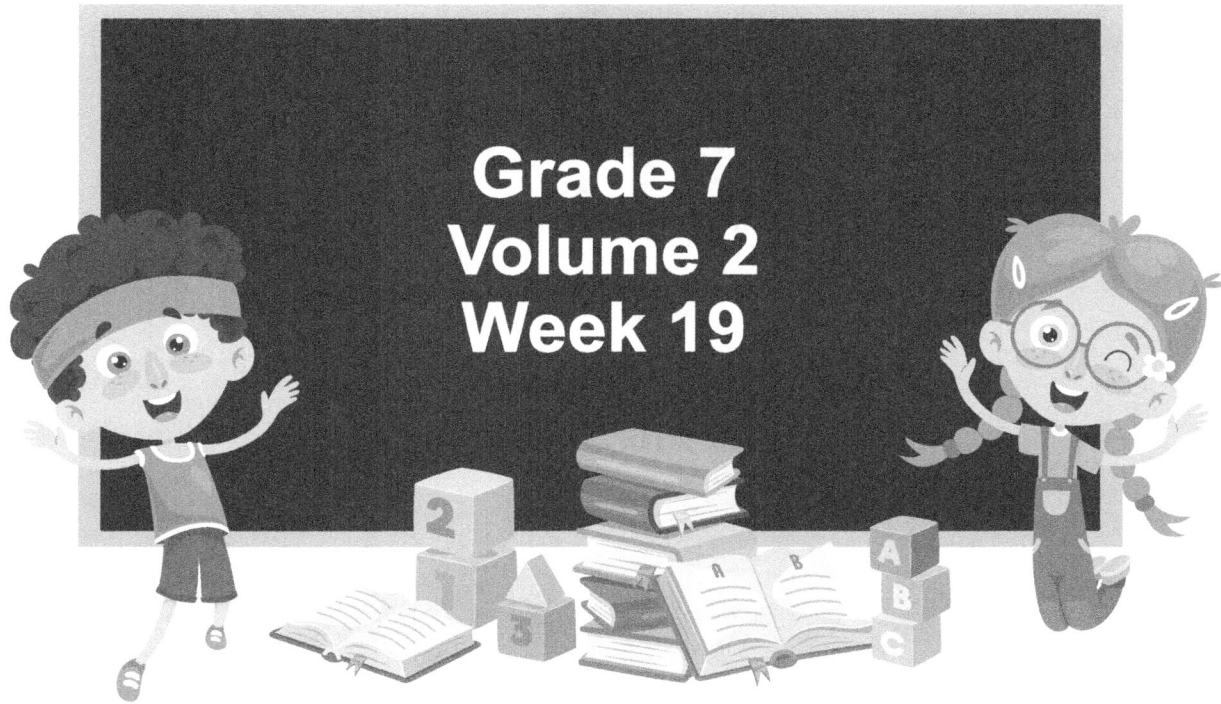

1) Solve the below given equation

$$x + 20 = 63$$

2) Solve the below given equation

$$8 - b = -8$$

3) Solve the below given equation

$$m + 41 = 57$$

4) Solve the below given equation

$$x + 8 = 31$$

5) Solve the below given equation

$$33 = p + 25$$

6) Solve the below given equation

$$n + 23 = 62$$

7) Solve the below given equation

$$m + 20 = -28$$

8) Solve the below given equation

$$-19 = k + 10$$

9) Solve the below given equation

$$15 = b + 38$$

13) Solve the below given equation

$$n + 32 = 27$$

10) Solve the below given equation

$$x - 23 = -6$$

14) Solve the below given equation

$$m - 20 = -70$$

11) Solve the below given equation

$$x + 30 = 9$$

15) Solve the below given equation

$$88 = a + 42$$

12) Solve the below given equation

$$x - 1 = -47$$

16) Solve the below given equation

$$v - 41 = -25$$

17) Solve the below given equation

$$-7 = x - 15$$

18) Solve the below given equation

$$-1 = x + 13$$

19) Solve the below given equation

$$-38 = p - 4$$

20) Solve the below given equation

$$k - 7 = 31$$

21) Solve the below given equation

$$-6 = -37 - n$$

22) Solve the below given equation

$$40 - r = 13$$

23) Solve the below given equation

$$-37 = x + 8$$

24) Solve the below given equation

$$35 = 1 + b$$

25) Solve the below given equation

$$-36 = a - 18$$

29) Solve the below given equation

$$6 = n - 31$$

26) Solve the below given equation

$$-47 + b = -35$$

30) Solve the below given equation

$$x - 47 = -87$$

27) Solve the below given equation

$$-56 = r - 39$$

31) Solve the below given equation

$$p - 24 = -72$$

28) Solve the below given equation

$$47 = k + 31$$

32) Solve the below given equation

$$n - 41 = -81$$

33) Solve the below given equation

$$-4 = n + 3$$

37) Solve the below given equation

$$b - 9 = 37$$

34) Solve the below given equation

$$-18 = 11 + m$$

38) Solve the below given equation

$$-7 + n = -28$$

35) Solve the below given equation

$$x - 29 = -57$$

39) Solve the below given equation

$$-64 = m - 39$$

36) Solve the below given equation

$$x - 43 = -80$$

40) Solve the below given equation

$$30 = n - 12$$

     www.math-knots.com | www.a4ace.com

41) Solve the below given equation

$$m - (-50) = 7$$

45) Solve the below given equation

$$x + 34 = 16$$

42) Solve the below given equation

$$x - (-36) = 83$$

46) Solve the below given equation

$$b - 15 = -52$$

43) Solve the below given equation

$$n - 13 = -51$$

47) Solve the below given equation

$$-8 = n - 28$$

44) Solve the below given equation

$$r + 43 = -7$$

48) Solve the below given equation

$$95 = v + 45$$

49) Solve the below given equation

$$23 = x - (-41)$$

53) Solve the below given equation

$$-37 = m - (-3)$$

50) Solve the below given equation

$$x - 49 = -1$$

54) Solve the below given equation

$$x - (-10) = 3$$

51) Solve the below given equation

$$3 + x = 46$$

55) Solve the below given equation

$$53 = 37 + k$$

52) Solve the below given equation

$$x + 43 = 50$$

56) Solve the below given equation

$$21 = k - 7$$

33   www.math-knots.com | www.a4ace.com

57) Solve the below given equation

$$m + 35 = 36$$

58) Solve the below given equation

$$p - 9 = 22$$

59) Solve the below given equation

$$-65 = v - 39$$

60) Solve the below given equation

$$-67 = n + (-38)$$

61) Solve the below given equation

$$-15 = v + 7$$

62) Solve the below given equation

$$21 = n - (-35)$$

63) Solve the below given equation

$$13 = m + (-7)$$

64) Solve the below given equation

$$r - 3 = -18$$

                                       www.math-knots.com | www.a4ace.com

65) Solve the below given equation

$$13 + v = 40$$

66) Solve the below given equation

$$-55 = n - 32$$

67) Solve the below given equation

$$n + (-8) = 1$$

68) Solve the below given equation

$$50 = x + 22$$

69) Solve the below given equation

$$k + (-11) = -33$$

70) Solve the below given equation

$$p + (-2) = 32$$

71) Solve the below given equation

$$-3 = n - 32$$

72) Solve the below given equation

$$n + 7 = 12$$

73) Solve the below given equation

$$2 = r - 46$$

77) Solve the below given equation

$$a + (-38) = -17$$

74) Solve the below given equation

$$k - 6 = -11$$

78) Solve the below given equation

$$m + (-26) = -69$$

75) Solve the below given equation

$$-41 = x - 41$$

79) Solve the below given equation

$$b + 34 = 9$$

76) Solve the below given equation

$$-12 = 12 + k$$

80) Solve the below given equation

$$v - 32 = -18$$

81) Solve the below given equation

$$34\,m = 952$$

82) Solve the below given equation

$$-816 = -17\,m$$

83) Solve the below given equation

$$-30 = \frac{b}{34}$$

84) Solve the below given equation

$$-517 = 11\,a$$

85) Solve the below given equation

$$\frac{32}{13} = \frac{n}{13}$$

86) Solve the below given equation

$$\frac{x}{27} = -18$$

87) Solve the below given equation

$$-14 = \frac{n}{5}$$

88) Solve the below given equation

$$-13\,x = -52$$

89) Solve the below given equation

$$-920 = 20\,n$$

90) Solve the below given equation

$$24 = -6\,a$$

91) Solve the below given equation

$$\frac{r}{28} = \frac{43}{28}$$

92) Solve the below given equation

$$-23 = \frac{v}{23}$$

93) Solve the below given equation

$$\frac{x}{10} = 23$$

94) Solve the below given equation

$$-50\,p = 2000$$

95) Solve the below given equation

$$-\frac{19}{12} = \frac{n}{24}$$

96) Solve the below given equation

$$-47 = \frac{n}{30}$$

97) Solve the below given equation

$$\frac{n}{11} = -\frac{46}{11}$$

98) Solve the below given equation

$$45k = -1575$$

99) Solve the below given equation

$$205 = 5v$$

100) Solve the below given equation

$$-\frac{50}{13} = \frac{x}{13}$$

101) Solve the below given equation

$$-24 = \frac{b}{44}$$

102) Solve the below given equation

$$\frac{v}{36} = 45$$

103) Solve the below given equation

$$41 = \frac{x}{15}$$

104) Solve the below given equation

$$\frac{a}{13} = -33$$

www.math-knots.com | www.a4ace.com

105) Solve the below given equation

$$-35r = -1645$$

109) Solve the below given equation

$$36 = \frac{n}{36}$$

106) Solve the below given equation

$$42 = \frac{x}{37}$$

110) Solve the below given equation

$$-\frac{4}{37} = \frac{x}{37}$$

107) Solve the below given equation

$$\frac{a}{36} = 16$$

111) Solve the below given equation

$$45r = -360$$

108) Solve the below given equation

$$-225 = -9n$$

112) Solve the below given equation

$$-46 = \frac{k}{39}$$

www.math-knots.com | www.a4ace.com

113) Solve the below given equation

$$300 = -10\,n$$

117) Solve the below given equation

$$-63 = -7b$$

114) Solve the below given equation

$$39 = \frac{r}{29}$$

118) Solve the below given equation

$$-9\,r = 126$$

115) Solve the below given equation

$$9\,n = -18$$

119) Solve the below given equation

$$\frac{b}{47} = 27$$

116) Solve the below given equation

$$26 = \frac{k}{23}$$

120) Solve the below given equation

$$\frac{x}{37} = 24$$

www.math-knots.com | www.a4ace.com

121) Solve the below given equation

$$-\frac{31}{42} = \frac{p}{42}$$

122) Solve the below given equation

$$9\,n = 72$$

123) Solve the below given equation

$$1020 = 34\,n$$

124) Solve the below given equation

$$\frac{p}{16} = 14$$

125) Solve the below given equation

$$216 = -12\,n$$

126) Solve the below given equation

$$-288 = 24\,x$$

127) Solve the below given equation

$$\frac{a}{38} = -\frac{23}{19}$$

128) Solve the below given equation

$$\frac{n}{16} = 31$$

www.math-knots.com | www.a4ace.com

129) Solve the below given equation

$$\frac{n}{34} = 30$$

133) Solve the below given equation

$$-2k = -80$$

130) Solve the below given equation

$$\frac{m}{40} = \frac{29}{40}$$

134) Solve the below given equation

$$1225 = -35a$$

131) Solve the below given equation

$$\frac{49}{36} = \frac{b}{36}$$

135) Solve the below given equation

$$-336 = -21n$$

132) Solve the below given equation

$$\frac{x}{5} = -42$$

136) Solve the below given equation

$$-22n = 858$$

       www.math-knots.com | www.a4ace.com

137) Solve the below given equation

$$28\,k = -476$$

141) Solve the below given equation

$$-48\,x = -96$$

138) Solve the below given equation

$$784 = -49\,b$$

142) Solve the below given equation

$$\frac{v}{5} = -45$$

139) Solve the below given equation

$$|p| = 34$$

143) Solve the below given equation

$$|n| = 19$$

140) Solve the below given equation

$$|p| = 5$$

144) Solve the below given equation

$$|k| = 10$$

 www.math-knots.com | www.a4ace.com

145) Solve the below given equation

$$|x| = 28$$

149) Solve the below given equation

$$|m| = 16$$

146) Solve the below given equation

$$|x| = 13$$

150) Solve the below given equation

$$|v| = 12$$

147) Solve the below given equation

$$|v| = 3$$

151) Solve the below given equation

$$|k| = 8$$

148) Solve the below given equation

$$|x| = 15$$

152) Solve the below given equation

$$|b| = 6$$

153) Solve the below given equation

$$|x| = 14$$

154) Solve the below given equation

$$|x| = 31$$

155) Solve the below given equation

$$-4|n| = -16$$

156) Solve the below given equation

$$\frac{|v|}{9} = 4$$

157) Solve the below given equation

$$|b| = 25$$

158) Solve the below given equation

$$2|x| = 12$$

159) Solve the below given equation

$$11|p| = 176$$

160) Solve the below given equation

$$|r| + 18 = 25$$

161) Solve the below given equation

$$18|x| = 324$$

162) Solve the below given equation

$$\frac{|n|}{12} = 8$$

163) Solve the below given equation

$$-12 + |x| = 5$$

164) Solve the below given equation

$$|x| - 6 = -5$$

165) Solve the below given equation

$$|b| + 17 = 25$$

166) Solve the below given equation

$$16 + |a| = 26$$

167) Solve the below given equation

$$|n| - 7 = 10$$

168) Solve the below given equation

$$12|p| = 216$$

169) Solve the below given equation

$$11\left|a\right| = 132$$

170) Solve the below given equation

$$\frac{\left|n\right|}{17} = 10$$

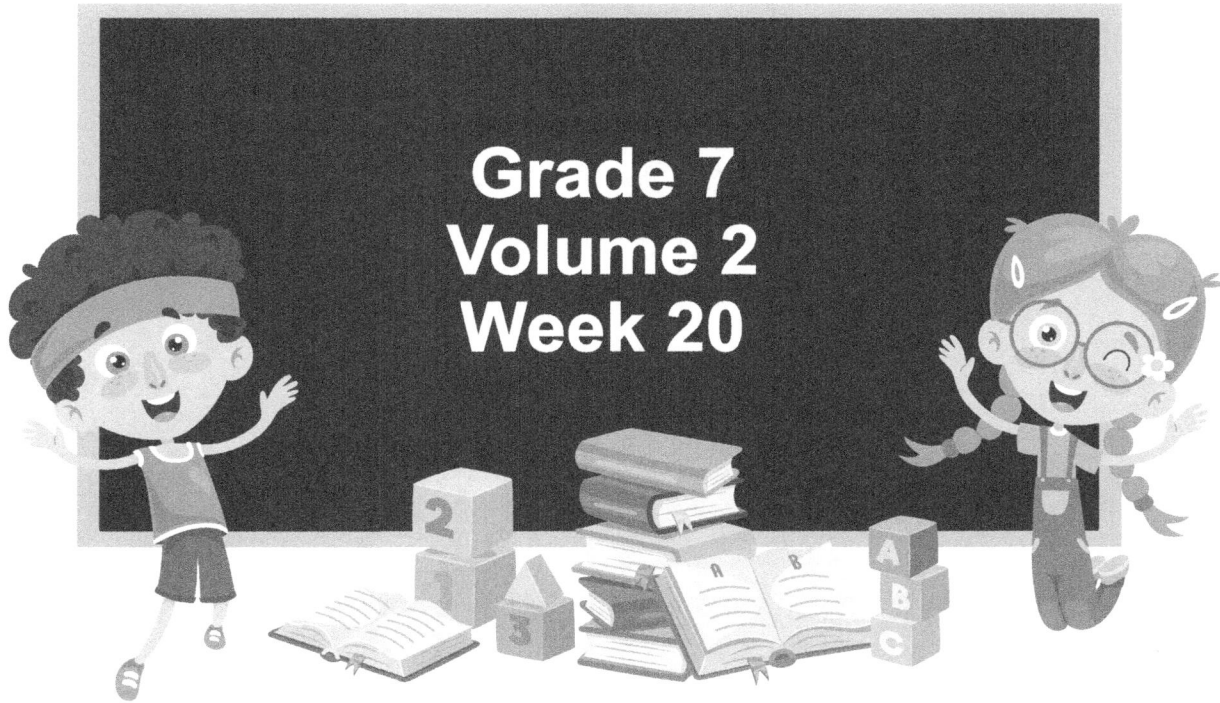

Grade 7
Volume 2
Week 20

www.math-knots.com | www.a4ace.com

50   www.math-knots.com | www.a4ace.com

1) Graph the below inequality.

$$0 \geq x$$

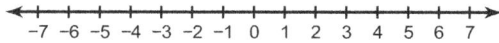

5) Graph the below inequality.

$$-1 > m$$

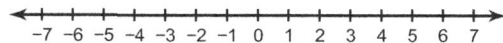

2) Graph the below inequality.

$$6 \leq -n$$

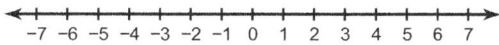

6) Graph the below inequality.

$$-n \leq -5$$

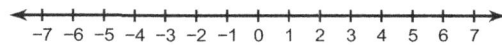

3) Graph the below inequality.

$$3 < -m$$

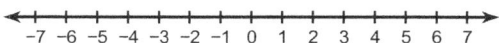

7) Graph the below inequality.

$$-m \geq 4$$

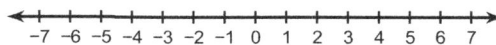

4) Graph the below inequality.

$$-n > -5$$

8) Graph the below inequality.

$$2 < -x$$

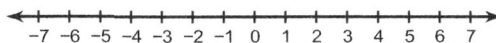

www.math-knots.com | www.a4ace.com

9) Graph the below inequality.

$$-n \leq -1$$

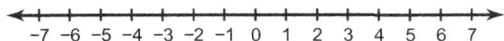

10) Graph the below inequality.

$$2 \geq x$$

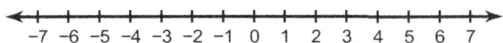

11) Graph the below inequality.

$$x \leq -5$$

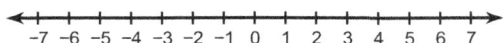

12) Graph the below inequality.

$$-a \geq 5$$

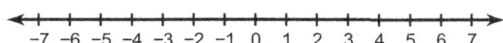

13) Graph the below inequality.

$$-3 \leq -k$$

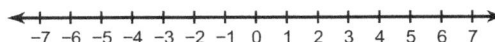

14) Graph the below inequality.

$$x > -3$$

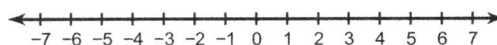

15) Graph the below inequality.

$$m < 0$$

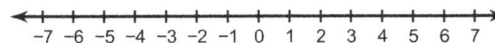

16) Graph the below inequality.

$$x \geq 4$$

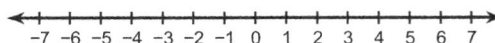

www.math-knots.com | www.a4ace.com

17) Graph the below inequality.

$$-3 > -v$$

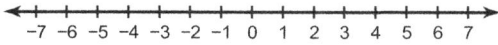

18) Graph the below inequality.

$$-4 > n$$

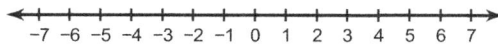

19) Graph the below inequality.

$$a \leq -6$$

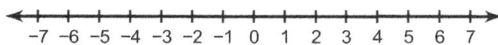

20) Graph the below inequality.

$$-r \geq 1$$

21) Graph the below inequality.

$$-6 < n$$

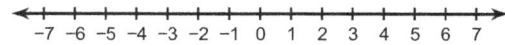

22) Graph the below inequality.

$$n \leq -1$$

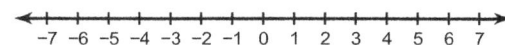

23) Graph the below inequality.

$$-n \leq -2$$

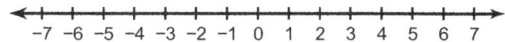

24) Graph the below inequality.

$$-r \leq 5$$

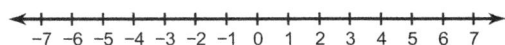

www.math-knots.com | www.a4ace.com

25) Graph the below inequality.

$$x < 5$$

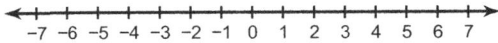

26) Graph the below inequality.

$$n > 2$$

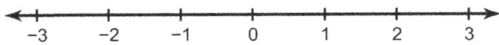

27) Graph the below inequality.

$$-2\frac{1}{2} \leq n$$

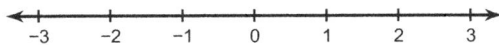

28) Graph the below inequality.

$$2 \leq n$$

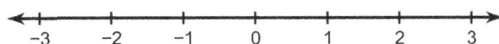

29) Graph the below inequality.

$$-m > -2\frac{1}{2}$$

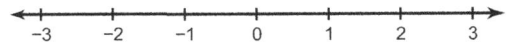

30) Graph the below inequality.

$$2\frac{1}{2} > n$$

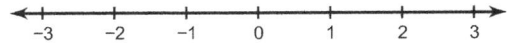

31) Graph the below inequality.

$$-k < 0$$

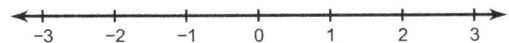

32) Graph the below inequality.

$$\frac{3}{2} > -n$$

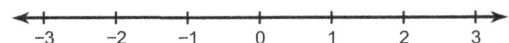

www.math-knots.com | www.a4ace.com

33) Graph the below inequality.

$$\frac{1}{2} > n$$

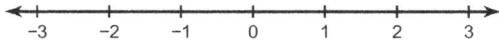

34) Graph the below inequality.

$$x \geq -1\frac{1}{2}$$

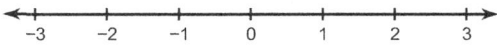

35) Graph the below inequality.

$$\frac{3}{2} < -x$$

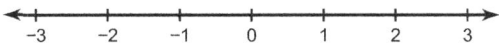

36) Graph the below inequality.

$$-p \geq \frac{1}{2}$$

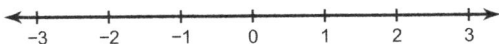

37) Graph the below inequality.

$$-r \leq 1\frac{1}{2}$$

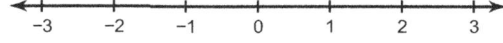

38) Graph the below inequality.

$$-1 > v$$

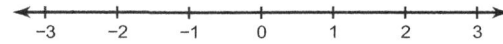

39) Graph the below inequality.

$$-2 > -a$$

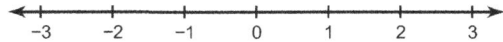

40) Graph the below inequality.

$$-k \leq -1\frac{1}{2}$$

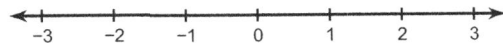

       www.math-knots.com | www.a4ace.com

41) Graph the below inequality.

$$-n \leq \frac{1}{2}$$

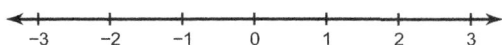

42) Graph the below inequality.

$$-n \leq 1$$

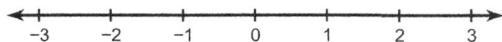

43) Graph the below inequality.

$$n \leq -2\frac{1}{2}$$

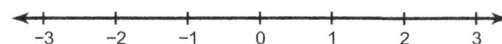

44) Choose the inequality from the given options for the below graph.

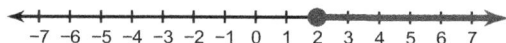

A) $x > -2$ B) $x \leq 2$

C) $x < -2$ D) $x \geq 2$

45) Graph the below inequality.

$$-r \geq -\frac{3}{2}$$

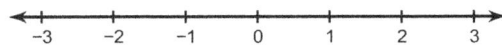

46) Graph the below inequality.

$$x \geq 2$$

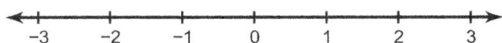

47) Choose the inequality from the given options for the below graph.

A) $n \geq -4$ B) $n < -4$

C) $n \leq -4$ D) $n > -4$

48) Choose the inequality from the given options for the below graph.

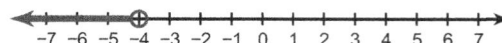

A) $b < -4$ B) $b > 4$

C) $b > -4$ D) $b \leq -4$

www.math-knots.com | www.a4ace.com

49) Choose the inequality from the given options for the below graph.

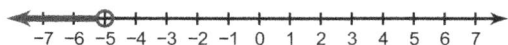

A) $n > 5$ B) $n < -5$

C) $n \leq 5$ D) $n \geq -5$

50) Choose the inequality from the given options for the below graph.

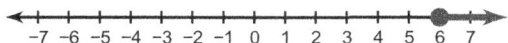

A) $m \geq 6$ B) $m < 6$

C) $m > -6$ D) $m \leq -6$

51) Choose the inequality from the given options for the below graph.

A) $b < 3$ B) $b > -3$

C) $b < -3$ D) $b \leq -3$

52) Choose the inequality from the given options for the below graph.

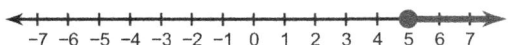

A) $a \geq -5$ B) $a < 5$

C) $a \leq 5$ D) $a \geq 5$

53) Choose the inequality from the given options for the below graph.

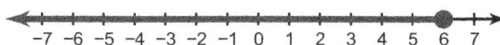

A) $a \leq 6$ B) $a > 6$

C) $a > -6$ D) $a < 6$

54) Choose the inequality from the given options for the below graph.

A) $k \leq -5$ B) $k \geq -5$

C) $k > 4$ D) $k < 4$

55) Choose the inequality from the given options for the below graph.

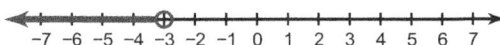

A) $b \leq -3$ B) $b \geq -3$

C) $b < -3$ D) $b < 3$

56) Choose the inequality from the given options for the below graph.

A) $n < 3$ B) $n \leq 3$

C) $n \leq 5$ D) $n < 5$

57) Choose the inequality from the given options for the below graph.

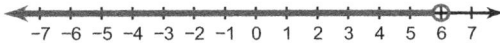

$$-7\ -6\ -5\ -4\ -3\ -2\ -1\ 0\ 1\ 2\ 3\ 4\ 5\ 6\ 7$$

A) $x \le 6$ B) $x < 6$

C) $x \ge -6$ D) $x > 6$

58) Choose the inequality from the given options for the below graph.

$$-7\ -6\ -5\ -4\ -3\ -2\ -1\ 0\ 1\ 2\ 3\ 4\ 5\ 6\ 7$$

A) $r \ge 0$ B) $r > 0$

C) $r \le 0$ D) $r < 0$

59) Choose the inequality from the given options for the below graph.

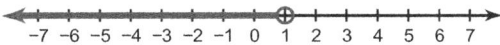

$$-7\ -6\ -5\ -4\ -3\ -2\ -1\ 0\ 1\ 2\ 3\ 4\ 5\ 6\ 7$$

A) $x \le -1$ B) $x \ge -1$

*C) $x < 1$ D) $x > -1$

60) Choose the inequality from the given options for the below graph.

$$-7\ -6\ -5\ -4\ -3\ -2\ -1\ 0\ 1\ 2\ 3\ 4\ 5\ 6\ 7$$

A) $n > 1$ B) $n \ge -1$

C) $n \ge 1$ *D) $n > -1$

61) Choose the inequality from the given options for the below graph.

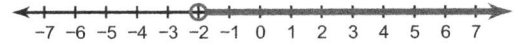

$$-7\ -6\ -5\ -4\ -3\ -2\ -1\ 0\ 1\ 2\ 3\ 4\ 5\ 6\ 7$$

A) $k < -2$ B) $k \le -2$

C) $k > -2$ D) $k \ge -2$

62) Choose the inequality from the given options for the below graph.

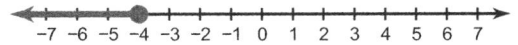

$$-7\ -6\ -5\ -4\ -3\ -2\ -1\ 0\ 1\ 2\ 3\ 4\ 5\ 6\ 7$$

A) $v \le -4$ B) $v < 4$

C) $v < -4$ D) $v \ge -4$

63) Choose the inequality from the given options for the below graph.

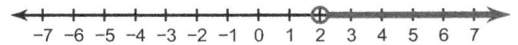

$$-7\ -6\ -5\ -4\ -3\ -2\ -1\ 0\ 1\ 2\ 3\ 4\ 5\ 6\ 7$$

A) $x \ge -2$ *B) $x > 2$

C) $x > -2$ D) $x < -2$

64) Choose the inequality from the given options for the below graph.

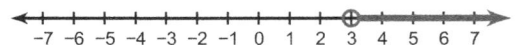

$$-7\ -6\ -5\ -4\ -3\ -2\ -1\ 0\ 1\ 2\ 3\ 4\ 5\ 6\ 7$$

A) $n \ge -3$ *B) $n > 3$

C) $n < -3$ D) $n < 3$

65) Choose the inequality from the given options for the below graph.

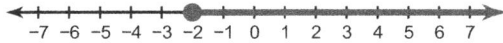

A) $p > -2$ B) $p \geq -2$

C) $p \geq 2$ D) $p < -2$

66) Solve the below inequality

$$x - 10 < -25$$

A) $x < -15$ B) $x > -250$

C) $x > -35$ D) $x > -15$

67) Solve the below inequality

$$11 > 8 + n$$

A) $n < 3$ B) $n > 19$

C) $n > -\dfrac{11}{8}$ D) $n < -\dfrac{11}{8}$

68) Solve the below inequality

$$-3 + r > -7$$

A) $r > \dfrac{7}{3}$ B) $r > -4$

C) $r < -4$ D) $r < \dfrac{7}{3}$

69) Solve the below inequality

$$44\,m < -528$$

A) $m < -484$ B) $m > -484$

C) $m > -12$ D) $m < -12$

70) Solve the below inequality

$$v + 4 \geq -19$$

A) $v \leq -23$ B) $v \leq -76$

C) $v \geq -76$ D) $v \geq -23$

71) Solve the below inequality

$$x + (-11) \geq -1$$

A) $x \leq 10$ B) $x \leq 11$

C) $x \geq 11$ D) $x \geq 10$

72) Solve the below inequality

$$32 \geq k + (-8)$$

A) $k \leq 40$ B) $k \leq -256$

C) $k \leq 24$ D) $k \leq 4$

73) Solve the below inequality

$$n - 31 > -58$$

A) $n > -27$ B) $n < -1798$

C) $n > -1798$ D) $n > 27$

74) Solve the below inequality

$$-34 + v \geq -49$$

A) $v \geq 1666$ B) $v \geq -\dfrac{49}{34}$

C) $v \geq -15$ D) $v \geq -83$

75) Solve the below inequality

$$-16 - p \geq 19$$

A) $p \geq -35$ B) $p \geq 3$

C) $p \leq -35$ D) $p \leq 3$

76) Solve the below inequality

$$-38 < -22 - m$$

A) $m > -60$ B) $m < 16$

C) $m > 836$ D) $m < 836$

77) Solve the below inequality

$$x - (-24) \geq 6$$

A) $x \geq -18$ B) $x \geq -\dfrac{1}{4}$

C) $x \leq -18$ D) $x \leq -\dfrac{1}{4}$

78) Solve the below inequality

$$x - 29 > 3$$

A) $x > 32$ B) $x < -26$

C) $x > -\dfrac{3}{29}$ D) $x < -\dfrac{3}{29}$

79) Solve the below inequality

$$-13 < n - 36$$

A) $n < -\dfrac{13}{36}$ B) $n > -23$

C) $n < -23$ D) $n > 23$

80) Solve the below inequality

$$b + (-1) \leq -10$$

A) $b \geq 10$ B) $b \geq -9$

C) $b \leq -9$ D) $b \leq 10$

        www.math-knots.com | www.a4ace.com

81) Solve the below inequality

$$-64 \geq -27 + n$$

A) $n \geq -\dfrac{64}{27}$ B) $n \leq -\dfrac{64}{27}$

C) $n \geq -37$ D) $n \leq -37$

82) Solve the below inequality

$$-20 \leq -32 + n$$

A) $n \geq -640$ B) $n \geq 52$

C) $n \geq 12$ D) $n \geq \dfrac{5}{8}$

83) Solve the below inequality

$$-69 \geq -39 + x$$

A) $x \geq \dfrac{23}{13}$ B) $x \leq \dfrac{23}{13}$

C) $x \geq -108$ D) $x \leq -30$

84) Solve the below inequality

$$-10 - x > -16$$

A) $x < 6$ B) $x > 6$

C) $x > -6$ D) $x > -160$

85) Solve the below inequality

$$72 \geq 38 + x$$

A) $x \leq \dfrac{36}{19}$ B) $x \geq \dfrac{36}{19}$

C) $x \leq 110$ D) $x \leq 34$

86) Solve the below inequality

$$-9 - p \geq 0$$

A) $p \geq 0$ B) $p \geq -9$

C) $p \leq -9$ D) $p \leq 0$

87) Solve the below inequality

$$-22 \geq p - 21$$

A) $p \leq 1$ B) $p \leq -1$

C) $p \leq \dfrac{22}{21}$ D) $p \geq -1$

88) Solve the below inequality

$$15 - r > 1$$

A) $r > -14$ B) $r < 14$

C) $r < -14$ D) $r > 14$

89) Solve the below inequality

$$-28 - n \le -44$$

A) $n \le 1232$ B) $n \ge 16$

C) $n \ge 1232$ D) $n \le 16$

90) Solve the below inequality

$$a - 18 \le -13$$

A) $a \ge 5$ B) $a \ge -234$

C) $a \ge -\dfrac{13}{18}$ D) $a \le 5$

91) Solve the below inequality

$$-24 \ge n - 2$$

A) $n \le -12$ B) $n \le -26$

C) $n \le -22$ D) $n \le -48$

92) Solve the below inequality

$$75 \le x + 36$$

A) $x \ge 39$ B) $x \ge 2700$

C) $x \ge 111$ D) $x \ge -39$

93) Solve the below inequality

$$-65 \le -25 + n$$

A) $n \le -40$ B) $n \le 90$

C) $n \ge 90$ D) $n \ge -40$

94) Solve the below inequality

$$48 > p - (-21)$$

A) $p > -1008$ B) $p < -1008$

C) $p < 27$ D) $p < 69$

95) Solve the below inequality

$$29 < p - (-13)$$

A) $p > 16$ B) $p > 42$

C) $p > -\dfrac{29}{13}$ D) $p < -\dfrac{29}{13}$

96) Solve the below inequality

$$n + (-39) < -35$$

A) $n < 4$ B) $n > -\dfrac{35}{39}$

C) $n > 4$ D) $n < -74$

97) Solve the below inequality

$$4 < -35 - n$$

A) $n > -140$ B) $n < -39$

C) $n < -\dfrac{4}{35}$ D) $n < -140$

98) Solve the below inequality

$$-18 < 7 - r$$

A) $r < \dfrac{18}{7}$ B) $r < -\dfrac{18}{7}$

C) $r < 25$ D) $r < -25$

99) Solve the below inequality

$$n - 29 < -39$$

A) $n < -\dfrac{39}{29}$ B) $n > -\dfrac{39}{29}$

C) $n < 68$ D) $n < -10$

100) Solve the below inequality

$$7 \geq x + (-29)$$

A) $x \leq 36$ B) $x \geq 203$

C) $x \leq 203$ D) $x \geq 36$

101) Solve the below inequality

$$-22 \leq 11 - r$$

A) $r \leq -2$ B) $r \leq 33$

C) $r \leq -242$ D) $r \leq 2$

102) Solve the below inequality

$$k - (-25) > 23$$

A) $k > -575$ B) $k < -575$

C) $k < -48$ D) $k > -2$

103) Solve the below inequality

$$-42 \leq n + (-18)$$

A) $n \geq -24$ B) $n \geq 756$

C) $n \geq -60$ D) $n \leq 756$

104) Solve the below inequality

$$16 + x \leq 51$$

A) $x \geq 35$ B) $x \leq 35$

C) $x \geq 816$ D) $x \geq 67$

105) Solve the below inequality

$$-31 \leq n - 32$$

A) $n \geq -992$ B) $n \leq -\dfrac{31}{32}$

C) $n \leq -992$ D) $n \geq 1$

106) Solve the below inequality

$$-6 \leq 19 + n$$

A) $n \geq 13$ B) $n \leq 13$

C) $n \leq -25$ D) $n \geq -25$

107) Solve the below inequality

$$9 \leq -22 - n$$

A) $n \leq -13$ B) $n \geq -13$

C) $n \leq -31$ D) $n \geq -31$

108) Solve the below inequality

$$-37 + n > -61$$

A) $n > -24$ B) $n > \dfrac{61}{37}$

C) $n > 24$ D) $n < -24$

109) Solve the below inequality

$$15 \leq a - (-15)$$

A) $a \geq -225$ B) $a \geq 0$

C) $a \leq -225$ D) $a \leq 0$

110) Solve the below inequality

$$-65 > v + (-29)$$

A) $v < -36$ B) $v > \dfrac{65}{29}$

C) $v > -94$ D) $v > -36$

111) Solve the below inequality

$$1 \leq -20 - x$$

A) $x \leq 21$ B) $x \geq 21$

C) $x \geq -20$ D) $x \leq -21$

112) Solve the below inequality

$$n - (-16) \leq 54$$

A) $n \geq 70$ B) $n \leq -864$

C) $n \leq 70$ D) $n \leq 38$

www.math-knots.com | www.a4ace.com

113) Solve the below inequality

$$n + 28 \leq 0$$

A) $n \geq -28$ B) $n \leq -28$

C) $n \geq 28$ D) $n \geq 0$

114) Solve the below inequality

$$-204 \leq -12v$$

A) $v \geq -216$ B) $v \geq -17$

C) $v \leq 17$ D) $v \geq 17$

115) Solve the below inequality

$$36 \geq 3n$$

A) $n \geq 39$ B) $n \geq 12$

C) $n \geq -39$ D) $n \leq 12$

116) Solve the below inequality

$$32 - p < 61$$

A) $p > \dfrac{61}{32}$ B) $p < 93$

C) $p > -29$ D) $p > 93$

117) Solve the below inequality

$$x - (-29) \geq 69$$

A) $x \geq -98$ B) $x \geq -\dfrac{69}{29}$

C) $x \geq 40$ D) $x \leq -98$

118) Solve the below inequality

$$-\dfrac{8}{15} < \dfrac{m}{15}$$

A) $m > -8$ B) $m < -\dfrac{233}{15}$

C) $m < -8$ D) $m > -\dfrac{233}{15}$

119) Solve the below inequality

$$-5 \geq \dfrac{k}{32}$$

A) $k \leq -160$ B) $k \geq -160$

C) $k \geq 27$ D) $k \geq -37$

120) Solve the below inequality

$$x - 11 < -28$$

A) $x < -39$ B) $x > -17$

C) $x < -17$ D) $x > -39$

 www.math-knots.com | www.a4ace.com

121) Solve the below inequality

$$21x \geq 210$$

A) $x \geq 10$

B) $x \leq 231$

C) $x \leq 10$

D) $x \geq 4410$

122) Solve the below inequality

$$\frac{b}{16} \leq \frac{15}{16}$$

A) $b \geq -15$

B) $b \geq \frac{271}{16}$

C) $b \geq 15$

D) $b \leq 15$

123) Solve the below inequality

$$36n \geq 1368$$

A) $n \leq 49248$

B) $n \geq 1404$

C) $n \geq 38$

D) $n \geq 49248$

124) Solve the below inequality

$$\frac{14}{9} \leq \frac{x}{18}$$

A) $x \geq -\frac{148}{9}$

B) $x \geq 28$

C) $x \leq \frac{7}{81}$

D) $x \leq -\frac{148}{9}$

125) Solve the below inequality

$$-4p < 96$$

A) $p > -24$

B) $p < -384$

C) $p < 92$

D) $p < -24$

126) Solve the below inequality

$$1440 \geq -32n$$

A) $n \geq -46080$

B) $n \leq -46080$

C) $n \leq -45$

D) $n \geq -45$

127) Solve the below inequality

$$-40v \geq 480$$

A) $v \geq 440$

B) $v \leq 440$

C) $v \leq -12$

D) $v \leq 520$

128) Solve the below inequality

$$-26p < 234$$

A) $p > 260$

B) $p > -260$

C) $p < -9$

D) $p > -9$

www.math-knots.com | www.a4ace.com

129) Solve the below inequality

$$\frac{x}{11} \leq 33$$

A) $x \leq 363$ B) $x \geq 363$

C) $x \geq 22$ D) $x \geq 3$

130) Solve the below inequality

$$-116 \geq -29n$$

A) $n \geq 3364$ B) $n \geq 145$

C) $n \geq -4$ D) $n \geq 4$

131) Solve the below inequality

$$-2162 < -46b$$

A) $b < 47$ B) $b < -2208$

C) $b < -47$ D) $b < 99452$

132) Solve the below inequality

$$-35n < -1330$$

A) $n > 46550$ B) $n > 38$

C) $n < -1365$ D) $n > -1365$

133) Solve the below inequality

$$-37 > \frac{b}{23}$$

A) $b < -60$ B) $b < 60$

C) $b < -14$ D) $b < -851$

134) Solve the below inequality

$$\frac{p}{3} > 34$$

A) $p < -37$ B) $p < 31$

C) $p > 102$ D) $p < 102$

135) Solve the below inequality

$$-11x \geq -385$$

A) $x \leq -35$ B) $x \leq 35$

C) $x \geq -396$ D) $x \leq -396$

136) Solve the below inequality

$$\frac{m}{15} < -8$$

A) $m < -120$ B) $m < 7$

C) $m < \frac{8}{15}$ D) $m > -120$

www.math-knots.com | www.a4ace.com

137) Solve the below inequality

$$\frac{x}{14} \geq \frac{11}{7}$$

A) $x \geq -\frac{87}{7}$ B) $x \leq 22$

C) $x \geq 22$ D) $x \leq -\frac{87}{7}$

138) Solve the below inequality

$$-3x \leq -30$$

A) $x \geq -33$ B) $x \geq 10$

C) $x \leq -33$ D) $x \geq 27$

139) Solve the below inequality

$$-242 < -11r$$

A) $r > 2662$ B) $r < 22$

C) $r > -253$ D) $r > 22$

140) Solve the below inequality

$$-1014 < -26n$$

A) $n > 26364$ B) $n > 39$

C) $n > -39$ D) $n < 39$

141) Solve the below inequality

$$-7p \geq -322$$

A) $p \geq 46$ B) $p \leq 46$

C) $p \geq 2254$ D) $p \geq 315$

142) Solve the below inequality

$$36n > -180$$

A) $n < -6480$ B) $n > -6480$

C) $n > -5$ D) $n > -216$

143) Solve the below inequality

$$43 > \frac{r}{48}$$

A) $r < 91$ B) $r < -5$

C) $r < \frac{43}{48}$ D) $r < 2064$

144) Solve the below inequality

$$-28 \leq \frac{v}{48}$$

A) $v \geq -\frac{7}{12}$ B) $v \geq -20$

C) $v \geq -1344$ D) $v \geq 20$

www.math-knots.com | www.a4ace.com

Grade 7
Volume 2
Week 21

www.math-knots.com | www.a4ace.com

1) Solve the below inequality

$$\frac{3}{20} x < \frac{39}{56}$$

A) $x > \dfrac{153}{280}$ B) $x > \dfrac{117}{1120}$

C) $x < \dfrac{117}{1120}$ D) $x < \dfrac{65}{14}$

2) Solve the below inequality

$$\frac{83}{6} a \leq \frac{83}{28}$$

A) $a \leq \dfrac{3}{14}$ B) $a \leq -\dfrac{913}{84}$

C) $a \leq \dfrac{6889}{168}$ D) $a \leq -\dfrac{1411}{84}$

3) Solve the below inequality

$$-\frac{11}{8} r \leq \frac{209}{64}$$

A) $r \geq -\dfrac{19}{8}$ B) $r \leq \dfrac{297}{64}$

C) $r \leq \dfrac{121}{64}$ D) $r \leq -\dfrac{19}{8}$

4) Solve the below inequality

$$2p \leq -\frac{45}{7}$$

A) $p \leq \dfrac{45}{14}$ B) $p \leq -\dfrac{97}{14}$

C) $p \leq -\dfrac{83}{14}$ D) $p \leq -\dfrac{45}{14}$

5) Solve the below inequality

$$-\frac{31}{30} a \leq -\frac{341}{150}$$

A) $a \geq -\dfrac{248}{75}$ B) $a \leq -\dfrac{248}{75}$

C) $a \leq \dfrac{11}{5}$ D) $a \geq \dfrac{11}{5}$

6) Solve the below inequality

$$\frac{395}{184} > \frac{5x}{8}$$

A) $x < \dfrac{79}{23}$ B) $x < -\dfrac{503}{920}$

C) $x < -\dfrac{79}{23}$ D) $x < \dfrac{3447}{920}$

7) Solve the below inequality

$$-\frac{3683}{165} \geq -\frac{29}{22}n$$

A) $n \leq -\frac{106807}{3630}$

B) $n \leq \frac{254}{15}$

C) $n \geq \frac{254}{15}$

D) $n \leq -\frac{6931}{330}$

8) Solve the below inequality

$$\frac{35}{27}a > -\frac{70}{27}$$

A) $a < 2$ B) $a > -2$

C) $a > -\frac{35}{27}$ D) $a > 2$

9) Solve the below inequality

$$-\frac{2}{3}r > -\frac{59}{6}$$

A) $r > -\frac{34}{3}$ B) $r < \frac{25}{3}$

C) $r < \frac{59}{4}$ D) $r > \frac{25}{3}$

10) Solve the below inequality

$$\frac{79}{10}n \leq \frac{2291}{240}$$

A) $n \geq -\frac{180989}{2400}$ B) $n \geq \frac{29}{24}$

C) $n \geq \frac{180989}{2400}$ D) $n \leq \frac{29}{24}$

11) Solve the below inequality

$$\frac{85}{7} \geq 10\,v$$

A) $v \leq \frac{857}{70}$ B) $v \geq \frac{857}{70}$

C) $v \leq -\frac{843}{70}$ D) $v \leq \frac{17}{14}$

12) Solve the below inequality

$$\frac{16\,a}{245} \geq \frac{136}{2695}$$

A) $a \geq \frac{17}{22}$

B) $a \geq \frac{2176}{660275}$

C) $a \geq -\frac{662451}{43120}$

D) $a \geq -\frac{2176}{660275}$

13) Solve the below inequality

$$-\frac{1369}{319} \geq \frac{37}{29}r$$

A) $r \leq -\frac{37}{11}$

B) $r \leq \frac{1776}{319}$

C) $r \leq -\frac{962}{319}$

D) $r \geq -\frac{962}{319}$

14) Solve the below inequality

$$-\frac{816}{13} < -4a$$

A) $a < -\frac{3251}{52}$

B) $a > -\frac{3251}{52}$

C) $a > -\frac{3277}{52}$

D) $a < \frac{204}{13}$

15) Solve the below inequality

$$\frac{215}{26}m > -\frac{13545}{442}$$

A) $m > \frac{2912175}{11492}$

B) $m > \frac{4945}{221}$

C) $m > -\frac{8600}{221}$

D) $m > -\frac{63}{17}$

16) Solve the below inequality

$$\frac{36332}{375} \leq \frac{124}{15}v$$

A) $v \geq \frac{293}{25}$

B) $v \leq -\frac{293}{25}$

C) $v \leq \frac{33232}{375}$

D) $v \geq \frac{33232}{375}$

17) Solve the below inequality

$$-\frac{229}{64} \leq -\frac{1}{4}b$$

A) $b \geq \frac{229}{16}$

B) $b \geq \frac{229}{256}$

C) $b \leq \frac{229}{16}$

D) $b \geq -\frac{229}{256}$

18) Solve the below inequality

$$-29n > -\frac{1537}{27}$$

A) $n < -\frac{754}{27}$

B) $n < -\frac{53}{27}$

C) $n < \frac{53}{27}$

D) $n > -\frac{754}{27}$

19) Solve the below inequality

$$-\frac{180}{437} < \frac{10}{19}n$$

A) $n > \frac{50}{437}$ B) $n > -\frac{1800}{8303}$

C) $n > -\frac{18}{23}$ D) $n > -\frac{410}{437}$

20) Solve the below inequality

$$-\frac{4060}{27} \geq -28p$$

A) $p \leq \frac{145}{27}$

B) $p \leq -\frac{113653}{756}$

C) $p \geq -\frac{113653}{756}$

D) $p \geq \frac{145}{27}$

21) Solve the below inequality

$$-\frac{8785}{529} \geq -\frac{35}{23}x$$

A) $x \leq \frac{307475}{12167}$ B) $x \geq -\frac{9590}{529}$

C) $x \geq \frac{251}{23}$ D) $x \geq \frac{307475}{12167}$

22) Solve the below inequality

$$\frac{20x}{257} > -\frac{145}{514}$$

A) $x > -\frac{29}{8}$ B) $x > \frac{29}{8}$

C) $x > -\frac{64599}{5140}$ D) $x < \frac{29}{8}$

23) Solve the below inequality

$$\frac{17}{12} < \frac{1}{12}x$$

A) $x < -\frac{4}{3}$ B) $x > \frac{4}{3}$

C) $x < \frac{4}{3}$ D) $x > 17$

24) Solve the below inequality

$$-\frac{47}{8} > 2x$$

A) $x > -\frac{47}{16}$ B) $x > -\frac{31}{8}$

C) $x < -\frac{31}{8}$ D) $x < -\frac{47}{16}$

25) Solve the below inequality

$$\frac{8}{7}x > \frac{172}{35}$$

A) $x > \frac{43}{10}$ B) $x > \frac{132}{35}$

C) $x < \frac{132}{35}$ D) $x < \frac{43}{10}$

26) Solve the below inequality

$$\frac{4500}{299} > \frac{25}{13}v$$

A) $v < \frac{112500}{3887}$ B) $v > \frac{112500}{3887}$

C) $v < \frac{180}{23}$ D) $v > \frac{180}{23}$

27) Solve the below inequality

$$-\frac{3}{11}x > \frac{57}{110}$$

A) $x < -\frac{19}{10}$ B) $x > \frac{27}{110}$

C) $x > -\frac{19}{10}$ D) $x > \frac{87}{110}$

28) Solve the below inequality

$$\frac{23}{40}a \leq \frac{3197}{1200}$$

A) $a \leq -\frac{121531}{27600}$

B) $a \leq \frac{121531}{27600}$

C) $a \leq \frac{139}{30}$

D) $a \leq \frac{73531}{48000}$

29) Solve the below inequality

$$-\frac{7}{4}a > \frac{49}{16}$$

A) $a < \frac{343}{64}$ B) $a < -\frac{7}{4}$

C) $a > \frac{343}{64}$ D) $a < -\frac{343}{64}$

30) Solve the below inequality

$$\frac{8257}{174} \geq \frac{23}{6}k$$

A) $k \leq \frac{359}{29}$ B) $k \geq \frac{1265}{29}$

C) $k \leq \frac{1265}{29}$ D) $k \geq \frac{359}{29}$

       www.math-knots.com | www.a4ace.com

31) Solve the below inequality

$$\frac{n}{5} + 1 < -2$$

A) $n < -30$ B) $n < -23$

C) $n < -26$ D) $n < -15$

32) Solve the below inequality

$$\frac{p}{4} + 5 < 9$$

A) $p < 16$ B) $p < -10$

C) $p < 10$ D) $p < -35$

33) Solve the below inequality

$$-120 < 8(m + 3)$$

A) $m > 5$ B) $m > -18$

C) $m < 5$ D) $m < -3$

34) Solve the below inequality

$$6 \geq 7 + \frac{r}{6}$$

A) $r \leq -50$ B) $r \geq -50$

C) $r \leq -6$ D) $r \geq -6$

35) Solve the below inequality

$$\frac{n}{10} + 7 < 5$$

A) $n > -29$ B) $n < -20$

C) $n < -27$ D) $n > -27$

36) Solve the below inequality

$$4(10 + n) < 108$$

A) $n > -40$ B) $n < 17$

C) $n < -40$ D) $n > 17$

37) Solve the below inequality

$$-10 \leq -5(n - 9)$$

A) $n \leq 11$ B) $n \geq -44$

C) $n \geq 11$ D) $n \leq -44$

38) Solve the below inequality

$$-28 > -4(n - 2)$$

A) $n < -44$ B) $n < 9$

C) $n < -4$ D) $n > 9$

www.math-knots.com | www.a4ace.com

39) Solve the below inequality

$$\frac{a}{9} + 9 \geq 10$$

A) $a \geq 9$ B) $a \leq 5$

C) $a \leq 9$ D) $a \leq -15$

40) Solve the below inequality

$$147 \leq -7\left(-10 + n\right)$$

A) $n \leq -11$ B) $n \leq -16$

C) $n \leq -1$ D) $n \leq 4$

41) Solve the below inequality

$$\frac{x}{4} - 3 < -7$$

A) $x < -16$ B) $x > -37$

C) $x > 1$ D) $x > -16$

42) Solve the below inequality

$$3x - 7 \geq -61$$

A) $x \leq -18$ B) $x \leq 4$

C) $x \leq -38$ D) $x \geq -18$

43) Solve the below inequality

$$94 \geq 10 + 7\,m$$

A) $m \leq -24$ B) $m \leq 12$

C) $m \geq -24$ D) $m \leq -1$

44) Solve the below inequality

$$8 + \frac{n}{6} > 5$$

A) $n < -18$ B) $n < 5$

C) $n > 5$ D) $n > -18$

45) Solve the below inequality

$$-38 \geq -7\,m - 3$$

A) $m \leq 1$ B) $m \geq 1$

C) $m \geq 5$ D) $m \leq 5$

46) Solve the below inequality

$$3 < \frac{k}{4} + 8$$

A) $k < -16$ B) $k > -20$

C) $k < 5$ D) $k < -20$

47) Solve the below inequality

$$-2(m+7) < -12$$

A) $m > -48$ B) $m > -43$

C) $m > -1$ D) $m < -48$

48) Solve the below inequality

$$0 \geq 2 + \frac{v}{4}$$

A) $v \geq -47$ B) $v \geq -8$

C) $v \leq -8$ D) $v \geq -43$

49) Solve the below inequality

$$-114 > 6(k-8)$$

A) $k > -20$ B) $k > -47$

C) $k < -11$ D) $k < -20$

50) Solve the below inequality

$$\frac{b}{6} + 10 \geq 11$$

A) $b \geq 4$ B) $b \geq 6$

C) $b \geq -6$ D) $b \geq -21$

51) Solve the below inequality

$$13 \geq 8 + \frac{p}{3}$$

A) $p \geq 1$ B) $p \leq 15$

C) $p \leq -42$ D) $p \leq 1$

52) Solve the below inequality

$$-2(-10+v) > -8$$

A) $v < -41$ B) $v > -46$

C) $v < 14$ D) $v < -46$

53) Solve the below inequality

$$1890 > 42p$$

A) $p > -79380$ B) $p < -79380$

C) $p > 1848$ D) $p < 45$

54) Solve the below inequality

$$-2 < \frac{v}{8} - 1$$

A) $v < -8$ B) $v > -8$

C) $v < -33$ D) $v > -33$

www.math-knots.com | www.a4ace.com

55) Solve the below inequality

$$-6 - 5a \leq -51$$

A) $a \leq -40$ B) $a \geq 9$

C) $a \leq -48$ D) $a \leq 9$

56) Solve the below inequality

$$-130 > -10 - 6v$$

A) $v < 20$ B) $v < 6$

C) $v < -49$ D) $v > 20$

57) Solve the below inequality

$$91 > -7 - 7v$$

A) $v > -14$ B) $v > -10$

C) $v < -10$ D) $v < -28$

58) Solve the below inequality

$$34 \leq 2(n + 4)$$

A) $n \geq -21$ B) $n \leq -21$

C) $n \geq -7$ D) $n \geq 13$

59) Solve the below inequality

$$7(v + 1) \leq 91$$

A) $v \leq -9$ B) $v \geq 12$

C) $v \leq -26$ D) $v \leq 12$

60) Solve the below inequality

$$-80 \geq -5(7 + n)$$

A) $n \geq -25$ B) $n \geq 9$

C) $n \geq -37$ D) $n \geq -10$

61) Solve the below inequality

$$3 + \frac{x}{6} \geq 4$$

A) $x \geq 6$ B) $x \geq -49$

C) $x \leq -49$ D) $x \leq 2$

62) Solve the below inequality

$$0 \geq 7x - 7x$$

A) { All real numbers. }:

B) $x \leq 20$:

C) $x \leq -7$:

D) $x \leq -37$:

63) Solve the below inequality

$$42 < -3n - 3n$$

A) $n < -7$:

B) $n < -78$:

C) No solution.:

D) $n > -15$:

64) Solve the below inequality

$$58 \leq 6n + 15 + 13$$

A) $n \geq -87$:

B) $n \geq -17$:

C) $n \geq 5$:

D) $n \geq -46$:

65) Solve the below inequality

$$-48 < -18x + 6x$$

A) $x < -61$:

B) $x > -61$:

C) $x > 4$:

D) $x < 4$:

66) Solve the below inequality

$$18 - 15r - 14 \leq 49$$

A) $r \geq -14$:

B) $r \geq -3$:

C) $r \geq -68$:

D) $r \geq -14$:

67) Solve the below inequality

$$7 - 19n - 7 < -19$$

A) $n > -97$:

B) $n > 1$:

C) No solution.:

D) $n > 4$:

68) Solve the below inequality

$$1 + 15n - 17n < 37$$

A) $n > 8$:

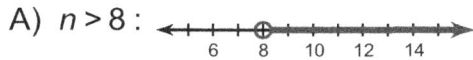

B) $n > -18$:

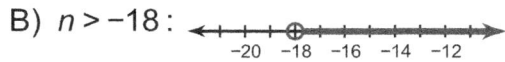

C) $n < 8$:

D) $n < -18$:

69) Solve the below inequality

$$20r - 6r > 0$$

A) $r > 3$:

B) { All real numbers. }:

C) $r > 0$:

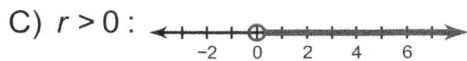

D) No solution.:

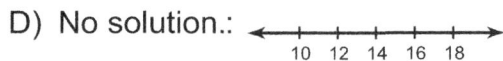

70) Solve the below inequality

$$31 < -19r - 12 + 5$$

A) $r < -98$:

B) $r < -2$:

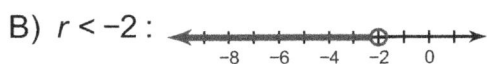

C) No solution.:

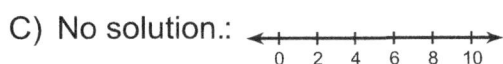

D) $r > -98$:

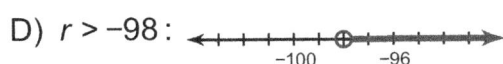

71) Solve the below inequality

$$-20 < 19r - 19r$$

A) $r \geq -66$:

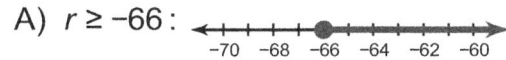

B) $r \geq -42$:

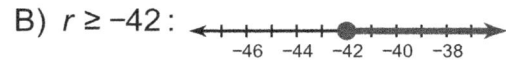

C) $r \geq -36$:

D) { All real numbers. }:

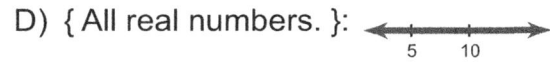

72) Solve the below inequality

$$28 < -15v - 13v$$

A) $v < -19$:

B) $v < -44$:

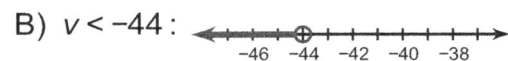

C) $v < -64$:

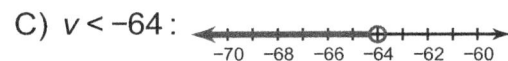

D) $v < -1$:

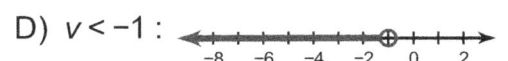

73) Solve the below inequality

$$16b + 6b \geq 0$$

A) $b \leq -14$:

B) No solution.:

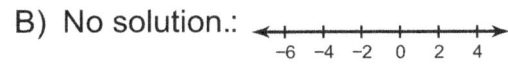

C) $b \geq 0$:

D) $b \leq -72$:

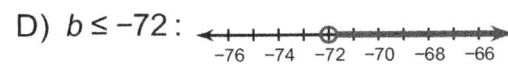

www.math-knots.com | www.a4ace.com

74) Solve the below inequality

$$19k - 10k \leq 0$$

A) { All real numbers. }:

B) $k \leq 0$:

C) $k \geq 11$:

D) $k \geq -38$:

75) Solve the below inequality

$$b + 15 + 17 > 45$$

A) $b < -16$:

B) $b > 13$:

C) $b > 13$:

D) $b > -16$:

76) Solve the below inequality

$$-32 < 14x + 18x$$

A) $x < -12$:

B) $x < -1$:

C) $x > -1$:

D) $x < -87$:

77) Solve the below inequality

$$-55 < 11n - 5 - 6$$

A) { All real numbers. }:

B) $n > -4$:

C) $n < -4$:

D) $n > -93$:

78) Solve the below inequality

$$1 + 8x - 8x > 1$$

A) $x < 20$:

B) No solution.:

C) $x < -20$:

D) $x < -44$:

79) Solve the below inequality

$$19x + 13 - 19x \geq 13$$

A) $x \geq 10$:

B) $x \geq -9$:

C) { All real numbers. }:

D) $x \geq 20$:

80) Solve the below inequality

$$-2 \le -6\,m + 6\,m$$

A) $m \le 17$:

B) { All real numbers. }:

C) $m \ge 20$:

D) $m \le 20$:

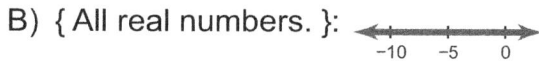

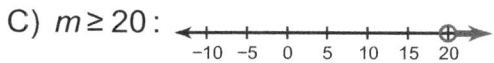

81) Solve the below inequality

$$-8 < n - n$$

A) $n < 20$:

B) $n < -49$:

C) { All real numbers. }:

D) $n > 20$:

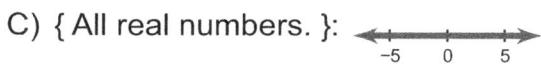

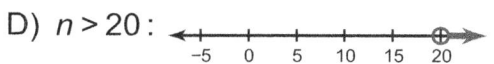

82) Solve the below inequality

$$14\,n - 6 + 1 > 37$$

A) $n > 3$:

B) $n > -87$:

C) $n > -30$:

D) $n > -30$:

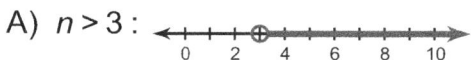

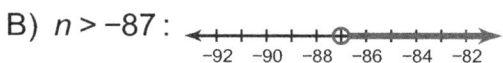

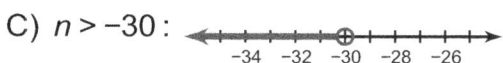

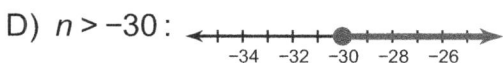

83) Solve the below inequality

$$1 - 8\,b + 5\,b < -5$$

A) { All real numbers. }:

B) $b > 2$:

C) $b > 2$:

D) No solution.:

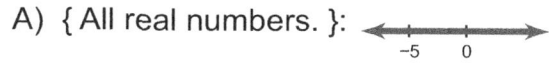

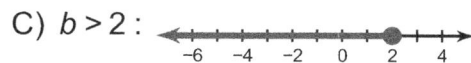

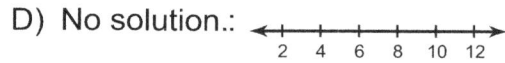

84) Solve the below inequality

$$-11 \le p - 11 - p$$

A) $p \le 5$:

B) $p \le -27$:

C) $p \le -52$:

D) { All real numbers. }:

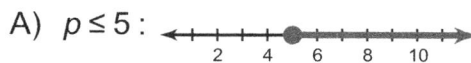

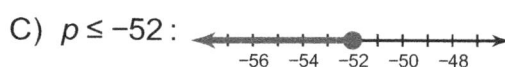

85) Solve the below inequality

$$-13 \le 14\,a + 13 + 12\,a$$

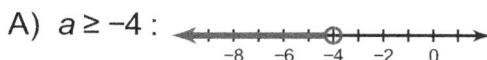

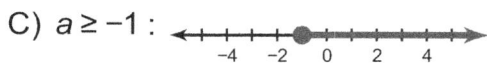

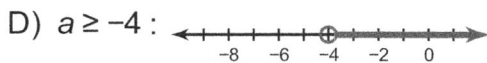

A) $a \ge -4$:

B) { All real numbers. }:

C) $a \ge -1$:

D) $a \ge -4$:

www.math-knots.com | www.a4ace.com

86) Solve the below inequality

$$-10x + 10x > -2$$

A) { All real numbers. }:

B) $x > -95$:

C) $x < -95$:

D) $x > 20$:

87) Solve the below inequality

$$1 - 2x + 20x \leq 1$$

A) $x \leq -99$:

B) $x \leq 0$:

C) $x \leq 15$:

D) $x \leq -37$:

88) Solve the below inequality

$$14a - 15a \leq -19$$

A) $a \geq -10$:

B) $a \geq -10$:

C) $a \geq 19$:

D) No solution.:

89) Solve the below inequality

$$2n + 11n \geq -39$$

A) $n \leq -85$:

B) $n \geq -3$:

C) $n \leq -85$:

D) $n \geq -85$:

90) Solve the below inequality

$$-2v + 2v \leq 10$$

A) $v > -94$:

B) $v > 0$:

C) { All real numbers. }:

D) $v < -94$:

91) Solve the below inequality

$$0 > -x + x$$

A) $x < -15$:

B) No solution.:

C) $x > -15$:

D) $x > 20$:

www.math-knots.com | www.a4ace.com

92) Solve the below inequality

$$-12(14n-8) > -744$$

A) $n > 5$ B) $n < 5$

C) $n > -41$ D) $n > -57$

96) Solve the below inequality

$$-9(n-6) < 144$$

A) $n > -35$ B) $n > -10$

C) $n > -46$ D) $n < -46$

93) Solve the below inequality

$$726 > 12 + 7(13n + 11)$$

A) $n < -44$ B) $n > -65$

C) $n > -44$ D) $n < 7$

97) Solve the below inequality

$$-283 \geq 5 + 9(2x - 12)$$

A) $x \leq -62$ B) $x \leq -57$

C) $x \leq -10$ D) $x \leq -9$

94) Solve the below inequality

$$-12(7n + 6) \leq -1164$$

A) $n \geq 13$ B) $n \geq -66$

C) $n \geq 3$ D) $n \geq -54$

98) Solve the below inequality

$$-12(-9 - 9n) \geq -432$$

A) $n \geq -12$ B) $n \geq -5$

C) $n \geq -25$ D) $n \geq -36$

95) Solve the below inequality

$$-620 \leq 8(12 + 8x) - 12$$

A) $x \geq 10$ B) $x \geq -11$

C) $x \geq -70$ D) $x \geq -29$

99) Solve the below inequality

$$14(n + 5) + 13n > 205$$

A) $n > -66$ B) $n > -41$

C) $n > -60$ D) $n > 5$

100) Solve the below inequality

$$198 \geq -6\left(-9r - 6\right)$$

A) No solution. B) $r \leq 3$

C) $r \geq -68$ D) $r \geq 3$

101) Solve the below inequality

$$14n + 10\left(2 - 9n\right) < 628$$

A) $n < -48$ B) $n > -8$

C) $n > -48$ D) $n > -51$

102) Solve the below inequality

$$143 \leq 13\left(3 - 8m\right)$$

A) $m \geq 3$ B) $m \leq -63$

C) $m \leq -1$ D) $m \leq 3$

103) Solve the below inequality

$$-220 < 8\left(2x - 14\right) - 7x$$

A) $x > -6$ B) $x > 5$

C) $x > -67$ D) $x > -12$

104) Solve the below inequality

$$-639 < 9\left(13 - 12r\right)$$

A) $r > 6$ B) $r < 6$

C) $r < 7$ D) $r > 7$

105) Solve the below inequality

$$11(x + 4) \geq 143$$

A) { All real numbers. }

B) $x \geq 9$

C) $x \geq -11$

D) No solution.

106) Solve the below inequality

$$6\left(-1 - 4p\right) \geq 306$$

A) $p \leq -13$ B) $p \leq -37$

C) $p \leq -50$ D) $p \geq -50$

107) Solve the below inequality

$$196 \leq 4\left(9 - 5b\right)$$

A) { All real numbers. }

B) $b \leq -48$

C) $b \geq -48$

D) $b \leq -8$

108) Solve the below inequality

$$-14(12-n) < -308$$

A) $n < -69$ B) $n < -10$

C) $n > -69$ D) $n < -1$

109) Solve the below inequality

$$14 - 3(10 + 7x) \geq -268$$

A) $x \leq 12$ B) No solution.

C) $x \leq 8$ D) $x \leq 4$

110) Solve the below inequality

$$-1147 < -14r + 11(13r + 13)$$

A) $r > -5$ B) $r > -10$

C) $r < -5$ D) $r < 10$

111) Solve the below inequality

$$524 < -5(9p + 14) + 9$$

A) $p > -13$ B) $p < -13$

C) No solution.   D) $p > -42$

112) Solve the below inequality

$$n + 5(1 - 4n) \geq 271$$

A) $n \leq -14$ B) $n \leq -15$

C) $n \geq -32$ D) $n \geq -15$

113) Solve the below inequality

$$-166 < -3(-4r + 12) - 10$$

A) $r > -17$

B) { All real numbers. }

C) $r > -10$

D) $r > -69$

114) Solve the below inequality

$$-10(-8 + 14n) > -340$$

A) $n < -69$ B) $n < 11$

C) $n < -18$ D) $n < 3$

115) Solve the below inequality

$$-226 < 7(1 - 4b) - 9$$

A) { All real numbers. }

B) $b < 1$

C) $b < 8$

D) $b < -31$

116) Solve the below inequality

$$4(-7n+11) < 212$$

A) $n > -29$ B) $n < -66$

C) $n > -6$ D) $n < -29$

117) Solve the below inequality

$$8(11b - 3) < 1120$$

A) $b < 13$

B) $b < -13$

C) $b < -8$

D) { All real numbers. }

118) Solve the below inequality

$$-570 \leq 10(8n - 9)$$

A) $n \leq -46$ B) $n \leq -15$

C) $n \leq -6$ D) $n \geq -6$

119) Solve the below inequality

$$-10(10v - 7) < -1230$$

A) $v > -58$ B) $v > 13$

C) $v > -64$ D) $v > -51$

120) Solve the below inequality

$$-7 + 11(1 + 11x) < 972$$

A) No solution.   B) $x < 8$

C) $x > 8$ D) $x > -37$

121) Solve the below inequality

$$9(-7b - 9) \leq -963$$

A) $b \geq 14$

B) $b \geq -7$

C) $b \geq -1$

D) { All real numbers. }

1) Simplify the below expression

$$-5(11x + 8)$$

A) $-55x - 40$ B) $67 - 91x$

C) $2 + 6x$ D) $77 - 91x$

2) Simplify the below expression

$$-8.7(-6.7 + 8.8n)$$

A) $-0.8 + 23.66n$

B) $58.29 - 73.86n$

C) $58.29 - 76.56n$

D) $2.6 + 23.66n$

3) Simplify the below expression

$$16 - 10(n + 10)$$

A) $80n + 108$ B) $-9n + 33$

C) $-6 + 28n$ D) $-84 - 10n$

4) Simplify the below expression

$$7(m - 6)$$

A) $3 - 18m$ B) $7m - 46$

C) $-2 + 6m$ D) $7m - 42$

5) Simplify the below expression

$$12(1 - 8x)$$

A) $-84x - 12$ B) $-96x - 12$

C) $12 - 96x$ D) $-96x$

6) Simplify the below expression

$$-\frac{5}{3}v + \frac{7}{5} - 2\frac{5}{8}$$

A) $\frac{23}{6}v + \frac{13}{8}$ B) $\frac{13}{6} - \frac{5}{18}v$

C) $-\frac{11}{12}v - \frac{49}{40}$ D) $-\frac{5}{3}v - \frac{49}{40}$

7) Simplify the below expression

$$-11(x + 1)$$

A) $-11x - 11$ B) $25 - 70x$

C) $36x + 36$ D) $-7 - 35x$

8) Simplify the below expression

$$-16(16 - 4v) - 19v$$

A) $19 - 340v$ B) $-256 + 45v$

C) $2v + 34$ D) $-63 + 98v$

www.math-knots.com | www.a4ace.com

9) Simplify the below expression

$$-9(1-11n)$$

A) $-20+99n$ B) $-12n-95$

C) $-12n-84$ D) $-9+99n$

10) Simplify the below expression

$$\frac{9}{8}x+1+4\frac{1}{2}$$

A) $\frac{1}{5}x$ B) $-\frac{13}{10}x$

C) $\frac{11}{2}+\frac{9}{8}x$ D) $\frac{11}{2}+\frac{21}{8}x$

11) Simplify the below expression

$$(7+14x)\cdot-4-14$$

A) $-42-56x$ B) $-36-56x$

C) $-54-56x$ D) $-45-56x$

12) Simplify the below expression

$$-3a+(1-15a)\cdot6$$

A) $-95a+6$ B) $-93a+6$

C) $-77a+32$ D) $-77a+18$

13) Simplify the below expression

$$-9a+14(1-13a)$$

A) $-191a+14$ B) $-191a+3$

C) $-191a$ D) $-191a+9$

14) Simplify the below expression

$$8(v-3.3)$$

A) $11.13-17.01v$

B) $8v-26.4$

C) $-75.116v-19.491$

D) $15.37-17.01v$

15) Simplify the below expression

$$-2(14x+3)-16$$

A) $-28x-22$ B) $-66+320x$

C) $-79+320x$ D) $-52+320x$

16) Simplify the below expression

$$-7(-4a-7)$$

A) $-99+66a$ B) $-4-8a$

C) $5-8a$ D) $28a+49$

www.math-knots.com | www.a4ace.com

17) Simplify the below expression

$$14x + (x - 11) \cdot 10$$

A) $24x - 91$ B) $24x - 110$

C) $29x + 119$ D) $19x - 91$

18) Simplify the below expression

$$-(m + 5)$$

A) $-117m + 126$

B) $-m - 5$

C) $-10m + 40$

D) $-10m + 28$

19) Write an inequality for the below graph

20) Write an inequality for the below graph

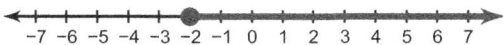

21) Simplify the below expression

$$5p + (-2 - 13p) \cdot 10$$

A) $-125p - 20$ B) $244p + 61$

C) $77p + 26$ D) $244p + 48$

22) Simplify the below expression

$$9(x + 13)$$

A) $9x + 117$ B) $9x + 125$

C) $-34 - 35x$ D) $-28 - 35x$

23) Write an inequality for the below graph

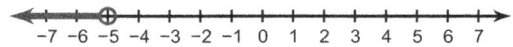

24) Write an inequality for the below graph

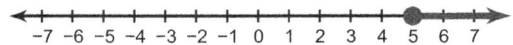

www.math-knots.com | www.a4ace.com

25) Write a graph for the below inequality

$$-x < -6$$

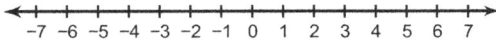

26) Write a graph for the below inequality

$$-a \geq 5$$

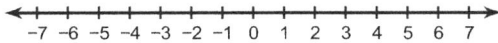

27) Write a graph for the below inequality

$$0 \leq -x$$

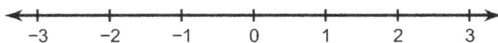

28) Write a graph for the below inequality

$$-2 < -v$$

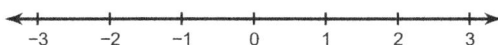

29) Write a graph for the below inequality

$$-n > -3$$

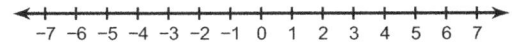

30) Write a graph for the below inequality

$$-6 < -n$$

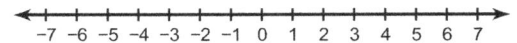

31) Write a graph for the below inequality

$$-k \geq 0$$

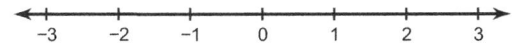

32) Write a graph for the below inequality

$$1\frac{1}{2} < n$$

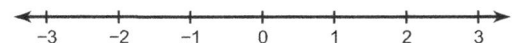

www.math-knots.com | www.a4ace.com

33) Write a graph for the below inequality

$$x < 2$$

37) Write a graph for the below inequality

$$-1\frac{1}{2} \geq b$$

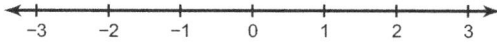

34) Solve the below inequality

$$19 + p > 51$$

A) $p > 969$　　　B) $p < 969$

C) $p < 32$　　　D) $p > 32$

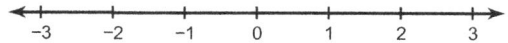

38) Solve the below inequality

$$14 \geq 13 + r$$

A) $r \leq 1$　　　B) $r \leq 182$

C) $r \geq \dfrac{14}{13}$　　　D) $r \leq \dfrac{14}{13}$

35) Solve the below inequality

$$p + 34 \leq 60$$

A) $p \geq 94$　　　B) $p \leq 26$

C) $p \geq 26$　　　D) $p \geq 2040$

39) Solve the below inequality

$$-19 - p > -45$$

A) $p < -64$　　　B) $p < -\dfrac{45}{19}$

C) $p < 26$　　　D) $p < 855$

36) Solve the below inequality

$$-12 - x \leq 5$$

A) $x \geq -7$　　　B) $x \geq 17$

C) $x \geq \dfrac{5}{12}$　　　D) $x \geq -17$

40) Solve the below inequality

$$-25 < -16 - p$$

A) $p < 9$　　　B) $p < -9$

C) $p > 9$　　　D) $p > -9$

41) Solve the below inequality

$$-35 \geq x - 32$$

A) $x \geq \dfrac{35}{32}$ B) $x \leq -3$

C) $x \geq 3$ D) $x \leq 3$

45) Solve the below inequality

$$-55 \geq -23 - p$$

A) $p \geq -1265$ B) $p \leq -78$

C) $p \geq 32$ D) $p \geq -78$

42) Solve the below inequality

$$19 - v < 43$$

A) $v > 62$ B) $v > -24$

C) $v < 24$ D) $v > 24$

46) Solve the below inequality

$$x - (-10) \geq -8$$

A) $x \leq -18$ B) $x \leq 2$

C) $x \geq -18$ D) $x \geq 2$

43) Solve the below inequality

$$r - (-24) < 64$$

A) $r < 40$ B) $r > 88$

C) $r > -1536$ D) $r < -1536$

47) Solve the below inequality

$$30 > 27 - r$$

A) $r < -3$ B) $r > -3$

C) $r < \dfrac{10}{9}$ D) $r > \dfrac{10}{9}$

44) Solve the below inequality

$$23 \geq x + 32$$

A) $x \leq \dfrac{23}{32}$ B) $x \leq -9$

C) $x \leq 55$ D) $x \leq 9$

48) Solve the below inequality

$$r - (-7) < -17$$

A) $r > -10$ B) $r > -\dfrac{17}{7}$

C) $r < -24$ D) $r < -\dfrac{17}{7}$

49) Solve the below inequality

$$-10 \geq 20 - a$$

A) $a \leq -\dfrac{1}{2}$

B) $a \geq -\dfrac{1}{2}$

C) $a \geq -200$

D) $a \geq 30$

50) Solve the below inequality

$$\dfrac{x}{30} < 33$$

A) $x > \dfrac{11}{10}$

B) $x > 990$

C) $x < 3$

D) $x < 990$

51) Solve the below inequality

$$644 > 23b$$

A) $b > 28$

B) $b < 667$

C) $b > 667$

D) $b < 28$

52) Solve the below inequality

$$\dfrac{x}{17} \leq -\dfrac{15}{17}$$

A) $x \geq -15$

B) $x \geq -\dfrac{304}{17}$

C) $x \geq -\dfrac{15}{289}$

D) $x \leq -15$

53) Solve the below inequality

$$-33r < -132$$

A) $r < 4$

B) $r > -99$

C) $r < -4356$

D) $r > 4$

54) Solve the below inequality

$$-33x \leq -132$$

A) $x \geq 4$

B) $x \geq 4356$

C) $x \geq -165$

D) $x \leq -165$

55) Solve the below inequality

$$17n \leq -136$$

A) $n \geq -153$

B) $n \geq 119$

C) $n \leq -153$

D) $n \leq -8$

56) Solve the below inequality

$$\dfrac{x}{40} < 34$$

A) $x > 1360$

B) $x < -6$

C) $x > -6$

D) $x < 1360$

57) Solve the below inequality

$$748 > 34\,m$$

A) $m < 25432$ B) $m > 714$

C) $m > 25432$ D) $m < 22$

58) Solve the below inequality

$$\frac{a}{13} \le 19$$

A) $a \le -247$ B) $a \le 6$

C) $a \ge 6$ D) $a \le 247$

59) Solve the below inequality

$$-\frac{6}{5}\,v < -\frac{177}{20}$$

A) $v > \frac{531}{50}$ B) $v > -\frac{201}{20}$

C) $v > \frac{201}{20}$ D) $v > \frac{59}{8}$

60) Solve the below inequality

$$30 \le 2\,b$$

A) $b \ge 15$ B) $b \le 28$

C) $b \le 15$ D) $b \le 60$

61) Solve the below inequality

$$\frac{7}{9}\,x > \frac{301}{36}$$

A) $x > \frac{2107}{324}$ B) $x > \frac{43}{4}$

C) $x > \frac{2431}{252}$ D) $x < \frac{2431}{252}$

62) Solve the below inequality

$$\frac{7}{16} \ge \frac{7}{8}\,m$$

A) $m \le \frac{1}{2}$ B) $m \le -\frac{49}{128}$

C) $m \le -\frac{177}{112}$ D) $m \le -\frac{79}{112}$

63) Solve the below inequality

$$\frac{199}{20}n > -\frac{199}{8}$$

A) $n < -\dfrac{597}{40}$

B) $n < -\dfrac{5}{2}$

C) $n > -\dfrac{597}{40}$

D) $n > -\dfrac{5}{2}$

64) Solve the below inequality

$$-\frac{3}{4}n \geq \frac{3}{2}$$

A) $n \geq -\dfrac{1}{6}$

B) $n \leq -2$

C) $n \geq -2$

D) $n \leq -\dfrac{1}{6}$

65) Solve the below inequality

$$\frac{15b}{109} \leq \frac{1530}{1199}$$

A) $b \leq \dfrac{22950}{130691}$

B) $b \leq -\dfrac{107741}{17985}$

C) $b \leq -\dfrac{153641}{17985}$

D) $b \leq \dfrac{102}{11}$

66) Solve the below inequality

$$-\frac{13}{3} \geq \frac{13}{18}p$$

A) $p \geq -\dfrac{169}{54}$

B) $p \geq -6$

C) $p \leq -6$

D) $p \geq \dfrac{65}{18}$

67) Solve the below inequality

$$-\frac{1705}{78} > \frac{110}{13}n$$

A) $n > \dfrac{1045}{78}$

B) $n < -\dfrac{31}{12}$

C) $n > -\dfrac{31}{12}$

D) $n < \dfrac{1045}{78}$

68) Solve the below inequality

$$15 < \frac{r+13}{2}$$

A) $r > -21$

B) $r > -6$

C) $r > -19$

D) $r > 17$

69) Solve the below inequality

$$\frac{x}{2} - 2 \le -6$$

A) $x \le -8$ B) $x \ge -39$

C) $x \le -39$ D) $x \ge -8$

70) Solve the below inequality

$$\frac{a}{7} + 8 > 5$$

A) $a < -21$ B) $a < -38$

C) $a < -22$ D) $a > -21$

71) Solve the below inequality

$$-32 < -4\left(-2 + x\right)$$

A) $x < 10$ B) $x > 10$

C) $x > 0$ D) $x < 0$

72) Solve the below inequality

$$8 + \frac{v}{25} > 7$$

A) $v > -36$ B) $v > -56$

C) $v > -17$ D) $v > -25$

73) Solve the below inequality

$$220 \le 4 + 8\,x$$

A) $x \le -40$ B) $x \ge -40$

C) $x \le 1$ D) $x \ge 27$

74) Solve the below inequality

$$\frac{x - 10}{38} \le -1$$

A) $x \ge -31$ B) $x \le -28$

C) $x \le -35$ D) $x \ge -35$

75) Solve the below inequality

$$5\,x + 11 > -94$$

A) $x < -56$ B) $x < -21$

C) $x > -21$ D) $x < -14$

76) Solve the below inequality

$$19 > \frac{n}{2} + 10$$

A) $n < 18$ B) $n < 9$

C) $n < -41$ D) $n < -47$

www.math-knots.com | www.a4ace.com

77) Solve the below inequality

$$186 \geq -6(n - 5)$$

A) $n \leq -26$ B) $n \leq 9$

C) $n \geq -26$ D) $n \leq -61$

78) Solve the below inequality

$$-2k \geq \frac{16}{3}$$

A) $k \leq \frac{32}{3}$ B) $k \leq \frac{35}{6}$

C) $k \leq -\frac{8}{3}$ D) $k \leq \frac{29}{6}$

79) Write a graph for the below inequality

$$-x > 1$$

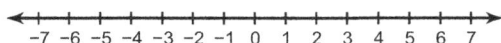

80) Write a graph for the below inequality

$$n \leq 0$$

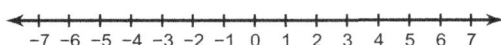

81) Solve the below inequality

$$\frac{6n}{19} \leq -\frac{4}{95}$$

A) $n \geq \frac{1781}{570}$ B) $n \leq \frac{1781}{570}$

C) $n \geq -\frac{1781}{570}$ D) $n \leq -\frac{2}{15}$

82) Write an inequality for the below graph

83) Write a graph for the below inequality

$$x \geq -4$$

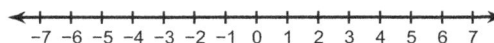

84) Write a graph for the below inequality

$$-5 < n$$

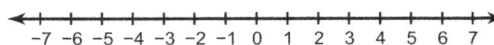

www.math-knots.com | www.a4ace.com

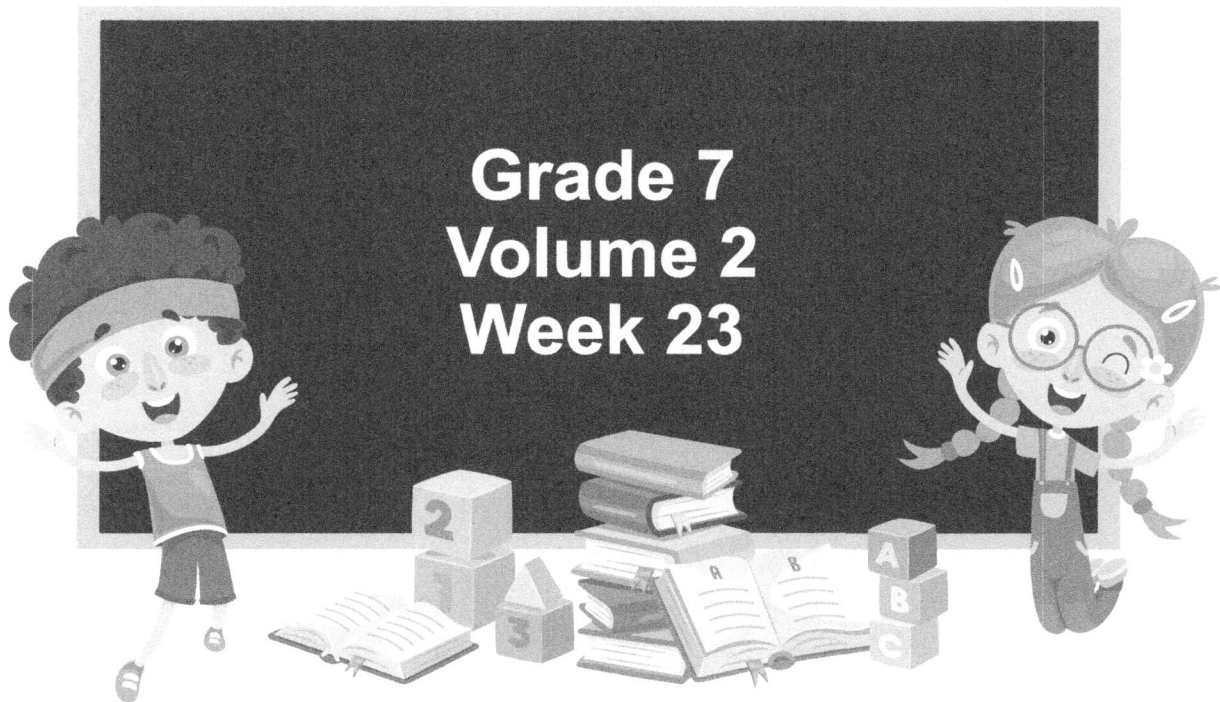

Grade 7
Volume 2
Week 23

www.math-knots.com | www.a4ace.com

1) State if the below three numbers can be the measures of the sides of a triangle.

16, 19, 5

5) State if the below three numbers can be the measures of the sides of a triangle.

25, 47, 20

2) State if the below three numbers can be the measures of the sides of a triangle.

23, 18, 19

6) State if the below three numbers can be the measures of the sides of a triangle.

7, 24, 27

3) State if the below three numbers can be the measures of the sides of a triangle.

18, 26, 24

7) State if the below three numbers can be the measures of the sides of a triangle.

22, 40, 18

4) State if the below three numbers can be the measures of the sides of a triangle.

45, 21, 23

8) State if the below three numbers can be the measures of the sides of a triangle.

22, 33, 16

www.math-knots.com | www.a4ace.com

9) State if the below three numbers can be the measures of the sides of a triangle.

26, 14, 18

10) State if the below three numbers can be the measures of the sides of a triangle.

16, 17, 1

11) State if the below three numbers can be the measures of the sides of a triangle.

25, 24, 19

12) State if the below three numbers can be the measures of the sides of a triangle.

40, 22, 16

13) State if the below three numbers can be the measures of the sides of a triangle.

22, 37, 16

14) State if the below three numbers can be the measures of the sides of a triangle.

9, 14, 14

15) State if the below three numbers can be the measures of the sides of a triangle.

28, 40, 27

16) State if the below three numbers can be the measures of the sides of a triangle.

7, 25, 22

17) State if the below three numbers can be the measures of the sides of a triangle.

6, 22, 25

18) State if the below three numbers can be the measures of the sides of a triangle.

22, 27, 46

19) State if the below three numbers can be the measures of the sides of a triangle.

28, 35, 19

20) State if the below three numbers can be the measures of the sides of a triangle.

17, 22, 14

21) State if the below three numbers can be the measures of the sides of a triangle.

24, 17, 27

22) State if the below three numbers can be the measures of the sides of a triangle.

23, 28, 29

23) State if the below three numbers can be the measures of the sides of a triangle.

7, 19, 26

24) State if the below three numbers can be the measures of the sides of a triangle.

28, 39, 19

25) State if the below three numbers can be the measures of the sides of a triangle.

20, 14, 7

26) Two sides of a triangle have the below measures. Find the range of possible measures for the third side.

14, 14

A) $0 < x < 28$ B) $1 < x < 24$

C) $1 < x < 28$ D) $1 < x < 27$

27) Two sides of a triangle have the below measures. Find the range of possible measures for the third side.

15, 11

A) $5 < x < 26$ B) $4 < x < 25$

C) $4 < x < 26$ D) $7 < x < 26$

28) Two sides of a triangle have the below measures. Find the range of possible measures for the third side.

11, 11

A) $0 < x < 22$ B) $1 < x < 22$

C) $0 < x < 18$ D) $0 < x < 21$

29) State if the below three numbers can be the measures of the sides of a triangle.

8, 13

A) $5 < x < 18$ B) $9 < x < 21$

C) $5 < x < 20$ D) $5 < x < 21$

30) Two sides of a triangle have the below measures. Find the range of possible measures for the third side.

10, 9

A) $1 < x < 19$ B) $3 < x < 19$

C) $2 < x < 16$ D) $2 < x < 15$

31) Two sides of a triangle have the below measures. Find the range of possible measures for the third side.

16, 10

A) $6 < x < 26$ B) $7 < x < 26$

C) $6 < x < 25$ D) $6 < x < 24$

32) Two sides of a triangle have the below measures. Find the range of possible measures for the third side.

9, 16

A) $8 < x < 21$ B) $8 < x < 22$

C) $7 < x < 24$ D) $7 < x < 25$

33) Two sides of a triangle have the below measures. Find the range of possible measures for the third side.

16, 13

A) $3 < x < 26$ B) $4 < x < 28$

C) $3 < x < 29$ D) $3 < x < 28$

34) Two sides of a triangle have the below measures. Find the range of possible measures for the third side.

8, 11

A) $7 < x < 18$ B) $3 < x < 19$

C) $3 < x < 18$ D) $4 < x < 18$

35) Two sides of a triangle have the below measures. Find the range of possible measures for the third side.

12, 16

A) $4 < x < 28$ B) $6 < x < 28$

C) $5 < x < 24$ D) $8 < x < 25$

36) Two sides of a triangle have the below measures. Find the range of possible measures for the third side.

8, 15

A) $8 < x < 20$ B) $7 < x < 19$

C) $7 < x < 22$ D) $7 < x < 23$

37) Two sides of a triangle have the below measures. Find the range of possible measures for the third side.

14, 8

A) $6 < x < 21$ B) $7 < x < 22$

C) $6 < x < 22$ D) $7 < x < 21$

38) Two sides of a triangle have the below measures. Find the range of possible measures for the third side.

14, 13

A) $1 < x < 27$ B) $1 < x < 23$

C) $5 < x < 26$ D) $1 < x < 26$

39) Two sides of a triangle have the below measures. Find the range of possible measures for the third side.

13, 11

A) $5 < x < 24$ B) $2 < x < 22$

C) $2 < x < 20$ D) $2 < x < 24$

40) Two sides of a triangle have the below measures. Find the range of possible measures for the third side.

10, 12

A) $2 < x < 22$ B) $5 < x < 18$

C) $6 < x < 19$ D) $2 < x < 21$

41) Find the area of the circle where radius
is 13 cm. (π = 3.14)
Round to the nearest tenth.

    A) 89695.1cm²   B) 530.7cm²

    C) 40.8cm²   D) 580.8cm²

42) Find the area of the circle where radius
is 10.7 km. (π = 3.14)
Round to the nearest tenth.

    A) 373.1km²   B) 429.8km²

    C) 33.6km²   D) 359.5km²

43) Find the area of the circle where radius
is 12.9 cm. (π = 3.14)
Round to the nearest tenth.

    A) 580.7cm²   B) 40.5cm²

    C) 86944.7cm²   D) 522.5cm²

44) Find the area of the circle where
diameter is 8.4 cm. (π = 3.14)
Round to the nearest tenth.

    A) 55.4cm²   B) 221.6cm²

    C) 977.4cm²   D) 78.5cm²

45) Find the area of the circle where radius
is 14.8 cm. (π = 3.14)
Round to the nearest tenth.

    A) 2751.2cm²   B) 172cm²

    C) 774cm²   D) 687.8cm²

46) Find the area of the circle where radius
is 14 mi. (π = 3.14)
Round to the nearest tenth.

    A) 697.1mi²   B) 615.4mi²

    C) 153.9mi²   D) 660.1mi²

47) Find the area of the circle where
diameter is 8 cm. (π = 3.14)
Round to the nearest tenth.

    A) 12.6cm²   B) 60.7cm²

    C) 63.5cm²   D) 50.2cm²

48) Find the area of the circle where
diameter is 25 m. (π = 3.14)
Round to the nearest tenth.

    A) 530.7m²   B) 598m²

    C) 89695.1m²   D) 538.9m²

www.math-knots.com | www.a4ace.com

49) Find the area of the circle where diameter is 10 cm. (π = 3.14) Round to the nearest tenth.

A) 78.5cm²　　B) 95cm²

C) 98.5cm²　　D) 109.3cm²

50) Find the area of the circle where circumference is 229 mi. (π = 3.14) Round to the nearest tenth.

A) 4182.5mi²

B) 4321.1mi²

C) 5571116.6mi²

D) 4367.9mi²

51) Find the area of the circle where circumference is 8.7 ft. (π = 3.14) Round to the nearest tenth.

A) 687.5ft²　　B) 615.2ft²

C) 650.9ft²　　D) 641.9ft²

52) Find the area of the circle where circumference is 81.6 m. (π = 3.14) Round to the nearest tenth.

A) 530.1m²　　B) 2120.4m²

C) 563.2m²　　D) 588.8m²

53) Find the area of the circle where diameter is 22 yd. (π = 3.14) Round to the nearest tenth.

A) 379.9yd²　　B) 437.2yd²

C) 1519.6yd²　　D) 452.1yd²

54) Find the area of the circle where circumference is 270 yd. (π = 3.14) Round to the nearest tenth.

A) 1451yd²　　B) 5804.1yd²

C) 6049.6yd²　　D) 5939.9yd²

55) Find the area of the circle where circumference is 131.9 mi. (π = 3.14) Round to the nearest tenth.

A) 1479.1mi²　　B) 1385.2mi²

C) 346.3mi²　　D) 66mi²

56) Find the area of the circle where circumference is 125.6 cm. (π = 3.14) Round to the nearest tenth.

A) 1256cm²　　B) 1294cm²

C) 1371.6cm²　　D) 1358.5cm²

www.math-knots.com | www.a4ace.com

57) Find the area of the circle where circumference is 260.6 cm. (π = 3.14) Round to the nearest tenth.

    A) 5407 cm²   B) 130.3 cm²

    C) 1351.8 cm²   D) 5485.5 cm²

58) Find the area of the circle where circumference is 194.7 yd. (π = 3.14) Round to the nearest tenth.

    A) 3018.2 yd²   B) 97.4 yd²

    C) 3216 yd²   D) 754.6 yd²

59) Find the circumference of the below circle.
Given area = 1296 π yd²

    A) 40π yd   B) 72π yd

    C) 38π yd   D) 68π yd

60) Find the circumference of the below circle.
Given area = 784 π km²

    A) 56π km   B) 68π km

    C) 82π km   D) 34π km

61) Find the area of the circle where circumference is 144.4 km. (π = 3.14) Round to the nearest tenth.

    A) 1747.9 km²   B) 1762.7 km²

    C) 1703.7 km²   D) 1660.1 km²

62) Find the area of the circle where circumference is 100.5 yd. (π = 3.14) Round to the nearest tenth.

    A) 804.2 yd²   B) 205967.4 yd²

    C) 50.3 yd²   D) 907.8 yd²

63) Find the circumference of the below circle.
Given area = 324 π in²

    A) 36π in   B) 28π in

    C) 50π in   D) 54π in

64) Find the circumference of the below circle.
Given area = 2116 π mi²

    A) 48π mi   B) 94π mi

    C) 92π mi   D) 72π mi

65) Find the circumference of the below circle.
Given area = 1600 π km²

A) 80π km   B) 84π km

C) 96π km   D) 44π km

66) Find the circumference of the below circle.
Given area = 1849 π m²

A) 68π m   B) 86π m

C) 74π m   D) 92π m

67) Find the circumference of the below circle.
Given area = 100 π m²

A) 16π m   B) 12π m

C) 20π m   D) 22π m

68) Find the diameter of the circle where circumference is 106.8 ft. (π = 3.14)
Round to the nearest tenth.

A) 578 ft   B) 8.2 ft

C) 17 ft   D) 34 ft

69) Find the circumference of the below circle.
Given area = 1444 π ft²

A) 38π ft   B) 64π ft

C) 76π ft   D) 58π ft

70) Find the circumference of the below circle.
Given area = 900 π mi²

A) 60π mi   B) 36π mi

C) 74π mi   D) 40π mi

71) Find the circumference of the below circle.
Given area = 576 π yd²

A) 34π yd   B) 40π yd

C) 52π yd   D) 48π yd

72) Find the diameter of the circle where circumference is 138.2 mi. (π = 3.14)
Round to the nearest tenth.

A) 88 mi   B) 45.4 mi

C) 44 mi   D) 45.2 mi

73) Find the diameter of the circle where circumference is 182.1 cm. (π = 3.14) Round to the nearest tenth.

A) 116 cm   B) 58.8 cm

C) 29 cm   D) 58 cm

74) Find the diameter of the circle where circumference is 157 km. (π = 3.14) Round to the nearest tenth.

A) 52 km   B) 50 km

C) 50.6 km   D) 50.8 km

75) Find the diameter of the circle where circumference is 244.3 ft. (π = 3.14) Round to the nearest tenth.

A) 155.6 ft   B) 79 ft

C) 78.2 ft   D) 77.8 ft

76) Find the diameter of the circle where circumference is 207.2 in. (π = 3.14) Round to the nearest tenth.

A) 33 in   B) 11.5 in

C) 66 in   D) 66.8 in

77) Find the diameter of the circle where circumference is 169.6 ft. (π = 3.14) Round to the nearest tenth.

A) 55.8 ft   B) 10.4 ft

C) 55.6 ft   D) 54 ft

78) Find the diameter of the circle where circumference is 277.6 ft. (π = 3.14) Round to the nearest tenth.

A) 88.4 ft   B) 176.8 ft

C) 13.3 ft   D) 44.2 ft

79) Find the diameter of the circle where circumference is 167 ft. (π = 3.14) Round to the nearest tenth.

A) 53.2 ft   B) 54 ft

C) 106.4 ft   D) 54.2 ft

80) Find the diameter of the circle where circumference is 135 in. (π = 3.14) Round to the nearest tenth.

A) 9.3 in   B) 43.2 in

C) 21.5 in   D) 43 in

81) Find the radius of the circle where area is 803.8 km². (π = 3.14) Round to the nearest tenth.

A) 16.2 km   B) 16 km

C) 16.3 km   D) 16.5 km

82) Find the radius of the circle where area is 606.7 km². (π = 3.14) Round to the nearest tenth.

A) 27.8 km   B) 13.9 km

C) 14.2 km   D) 3.7 km

83) Find the radius of the circle where area is 1017.4 m². (π = 3.14) Round to the nearest tenth.

A) 18 m   B) 4.2 m

C) 9 m   D) 36 m

84) Find the radius of the circle where area is 12.6 yd². (π = 3.14) Round to the nearest tenth.

A) 2.1 yd   B) 2.9 yd

C) 2.4 yd   D) 2 yd

85) Find the radius of the circle where area is 706.5 yd². (π = 3.14) Round to the nearest tenth.

A) 15.9 yd   B) 225 yd

C) 15 yd   D) 30 yd

86) Find the radius of the circle where area is 201 ft². (π = 3.14) Round to the nearest tenth.

A) 64 ft   B) 8 ft

C) 4 ft   D) 8.6 ft

87) Find the radius of the circle where area is 78.5 cm². (π = 3.14) Round to the nearest tenth.

A) 5.9 cm   B) 5 cm

C) 6 cm   D) 5.2 cm

88) Find the radius of the circle where area is 907.5 km². (π = 3.14) Round to the nearest tenth.

A) 17.3 km   B) 17.6 km

C) 17 km   D) 17.4 km

www.math-knots.com | www.a4ace.com

89) Find the radius of the circle where area is 379.9 mi². (π = 3.14) Round to the nearest tenth.

    A) 11 mi   B) 5.5 mi

    C) 11.8 mi   D) 3.3 mi

90) Find the radius of the circle where area is 844.5 m². (π = 3.14) Round to the nearest tenth.

    A) 8.2 m   B) 16.4 m

    C) 32.8 m   D) 17.2 m

91) Two circles having same centre have radii 210 inches and 350 inches respectively. What is the difference in their circumferences?

92) Diameter of a cycle wheel is 63 cm. How many times does the wheel revolve to cover a distance of 1980 m?

93) Find the radius of a circle whose area is 2,464 ft².

94) A horse is tied to a fixed pole with 14 ft long rope. The horse keeps moving keeping the rope tight. Find the area of ground swept by the horse.

95) Find the area of a circle whose diameter is 14 inches. (Take, Π = 22/7)

96) Find the circumference of a circle whose radius is 21 inches. (Take, Π = 22/7)

www.math-knots.com | www.a4ace.com

97) Find the area of a circle whose radius is 21 inches. (Take, Π = 22/7)

98) Find the circumference of a circle whose diameter is 35 inches. (Take, Π = 22/7)

99) Find the area of a circular park whose circumference is 44 ft. (Take, Π = 22/7)

100) Find the diameter of a circle whose area is 78.5 inches^2. (Take, Π = 3.14)

101) Find the radius of a circle whose circumference is 88 inches. (Take, Π = 22/7)

102) Fill in the blank: If the radius of a circle is doubled, its area is _____.

103) The areas of two circles are in the ratio 9:16. Find the ratio of their diameters.

104) The circumferences of two circles are in the ratio 5 : 6. Find the ratio of their areas.

105) Find the area of a circle whose circumference is the same as the perimeter of a rhombus of side 11 inches. (Take, ∏ = 22/7)

106) From a square sheet of side 14 inches, a circular sheet as big as possible was cut off. What is the area of the remaining sheet? (Take, π = 22/7)

107) A wire in circular shape of radius 35 inches is bent in the form of a square. Find the area of the square so formed, assuming no loss in wire. (Take, π = 22/7)

108) The radius of a circular park is 15 ft. A 2 ft wide circular path is laid inside the park along its circumference. Find the area of the circular path. (Take, ∏ = 22/7)

109) Two circles having the same centre have the radii 23 inches and 30 inches respectively. Find the difference in their circumferences. (Take, π = 22/7)

110) Find the area of a circle whose radius is 10.5 inches. (Consider, π = 22/7)

111) Find the circumference of a circle whose radius is 4.2 inches. (Consider, π = 22/7)

112) Find the area of a circle whose diameter is 8.4 inches. (Consider, π = 22/7)

113) Find the area of a circle whose radius is 4.9 inches. (Consider, π = 22/7)

114) Find the area of a circle whose diameter is 11.2 inches. (Consider, π = 22/7)

115) Find the circumference of a circle whose radius is 1.4 inches. (Consider, π = 3.14)

116) Find the circumference of a circle whose radius is 1.8 inches. (Consider, π = 3.14)

117) Find the circumference of a circle whose radius is 2.5 inches. (Consider, π = 3.14)

118) Find the circumference of a circle whose radius is 4.7 inches. (Consider, π = 3.14)

119) Find the circumference of a circle whose radius is 2.6 inches. (Consider, π = 3.14)

120) Find the area of a circle whose diameter is 18 inches. (Consider, π = 3.14)

121) Find the area of a circle whose diameter is 24 inches. (Consider, π = 3.14)

122) Find the circumference of a circle whose diameter is 20 inches. (Consider, π = 3.14)

123) Find the circumference of a circle whose diameter is 8 inches. (Consider, π = 3.14)

124) Find the area of a circle whose radius is 6 inches. (Consider, π = 3.14)

125) The area of a circle is 124.74 inches^2. Find the radius of the circle. (Take π = 22/7)

126) The area of a circle is 38.5 inches^2. Find the radius of the circle. (Take π = 22/7)

127) The area of a circle is 98.56 inches^2. Find the radius of the circle. (Take π = 22/7)

128) The area of a circle is 3,850 inches^2. Find the radius of the circle. (Take π = 22/7)

www.math-knots.com | www.a4ace.com

129) The area of a circle is 314 inches^2. Find the radius of the circle.

130) The circumference of a circle is 22 inches. Find the radius of the circle. (Consider, π = 22/7)

131) The circumference of a circle is 30.8 inches. Find the radius of the circle. (Consider, π = 22/7)

132) The circumference of a circle is 8.8 inches. Find the radius of the circle. (Consider, π = 22/7)

133) The circumference of a circle is 96.8 inches. Find the radius of the circle. (Consider, π = 22/7)

134) The circumference of a circle is 132 inches. Find the radius of the circle. (Consider, π = 22/7)

135) The area of a circle is 72.3456 inches^2. Find its circumference. (Consider, π = 3.14)

136) The area of a circle is 19.625 inches^2. Find its circumference. (Consider, π = 3.14)

137) The area of a circle is 12.56 inches^2.
Find its circumference.
(Consider, Π = 3.14)

138) The area of a circle is 153.86 inches^2.
Find its circumference.
(Consider, π = 3.14)

139) The area of a circle is 50.24 inches^2.
Find its circumference.
(Consider, π = 3.14)

140) The circumference of a circle is 75.36
inches. Find its area.
(Take π = 3.14)

141) The circumference of a circle is 50.24
inches. Find its area.
(Take π = 3.14)

142) The circumference of a circle is 34.54
inches. Find its area.
(Take π = 3.14)

143) The circumference of a circle is 94.2
inches. Find its area.
(Take π = 3.14)

144) The circumference of a circle is
87.92 inches. Find its area.
(Take Π = 3.14)

www.math-knots.com | www.a4ace.com

145) A wire in the form of a rectangle 10.4 inches long and 8.44 inches wide is reshaped and bent to form a circle. What is the radius of the circle so formed? (Take, Π = 3.14)

146) A wire in the form of a rectangle 15.12 inches long and 10 inches wide is reshaped and bent to form a circle. What is the radius of the circle so formed? (Take, Π = 3.14)

147) A wire in the form of a square 6.28 inches long on each side is reshaped and bent into a circle. What is the radius of the circle so formed? (Take, Π = 3.14)

148) A wire in the form of a square 18.84 inches long on each side is re-shaped and bent into a circle. What is the radius of the circle so formed? (Take, Π = 3.14)

149) A wire in the form of a rectangle 26 inches long and 11.68 inches wide is reshaped and bent into a circle. What is the radius of the circle so formed? (Take, π = 3.14)

150) A wire in the form of a rectangle 18.7 inches long and 14.27 inches wide is bent in the form of a circle. What is the area of the circle so formed? (Consider, Π = 3.14)

151) A wire in the form of a rectangle 18.6 inches long and 9.66 inches wide is bent in the form of a circle. What is the area of the circle so formed? (Consider, Π = 3.14)

152) A wire in the form of a rectangle 22.06 inches long and 15.62 inches wide is bent into the form of a circle. What is the area of the circle so formed? (Consider, Π = 3.14)

www.math-knots.com | www.a4ace.com

153) A wire in the form of a rectangle 9.7 inches long and 6 inches wide is bent into the form of a circle. What is the area of the circle so formed? (Consider, Π = 3.14)

154) A wire in the form of a rectangle 22.9 inches long and 21.06 inches wide is bent into the form of a circle. What is the area of the circle so formed? (Consider, Π = 3.14)

155) A wire in the form of a rectangle 18.7 inches long and 14.27 inches wide is bent in the form of a circle. What is the diameter of the circle so formed? (Consider, Π = 3.14)

156) A wire in the form of a rectangle 18.6 inches long and 9.66 inches wide is bent in the form of a circle. What is the diameter of the circle so formed? (Consider, Π = 3.14)

157) A wire in the form of a rectangle 22.06 inches long and 15.62 inches wide is bent into the form of a circle. What is the diameter of the circle so formed? (Consider, Π = 3.14)

158) A wire in the form of a rectangle 9.7 inches long and 6 inches wide is bent into the form of a circle. What is the diameter of the circle so formed? (Consider, Π = 3.14)

159) A wire in the form of a rectangle 22.9 inches long and 21.06 inches wide is bent into the form of a circle. What is the diameter of the circle so formed? (Consider, Π = 3.14)

160) What is the distance covered by the wheel of a truck in 1500 revolutions if the diameter of the wheel is 26.88 inches? Express the distance covered in miles. (Consider, Π = 22/7 and 1 mile = 1,760 yards)

161) What is the distance covered by the wheel of a car in 2000 revolutions if the diameter of the wheel is 18 inches? Express the distance covered in yards. (Consider, Π = 3.14)

162) The diameter of a wheel is 21 inches. How many revolutions will it make to travel 33 yards? (Consider, Π = 22/7)

163) The radius of a bicycle wheel is 15 inches. How many revolutions will it make to travel 3.5 miles? (Consider, Π = 22/7 and 1 mile = 1,760 yards)

164) Find the area of space enclosed by two concentric circles of radii 15 inches and 6 inches. (Consider, Π = 22/7)

165) Find the area of space enclosed by two concentric circles of radii 15 inches and 10 inches. (Consider, Π = 3.14)

166) Find the area of space enclosed by two concentric circles of radii 18 inches and 15 inches. (Consider, Π = 3.14)

167) Find the area of space enclosed by two concentric circles of radii 25 inches and 20 inches. (Consider, Π = 3.14)

168) Find the area of space enclosed by two concentric circles of radii 14 inches and 7 inches. (Consider, Π = 22/7)

169) The diameter of a circular park is 46 yards. A 2 yards wide road runs outside around the park. Find the cost of constructing the road at $3 per square yard. (Consider, Π = 3.14)

170) Find the area of a circle inscribed in a square of side 4.9 inches. (Consider, Π = 22/7)

171) Find the area of a circle inscribed in a square of side 7 inches. (Consider, Π = 22/7)

172) Find the area of the circle inscribed in a square of side 8.4 inches. (Consider, Π = 22/7)

173) The area of a circle is 25 times the area of another circle. What is the ratio of their circumferences?

174) The area of a circle is 49 times the area of another circle. What is the ratio of their circumference?

175) The area of a circle is 9 times the area of another circle. If the radius of the bigger circle is 15 inches, what is the radius of the smaller circle?

176) The area of a circle is 16 times the area of another circle. If the diameter of the smaller circle is 8 inches, what is the radius of the bigger circle?

177) The circumference of a circle is 6 times the circumference of another circle. What is the ratio of their areas?

178) The radius of a circular playground is 21 yards. On the outside, a 4 yard wide path is running around it. Find the cost of turfing the path at $1.50 per square yard. (Consider, π = 3.14)

179) The diameter of a circular sheet of cardboard is 14 inches. From it, 105 circular pieces of 0.5 inch radius have been cut. What is the area of the remaining sheet? (Consider, Π = 22/7)

180) Find the radius of a circle whose circumference is 25.12 inches. (Use, Π = 3.14)

181) Find the radius of a circle whose circumference is 37.68 inches. (Use, Π = 3.14)

182) Find the radius of a circle whose circumference is 56.52 inches. (Use Π = 3.14)

183) Find the circumference of a circle whose diameter is 7 cm. (Use Π = 3.14)

184) Find the circumference of a circle whose diameter is 5 cm. (Use Π = 3.14)

185) Find the circumference of a circle whose diameter is 8 cm.
(Use Π = 3.14)

186) The diameter of a wheel of a bike is 56 cm. Find the distance traveled by the bike during the period in which the wheel makes 1000 revolutions.
(Use Π = 22/7)

187) The diameter of a wheel of a bike is 49 cm. Find the distance traveled by the bike during the period in which the wheel makes 100 revolutions.
(Use Π = 22/7)

188) The diameter of a wheel of a car is 35 cm. Find the distance traveled by the car during the period in which the wheel makes 2500 revolutions.
(Use Π = 22/7)

189) The radius of a wheel of a truck is 63 cm. Find the distance traveled by the truck during the period in which the wheel makes 5000 revolutions. (Use Π = 22/7)

190) Find the area of a circle whose radius is 11 cm.
(Use Π = 3.14)

191) Find the area of a circle whose radius is 13 cm.
(Use Π = 3.14)

192) Find the area of a circle whose radius is 16 cm.
(Use Π = 3.14)

193) The circumference of a circle is 138.16 cm. Find the area of the circle. (Use, Π = 3.14)

194) The circumference of a circle is 94.2 cm. Find the area of the circle. (Use, Π = 3.14)

195) The circumference of a circle is 62.8 cm. Find the area of the circle. (Use, Π = 3.14)

130   www.math-knots.com | www.a4ace.com

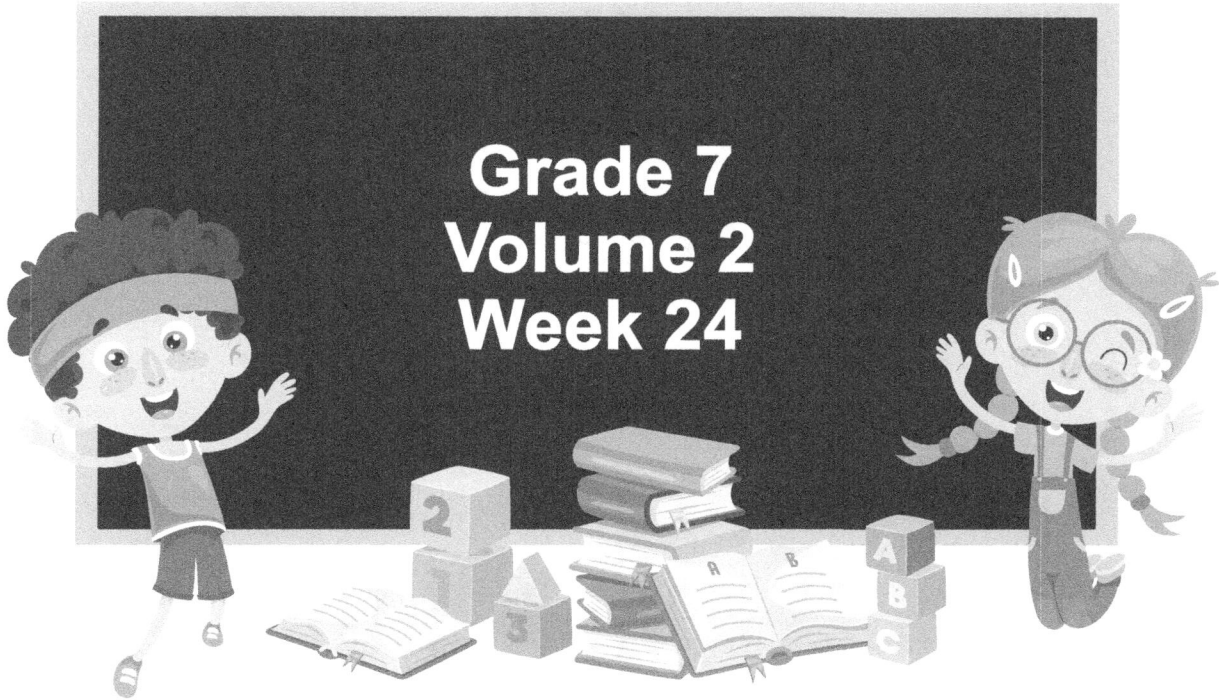

Grade 7
Volume 2
Week 24

www.math-knots.com | www.a4ace.com

Grade 7
Volume 2
Week 24

©All rights reserved-Math-Knots LLC., VA-USA   132   www.math-knots.com | www.a4ace.com

1) Find the area of the given figure below.

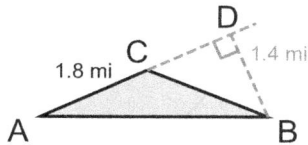

2) Find the area of the given figure below.

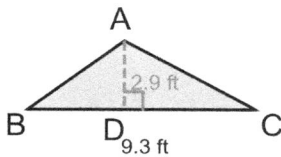

3) Find the area of the given figure below.

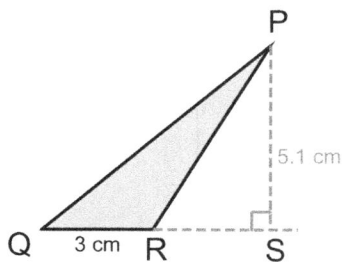

4) Find the area of the given figure below.

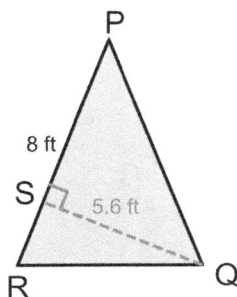

5) Find the area of the given figure below.

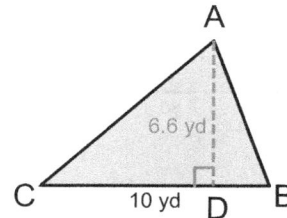

6) Find the area of the given figure below.

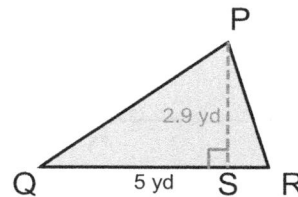

7) Find the area of the given figure below.

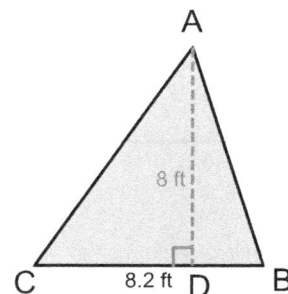

8) Find the area of the given figure below.

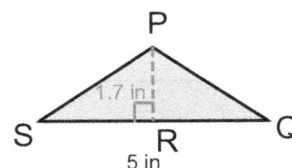

9) Find the area of the given figure below.

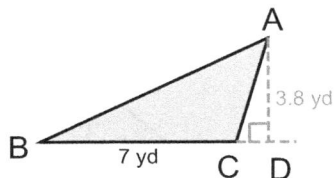

10) Find the area of the given figure below.

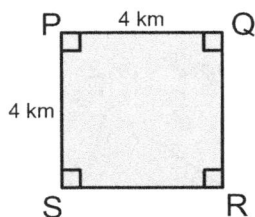

11) Find the area of the given figure below.

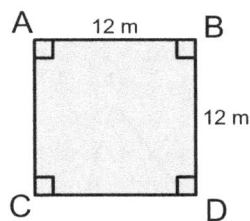

12) Find the area of the given figure below.

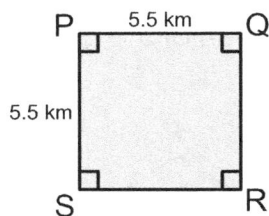

13) Find the area of the given figure below.

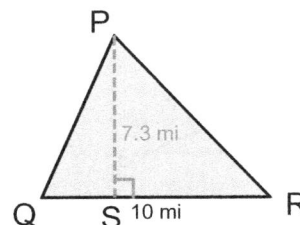

14) Find the area of the given figure below.

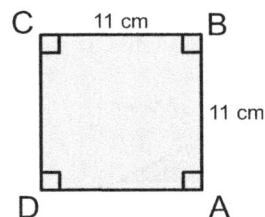

15) Find the area of the given figure below.

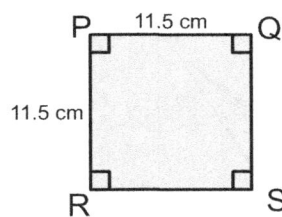

16) Find the area of the given figure below.

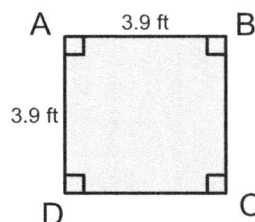

www.math-knots.com | www.a4ace.com

17) Find the area of the given figure below.

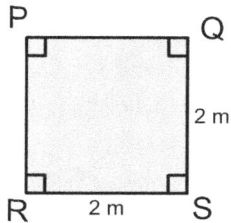

P   Q

2 m

R   2 m   S

21) Find the area of the given figure below.

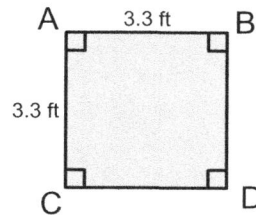

A   3.3 ft   B

3.3 ft

C   D

18) Find the area of the given figure below.

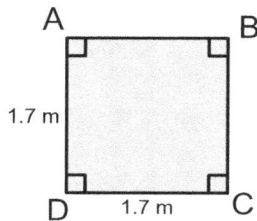

A   B

1.7 m

D   1.7 m   C

22) Find the area of the given figure below.

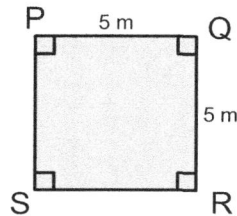

P   5 m   Q

5 m

S   R

19) Find the area of the given figure below.

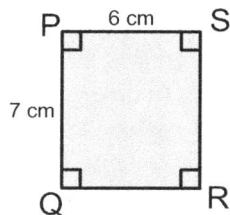

P   6 cm   S

7 cm

Q   R

23) Find the area of the given figure below.

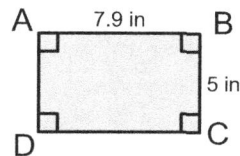

A   7.9 in   B

5 in

D   C

20) Find the area of the given figure below.

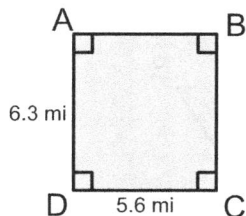

A   B

6.3 mi

D   5.6 mi   C

24) Find the area of the given figure below.

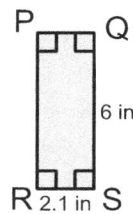

P   Q

6 in

R 2.1 in S

www.math-knots.com | www.a4ace.com

25) Find the area of the given figure below.

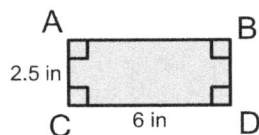

A _____ B
2.5 in
C   6 in   D

26) Find the area of the given figure below.

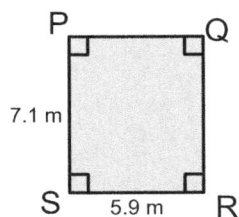

P _____ Q
7.1 m
S   5.9 m   R

27) Find the area of the given figure below.

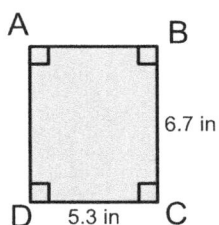

A   B
6.7 in
D   5.3 in   C

28) Find the area of the given figure below.

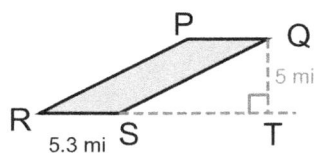

P _____ Q
            5 mi
R   T
5.3 mi S

29) Find the area of the given figure below.

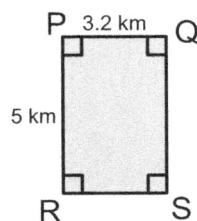

P 3.2 km Q
5 km
R   S

30) Find the area of the given figure below.

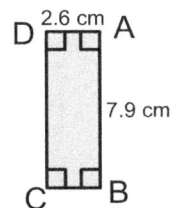

D 2.6 cm A
          7.9 cm
C   B

31) Find the area of the given figure below.

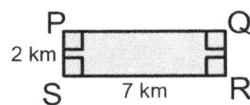

P _____ Q
2 km
S   7 km   R

32) Find the area of the given figure below.

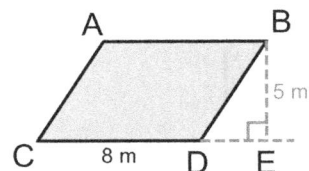

A   B
            5 m
C   8 m   D E

33) Find the area of the given figure below.

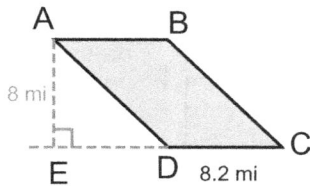

34) Find the area of the given figure below.

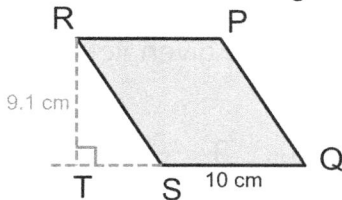

35) Find the area of the given figure below.

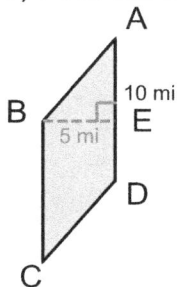

36) Find the area of the given figure below.

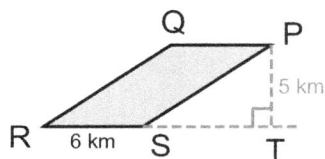

37) Find the area of the given figure below.

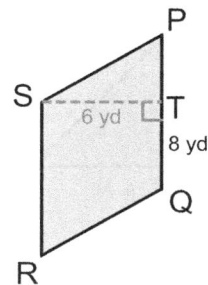

38) Find the area of the given figure below.

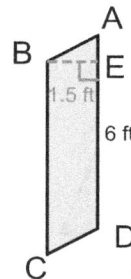

39) Find the area of the given figure below.

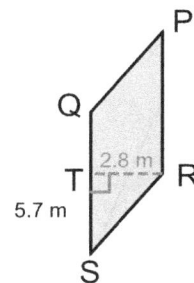

40) Find the area of the given figure below.

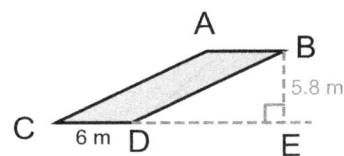

41) Find the area of the given figure below.

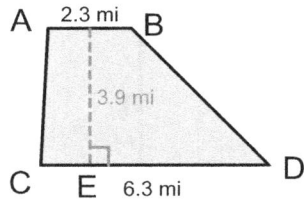

A 2.3 mi B
3.9 mi
C E 6.3 mi D

42) Find the area of the given figure below.

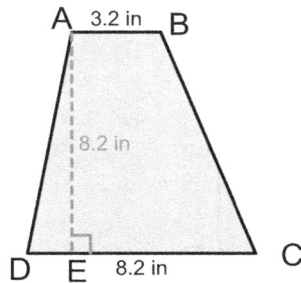

A 3.2 in B
8.2 in
D E 8.2 in C

43) Find the area of the given figure below.

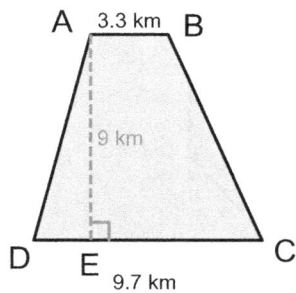

A 3.3 km B
9 km
D E 9.7 km C

44) Find the area of the given figure below.

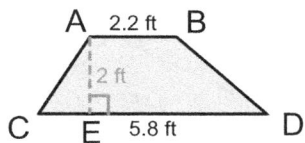

A 2.2 ft B
2 ft
C E 5.8 ft D

45) Find the area of the given figure below.

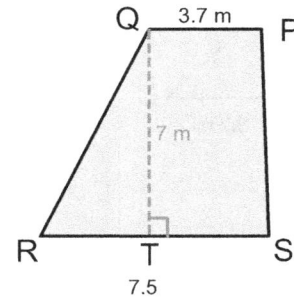

Q 3.7 m P
7 m
R T S
7.5

46) Find the area of the given figure below.

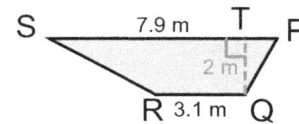

S 7.9 m T P
2 m
R 3.1 m Q

47) Find the area of the given figure below.

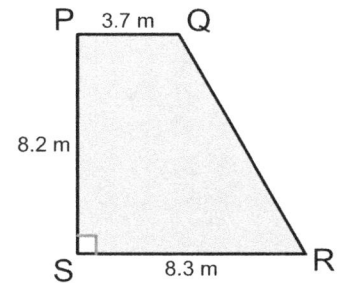

P 3.7 m Q
8.2 m
S 8.3 m R

48) Find the area of the given figure below.

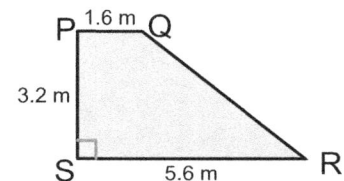

P 1.6 m Q
3.2 m
S 5.6 m R

49) Find the area of the given figure below.

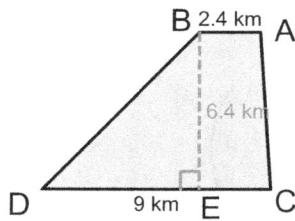

50) Find the area of the given circle below in terms of Pi.

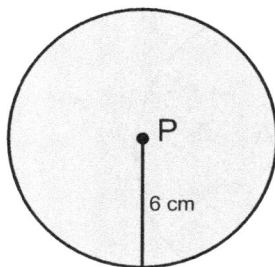

51) Find the area of the given circle below in terms of Pi.

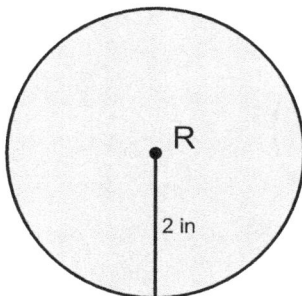

52) Find the area of the given figure below.

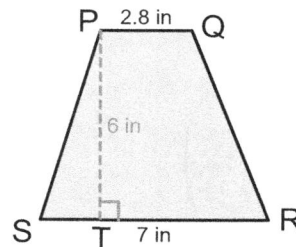

53) Find the area of the given circle below in terms of Pi.

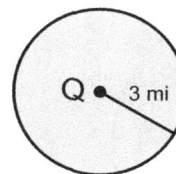

54) Find the area of the given circle below in terms of Pi.

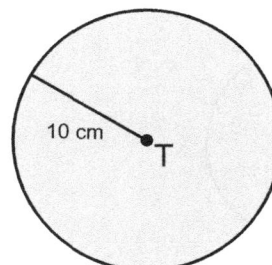

www.math-knots.com | www.a4ace.com

55) Find the area of the given circle below in terms of Pi.

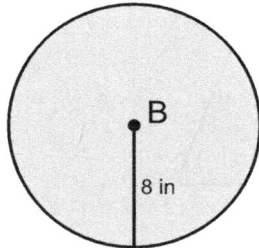

56) Find the area of the given circle below in terms of Pi.

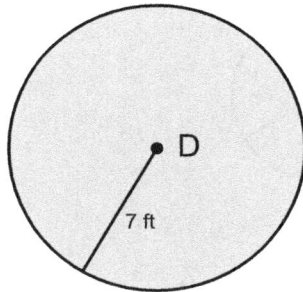

57) Find the area of the given circle below in terms of Pi.

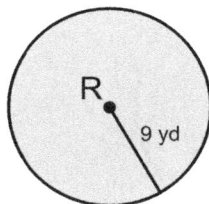

58) Find the area of the given circle below in terms of Pi.

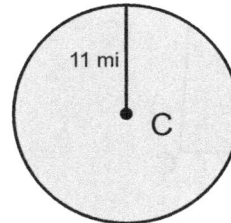

59) Find the area of the given circle below in terms of Pi.

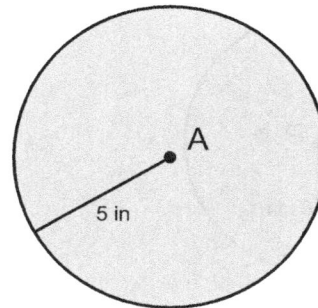

60) Find the area of the given circle below in terms of Pi.

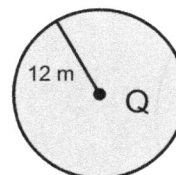

www.math-knots.com | www.a4ace.com

61) Find the circumference of the given circle below in terms of Pi.

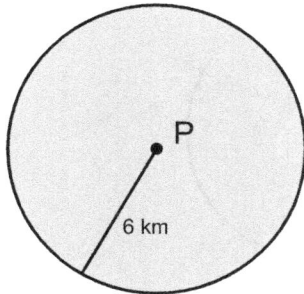

6 km

P

62) Find the circumference of the given circle below in terms of Pi.

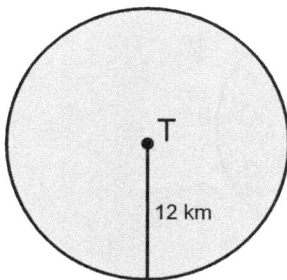

T

12 km

63) Find the circumference of the given circle below in terms of Pi.

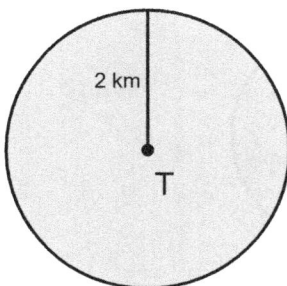

2 km

T

64) Find the circumference of the given circle below in terms of Pi.

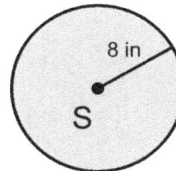

8 in

S

65) Find the circumference of the given circle below in terms of Pi.

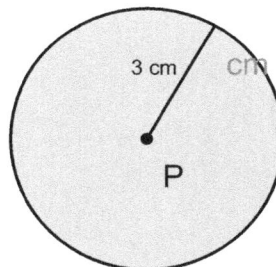

3 cm

cm

P

66) Find the circumference of the given circle below in terms of Pi.

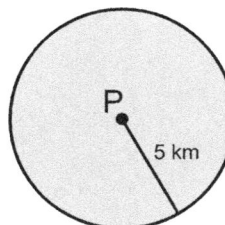

P

5 km

www.math-knots.com | www.a4ace.com

67) Find the circumference of the given circle below in terms of Pi.

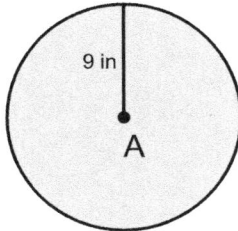

9 in

A

68) Find the circumference of the given circle below in terms of Pi.

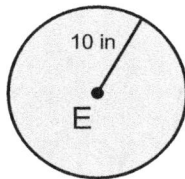

10 in

E

69) Find the area of the given circle below. (Round your answer to the nearest tenth)

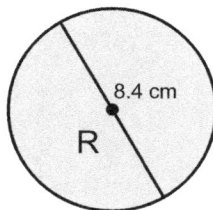

8.4 cm

R

70) Find the circumference of the given circle below in terms of Pi.

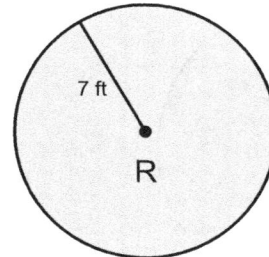

7 ft

R

71) Find the circumference of the given circle below in terms of Pi.

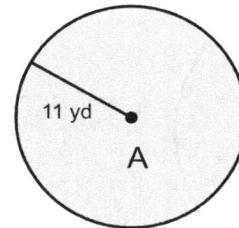

11 yd

A

72) Find the area of the given circle below. (Round your answer to the nearest tenth)

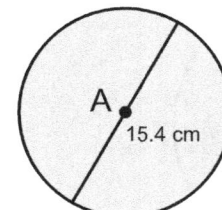

A

15.4 cm

www.math-knots.com | www.a4ace.com

73) Find the area of the given circle below. (Round your answer to the nearest tenth)

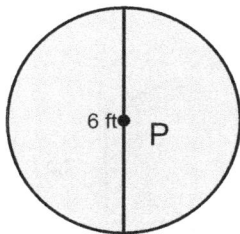

76) Find the area of the given circle below. (Round your answer to the nearest tenth)

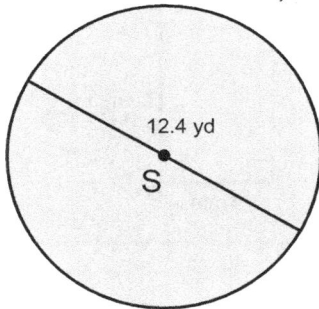

74) Find the area of the given circle below. (Round your answer to the nearest tenth)

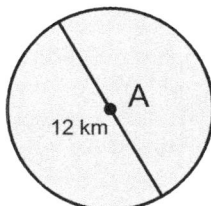

77) Find the circumference of the given circle below. (Round your answer to the nearest tenth)

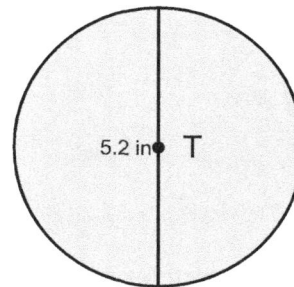

75) Find the circumference of the given circle below. (Round your answer to the nearest tenth)

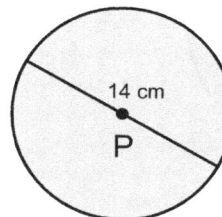

78) Find the circumference of the given circle below. (Round your answer to the nearest tenth)

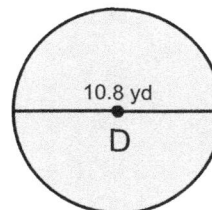

79) Find the circumference of the given circle below. (Round your answer to the nearest tenth)

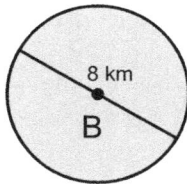

8 km

B

80) Find the circumference of the given circle below. (Round your answer to the nearest tenth)

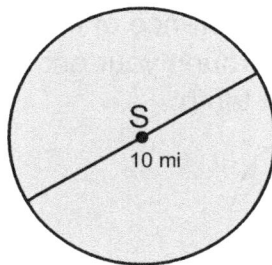

S
10 mi

81) Find the area and perimeter of the figure given below

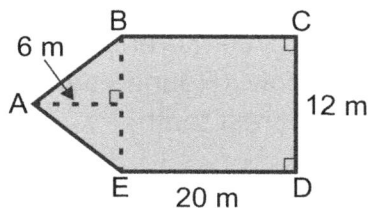

6 m

B   C

A

12 m

E   20 m   D

82) Find the area and perimeter of the figure given below

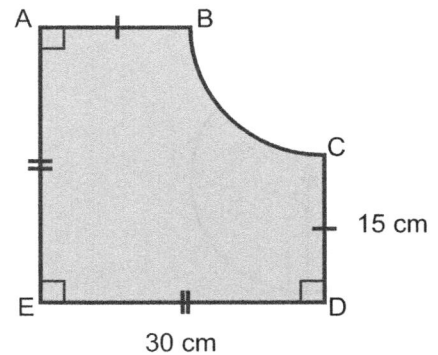

A   B

C

15 cm

E   D

30 cm

83) Find the area and perimeter of the figure given below

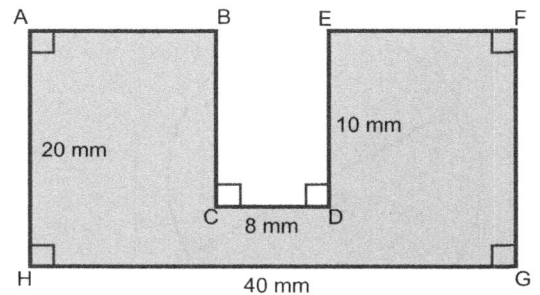

A   B   E   F

20 mm   10 mm

C   8 mm   D

H   40 mm   G

84) Find the area and perimeter of the figure given below

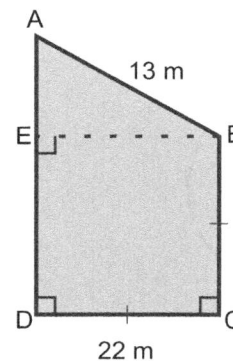

A

13 m

E - - - - - - B

D   C

22 m

www.math-knots.com | www.a4ace.com

85) Find the area and perimeter of the figure given below

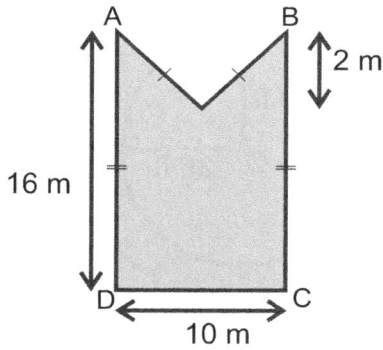

86) Find the area and perimeter of the figure given below

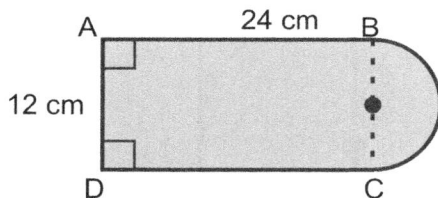

87) Find the area and perimeter of the figure given below

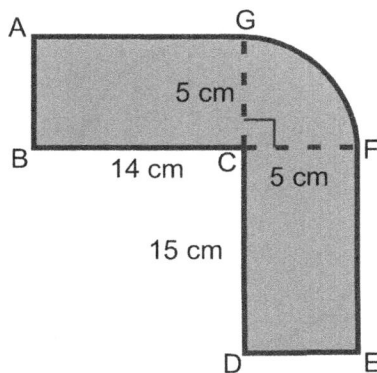

88) Find the area and perimeter of the figure given below

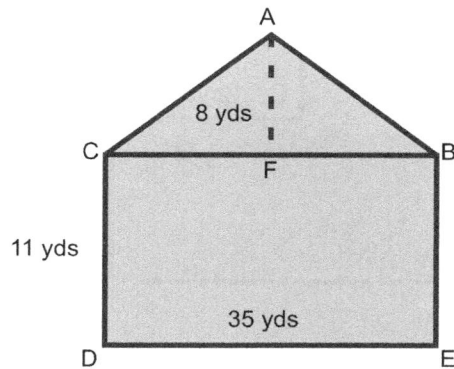

89) Find the area and perimeter of the figure given below

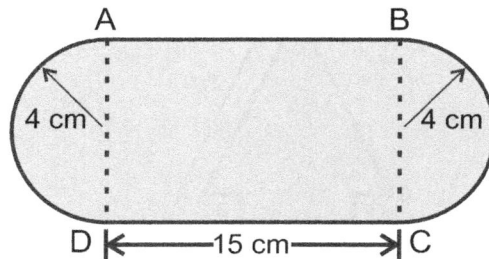

90) Find the area and perimeter of the figure given below

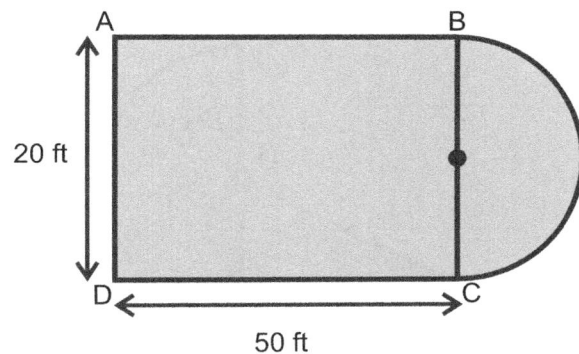

www.math-knots.com | www.a4ace.com

91) Find the area and perimeter of the figure given below

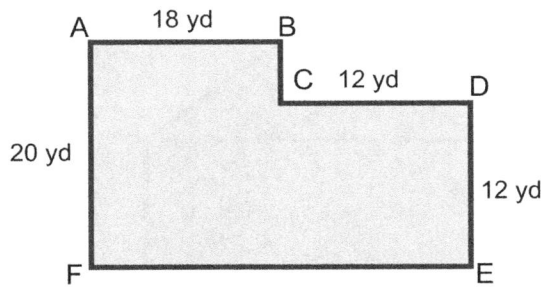

A ─18 yd─ B
C 12 yd D
20 yd
12 yd
F E

92) Find the perimeter of the figure given below

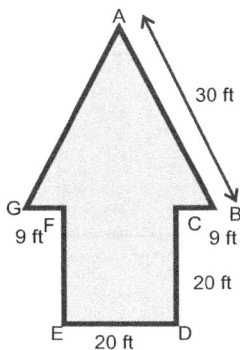

A
30 ft
G B
9 ft F C 9 ft
20 ft
E 20 ft D

93) Find the area of the figure given below

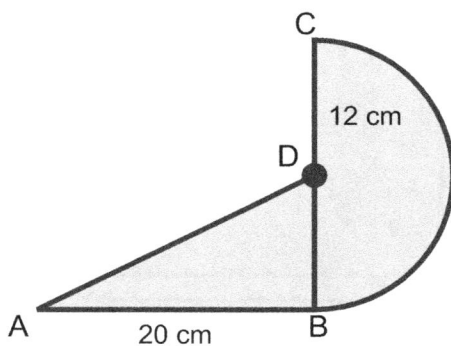

C
12 cm
D
A 20 cm B

94) Find the area of the shaded region to the nearest tenth

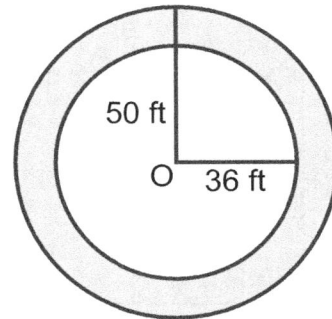

50 ft
O 36 ft

95) Find the area of the shaded region to the nearest tenth

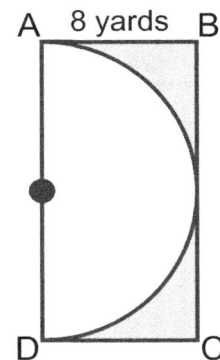

A 8 yards B

D C

96) Find the area of the shaded region to the nearest tenth

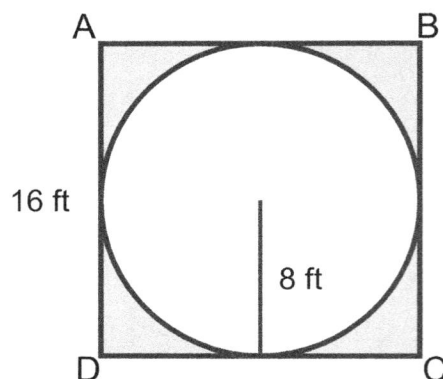

A B
16 ft
8 ft
D C

97) Find the area of the shaded region to the nearest tenth

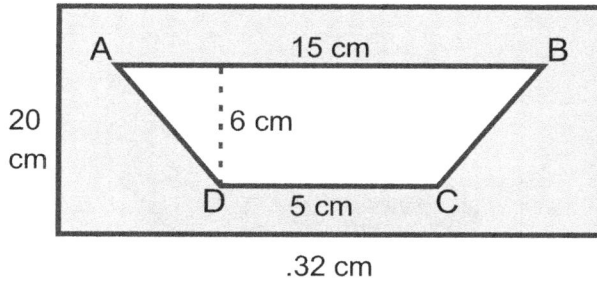

98) Find the area of the figure given below

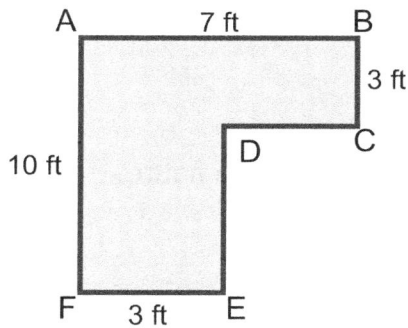

99) Find the area of the shaded region to the nearest tenth

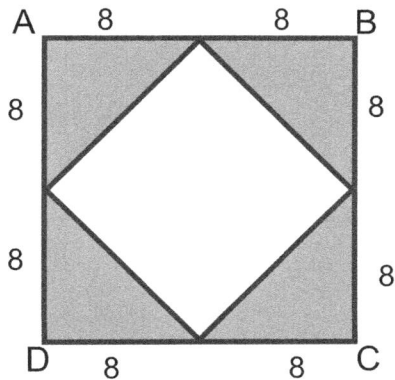

100) Find the area of the figure given below

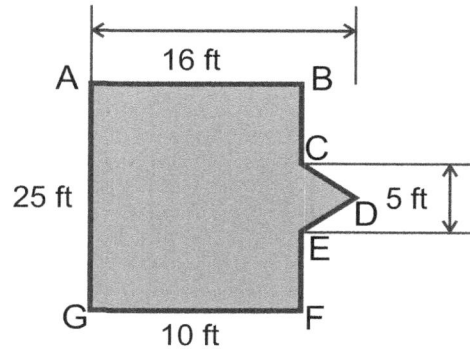

101) Find the area of the figure given below

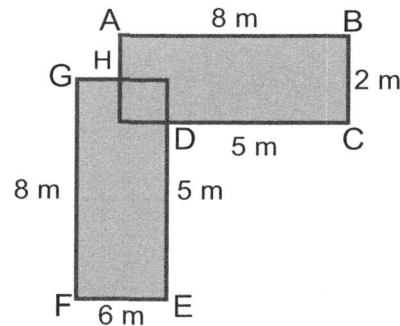

102) Find the area of the figure given below

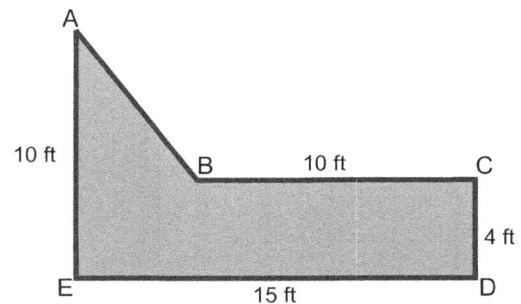

www.math-knots.com | www.a4ace.com

103) Find the area of the figure given below

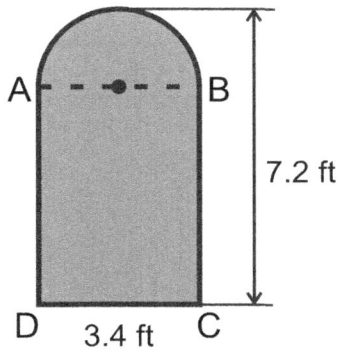

7.2 ft

3.4 ft

104) Find the perimeter of the figure given below

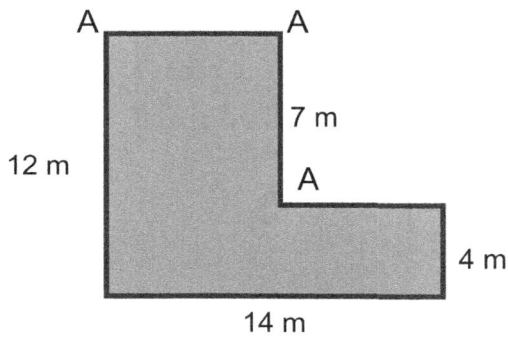

7 m

12 m

4 m

14 m

105) Find the area of the figure given below

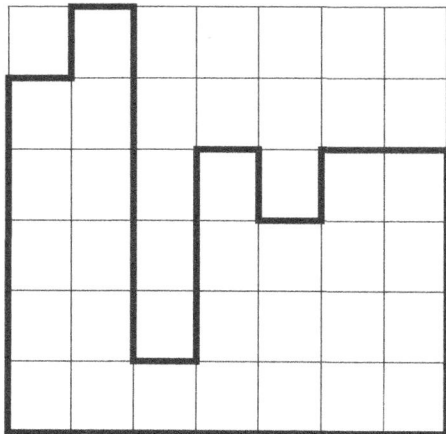

106) Find the area of the figure given below

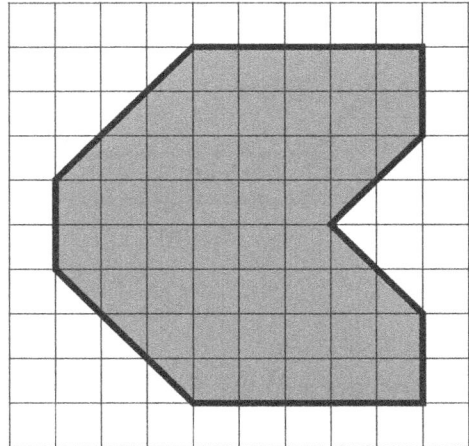

107) Find the area of the figure given below

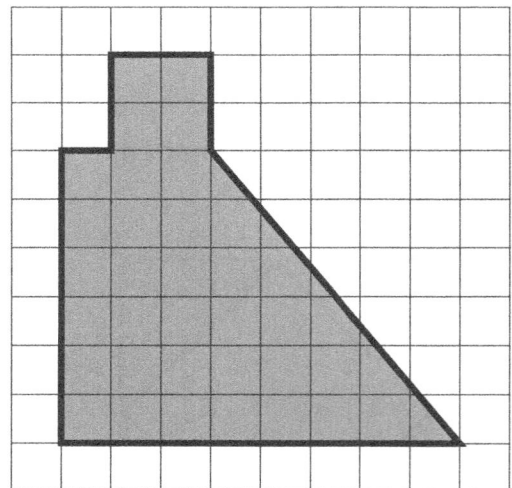

108) Find the area of the figure given below

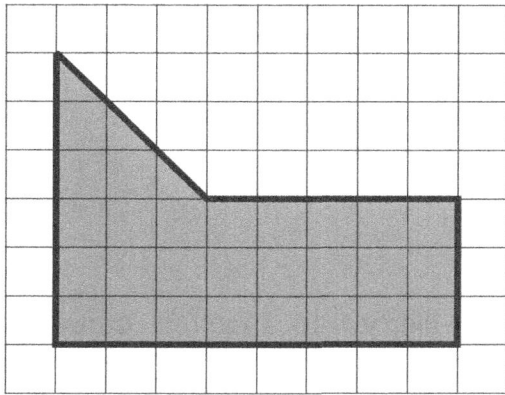

109) Find the area of the figure given below

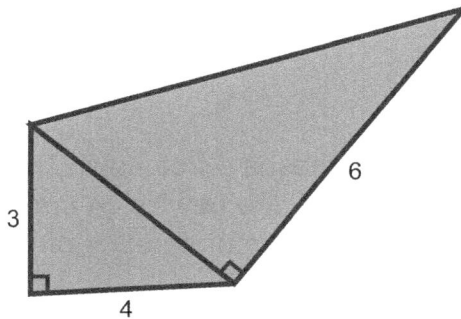

110) Find the area of the figure given below

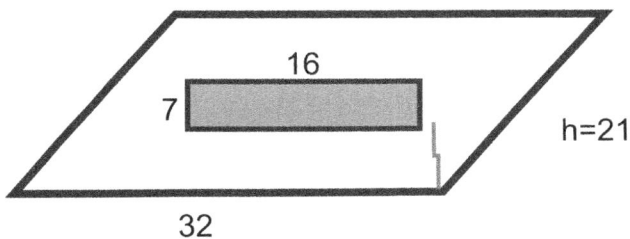

111) Find the perimeter of the composite figure given below below

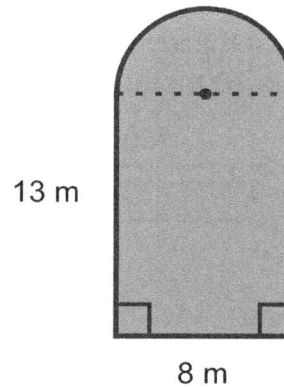

13 m

8 m

112) Find the perimeter of the composite figure given below below

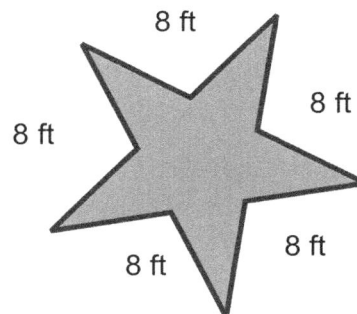

8 ft

8 ft

8 ft

8 ft

8 ft

8 ft

113) Find the perimeter of the composite figure given below below

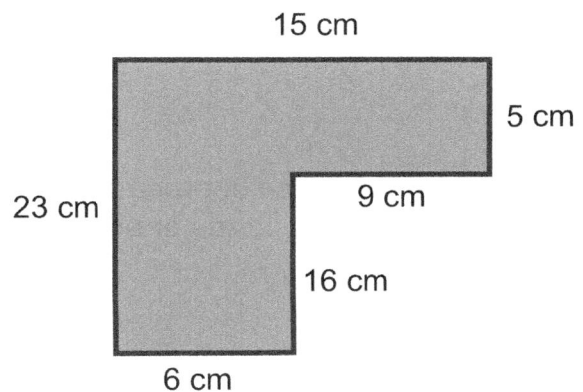

15 cm

5 cm

23 cm

9 cm

16 cm

6 cm

114) Here is a diagram of the track King's is thinking of adding around the new field. It consists of two parallel lines and a semicircle at each end. The track is 10 meters wide.

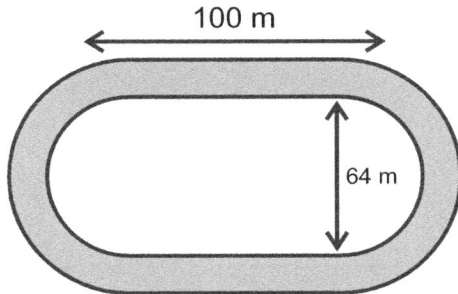

100 m

64 m

a) If someone runs one lap on the track , how far will they have run ?

b) If someone runs one lap on the outside of the track , how far will they have run ?

c) Find the difference between the distances of running on the inside or outside of the track.

115) Tom buys a round table. The radius of the table is 6 meters. What is the area of table?

116) Harry has a circular carpet in his drawing room. He wants to put a circular table in middle of the carpet. The diameter of the carpet is 12 meters and the diameter of the table is 4 meters. Calculate how much area of carpet is left after putting the table in place?

117) Will purchases a fruit bowl. The diameter of the bowl is 14 cm. What is the circumference of the bowl?

118) Lola bakes cookies for her friend. The radius of a cookie is 5 inches. What is the cookie's circumference?

119) Beth makes a round pizza. She wants to put a cheese layer on the pizza. If the cake is 8 cm in diameter, how many square cm of cheese layer does she need to put on the pizza?

123) Johnbuys a big drum. The diameter of a drum circle is 12 feet. What is the area of the drum?

120) Maria buys a round photo frame . The radius of the photo frame is 9 cm. What is the photo frame's circumference?

124) Nancy wants to buy round dinner plates for Christmas dinner party at her home. The radius of plates is 1 foot. What is the plate's circumference?

121) Ben made a tasty burger. The diameter of the burger was 5 cm. What was the area of burger?

125) Andy made a cake. The circumferences of the cake is 6 cm. What is the diameter of the cake?

122) Ron purchases a round wall clock. The clock's radius is 10m. What is the circumference of the clock?

126) Zade makes a round chocolate cake. She wants to put a cream layer on cake. If the cake is 6 cm in diameter, how many square cm of cream layer does she need to put on the chocolate cake?

127) Jade wants to change tire for her Tesla car. The Tesla cars wheel has a radius of 35', what is the area of the Tesla cars wheel?

128) Ms. Mary has a flower garden. There is a circular fountain with a 10m radius in the center of a circular park with a 200 m radius. Calculate the total walking area available to the park visitors.

129) Mary has a circular fountain in her garden. She wants to put a statue in middle of the fountain. The diameter of fountain is 16 meters and diameter of statue is 2 meters. What is the area of the fountain?

130) A Cow is tied with rope in the center of grassland to graze. The length of rope is 5m. The diameter of circular garden is 50m. Find the area in which the horse cannot graze.

131) Olivia made a round strawberry shortcake. The diameter of the cake is 8 cm. What is the area of the cake?

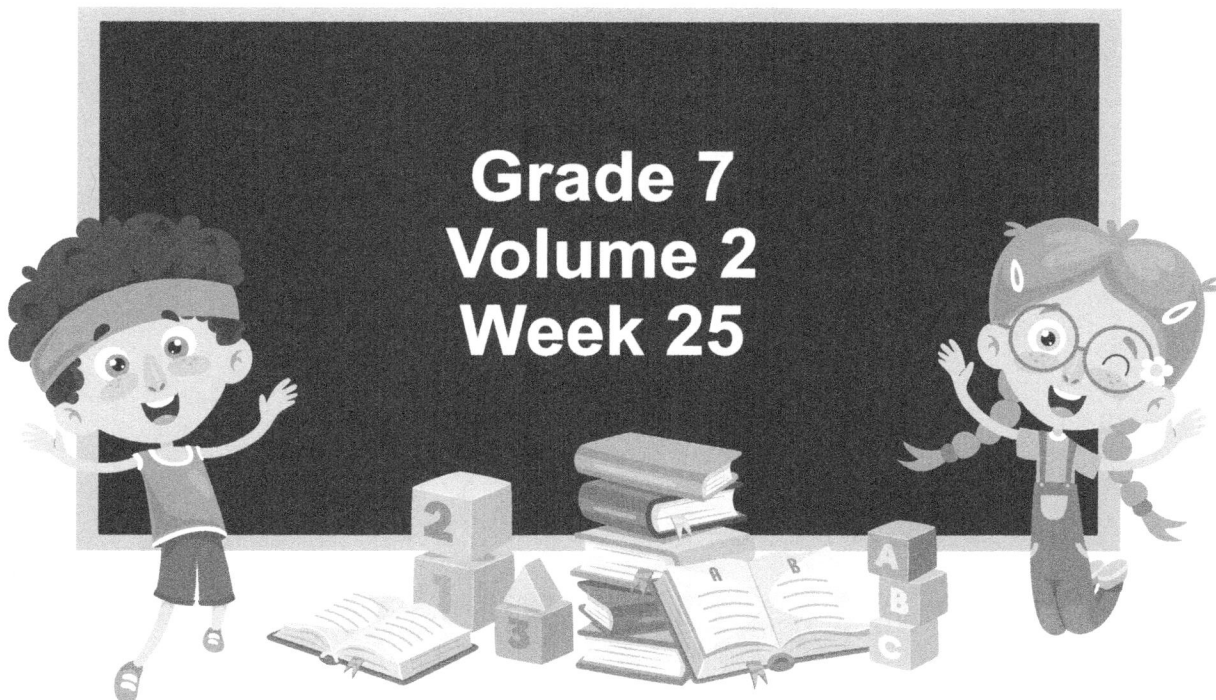

Grade 7
Volume 2
Week 25

1) A square prism measuring 26 ft along each edge of the base and 22 ft tall. Find the volume.

   A) 9689 ft³   B) 14449 ft³

   C) 15467 ft³   D) 14872 ft³

2) A square prism measuring 19 ft along each edge of the base and 16 ft tall. Find the volume.

   A) 6040 ft³   B) 5776 ft³

   C) 5589 ft³   D) 8524 ft³

3) A square prism measuring 3 in along each edge of the base and 8 in tall. Find the volume.

   A) 75 in³   B) 61 in³

   C) 72 in³   D) 98 in³

4) A square prism measuring 9 m along each edge of the base and 24 m tall. Find the volume.

   A) 1773 m³   B) 2046 m³

   C) 2219 m³   D) 1944 m³

5) A square prism measuring 17 m along each edge of the base and 8 m tall. Find the volume.

   A) 2312 m³   B) 2518 m³

   C) 2591 m³   D) 3356 m³

6) A square prism measuring 13 m along each edge of the base and 30 m tall. Find the volume.

   A) 5070 m³   B) 2550 m³

   C) 3079 m³   D) 4758 m³

7) A square prism measuring 9 in along each edge of the base and 23 in tall. Find the volume.

   A) 2107 in³   B) 1863 in³

   C) 1763 in³   D) 2609 in³

8) A square prism measuring 7 in along each edge of the base and 13 in tall. Find the volume.

   A) 558 in³   B) 637 in³

   C) 807 in³   D) 688 in³

         www.math-knots.com | www.a4ace.com

9) A square prism measuring 8 cm along each edge of the base and 6 cm tall. Find the volume.

A) 490 cm³   B) 256 cm³

C) 384 cm³   D) 488 cm³

10) A square prism measuring 19 m along each edge of the base and 28 m tall. Find the volume.

A) 10108 m³   B) 13620 m³

C) 9186 m³   D) 11359 m³

11) A square prism measuring 21 km along each edge of the base and 22 km tall. Find the volume.

A) 9702 km³   B) 11314 km³

C) 10604 km³   D) 5946 km³

12) A square prism measuring 8 yd along each edge of the base and 2 yd tall. Find the volume.

A) 128 yd³   B) 192 yd³

C) 73 yd³   D) 69 yd³

13) A square prism measuring 24 m along each edge of the base and 15 m tall. Find the volume.

A) 10327 m³   B) 10450 m³

C) 9347 m³   D) 8640 m³

14) A square prism measuring 11 cm along each edge of the base and 21 cm tall. Find the volume.

A) 2541 cm³   B) 3752 cm³

C) 2579 cm³   D) 1581 cm³

15) A square prism measuring 26 m along each edge of the base and 25 m tall. Find the volume.

A) 21435 m³   B) 12689 m³

C) 13749 m³   D) 16900 m³

16) A square prism measuring 29 in along each edge of the base and 28 in tall. Find the volume.

A) 16215 in³   B) 13891 in³

C) 23548 in³   D) 31841 in³

17) A square prism measuring 30 cm along each edge of the base and 26 cm tall. Find the volume.

   A) 18172 cm³   B) 23400 cm³

   C) 23654 cm³   D) 22040 cm³

21) A square prism measuring 26 yd along each edge of the base and 17 yd tall. Find the volume.

   A) 11492 yd³   B) 11406 yd³

   C) 14662 yd³   D) 15874 yd³

18) A square prism measuring 12 m along each edge of the base and 20 m tall. Find the volume.

   A) 3699 m³   B) 3395 m³

   C) 1509 m³   D) 2880 m³

22) A square prism measuring 26 km along each edge of the base and 29 km tall. Find the volume.

   A) 27149 km³   B) 19604 km³

   C) 25168 km³   D) 26481 km³

19) A square prism measuring 29 km along each edge of the base and 10 km tall. Find the volume.

   A) 8410 km³   B) 6880 km³

   C) 6068 km³   D) 12280 km³

23) A square prism measuring 16 mi along each edge of the base and 17 mi tall. Find the volume.

   A) 4352 mi³   B) 3592 mi³

   C) 3893 mi³   D) 6130 mi³

20) A square prism measuring 20 ft along each edge of the base and 4 ft tall. Find the volume.

   A) 2291 ft³   B) 1600 ft³

   C) 1516 ft³   D) 1608 ft³

24) A square prism measuring 25 km along each edge of the base and 22 km tall. Find the volume.

   A) 17537 km³   B) 13750 km³

   C) 11131 km³   D) 10959 km³

www.math-knots.com | www.a4ace.com

25) A square prism measuring 13 cm along each edge of the base and 26 cm tall. Find the volume.

A) 6226 cm³   B) 3620 cm³

C) 3059 cm³   D) 4394 cm³

26) A square prism measuring 13 yd along each edge of the base and 27 yd tall. Find the volume.

A) 6502 yd³   B) 4407 yd³

C) 2988 yd³   D) 4563 yd³

27) A square prism measuring 25 cm along each edge of the base and 24 cm tall. Find the volume.

A) 15000 cm³   B) 17711 cm³

C) 13796 cm³   D) 14669 cm³

28) A square prism measuring 16 mi along each edge of the base and 11 mi tall. Find the volume.

A) 2816 mi³   B) 3039 mi³

C) 3606 mi³   D) 2314 mi³

29) A square prism measuring 25 km along each edge of the base and 20 km tall. Find the volume.

A) 15503 km³   B) 12500 km³

C) 10197 km³   D) 18523 km³

30) A square prism measuring 12 cm along each edge of the base and 13 cm tall. Find the volume.

A) 1272 cm³   B) 2571 cm³

C) 2672 cm³   D) 1872 cm³

31) A rectangular prism measuring 6 cm and 4 cm along the base and 19 cm tall. Find the volume.

A) 456 cm³   B) 659 cm³

C) 531 cm³   D) 488 cm³

32) A rectangular prism measuring 5 ft and 12 ft along the base and 11 ft tall. Find the volume.

A) 923 ft³   B) 660 ft³

C) 648 ft³   D) 687 ft³

33) A rectangular prism measuring 14 cm and 15 cm along the base and 16 cm tall. Find the volume.

    A) 2136 cm³   B) 2504 cm³

    C) 3360 cm³   D) 2708 cm³

34) A rectangular prism measuring 17 mi and 15 mi along the base and 8 mi tall. Find the volume.

    A) 2950 mi³   B) 2503 mi³

    C) 1336 mi³   D) 2040 mi³

35) A rectangular prism measuring 9 in and 5 in along the base and 2 in tall. Find the volume.

    A) 102 in³   B) 96 in³

    C) 109 in³   D) 90 in³

36) A rectangular prism measuring 5 mi and 6 mi along the base and 11 mi tall. Find the volume.

    A) 410 mi³   B) 396 mi³

    C) 330 mi³   D) 171 mi³

37) A rectangular prism measuring 17 yd and 12 yd along the base and 9 yd tall. Find the volume.

    A) 2744 yd³   B) 1834 yd³

    C) 1836 yd³   D) 1394 yd³

38) A rectangular prism measuring 15 in and 20 in along the base and 5 in tall. Find the volume.

    A) 1500 in³   B) 885 in³

    C) 1418 in³   D) 862 in³

39) A rectangular prism measuring 17 ft and 12 ft along the base and 7 ft tall. Find the volume.

    A) 1129 ft³   B) 1338 ft³

    C) 1428 ft³   D) 2106 ft³

40) A rectangular prism measuring 14 mi and 5 mi along the base and 14 mi tall. Find the volume.

    A) 814 mi³   B) 980 mi³

    C) 983 mi³   D) 660 mi³

        www.math-knots.com | www.a4ace.com

41) A rectangular prism measuring 2 mi and 13 mi along the base and 2 mi tall. Find the volume.

    A) 29 mi³   B) 56 mi³

    C) 52 mi³   D) 49 mi³

42) A rectangular prism measuring 8 cm and 9 cm along the base and 11 cm tall. Find the volume.

    A) 907 cm³   B) 669 cm³

    C) 803 cm³   D) 792 cm³

43) A rectangular prism measuring 16 m and 15 m along the base and 17 m tall. Find the volume.

    A) 3705 m³   B) 4080 m³

    C) 2165 m³   D) 2754 m³

44) A rectangular prism measuring 8 mi and 2 mi along the base and 11 mi tall. Find the volume.

    A) 206 mi³   B) 176 mi³

    C) 222 mi³   D) 231 mi³

45) A rectangular prism measuring 13 cm and 18 cm along the base and 7 cm tall. Find the volume.

    A) 1638 cm³   B) 1430 cm³

    C) 2225 cm³   D) 831 cm³

46) A rectangular prism measuring 11 in and 15 in along the base and 13 in tall. Find the volume.

    A) 3056 in³   B) 3188 in³

    C) 1542 in³   D) 2145 in³

47) A rectangular prism measuring 20 cm and 13 cm along the base and 6 cm tall. Find the volume.

    A) 1560 cm³   B) 1687 cm³

    C) 1544 cm³   D) 2038 cm³

48) A rectangular prism measuring 20 km and 14 km along the base and 14 km tall. Find the volume.

    A) 4608 km³   B) 4876 km³

    C) 3920 km³   D) 3697 km³

www.math-knots.com | www.a4ace.com

49) A rectangular prism measuring 15 mi and 10 mi along the base and 12 mi tall. Find the volume.

A) 1590 mi³   B) 1800 mi³

C) 1316 mi³   D) 2360 mi³

50) A rectangular prism measuring 12 m and 9 m along the base and 13 m tall. Find the volume.

A) 834 m³   B) 1404 m³

C) 1221 m³   D) 1626 m³

51) A rectangular prism measuring 13 yd and 12 yd along the base and 20 yd tall. Find the volume.

A) 3120 yd³   B) 1609 yd³

C) 2577 yd³   D) 1828 yd³

52) A rectangular prism measuring 6 m and 8 m along the base and 8 m tall. Find the volume.

A) 256 m³   B) 277 m³

C) 406 m³   D) 384 m³

53) A rectangular prism measuring 16 cm and 6 cm along the base and 9 cm tall. Find the volume.

A) 741 cm³   B) 589 cm³

C) 864 cm³   D) 1079 cm³

54) A rectangular prism measuring 9 km and 6 km along the base and 17 km tall. Find the volume.

A) 1192 km³   B) 918 km³

C) 1053 km³   D) 654 km³

55) A rectangular prism measuring 19 km and 18 km along the base and 3 km tall. Find the volume.

A) 656 km³   B) 1216 km³

C) 584 km³   D) 1026 km³

56) A rectangular prism measuring 20 cm and 16 cm along the base and 4 cm tall. Find the volume.

A) 960 cm³   B) 881 cm³

C) 657 cm³   D) 1280 cm³

57) A rectangular prism measuring 16 yd and 9 yd along the base and 3 yd tall. Find the volume.

    A) 390 yd³   B) 542 yd³

    C) 478 yd³   D) 432 yd³

58) A rectangular prism measuring 9 ft and 14 ft along the base and 6 ft tall. Find the volume.

    A) 1092 ft³   B) 525 ft³

    C) 565 ft³   D) 756 ft³

59) A rectangular prism measuring 16 in and 19 in along the base and 16 in tall. Find the volume.

    A) 3233 in³   B) 4864 in³

    C) 6379 in³   D) 7231 in³

60) A rectangular prism measuring 17 ft and 16 ft along the base and 11 ft tall. Find the volume.

    A) 2992 ft³   B) 3359 ft³

    C) 3667 ft³   D) 4479 ft³

61) A rectangluar pyramid of height 20 yd measuring 26 yd and 28 yd along the base. Find the volume.

    A) 3118.22 yd³   B) 2883.33 yd³

    C) 14560 yd³   D) 4853.33 yd³

62) A rectangluar pyramid of height 25 cm measuring 26 cm and 27 cm along the base. Find the volume.

    A) 5850 cm³   B) 7345 cm³

    C) 17550 cm³   D) 3676 cm³

63) A rectangluar pyramid of height 19 yd measuring 12 yd and 21 yd along the base. Find the volume.

    A) 4788 yd³   B) 1596 yd³

    C) 2335 yd³   D) 1329 yd³

64) A rectangluar pyramid of height 7 in measuring 8 in and 16 in along the base. Find the volume.

    A) 896 in³   B) 191.84 in³

    C) 298.67 in³   D) 301.43 in³

65) A rectangluar pyramid of height 22 cm measuring 9 cm and 23 cm along the base. Find the volume.

   A) 4554 cm³   B) 1483 cm³

   C) 1518 cm³   D) 2245 cm³

66) A rectangluar pyramid of height 16 cm measuring 10 cm and 14 cm along the base. Find the volume.

   A) 746.67 cm³   B) 519.93 cm³

   C) 949.93 cm³   D) 2240 cm³

67) A rectangluar pyramid of height 21 in measuring 14 in and 18 in along the base. Find the volume.

   A) 5292 in³   B) 1317 in³

   C) 1764 in³   D) 1432 in³

68) A rectangluar pyramid of height 14 m measuring 16 m and 19 m along the base. Find the volume.

   A) 1418.67 m³   B) 4256 m³

   C) 1351.63 m³   D) 1990.11 m³

69) A rectangluar pyramid of height 13 in measuring 8 in and 13 in along the base. Find the volume.

   A) 396.4 in³   B) 450.67 in³

   C) 1352 in³   D) 231.08 in³

70) A rectangluar pyramid of height 19 ft measuring 24 ft and 30 ft along the base. Find the volume.

   A) 2365 ft³   B) 13680 ft³

   C) 3424 ft³   D) 4560 ft³

71) A rectangluar pyramid of height 9 mi measuring 11 mi and 21 mi along the base. Find the volume.

   A) 354 mi³   B) 2079 mi³

   C) 700 mi³   D) 693 mi³

72) A rectangluar pyramid of height 25 km measuring 21 km and 28 km along the base. Find the volume.

   A) 5982 km³   B) 5611 km³

   C) 4900 km³   D) 14700 km³

73) A rectangluar pyramid of height 22 yd measuring 13 yd and 21 yd along the base. Find the volume.

   A) 1862 yd³   B) 2002 yd³

   C) 6006 yd³   D) 1691 yd³

74) A rectangluar pyramid of height 23 mi measuring 17 mi and 29 mi along the base. Find the volume.

   A) 11339 mi³   B) 3779.67 mi³

   C) 2873.13 mi³   D) 3708.57 mi³

75) A rectangluar pyramid of height 22 yd measuring 21 yd and 23 yd along the base. Find the volume.

   A) 10626 yd³   B) 1815 yd³

   C) 3778 yd³   D) 3542 yd³

76) A rectangluar pyramid of height 22 km measuring 8 km and 17 km along the base. Find the volume.

   A) 1284.15 km³   B) 895.01 km³

   C) 2992 km³   D) 997.33 km³

77) A rectangluar pyramid of height 11 km measuring 12 km and 17 km along the base. Find the volume.

   A) 748 km³   B) 397 km³

   C) 601 km³   D) 2244 km³

78) A rectangluar pyramid of height 18 mi measuring 6 mi and 17 mi along the base. Find the volume.

   A) 441 mi³   B) 612 mi³

   C) 648 mi³   D) 1836 mi³

79) A rectangluar pyramid of height 15 cm measuring 17 cm and 30 cm along the base. Find the volume.

   A) 2550 cm³   B) 3338 cm³

   C) 1575 cm³   D) 7650 cm³

80) A rectangluar pyramid of height 21 cm measuring 15 cm and 24 cm along the base. Find the volume.

   A) 3379 cm³   B) 2872 cm³

   C) 2520 cm³   D) 7560 cm³

www.math-knots.com | www.a4ace.com

81) A rectangluar pyramid of height 25 ft measuring 25 ft and 30 ft along the base. Find the volume.

   A) 18750 ft³   B) 7021 ft³

   C) 6250 ft³   D) 5495 ft³

82) A rectangluar pyramid of height 23 cm measuring 24 cm and 30 cm along the base. Find the volume.

   A) 5520 cm³   B) 16560 cm³

   C) 6700 cm³   D) 3117 cm³

83) A rectangluar pyramid of height 20 in measuring 27 in and 28 in along the base. Find the volume.

   A) 15120 in³   B) 3216 in³

   C) 5075 in³   D) 5040 in³

84) A rectangluar pyramid of height 24 in measuring 15 in and 20 in along the base. Find the volume.

   A) 3056 in³   B) 2691 in³

   C) 7200 in³   D) 2400 in³

85) A rectangluar pyramid of height 29 cm measuring 14 cm and 15 cm along the base. Find the volume.

   A) 2057 cm³   B) 2026 cm³

   C) 6090 cm³   D) 2030 cm³

86) A rectangluar pyramid of height 30 yd measuring 16 yd and 23 yd along the base. Find the volume.

   A) 3680 yd³   B) 11040 yd³

   C) 2826 yd³   D) 3677 yd³

87) A rectangluar pyramid of height 12 mi measuring 10 mi and 11 mi along the base. Find the volume.

   A) 440 mi³   B) 1320 mi³

   C) 288 mi³   D) 654 mi³

88) A rectangluar pyramid of height 20 ft measuring 15 ft and 27 ft along the base. Find the volume.

   A) 8100 ft³   B) 2700 ft³

   C) 2280 ft³   D) 2585 ft³

www.math-knots.com | www.a4ace.com

89) A rectangluar pyramid of height 30 cm measuring 22 cm and 29 cm along the base. Find the volume.

A) 6380 cm³   B) 4021 cm³

C) 19140 cm³   D) 6468 cm³

90) A rectangluar pyramid of height 29 in measuring 17 in and 25 in along the base. Find the volume.

A) 4108.33 in³   B) 3246.19 in³

C) 12325 in³   D) 3482.11 in³

91) Find the surface area of the below figure. Round your answer to the nearest hundredth, if necessary.

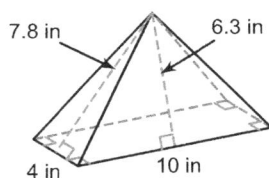

A) 134.2 in²   B) 149.8 in²

C) 123.9 in²   D) 128.1 in²

92) Find the surface area of the below figure. Round your answer to the nearest hundredth, if necessary.

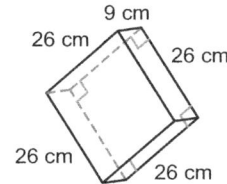

A) 2262 cm²   B) 1612 cm²

C) 3055 cm²   D) 2288 cm²

93) Find the surface area of the below figure. Round your answer to the nearest hundredth, if necessary.

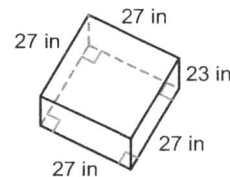

A) 3942 in²   B) 3213 in²

C) 3447 in²   D) 2642 in²

94) Find the surface area of the below figure. Round your answer to the nearest hundredth, if necessary.

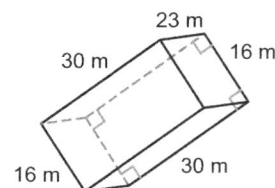

A) 3056 m²   B) 2698 m²

C) 2596 m²   D) 3076 m²

www.math-knots.com | www.a4ace.com

95) Find the surface area of the below figure. Round your answer to the nearest hundredth, if necessary.

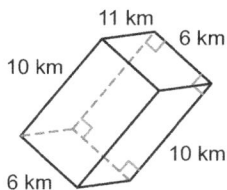

A) 412 km² B) 507 km²

C) 472 km² D) 449 km²

96) Find the surface area of the below figure. Round your answer to the nearest hundredth, if necessary.

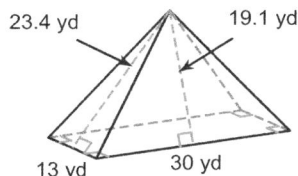

A) 1325.5 yd² B) 1143.6 yd²

C) 1267.2 yd² D) 1282.8 yd²

97) Find the surface area of the below figure. Round your answer to the nearest hundredth, if necessary.

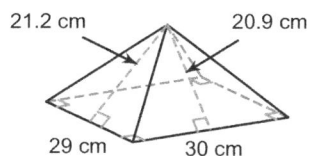

A) 2111.8 cm² B) 1679.9 cm²

C) 1248.2 cm² D) 1185.1 cm²

98) Find the surface area of the below figure. Round your answer to the nearest hundredth, if necessary.

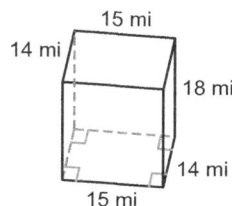

A) 1742 mi² B) 2175 mi²

C) 1464 mi² D) 1254 mi²

99) Find the surface area of the below figure. Round your answer to the nearest hundredth, if necessary.

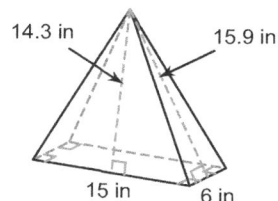

A) 566.4 in² B) 491.4 in²

C) 399.9 in² D) 245.6 in²

100) Find the surface area of the below figure. Round your answer to the nearest hundredth, if necessary.

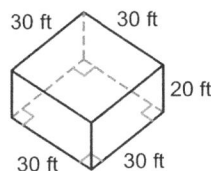

A) 3300 ft² B) 4604 ft²

C) 5491 ft² D) 4200 ft²

www.math-knots.com | www.a4ace.com

101) Find the surface area of the below figure. Round your answer to the nearest hundredth, if necessary.

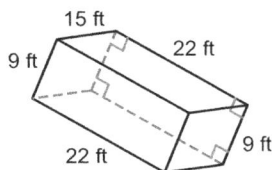

A) 1326 ft²   B) 1211 ft²

C) 1565 ft²   D) 1128 ft²

102) Find the surface area of the below figure. Round your answer to the nearest hundredth, if necessary.

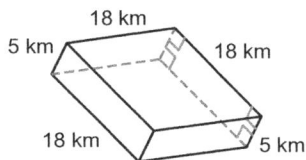

A) 1176 km²   B) 918 km²

C) 1052 km²   D) 1008 km²

103) Find the surface area of the below figure. Round your answer to the nearest hundredth, if necessary.

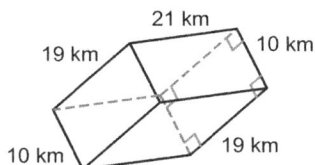

A) 932 km²   B) 1483 km²

C) 1408 km²   D) 1598 km²

104) Find the surface area of the below figure. Round your answer to the nearest hundredth, if necessary.

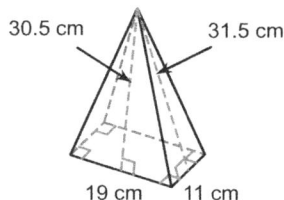

A) 1599 cm²   B) 931 cm²

C) 1135 cm²   D) 1099 cm²

105) Find the surface area of the below figure. Round your answer to the nearest hundredth, if necessary.

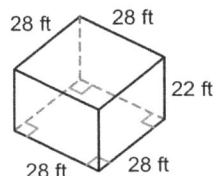

A) 2889 ft²   B) 2153 ft²

C) 3248 ft²   D) 4032 ft²

106) Find the surface area of the below figure. Round your answer to the nearest hundredth, if necessary.

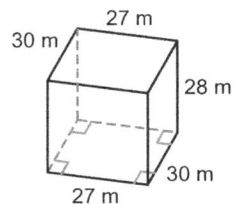

A) 4812 m²   B) 4002 m²

C) 3940 m²   D) 2640 m²

www.math-knots.com | www.a4ace.com

107) Find the surface area of the below figure. Round your answer to the nearest hundredth, if necessary.

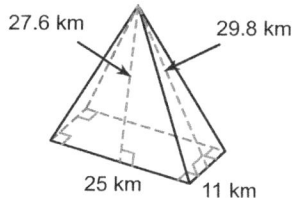

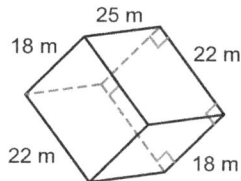

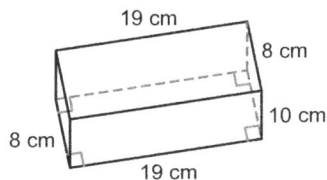

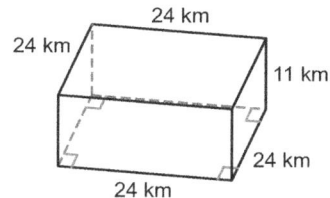

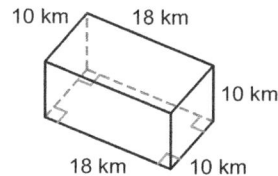

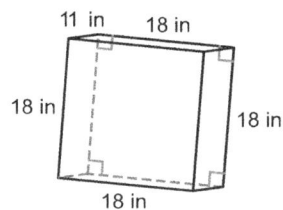

27.6 km   29.8 km

25 km   11 km

A) 1292.8 km²   B) 1639.6 km²

C) 1388.4 km²   D) 1768.2 km²

108) Find the surface area of the below figure. Round your answer to the nearest hundredth, if necessary.

25 m
18 m   22 m

22 m   18 m

A) 2792 m²   B) 1609 m²

C) 2396 m²   D) 3963 m²

109) Find the surface area of the below figure. Round your answer to the nearest hundredth, if necessary.

19 cm
8 cm
10 cm
8 cm
19 cm

A) 1231 cm²   B) 844 cm²

C) 987 cm²   D) 692 cm²

110) Find the surface area of the below figure. Round your answer to the nearest hundredth, if necessary.

24 km
24 km   11 km
24 km
24 km

A) 1632 km²   B) 1448 km²

C) 2208 km²   D) 2763 km²

111) Find the surface area of the below figure. Round your answer to the nearest hundredth, if necessary.

10 km   18 km
10 km
18 km   10 km

A) 606 km²   B) 920 km²

C) 1239 km²   D) 740 km²

112) Find the surface area of the below figure. Round your answer to the nearest hundredth, if necessary.

11 in   18 in
18 in   18 in
18 in

A) 1116 in²   B) 1000 in²

C) 2031 in²   D) 1440 in²

       www.math-knots.com | www.a4ace.com

113) Find the surface area of the below figure. Round your answer to the nearest hundredth, if necessary.

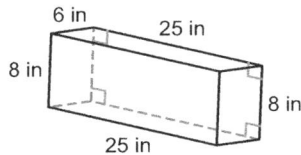

A) 796 in²   B) 596 in²

C) 907 in²   D) 815 in²

114) Find the surface area of the below figure. Round your answer to the nearest hundredth, if necessary.

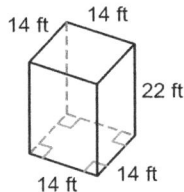

A) 2374 ft²   B) 1624 ft²

C) 1428 ft²   D) 1306 ft²

115) Find the surface area of the below figure. Round your answer to the nearest hundredth, if necessary.

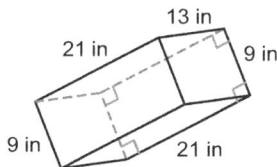

A) 594 in²   B) 969 in²

C) 1158 in²   D) 1024 in²

116) Find the surface area of the below figure. Round your answer to the nearest hundredth, if necessary.

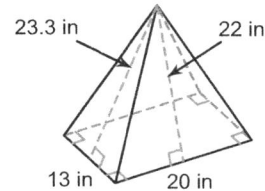

A) 1122.6 in²   B) 1413 in²

C) 1306.1 in²   D) 1002.9 in²

117) Find the surface area of the below figure. Round your answer to the nearest hundredth, if necessary.

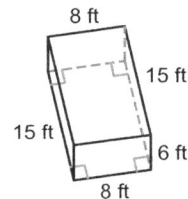

A) 396 ft²   B) 468 ft²

C) 516 ft²   D) 480 ft²

118) Find the surface area of the below figure. Round your answer to the nearest hundredth, if necessary.

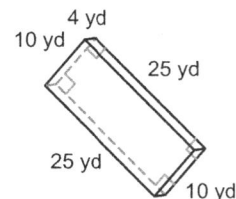

A) 1027 yd²   B) 530 yd²

C) 780 yd²   D) 1024 yd²

119) Find the surface area of the below figure. Round your answer to the nearest hundredth, if necessary.

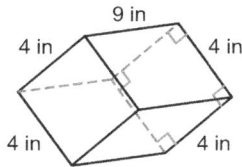

A) 129 in²   B) 160 in²

C) 176 in²   D) 173 in²

120) Find the surface area of the below figure. Round your answer to the nearest hundredth, if necessary.

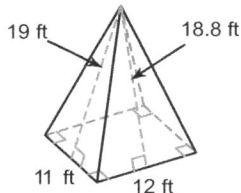

A) 741.1 ft²   B) 566.6 ft²

C) 447.4 ft²   D) 483.1 ft²

121) Find the surface area of the below figure. Round your answer to the nearest hundredth, if necessary.

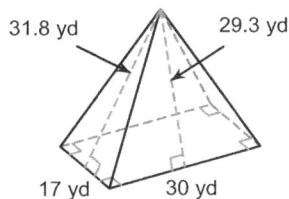

A) 2704.2 yd²   B) 1546.4 yd²

C) 1929.6 yd²   D) 1162.5 yd²

122) Find the surface area of the below figure. Round your answer to the nearest hundredth, if necessary.

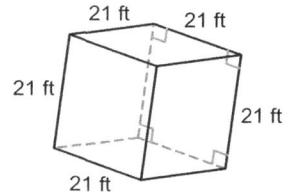

A) 2205 ft²   B) 1943 ft²

C) 2646 ft²   D) 3542 ft²

123) Find the surface area of the below figure. Round your answer to the nearest hundredth, if necessary.

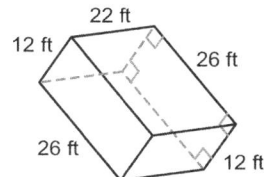

A) 2097 ft²   B) 1984 ft²

C) 2719 ft²   D) 2296 ft²

124) Find the surface area of the below figure. Round your answer to the nearest hundredth, if necessary.

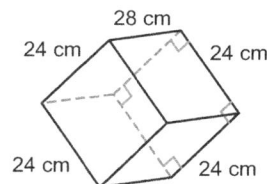

A) 3264 cm²   B) 2998 cm²

C) 3840 cm²   D) 3585 cm²

125) Find the surface area of the below figure. Round your answer to the nearest hundredth, if necessary.

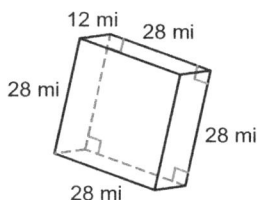

12 mi   28 mi
28 mi
28 mi
28 mi

A) 2912 mi²   B) 2128 mi²

C) 2792 mi²   D) 1984 mi²

126) Find the surface area of the below figure. Round your answer to the nearest hundredth, if necessary.

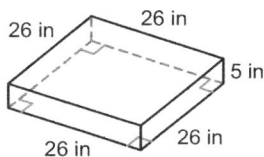

26 in   26 in
26 in
5 in
26 in   26 in

A) 1785 in²   B) 1196 in²

C) 1872 in²   D) 1257 in²

127) Find the surface area of the below figure. Round your answer to the nearest hundredth, if necessary.

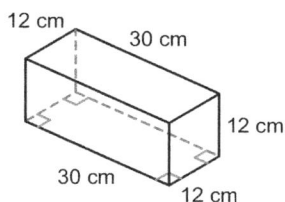

12 cm   30 cm
12 cm
30 cm   12 cm

A) 1094 cm²   B) 1728 cm²

C) 1640 cm²   D) 1368 cm²

128) Find the surface area of the below figure. Round your answer to the nearest hundredth, if necessary.

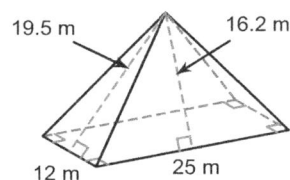

19.5 m   16.2 m
12 m   25 m

A) 500 m²   B) 613 m²

C) 939 m²   D) 1045 m²

129) Find the surface area of the below figure. Round your answer to the nearest hundredth, if necessary.

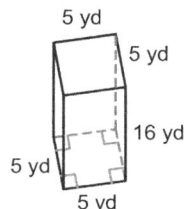

5 yd
5 yd
16 yd
5 yd
5 yd

A) 295 yd²   B) 370 yd²

C) 345 yd²   D) 521 yd²

130) Find the surface area of the below figure. Round your answer to the nearest hundredth, if necessary.

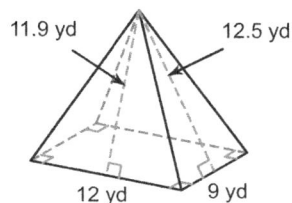

11.9 yd   12.5 yd
12 yd   9 yd

A) 451 yd²   B) 363.3 yd²

C) 332.7 yd²   D) 418 yd²

131) Find the surface area of the below figure. Round your answer to the nearest hundredth, if necessary.

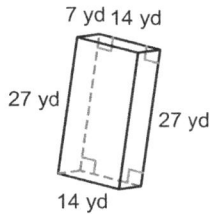

7 yd 14 yd
27 yd
27 yd
14 yd

A) 952 yd²   B) 1163 yd²

C) 932 yd²   D) 1330 yd²

132) Find the surface area of the below figure. Round your answer to the nearest hundredth, if necessary.

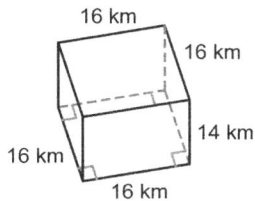

16 km
16 km
14 km
16 km
16 km

A) 1152 km²   B) 1361 km²

C) 2067 km²   D) 1408 km²

133) Find the surface area of the below figure. Round your answer to the nearest hundredth, if necessary.

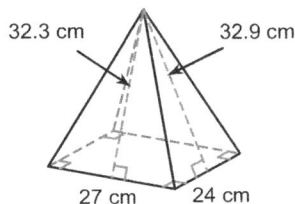

32.3 cm   32.9 cm
27 cm   24 cm

A) 1426.3 cm²   B) 2517.5 cm²

C) 2309.7 cm²   D) 1730 cm²

134) Find the surface area of the below figure. Round your answer to the nearest hundredth, if necessary.

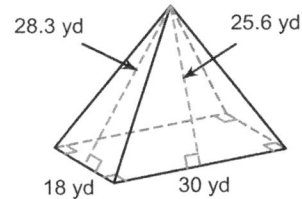

28.3 yd   25.6 yd
18 yd   30 yd

A) 1887.9 yd²   B) 2251.8 yd²

C) 958.9 yd²   D) 1817.4 yd²

135) Find the surface area of the below figure. Round your answer to the nearest hundredth, if necessary.

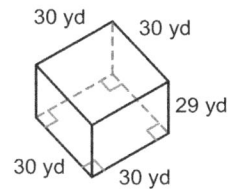

30 yd   30 yd
29 yd
30 yd   30 yd

A) 5280 yd²   B) 3385 yd²

C) 2678 yd²   D) 4380 yd²

136) Find the surface area of the below figure. Round your answer to the nearest hundredth, if necessary.

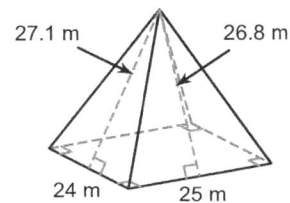

27.1 m   26.8 m
24 m   25 m

A) 1920.4 m²   B) 1181.3 m²

C) 1140.4 m²   D) 1045.4 m²

137) Find the surface area of the below figure. Round your answer to the nearest hundredth, if necessary.

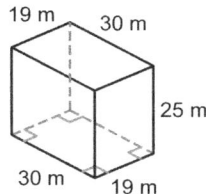

A) 3749 m²   B) 3590 m²

C) 3020 m²   D) 2487 m²

138) Find the surface area of the below figure. Round your answer to the nearest hundredth, if necessary.

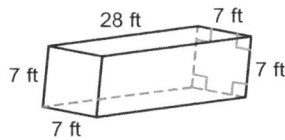

A) 833 ft²   B) 463 ft²

C) 882 ft²   D) 893 ft²

139) Find the surface area of the below figure. Round your answer to the nearest hundredth, if necessary.

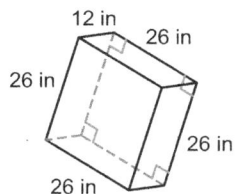

A) 2530 in²   B) 2600 in²

C) 1924 in²   D) 2754 in²

140) Find the surface area of the below figure. Round your answer to the nearest hundredth, if necessary.

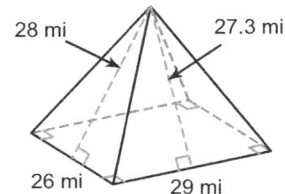

A) 1514.8 mi²   B) 2323.8 mi²

C) 2327.8 mi²   D) 2273.7 mi²

141) The manager of Scents 4 Cents needs to manufacture their new perfume. The bottle that they are filling is in the shape of a cone. The height of the cone is 9 centimeters and the radius of the base is 4.5 centimeters. How many cubic centimeters of perfume will fit in each bottle?

142) A traffic cone is made from a cone and a square prism. If the cone has a diameter of 18 inches and a height of 40 inches, how much rubber is needed to make just the cone? Remember the cone sits on a square prism base, so there is no base for the cone.

143) Eli just turned two and wants to have his first ice cream cone. How many cubic inches of ice cream can fit inside the cone? How many square inches of waffle will be needed to make the cone?

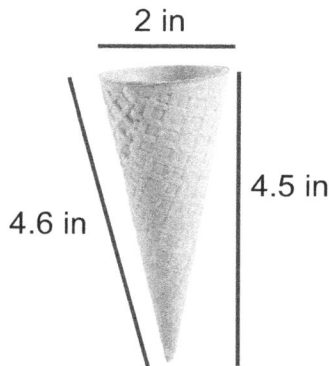

2 in

4.6 in

4.5 in

144) As runners in a marathon go by, volunteers hand them small cone shaped cups of water. The cups have the dimensions shown. How much paper is needed to make each cup?

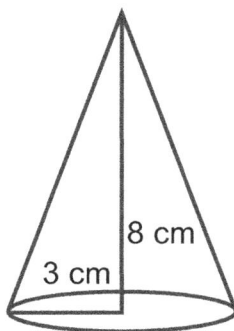

8 cm

3 cm

145) A cone has radius of 4 inches. The volume of the cone is 120.576 cubic inches. Find the height of the cone

146) Birthday Parties R Us' made hats in the shape of a cone for Yousef's 7th birthday. If they used 141.3 square inches of cardboard to make each hat, and each hat has a diameter of 10 inches, what is the slant height of the hat?

147) Find the length of a rectangular prism with a height of 7 inches, a width of 6 inches and a volume of 546 cubic inches. Once you have found the length, find the surface area of the rectangular prism. Hint: Start by drawing a diagram.

www.math-knots.com | www.a4ace.com

148) Avery's aquarium is twenty inches long and fourteen and one-half inches wide. It has a height of sixteen inches. How many cubic inches of water will she need to fill the aquarium to three-fourths of the capacity?

149) If the volume of a cube is 64 m^3, what is the surface area?

150) A cylindrical bucket has a diameter of eighteen inches and a height of fifteen inches. How many cubic inches of water are needed to fill it halfway?

151) Logan has a can that he needs to paint. He wants to leave the top and bottom unpainted. The can has a radius of seven inches and a height of twenty inches. How many square inches will he need to paint?

152) You know the area of the base of a cylindrical tower is 1570 square feet. The volume of the cylinder is 62,800 cubic feet. What is the height of the tower?

153) Diya wanted to put a skylight in her new house. The skylight is made of all glass and is in the shape of a square pyramid. The perimeter of the base is 60 feet and the skylight has a slant height of 12.5 feet. Find the amount of glass needed to make the skylight.

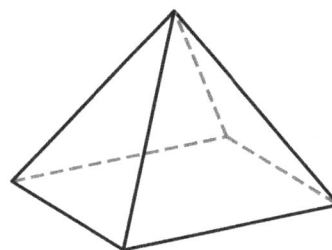

154) Aditiya is starting a candle business. He plans on making candles in the shape of square pyramid. The base has side lengths of 6 inches and the candle contains 96 cubic inches of wax. What is the height of each candle?

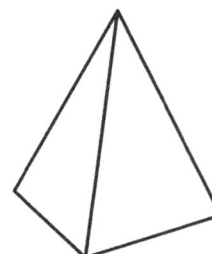

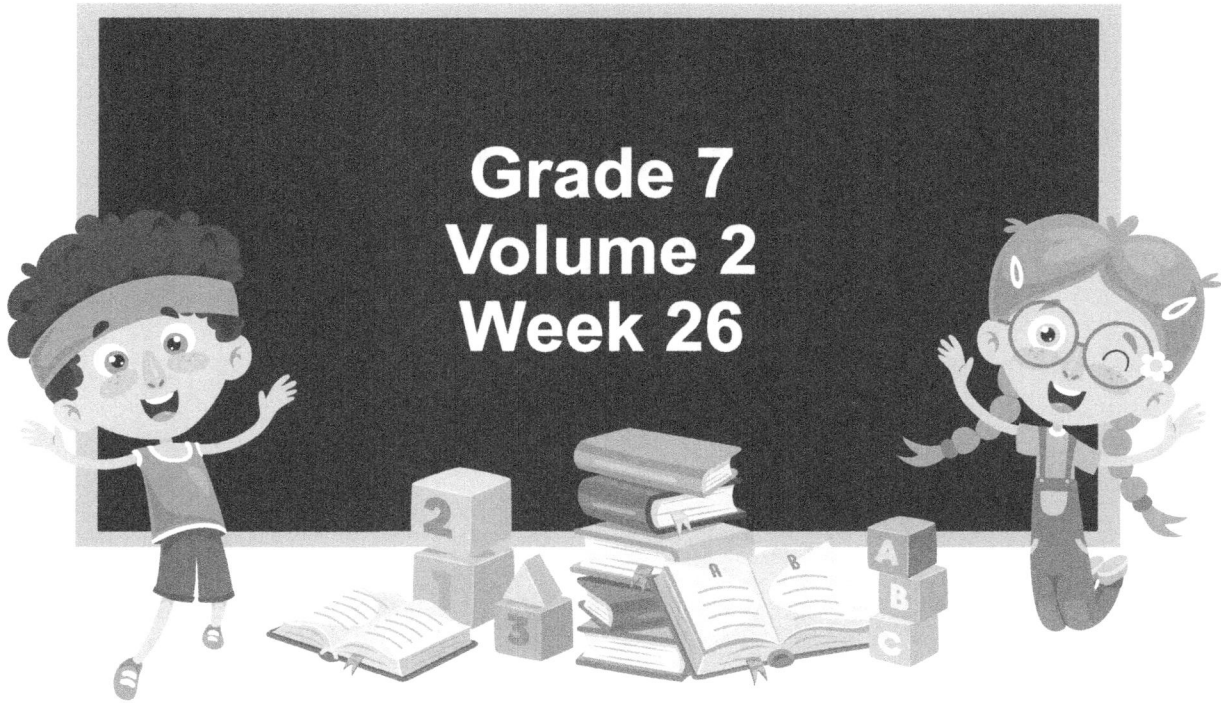

Grade 7
Volume 2
Week 26

www.math-knots.com | www.a4ace.com

178   www.math-knots.com | www.a4ace.com

1) Find the measure of angle b

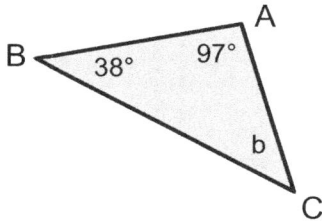

A) 58°   B) 45°

C) 52°   D) 53°

2) Find the measure of angle b

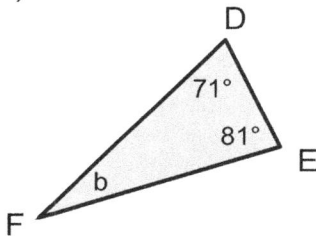

A) 29°   B) 36°

C) 26°   D) 28°

3) Find the measure of angle b

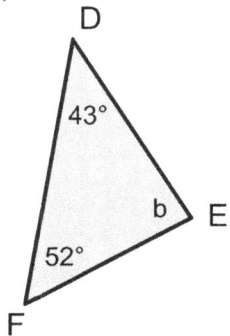

A) 76°   B) 85°

C) 63°   D) 71°

4) Find the measure of angle b

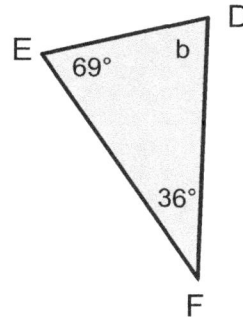

A) 78°   B) 83°

C) 75°   D) 87°

5) Find the measure of angle b

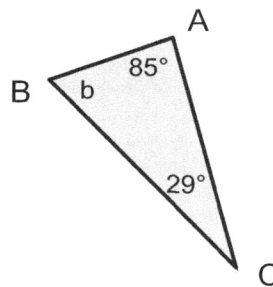

A) 75°   B) 65°

C) 55°   D) 66°

6) Find the measure of angle b

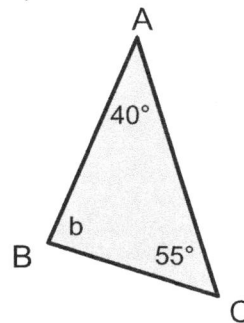

A) 85°   B) 74°

C) 81°   D) 76°

www.math-knots.com | www.a4ace.com

7) Find the measure of angle b

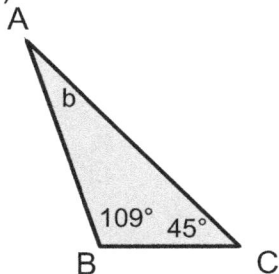

A

b

109° 45°

B   C

A) 16°   B) 26°

C) 21°   D) 31°

8) Find the measure of angle b

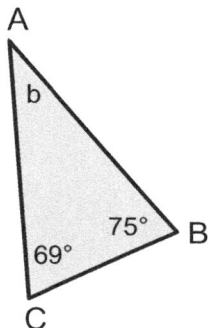

A

b

75° B

69°

C

A) 44°   B) 41°

C) 36°   D) 34°

9) Find the measure of angle b

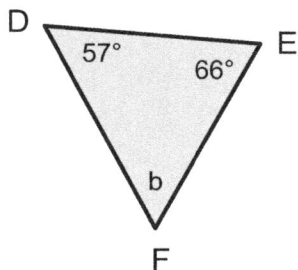

D   E
57°
66°

b

F

A) 70°   B) 57°

C) 65°   D) 78°

10) Find the measure of angle b

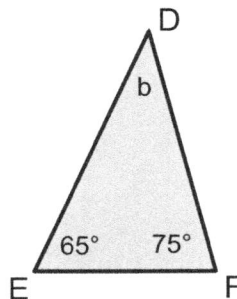

D

b

65°   75°

E   F

A) 44°   B) 34°

C) 52°   D) 40°

11) Find the measure of angle b

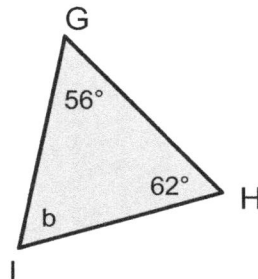

G

56°

62° H

b

I

A) 78°   B) 68°

C) 62°   D) 60°

12) Find the measure of angle b

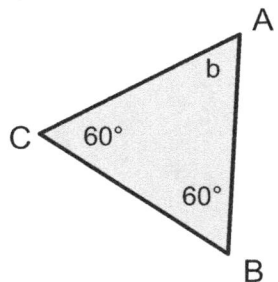

A

b

C   60°

60°

B

A) 76°   B) 65°

C) 60°   D) 70°

13) Find the measure of angle b

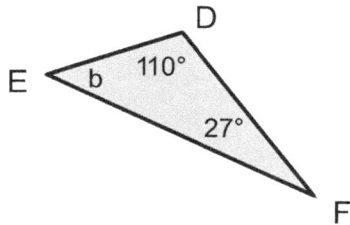

A) 40° B) 34°

C) 43° D) 33°

14) Find the measure of angle b

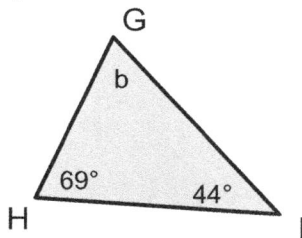

A) 51° B) 59°

C) 60° D) 67°

15) Find the measure of angle b

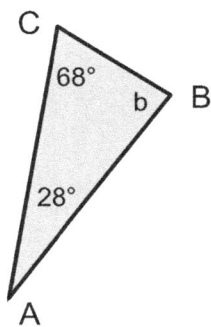

A) 93° B) 85°

C) 84° D) 76°

16) Find the measure of angle b

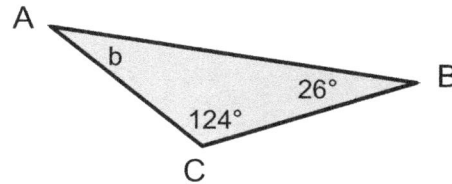

A) 28° B) 36°

C) 37° D) 30°

17) Find the measure of angle b

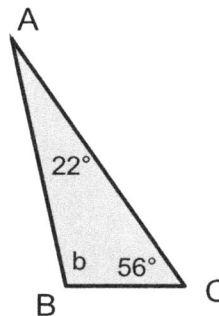

A) 110° B) 103°

C) 96° D) 102°

18) Find the measure of angle b

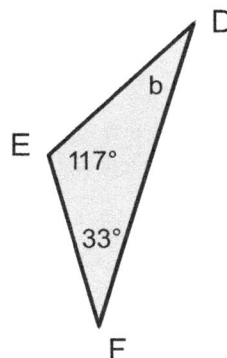

A) 41° B) 40°

C) 30° D) 48°

19) Find the measure of angle b

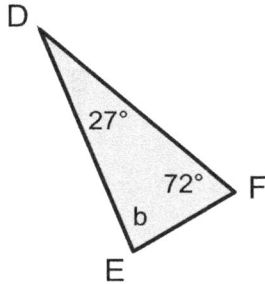

A) 81°   B) 80°

C) 72°   D) 66°

20) Find the measure of angle b

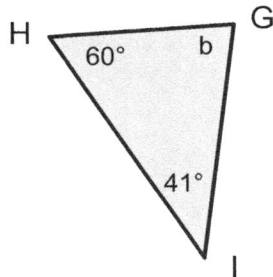

A) 77°   B) 84°

C) 82°   D) 79°

21) Find the measure of angle b

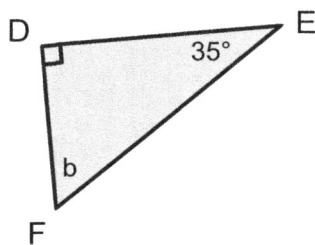

A) 50°   B) 40°

C) 55°   D) 31°

22) Find the measure of angle b

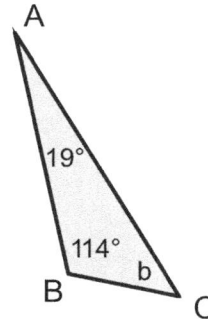

A) 38°   B) 41°

C) 31°   D) 47°

23) Find the measure of angle b

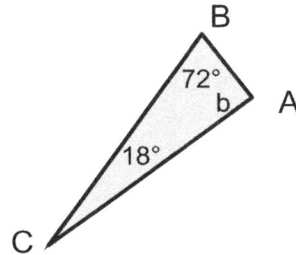

A) 99°   B) 107°

C) 90°   D) 113°

24) Find the measure of angle b

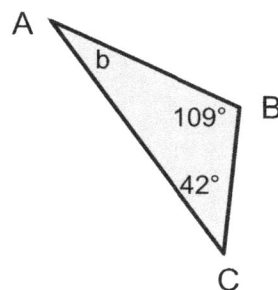

A) 21°   B) 29°

C) 15°   D) 7°

25) Find the measure of angle b

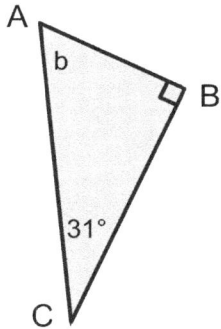

A) 68°   B) 71°

C) 59°   D) 63°

26) Find the measure of angle b

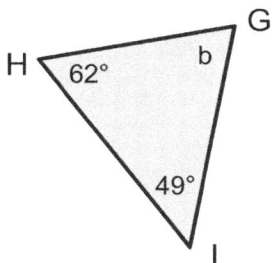

A) 76°   B) 68°

C) 69°   D) 75°

27) Find the measure of angle b

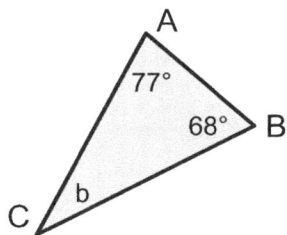

A) 45°   B) 35°

C) 55°   D) 50°

28) Find the measure of angle b

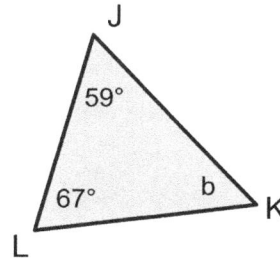

A) 55°   B) 65°

C) 54°   D) 47°

29) Find the measure of angle b

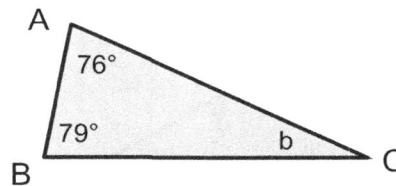

A) 31°   B) 20°

C) 30°   D) 25°

30) Find the measure of angle b

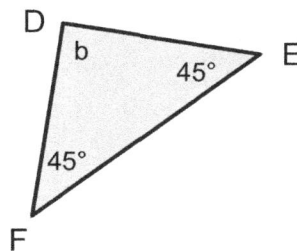

A) 68°   B) 90°

C) 82°   D) 73°

www.math-knots.com | www.a4ace.com

31) Find the value of x

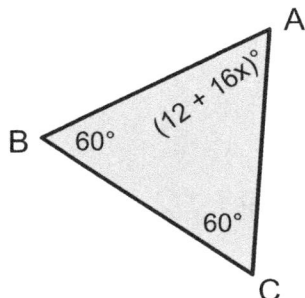

Triangle with B 60°, (12 + 16x)° at A, 60° at C

A) 3   B) 9

C) 0   D) 8

32) Find the value of x

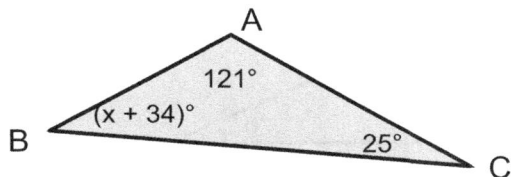

Triangle with A 121°, (x + 34)° at B, 25° at C

A) 1   B) 6

C) 10   D) 0

33) Find the value of x

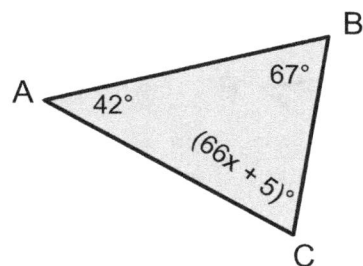

Triangle with A 42°, B 67°, (66x + 5)° at C

A) 12   B) 8

C) 1   D) 3

34) Find the value of x

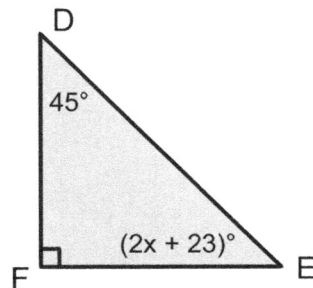

Triangle with D 45°, right angle at F, (2x + 23)° at E

A) 17   B) 22

C) 30   D) 11

35) Find the value of x

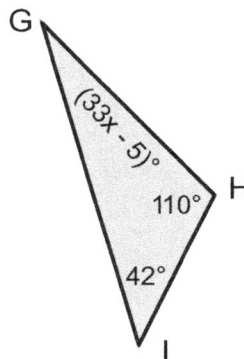

Triangle with (33x - 5)° at G, 110° at H, 42° at I

A) 9   B) 23

C) 16   D) 1

36) Find the value of x

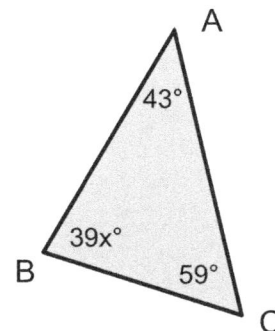

Triangle with A 43°, 39x° at B, 59° at C

A) 12   B) 10

C) 5   D) 2

37) Find the value of x

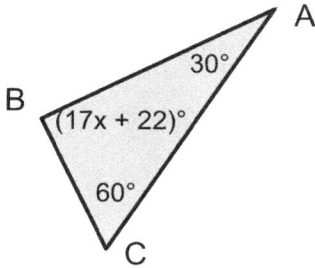

A) 12   B) 4

C) 14   D) 5

38) Find the value of x

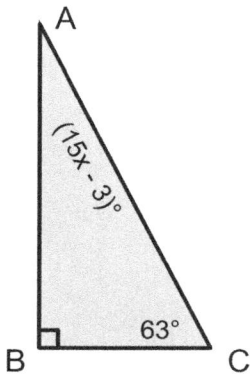

A) 2   B) 10

C) 8   D) 17

39) Find the value of x

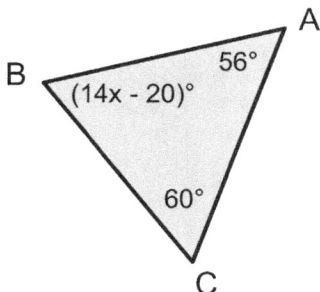

A) 15   B) 9

C) 2   D) 6

40) Find the value of x

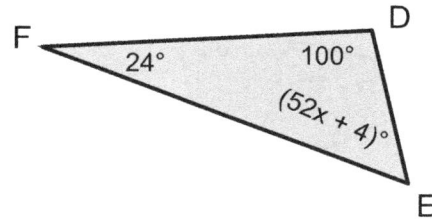

A) 9   B) 1

C) 16   D) 26

41) Find the value of x

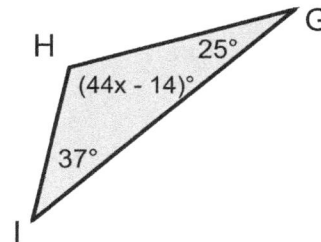

A) 2   B) 7

C) 3   D) 1

42) Find the value of x

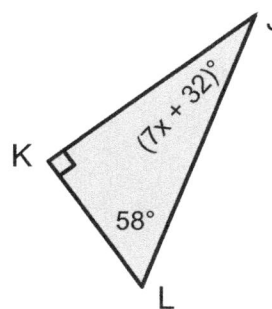

A) 5   B) 13

C) 0   D) 21

www.math-knots.com | www.a4ace.com

43) Find the value of x

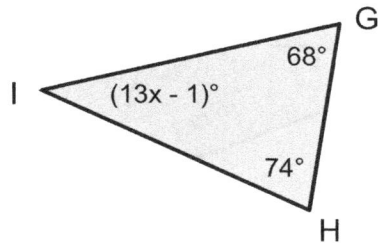

G
68°
I
(13x - 1)°
74°
H

A) 2   B) 9

C) 3   D) 7

44) Find the value of x

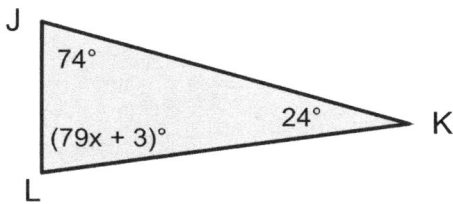

J
74°
(79x + 3)°
24°   K
L

A) 4   B) 6

C) 1   D) 14

45) Find the value of x

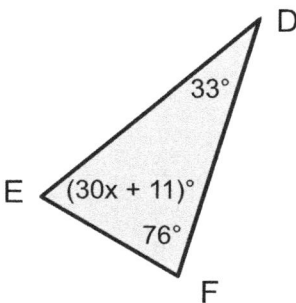

D
33°
E
(30x + 11)°
76°
F

A) 2   B) 13

C) 3   D) 5

46) Find the value of x

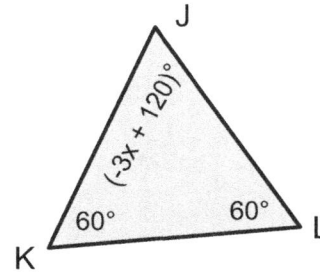

J
(-3x + 120)°
60°   60°
K   L

A) 9   B) 19

C) 12   D) 20

47) Find the value of x

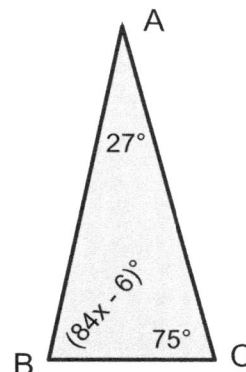

A
27°
(84x - 6)°
75°
B   C

A) 5   B) 1

C) 2   D) 3

48) Find the value of x

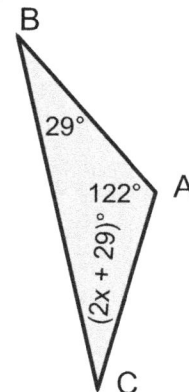

B
29°
122°   A
(2x + 29)°
C

A) 12   B) 6

C) 19   D) 0

49) Find the value of x

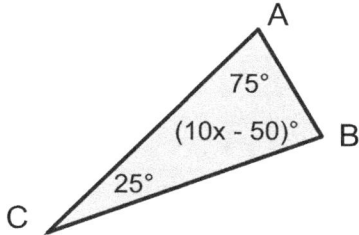

A
75°
(10x - 50)° B
25°
C

A) 13   B) 19

C) 12   D) 5

50) Find the value of x

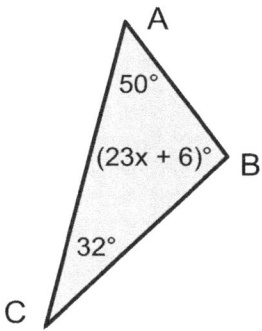

A
50°
(23x + 6)° B
32°
C

A) 16   B) 2

C) 8   D) 4

51) Find the value of x

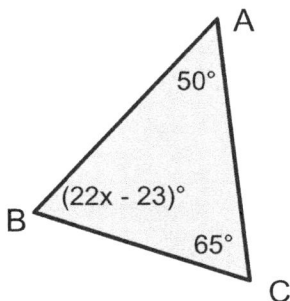

A
50°
(22x - 23)°
B
65°
C

A) 17   B) 22

C) 10   D) 4

52) Find the value of x

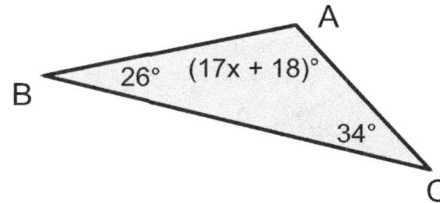

A
26° (17x + 18)°
B
34°
C

A) 20   B) 6

C) 0   D) 10

53) Find the value of x

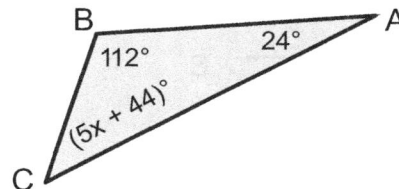

B   24° A
112°
(5x + 44)°
C

A) 8   B) 2

C) 3   D) 0

54) Find the value of x

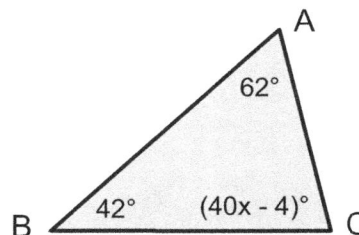

A
62°
42° (40x - 4)°
B   C

A) 8   B) 5

C) 2   D) 1

55) Find the value of x

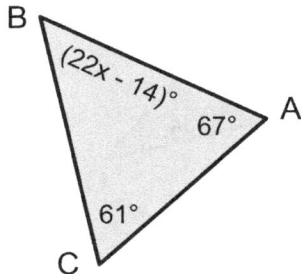

B
(22x - 14)°
67° A
61°
C

A) 14   B) 3

C) 7   D) 24

56) Find the value of x

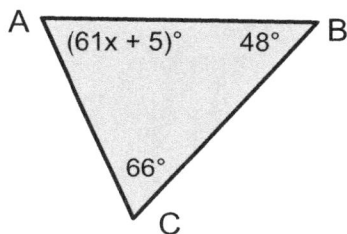

A
(61x + 5)°   48° B
66°
C

A) 17   B) 7

C) 12   D) 1

57) Find the value of x

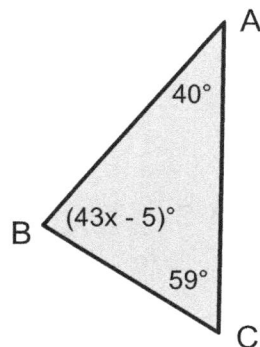

A
40°
B
(43x - 5)°
59°
C

A) 2   B) 14

C) 7   D) 20

58) Find the value of x

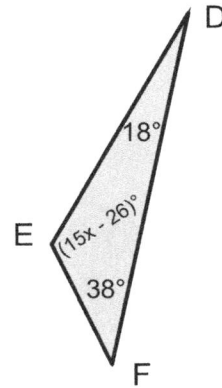

D
18°
E
(15x - 26)°
38°
F

A) 0   B) 12

C) 6   D) 10

59) Find the value of x

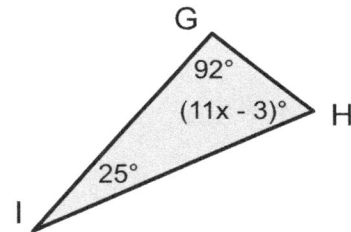

G
92°
(11x - 3)°   H
25°
I

A) 20   B) 12

C) 6   D) 28

60) Find the value of x

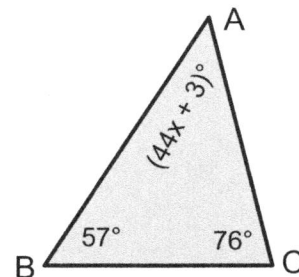

A
(44x + 3)°
57°   76°
B   C

A) 15   B) 1

C) 9   D) 25

61) Find the measure of angle b

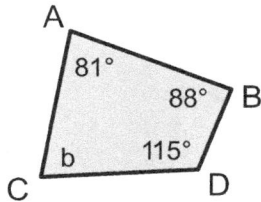

A) 66°   B) 58°

C) 84°   D) 76°

64) Find the measure of angle b

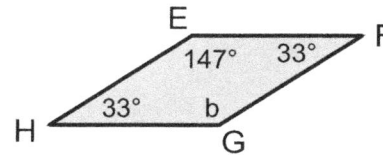

A) 147°   B) 137°

C) 139°   D) 130°

62) Find the measure of angle b

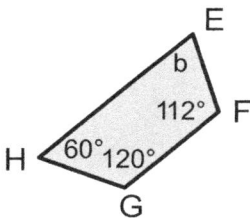

A) 49°   B) 68°

C) 58°   D) 40°

65) Find the measure of angle b

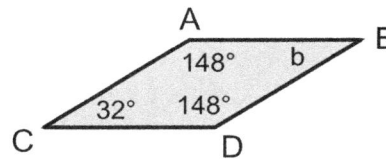

A) 34°   B) 25°

C) 32°   D) 43°

63) Find the measure of angle b

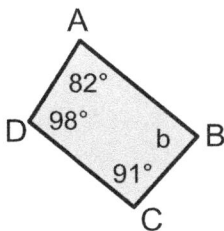

A) 89°   B) 78°

C) 84°   D) 88°

66) Find the measure of angle b

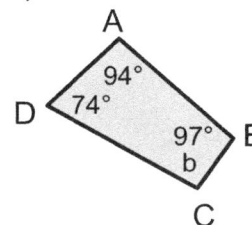

A) 95°   B) 83°

C) 85°   D) 78°

67) Find the measure of angle b

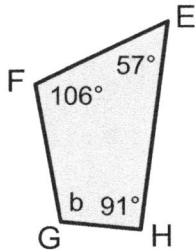

A) 91°   B) 106°

C) 96°   D) 101°

70) Find the measure of angle b

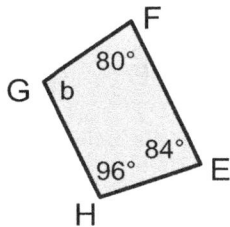

A) 45°   B) 62°

C) 54°   D) 52°

68) Find the measure of angle b

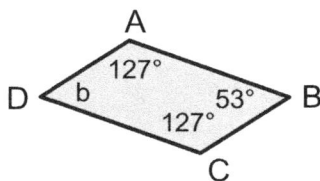

A) 83°   B) 91°

C) 78°   D) 100°

71) Find the measure of angle b

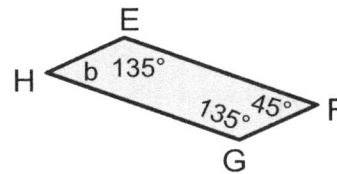

A) 90°   B) 92°

C) 83°   D) 85°

69) Find the measure of angle b

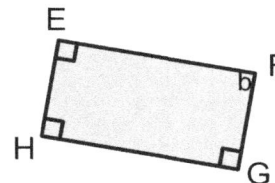

A) 62°   B) 63°

C) 72°   D) 53°

72) Find the measure of angle b

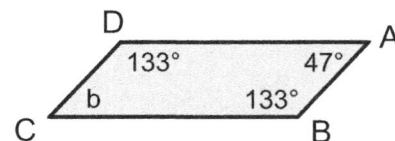

A) 45°   B) 39°

C) 47°   D) 55°

                   www.math-knots.com | www.a4ace.com

73) Find the measure of angle b

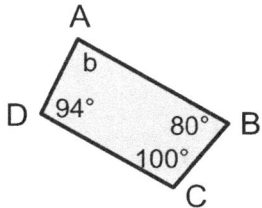

A
b
D 94°
80° B
100°
C

A) 86°   B) 79°

C) 77°   D) 89°

76) Find the measure of angle b

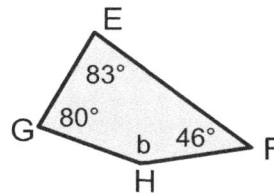

E
83°
G 80°
b 46°
F
H

A) 146°   B) 155°

C) 151°   D) 164°

74) Find the measure of angle b

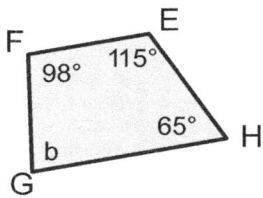

F   E
98° 115°
65° H
b
G

A) 96°   B) 82°

C) 89°   D) 102°

77) Find the measure of angle b

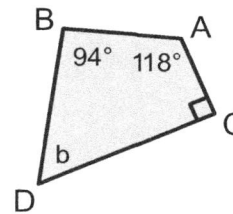

B   A
94° 118°
C
b
D

A) 48°   B) 41°

C) 58°   D) 32°

75) Find the measure of angle b

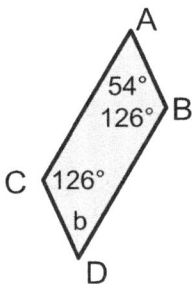

A
54°
126° B
C 126°
b
D

A) 54°   B) 58°

C) 48°   D) 49°

78) Find the measure of angle b

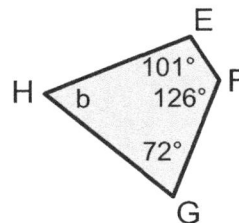

E
101°
H   b   126° F
72°
G

A) 68°   B) 62°

C) 67°   D) 61°

191

79) Find the measure of angle b

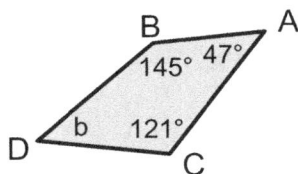

B 47° A
145°
b 121°
D C

A) 47°   B) 68°

C) 53°   D) 62°

82) Find the measure of angle b

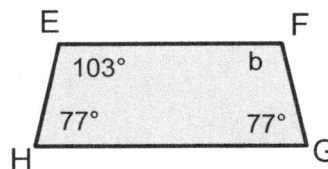

E   F
103°   b
77°   77°
H   G

A) 106°   B) 103°

C) 94°   D) 101°

80) Find the measure of angle b

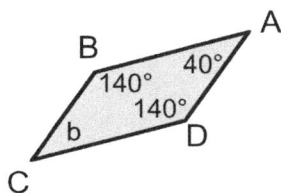

B 40° A
140°
140°
b D
C

A) 47°   B) 40°

C) 31°   D) 38°

83) Find the measure of angle b

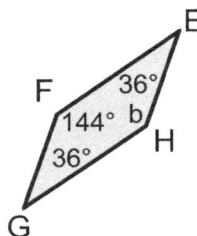

E
F 36°
144° b
36° H
G

A) 135°   B) 143°

C) 144°   D) 148°

81) Find the measure of angle b

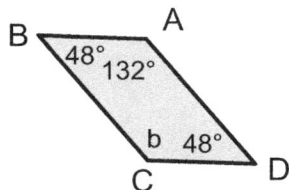

B A
48° 132°
b 48°
C D

A) 124°   B) 130°

C) 137°   D) 132°

84) Find the measure of angle b

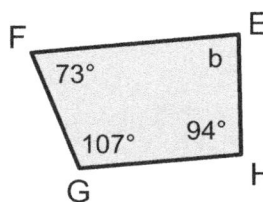

F   E
73°   b
107°   94°
G   H

A) 86°   B) 98°

C) 87°   D) 92°

85) Find the measure of angle b

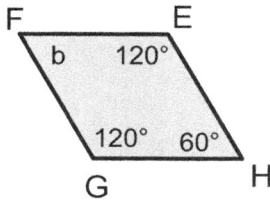

A) 75°   B) 65°

C) 55°   D) 60°

86) Find the measure of angle b

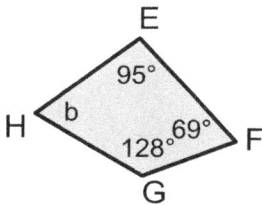

A) 95°   B) 78°

C) 85°   D) 68°

87) Find the measure of angle b

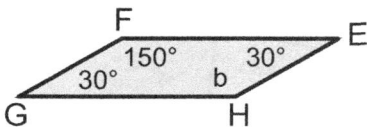

A) 141°   B) 150°

C) 136°   D) 143°

88) Find the measure of angle b

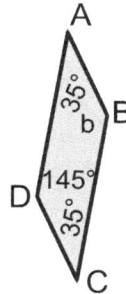

A) 141°   B) 145°

C) 151°   D) 149°

89) Find the measure of angle b

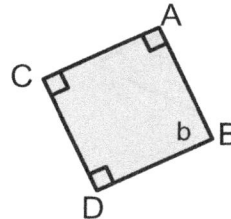

A) 81°   B) 90°

C) 75°   D) 80°

90) Find the measure of angle b

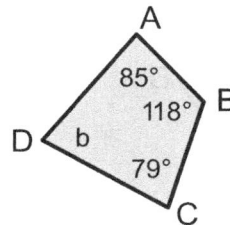

A) 78°   B) 68°

C) 59°   D) 88°

                   www.math-knots.com | www.a4ace.com

91) Find the value of x

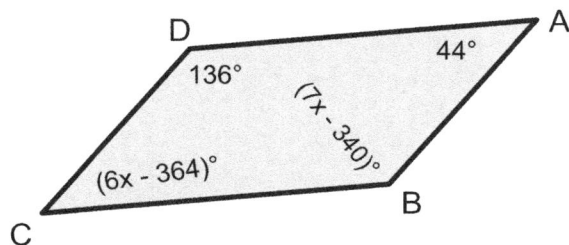

D 136°   44° A
(7x - 340)°
(6x - 364)°   B
C

A) 63   B) 62

C) 68   D) 55

94) Find the value of x

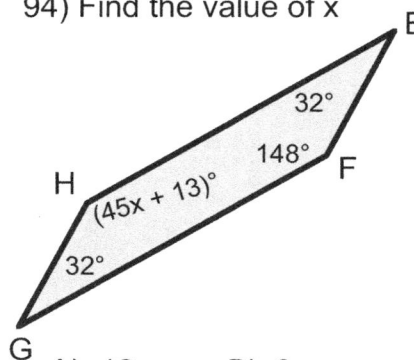

E
32°
H 148° F
(45x + 13)°
32°
G

A) 12   B) 3

C) 7   D) 13

92) Find the value of x

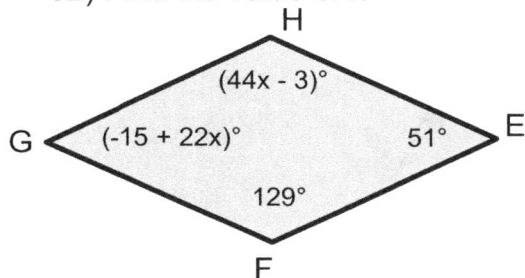

H
(44x - 3)°
G (-15 + 22x)°   51° E
129°
F

A) 6   B) 11

C) -4   D) 3

95) Find the value of x

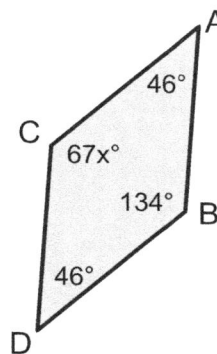

A
46°
C
67x°
134° B
46°
D

A) 2   B) 12

C) 19   D) 7

93) Find the value of x

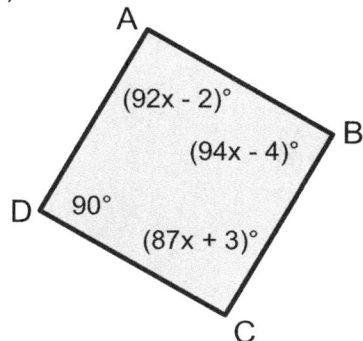

A
(92x - 2)°
(94x - 4)° B
D 90°
(87x + 3)°
C

A) 3   B) 8

C) 9   D) 1

96) Find the value of x

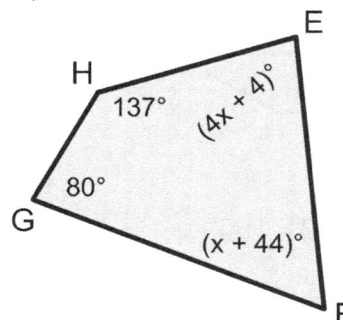

E
H 137° (4x + 4)°
80°
G
(x + 44)°
F

A) -3   B) 9

C) 2   D) 19

194

97) Find the value of x

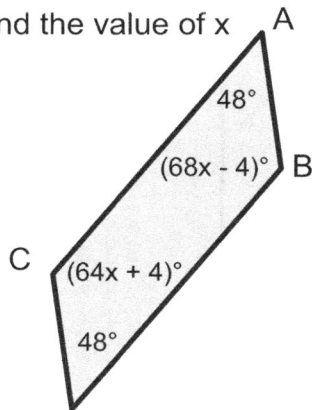

A
48°
(68x - 4)° B
C
(64x + 4)°
48°
D

A) -8   B) -23

C) -14   D) 2

98) Find the value of x

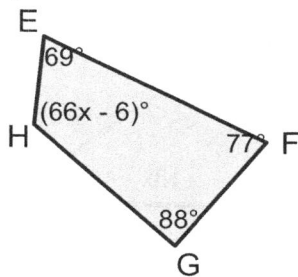

E
69°
(66x - 6)°
H
77° F
88°
G

A) -3   B) 2

C) 7   D) -8

99) Find the value of x

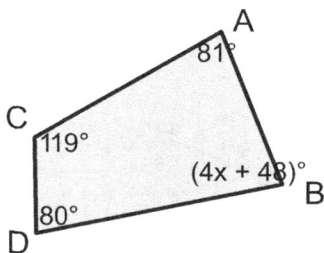

A
81°
C
119°
(4x + 48)°
B
80°
D

A) 0   B) 8

C) 4   D) 9

100) Find the value of x

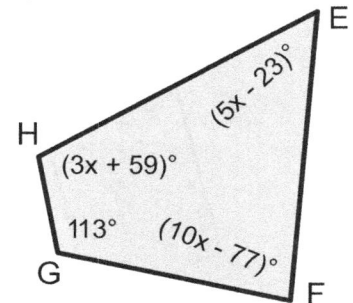

E
(5x - 23)°
H
(3x + 59)°
113°   (10x - 77)°
G   F

A) 16   B) 24

C) 14   D) 23

101) Find the value of x

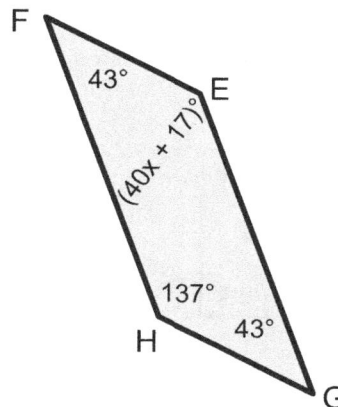

F
43°   E
(40x + 17)°
137°
H   43°
G

A) 6   B) 3

C) -2   D) 14

102) Find the value of x

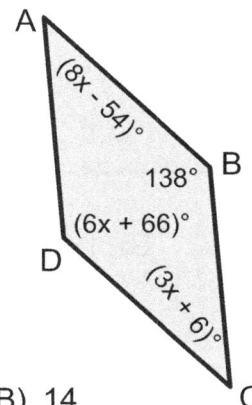

A
(8x - 54)°
138°   B
(6x + 66)°
D
(3x + 6)°
C

A) 12   B) 14

C) 1   D) 7

195

103) Find the value of x

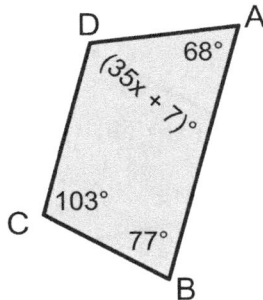

A) 3   B) 12

C) 6   D) 14

104) Find the value of x

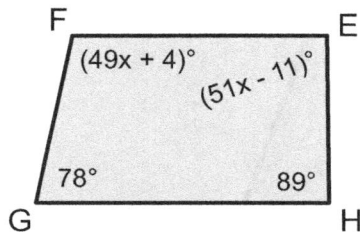

A) 2   B) 4

C) -6   D) 10

105) Find the value of x

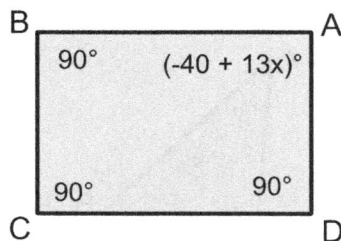

A) -4   B) 1

C) 2   D) 10

106) Find the value of x

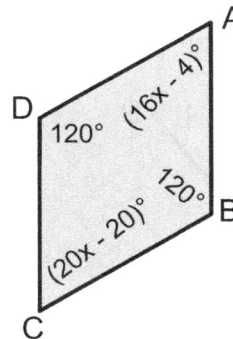

A) 4   B) 13

C) 23   D) 18

107) Find the value of x

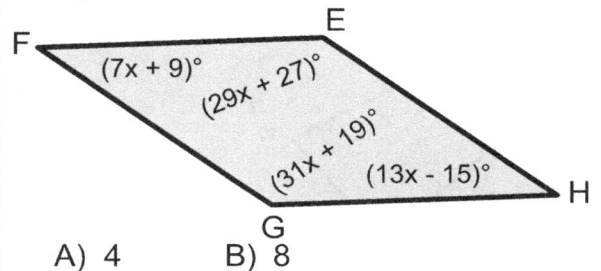

A) 4   B) 8

C) -1   D) 16

108) Find the value of x

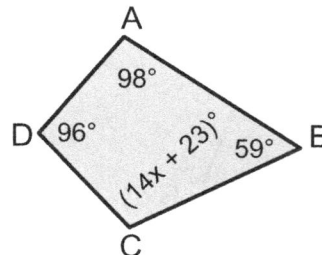

A) 20   B) 6

C) 12   D) 26

       www.math-knots.com | www.a4ace.com

109) Find the value of x

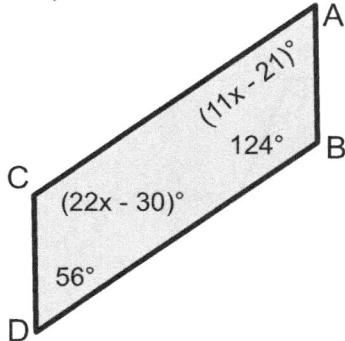

(11x - 21)°
124°
(22x - 30)°
56°

A) -2   B) -11

C) -3   D) 7

110) Find the value of x

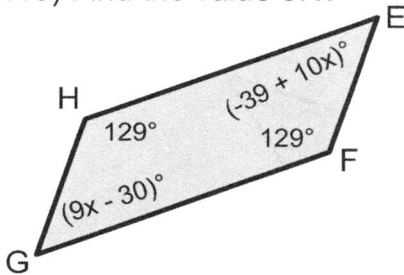

(-39 + 10x)°
129°
129°
(9x - 30)°

A) 17   B) 14

C) 9   D) 8

111) Find the value of x

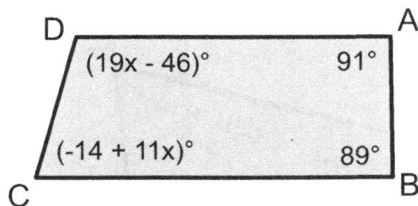

(19x - 46)°   91°
(-14 + 11x)°   89°

A) -4   B) 2

C) -9   D) 8

112) Find the value of x

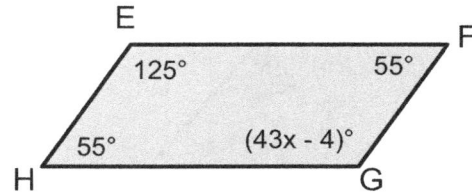

125°   55°
55°   (43x - 4)°

A) 18   B) 9

C) 3   D) 12

113) Find the value of x

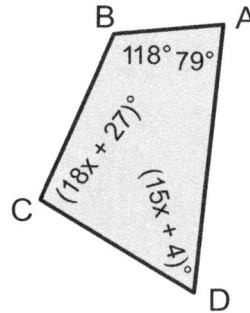

118° 79°
(18x + 27)°
(15x + 4)°

A) -7   B) 4

C) 3   D) -5

114) Find the value of x

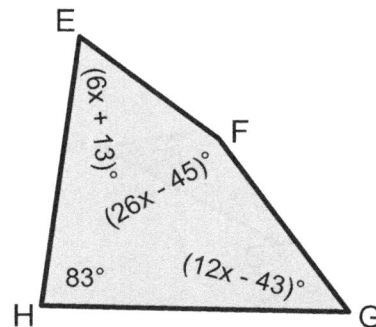

(6x + 13)°
(26x - 45)°
83°   (12x - 43)°

A) 13   B) 7

C) -2   D) 8

115) Find the value of x

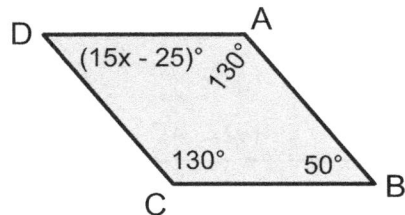

A) -12   B) 5

C) -7   D) -3

118) Find the value of x

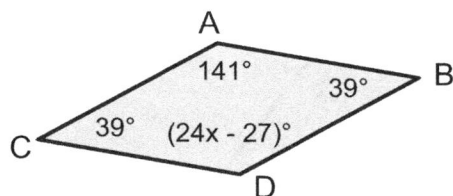

A) 7   B) 3

C) -2   D) -3

116) Find the value of x

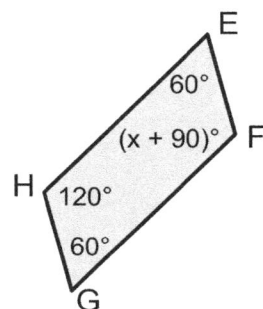

A) 42   B) 27

C) 30   D) 36

119) Find the value of x

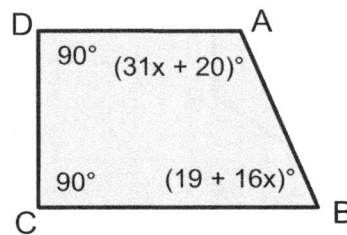

A) 16   B) -3

C) 7   D) 6

117) Find the value of x

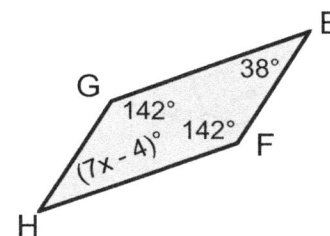

A) 14   B) 11

C) 6   D) 7

120) Find the value of x

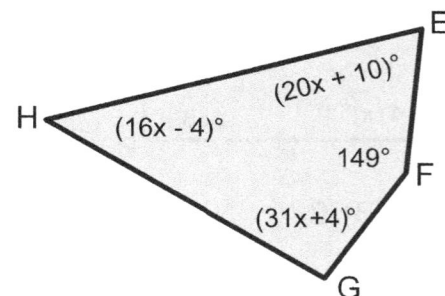

A) 3   B) 6

C) -7   D) -2

       www.math-knots.com | www.a4ace.com

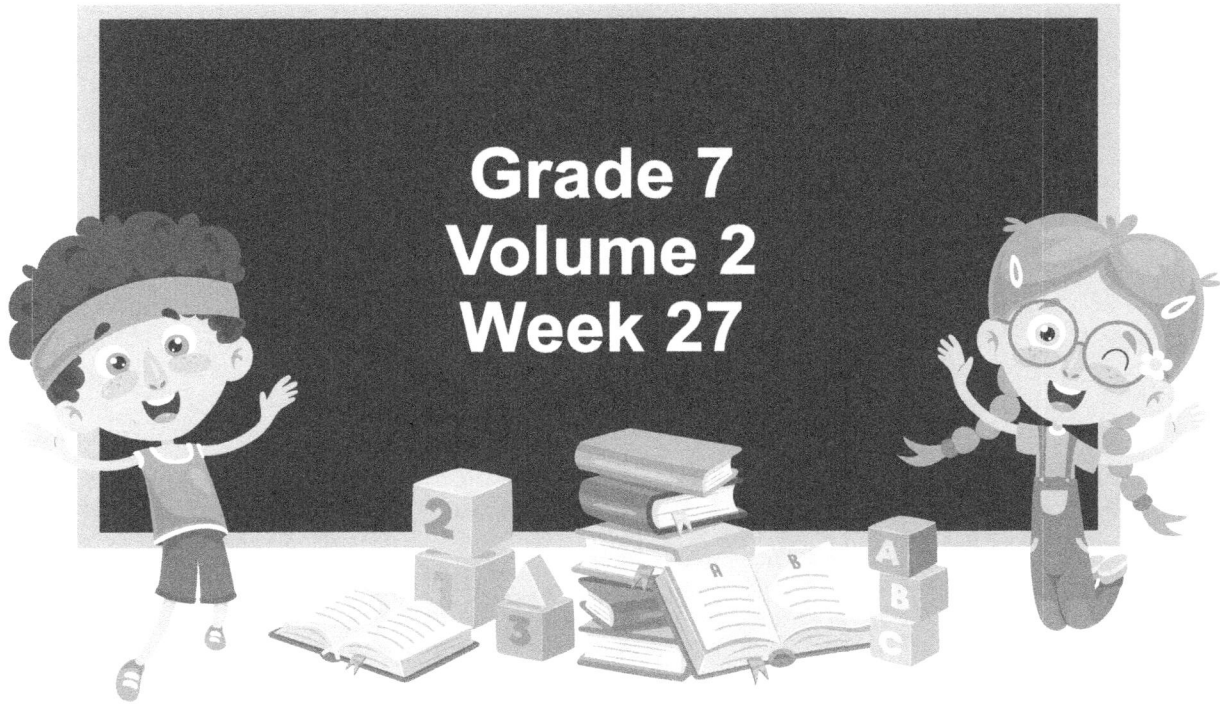

1) Find the value of x

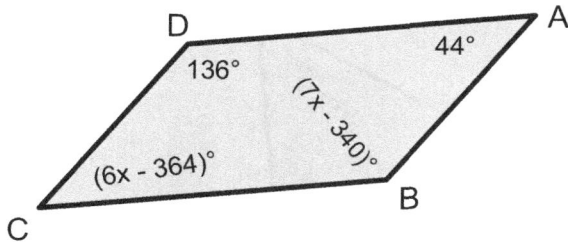

D   136°   44°   A
(7x - 340)°
(6x - 364)°   B
C

A) 63   B) 62

C) 68   D) 55

4) Find the value of x

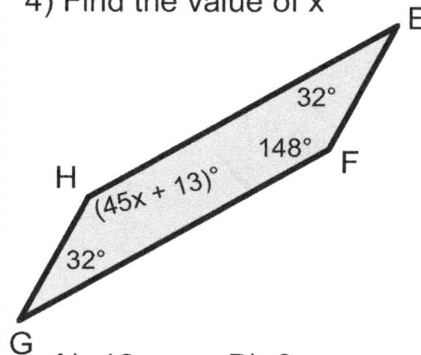

E
32°
148°   F
H
(45x + 13)°
32°
G

A) 12   B) 3

C) 7   D) 13

2) Find the value of x

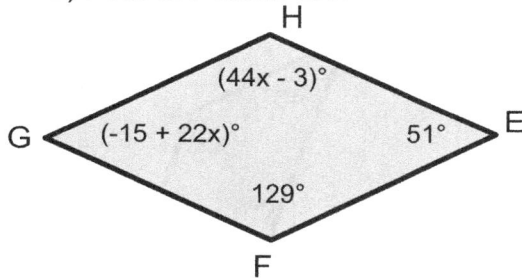

H
(44x - 3)°
G   (-15 + 22x)°   51°   E
129°
F

A) 6   B) 11

C) -4   D) 3

5) Find the value of x

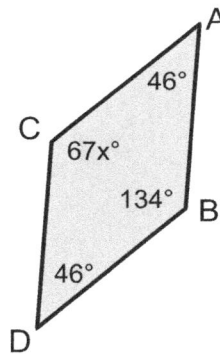

A
46°
C
67x°
134°   B
46°
D

A) 2   B) 12

C) 19   D) 7

3) Find the value of x

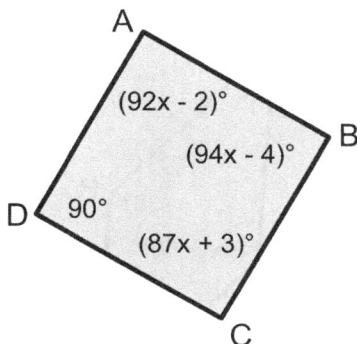

A
(92x - 2)°
(94x - 4)°   B
D   90°
(87x + 3)°
C

A) 3   B) 8

C) 9   D) 1

6) Find the value of x

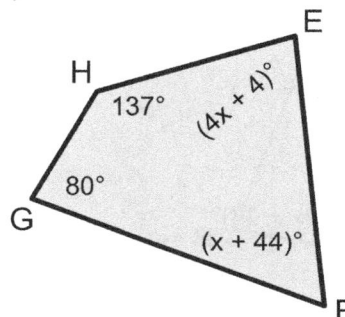

E
H   137°   (4x + 4)°
80°
G
(x + 44)°
F

A) -3   B) 9

C) 2   D) 19

       www.math-knots.com | www.a4ace.com

7) Find the value of x

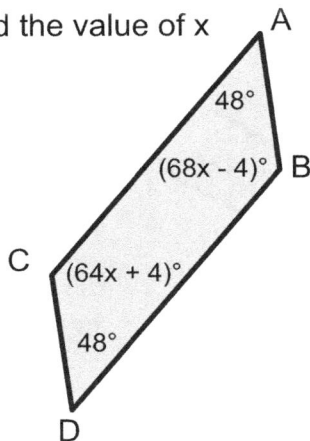

A 48°
(68x - 4)° B
C (64x + 4)°
48°
D

A) -8   B) -23

C) -14   D) 2

8) Find the value of x

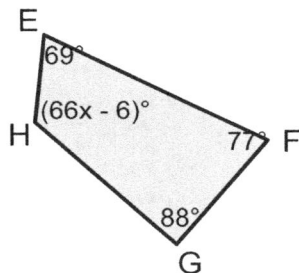

E 69°
(66x - 6)°
H   77° F
88°
G

A) -3   B) 2

C) 7   D) -8

9) Find the value of x

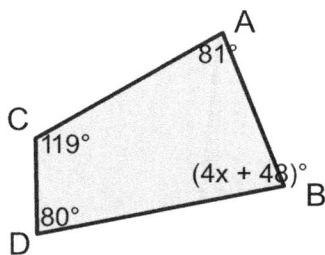

A 81°
C 119°
(4x + 48)° B
80°
D

A) 0   B) 8

C) 4   D) 9

10) Find the value of x

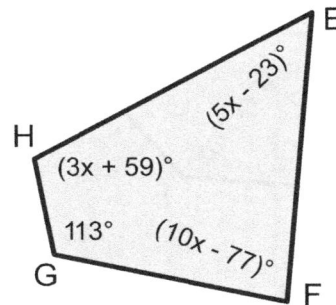

E
(5x - 23)°
H
(3x + 59)°
113°   (10x - 77)°
G   F

A) 16   B) 24

C) 14   D) 23

11) Find the value of x

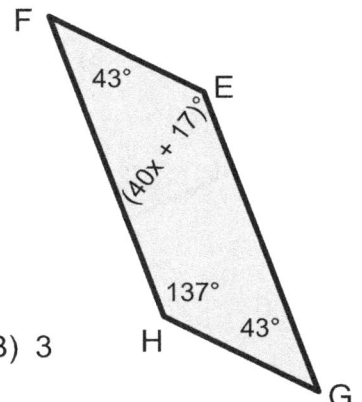

F
43°   E
(40x + 17)°
137°
H   43°
G

A) 6   B) 3

C) -2   D) 14

12) Find the value of x

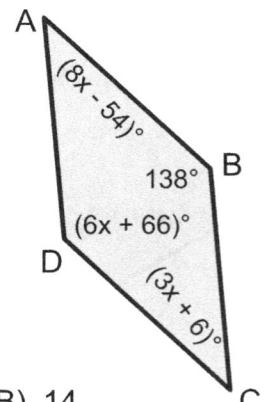

A
(8x - 54)°
138° B
(6x + 66)°
D
(3x + 6)°
C

A) 12   B) 14

C) 1   D) 7

13) Find the value of x

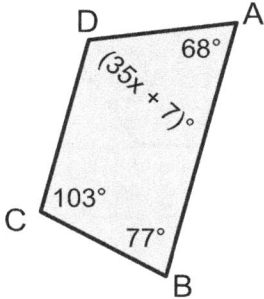

D ___ A
68°
(35x + 7)°
103°
77°
C ___ B

A) 3   B) 12

C) 6   D) 14

14) Find the value of x

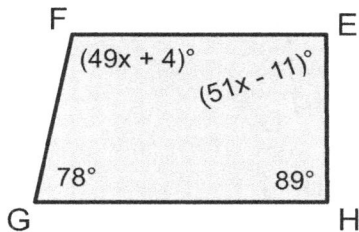

F ___ E
(49x + 4)°
(51x - 11)°
78°   89°
G ___ H

A) 2   B) 4

C) -6   D) 10

15) Find the value of x

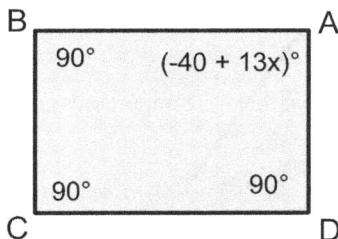

B ___ A
90°   (-40 + 13x)°
90°   90°
C ___ D

A) -4   B) 1

C) 2   D) 10

16) Find the value of x

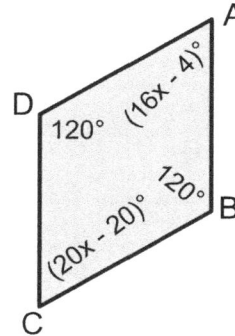

A
D
120°   (16x - 4)°
120°   B
(20x - 20)°
C

A) 4   B) 13

C) 23   D) 18

17) Find the value of x

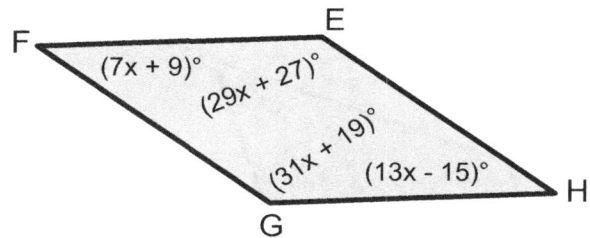

F ___ E
(7x + 9)°
(29x + 27)°
(31x + 19)°   (13x - 15)°   H
G

A) 4   B) 8

C) -1   D) 16

18) Find the value of x

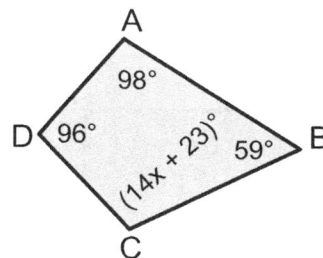

A
98°
D   96°
(14x + 23)°   59°   B
C

A) 20   B) 6

C) 12   D) 26

19) Find the value of x

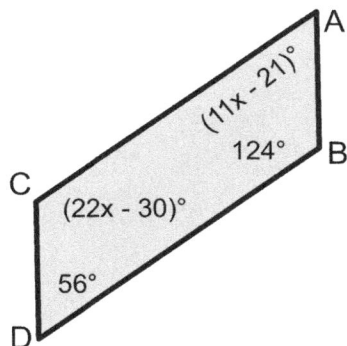

(11x - 21)°
124°
(22x - 30)°
56°

A) -2   B) -11

C) -3   D) 7

20) Find the value of x

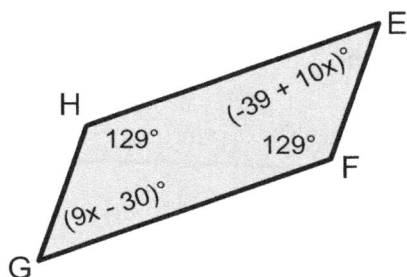

(-39 + 10x)°
129°
129°
(9x - 30)°

A) 17   B) 14

C) 9   D) 8

21) Find the value of x

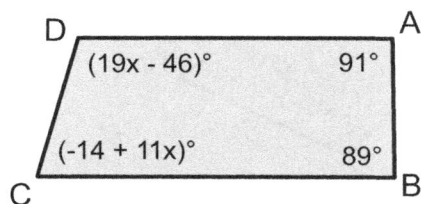

(19x - 46)°   91°
(-14 + 11x)°   89°

A) -4   B) 2

C) -9   D) 8

22) Find the value of x

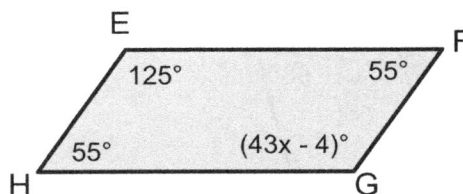

125°   55°
55°   (43x - 4)°

A) 18   B) 9

C) 3   D) 12

23) Find the value of x

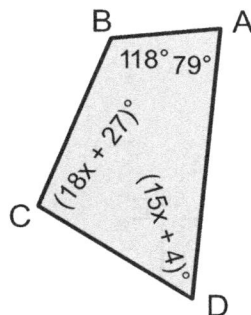

118° 79°
(18x + 27)°
(15x + 4)°

A) -7   B) 4

C) 3   D) -5

24) Find the value of x

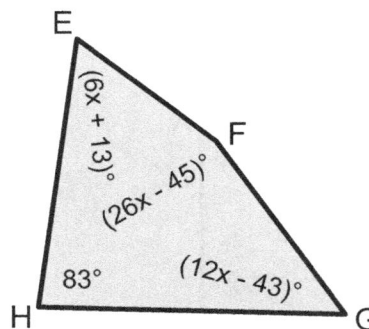

(6x + 13)°
(26x - 45)°
83°   (12x - 43)°

A) 13   B) 7

C) -2   D) 8

www.math-knots.com | www.a4ace.com

25) Find the value of x

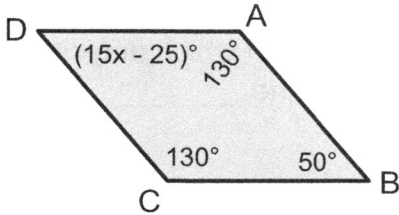

A) -12   B) 5

C) -7   D) -3

26) Find the value of x

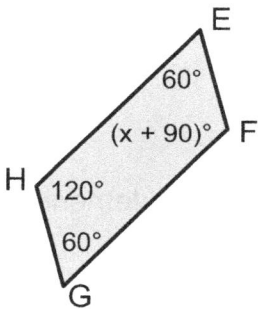

A) 42   B) 27

C) 30   D) 36

27) Find the value of x

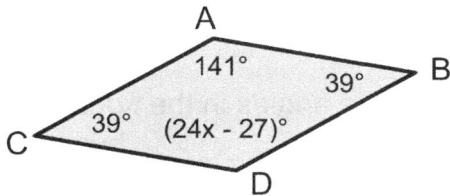

A) 14   B) 11

C) 6   D) 7

28) Find the value of x

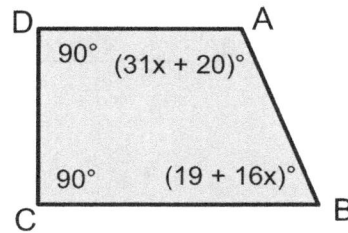

A) 7   B) 3

C) -2   D) -3

29) Find the value of x

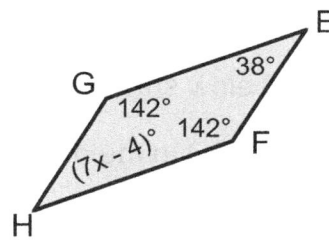

A) 16   B) -3

C) 7   D) 6

30) Find the value of x

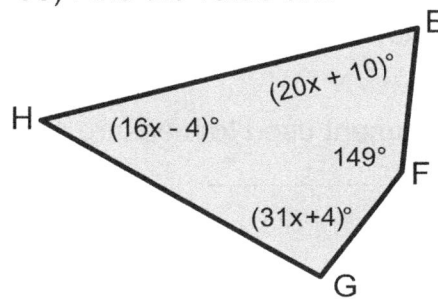

A) 3   B) 6

C) -7   D) -2

31) Complete the below statement.

The figure formed by two rays from the same endpoint is an _____

32) Complete the below statement.

The intersection of the two sides of an angle is called its _____

33) Complete the below statement.

The vertex of ∟COD in the drawing below is point _____

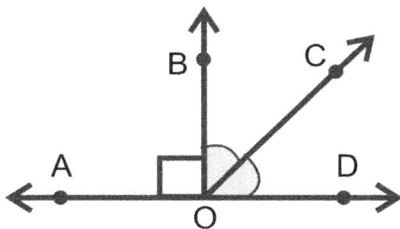

34) Complete the below statement.

The instrument used to measure angles is called a _____

35) Complete the below statement.

The basic unit in which angles are measured is the _____

36) Complete the below statement.

∟AOB has a measure of 90^0 and is called a _____

37) Complete the below statement.

An angle whose measure is between 0^0 and 90^0 is an _____ angle

38) Complete the below statement.

Two acute angles in the figure are ∟BOC and _____ angle

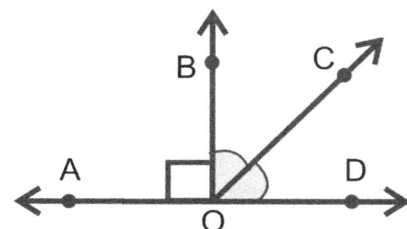

39) Complete the below statement.

An angle whose measure is between 90^0 and 180^0 is an _____ angle

40) Complete the below statement.

An obtuse angle in the figure below is _____

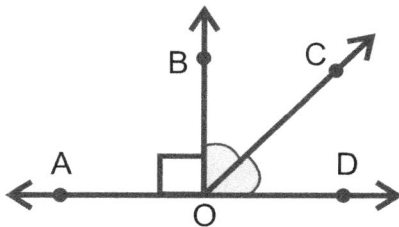

41) Complete the below statement.
Two angles are complementary if the sum of their measure is _____

42) Complete the below statement.

Two angles are supplementary if the sum of their measure is _____

43) Complete the below statement.

The complement of a 30^0 angle has a measure of _____

44) Complete the below statement.

The supplement of a 65^0 angle has a measure of _____

45) Find the missing angle.

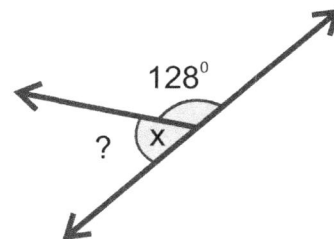

46) Find the missing angle.

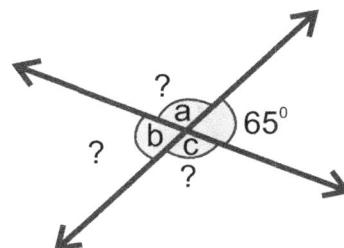

47) Find the missing angle.

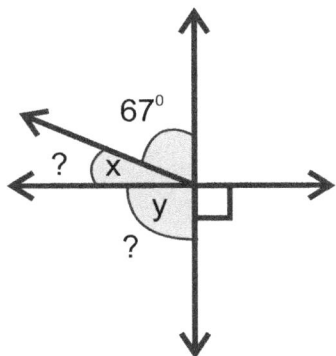

67⁰ — rendered as 67^0

67^0

? x y ?

48) Find the missing angle.

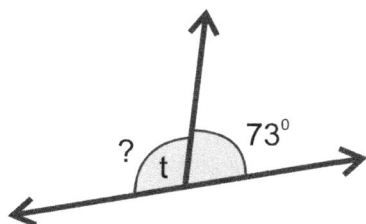

? t 73^0

49) Find the missing angle.

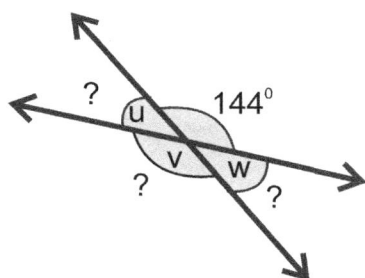

? u 144^0 v w ?

50) Find the missing angle.

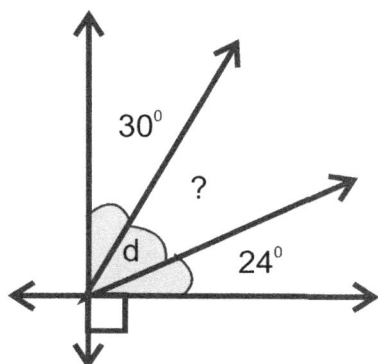

30^0 ? d 24^0

51) Find the missing angle.

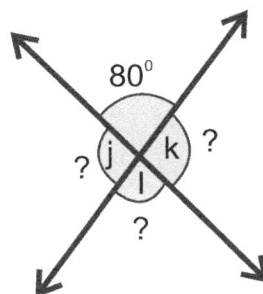

80^0 ? j k l ? ?

52) Find the missing angle.

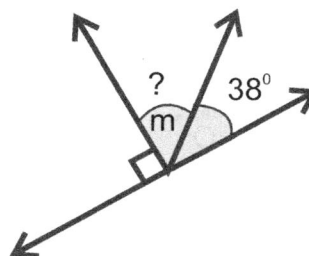

? m 38^0

53) Find the missing angle.

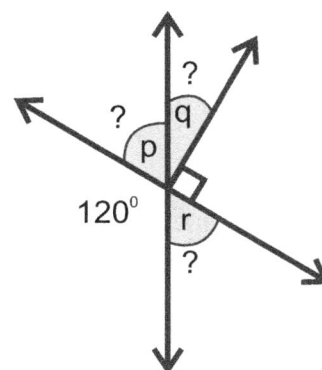

? ? q p r ? 120^0

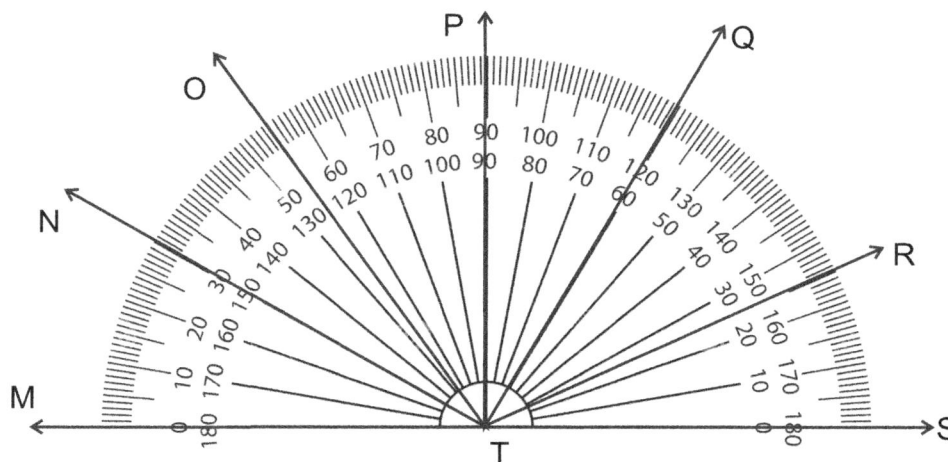

Find the below measured angles

54) ∟MTN

55) ∟MTP

56) ∟NTQ

57) ∟PTQ

58) ∟QTR

59) ∟RTS

60) ∟QTS

61) ∟OTR

62) ∟OTQ

63) ∟NTO

64) ∟NTQ

65) ∟MTO

66) ∟PTS

67) ∟MTS

68) ∟QTO

69) ∟NTR

70) ∟PTR

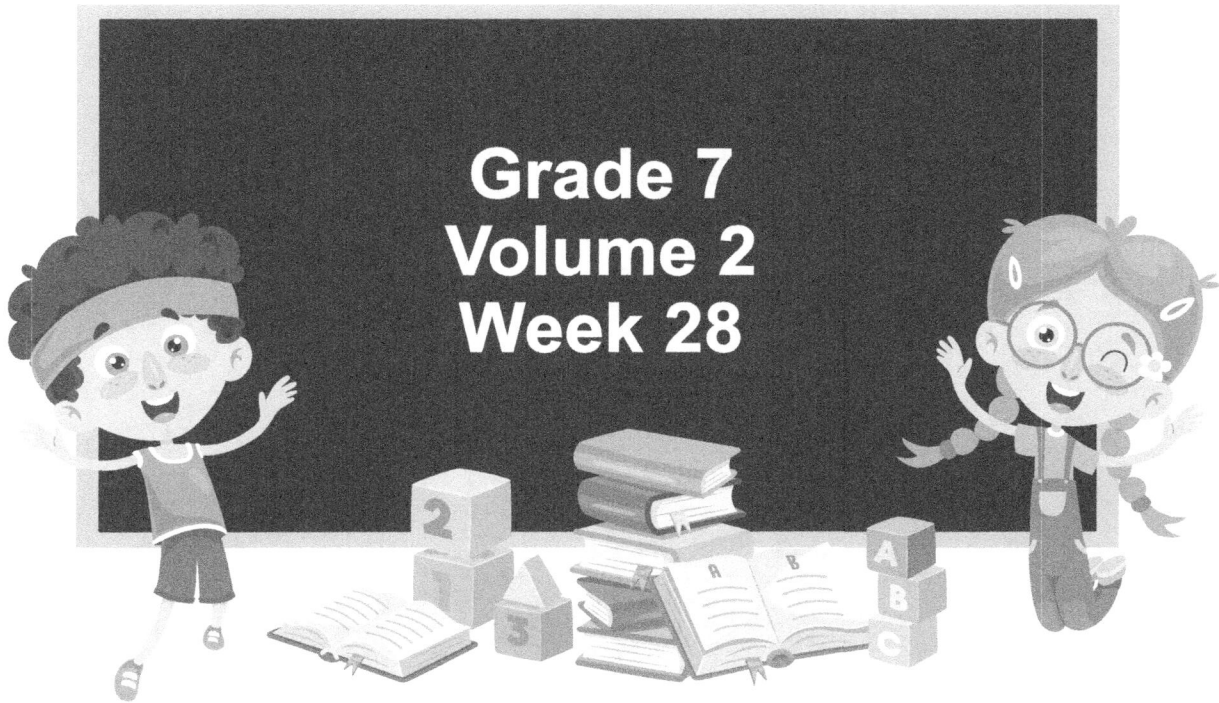

Grade 7
Volume 2
Week 28

210   www.math-knots.com | www.a4ace.com

1) A triangle with the angles: 148°, 11° and 10°.

5) A triangle with the angles: 42°, 40° and 68°.

2) A triangle with the angles: 126°, 11° and 43°.

6) A triangle with the angles: 111°, 32° and 21°.

3) A triangle with the angles: 43°, 34° and 75°.

7) A triangle with the angles: 73°, 22° and 85°.

4) A triangle with the angles: 30°, 1° and 149°.

8) A triangle with the angles: 22°, 90° and 68°.

9) A triangle with the angles: 32°, 19° and 129°.

13) A triangle with the sides: 5in, 5in and 4in.

10) A triangle with the angles: 101°, 21° and 52°.

14) A triangle with the sides: 5in, 10in and 4in.

11) A triangle with the sides: 6ft, 9ft and 5ft.

15) A triangle with the sides: 9mm, 9mm and 5mm.

12) A triangle with the sides: 3ft, 4ft and 2ft.

16) A triangle with the sides: 4mm, 10mm and 3mm.

17) A triangle with the sides: 1ft, 1ft and 1ft.

18) A triangle with the sides: 6ft, 3ft and 7ft.

19) A triangle with the angles: 45°, 56° and 79°.

20) A triangle with the angles: 99°, 58° and 23°.

21) A triangle with the angles: 19°, 102° and 30°.

22) A triangle with the angles: 15°, 60° and 105°.

23) A triangle with the angles: 3°, 75° and 102°.

24) A triangle with the angles: 16°, 112° and 52°.

25) A triangle with the angles: 25°, 141° and 14°.

26) A triangle with the angles: 5°, 144° and 31°.

27) A triangle with the angles: 133°, 9° and 34°.

28) A triangle with the angles: 14°, 57° and 103°.

29) A triangle with the angles: 31°, 131° and 18°.

30) A triangle with the angles: 29°, 83° and 53°.

31) A triangle with the angles: 100°, 14° and 66°.

32) A triangle with the angles: 76°, 50° and 26°.

33) A triangle with the sides: 3mm, 8mm and 2mm.

34) A triangle with the sides: 9mm, 5mm and 4mm.

35) A triangle with the sides: 8ft, 3ft and 9ft.

36) A triangle with the sides: 8ft, 2ft and 1ft.

37) A triangle with the sides: 10in, 2in and 1in.

38) A triangle with the sides: 3in, 3in and 1in.

39) A triangle with the angles: 47°, 22° and 98°.

40) A triangle with the angles: 40°, 65° and 51°.

www.math-knots.com | www.a4ace.com

41) A triangle with the angles: 50°, 84° and 46°.

42) A triangle with the angles: 48°, 33° and 99°.

43) Find the value of A in the below complementary angle.

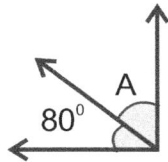

80°, A

44) Find the value of A in the below complementary angle.

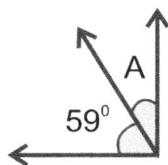

59°, A

45) Find the value of A in the below complementary angle.

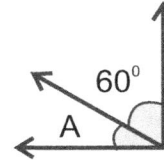

60°, A

46) Find the value of A in the below complementary angle.

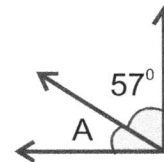

57°, A

47) Find the value of A in the below complementary angle.

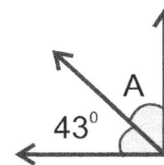

43°, A

48) Find the value of A in the below complementary angle.

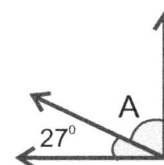

27°, A

www.math-knots.com | www.a4ace.com

49) Find the value of A in the below complementary angle.

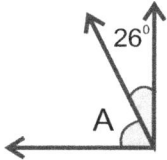

26°

A

50) Find the value of A in the below complementary angle.

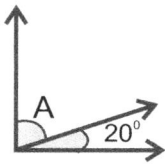

A

20°

51) Find the value of A in the below complementary angle.

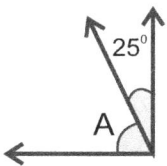

25°

A

52) Find the value of A in the below complementary angle.

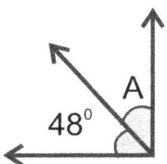

A

48°

53) Find the value of A in the below complementary angle.

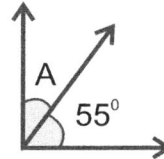

A

55°

54) Find the value of A in the below complementary angle.

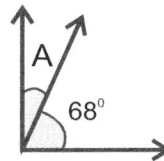

A

68°

55) Find the value of A in the below complementary angle.

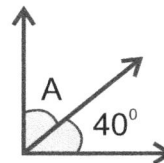

A

40°

56) Find the value of A in the below complementary angle.

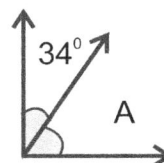

34°

A

57) Find the value of A in the below complementary angle.

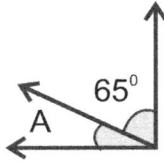

65^0

A

58) Find the value of A in the below complementary angle.

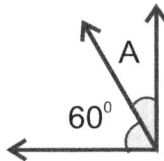

A

60^0

59) Find the value of A in the below complementary angle.

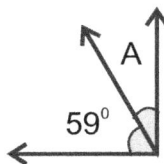

A

59^0

60) Find the value of A in the below complementary angle.

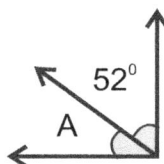

52^0

A

61) Find the value of A in the below complementary angle.

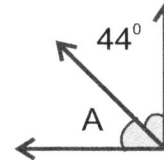

44^0

A

62) Find the value of A in the below complementary angle.

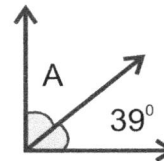

A

39^0

63) Find the value of A in the below complementary angle.

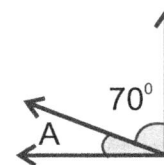

70^0

A

64) Find the value of A in the below complementary angle.

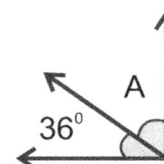

A

36^0

www.math-knots.com | www.a4ace.com

65) Find the value of A in the below complementary angle.

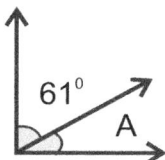

66) Find the value of A in the below complementary angle.

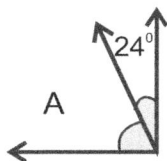

67) The complementary angle of 45° is _____

68) The complementary angle of 49° is _____

69) The complementary angle of 23° is _____

70) The supplementary angle of 112° is _____

71) The supplementary angle of 171° is _____

72) The supplementary angle of 29° is _____

www.math-knots.com | www.a4ace.com

73) The supplementary angle of 147°
is _____

74) The supplementary angle of 164°
is _____

75) The complementary angle of 34°
is _____

76) The complementary angle of 77°
is _____

77) The complementary angle of 70°
is _____

78) The complementary angle of 28°
is _____

79) The complementary angle of 68°
is _____

80) The complementary angle of 45°
is _____

www.math-knots.com | www.a4ace.com

81) The supplementary angle of 122°
   is _____

82) The supplementary angle of 72°
   is _____

83) The supplementary angle of 166°
   is _____

84) The supplementary angle of 59°
   is _____

85) The supplementary angle of 93°
   is _____

86) The complementary angle of 35°
   is _____

87) The complementary angle of 5°
   is _____

88) The complementary angle of 13°
   is _____

89) The complementary angle of 60°
   is _____

90) The supplementary angle of 106°
   is _____

91) The supplementary angle of 84°
   is _____

92) The supplementary angle of 69°
   is _____

93) The supplementary angle of 29°
   is _____

94) Determine the 2D shape that would be
   created if the 3d shape were sliced as
   shown

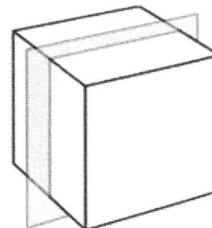

95) Determine the 2D shape that would be
   created if the 3d shape were sliced as
   shown

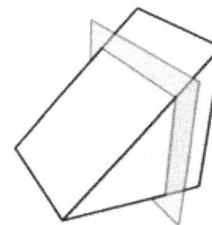

96) Determine the 2D shape that would be
   created if the 3d shape were sliced as
   shown

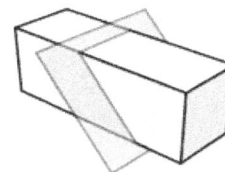

www.math-knots.com | www.a4ace.com

97) Determine the 2D shape that would be created if the 3d shape were sliced as shown

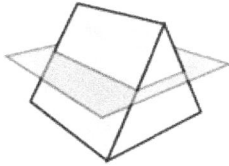

98) Determine the 2D shape that would be created if the 3d shape were sliced as shown

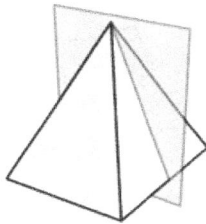

99) Determine the 2D shape that would be created if the 3d shape were sliced as shown

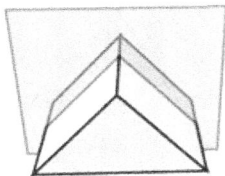

100) Determine the 2D shape that would be created if the 3d shape were sliced as shown

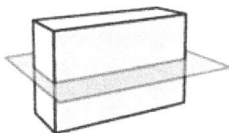

101) Determine the 2D shape that would be created if the 3d shape were sliced as shown

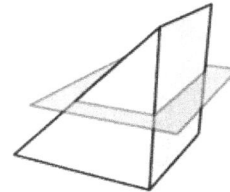

102) Determine the 2D shape that would be created if the 3d shape were sliced as shown

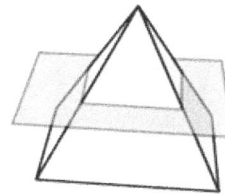

103) Determine the 2D shape that would be created if the 3d shape were sliced as shown

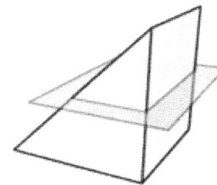

104) Determine the 2D shape that would be created if the 3d shape were sliced as shown

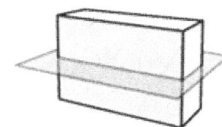

www.math-knots.com | www.a4ace.com

105) Determine the 2D shape that would be created if the 3d shape were sliced as shown

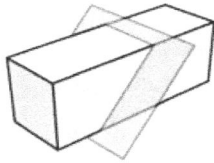

106) Determine the 2D shape that would be created if the 3d shape were sliced as shown

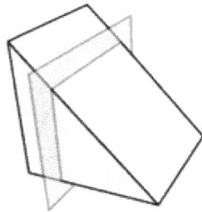

107) Determine the 2D shape that would be created if the 3d shape were sliced as shown

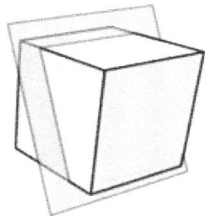

108) Determine the 2D shape that would be created if the 3d shape were sliced as shown

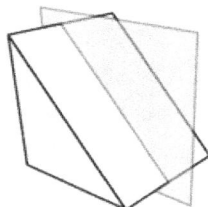

109) Determine the 2D shape that would be created if the 3d shape were sliced as shown

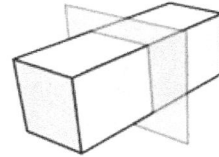

110) Determine the 2D shape that would be created if the 3d shape were sliced as shown

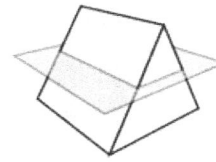

111) Determine the 2D shape that would be created if the 3d shape were sliced as shown

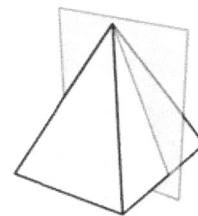

112) Determine the 2D shape that would be created if the 3d shape were sliced as shown

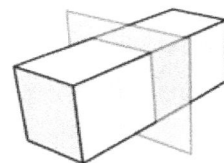

113) Determine the 2D shape that would be created if the 3d shape were sliced as shown

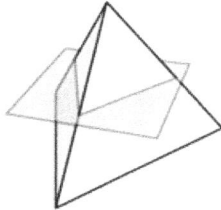

114) Determine the 2D shape that would be created if the 3d shape were sliced as shown

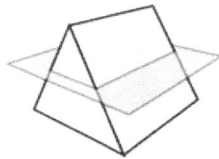

115) Determine the 2D shape that would be created if the 3d shape were sliced as shown

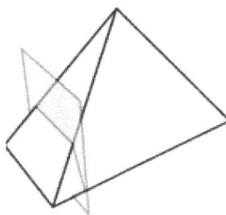

116) Determine the 2D shape that would be created if the 3d shape were sliced as shown

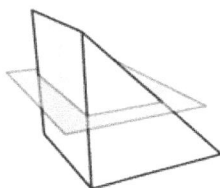

117) Determine the 2D shape that would be created if the 3d shape were sliced as shown

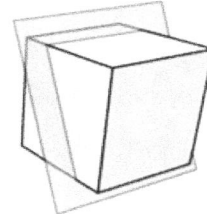

118) Determine the 2D shape that would be created if the 3d shape were sliced as shown

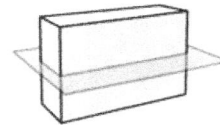

119) Determine the 2D shape that would be created if the 3d shape were sliced as shown

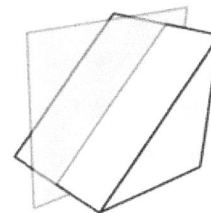

120) Determine the 2D shape that would be created if the 3d shape were sliced as shown

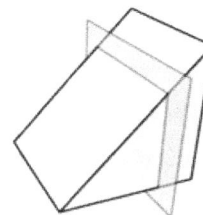

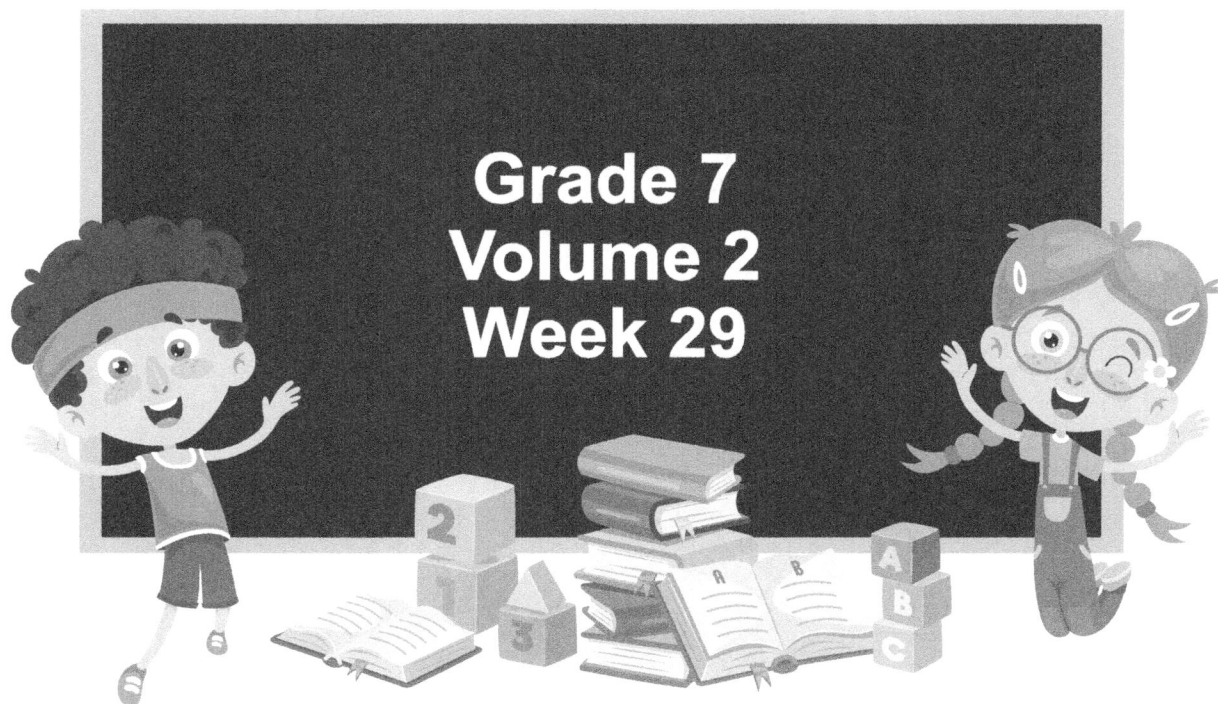

Grade 7
Volume 2
Week 29

228   www.math-knots.com | www.a4ace.com

1) Find the value of angle A and angle B from the figure given below.

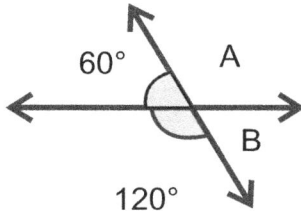

60°   A
120°   B

2) Find the value of angle X and angle Y from the figure given below.

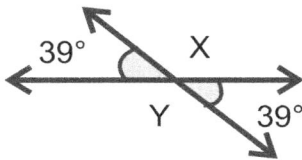

39°   X
Y   39°

3) Find the value of angle A and angle B from the figure given below.

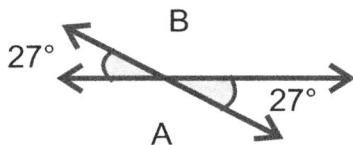

27°   B
A   27°

4) Find the value of angle X and angle Y from the figure given below.

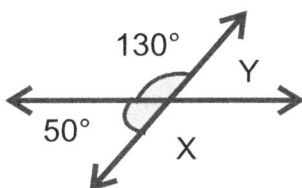

130°   Y
50°   X

5) Find the value of angle A and angle B from the figure given below.

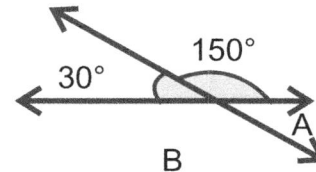

30°   150°
B   A

6) Find the value of angle X and angle Y from the figure given below.

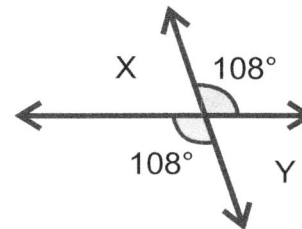

X   108°
108°   Y

7) Find the value of angle A and angle B from the figure given below.

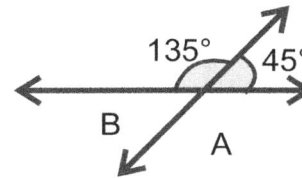

135°   45°
B   A

8) Find the value of angle X and angle Y from the figure given below.

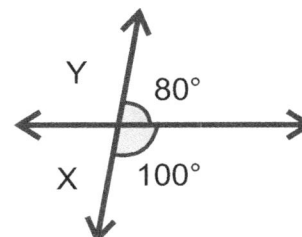

Y   80°
X   100°

www.math-knots.com | www.a4ace.com

9) Find the value of angle A and angle B from the figure given below.

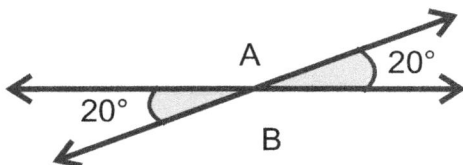

10) Find the value of angle X and angle Y from the figure given below.

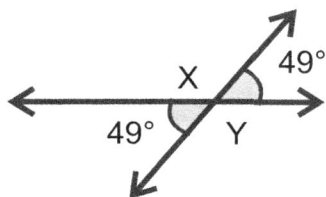

11) Find the value of angle A and angle B from the figure given below.

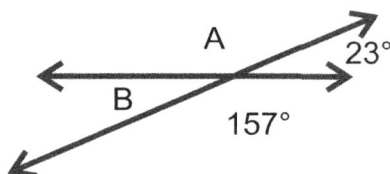

12) Find the value of angle X and angle Y from the figure given below.

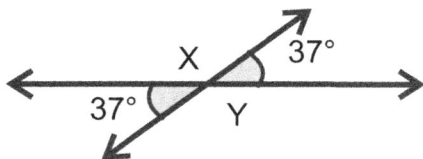

13) Find the value of angle A and angle B from the figure given below.

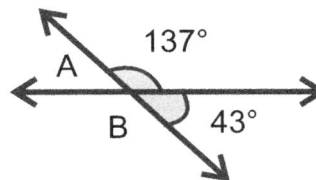

14) Find the value of angle X and angle Y from the figure given below.

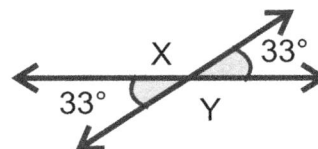

15) Find the value of angle A and angle B from the figure given below.

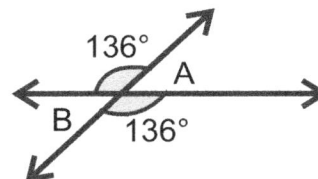

16) Find the value of angle X and angle Y from the figure given below.

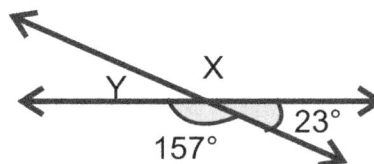

   www.math-knots.com | www.a4ace.com

17) Find the value of a and b.
Angle PQR is 180°.

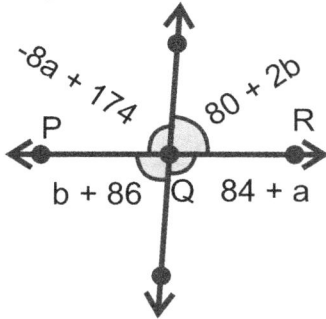

$-8a + 174$
$80 + 2b$
P
R
$b + 86$ Q $84 + a$

18) Find the value of a and b.
Angle PQR is 180°.

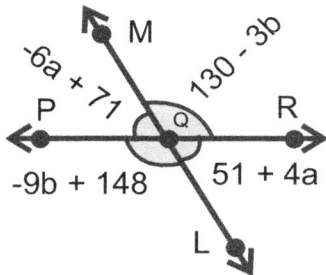

M
$-6a + 71$
$130 - 3b$
P
R
Q
$-9b + 148$
$51 + 4a$
L

19) Find the value of a and b.
Angle PQR is 180°.

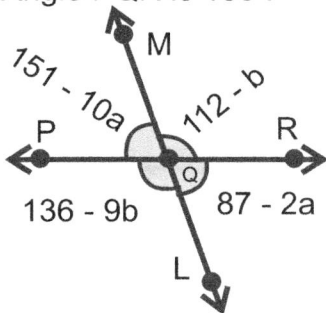

M
$151 - 10a$
$112 - b$
P
R
Q
$136 - 9b$
$87 - 2a$
L

20) Find the value of a and b.
Angle PQR is 180°.

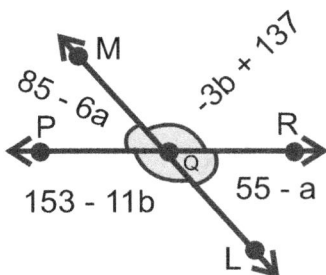

M
$85 - 6a$
$-3b + 137$
P
R
Q
$153 - 11b$
$55 - a$
L

21) Find the value of a and b.
Angle PQR is 180°.

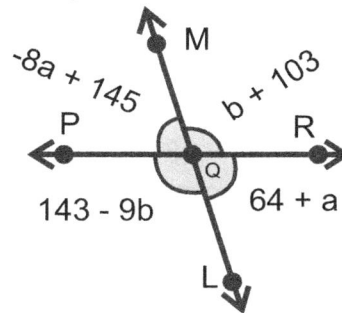

M
$-8a + 145$
$b + 103$
P
R
Q
$143 - 9b$
$64 + a$
L

22) Find the value of a and b.
Angle PQR is 180°.

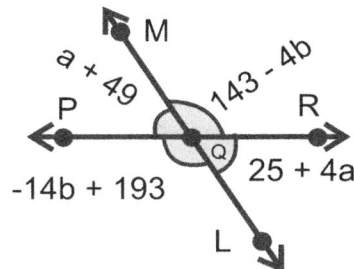

M
$a + 49$
$143 - 4b$
P
R
Q
$-14b + 193$
$25 + 4a$
L

23) Find the value of a and b.
Angle PQR is 180°.

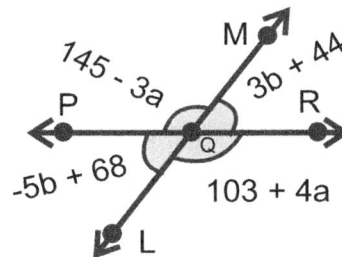

M
$145 - 3a$
$3b + 44$
P
R
Q
$-5b + 68$
$103 + 4a$
L

24) Find the value of a and b.
Angle PQR is 180°.

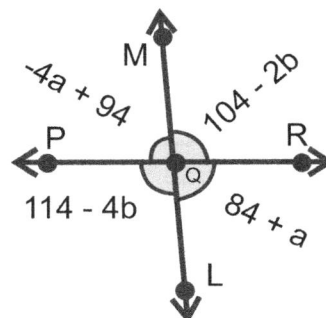

M
$-4a + 94$
$104 - 2b$
P
R
Q
$114 - 4b$
$84 + a$
L

25) Find the value of a and b.
Angle PQR is 180^0.

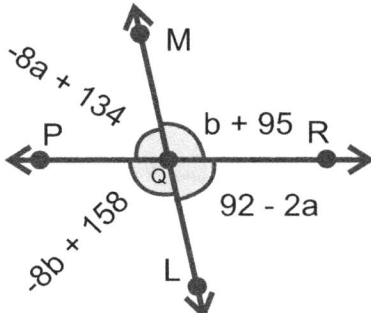

-8a + 134
b + 95
92 - 2a
-8b + 158

26) Find the value of a and b.
Angle PQR is 180^0.

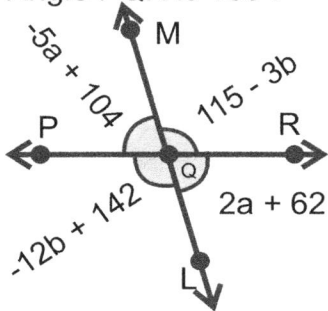

-5a + 104
115 - 3b
-12b + 142
2a + 62

27) Find the value of a and b.
Angle PQR is 180^0.

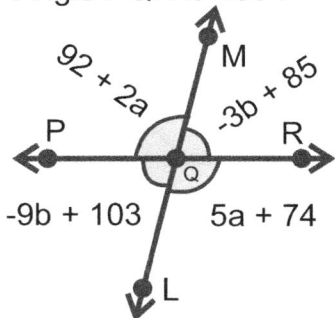

92 + 2a
-3b + 85
-9b + 103
5a + 74

28) Find the value of a and b.
Angle PQR is 180^0.

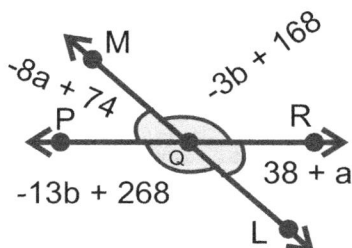

-8a + 74
-3b + 168
-13b + 268
38 + a

29) Find the value of a and b.
Angle PQR is 180^0.

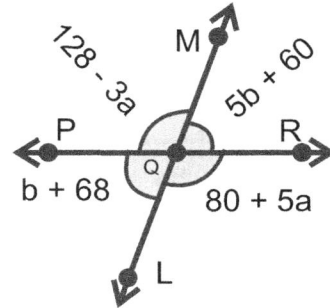

128 - 3a
5b + 60
b + 68
80 + 5a

30) Find the value of a and b.
Angle PQR is 180^0.

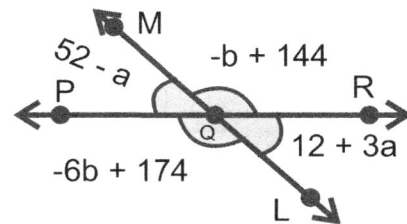

52 - a
-b + 144
-6b + 174
12 + 3a

31) Find the value of a and b.
Angle PQR is 180^0.

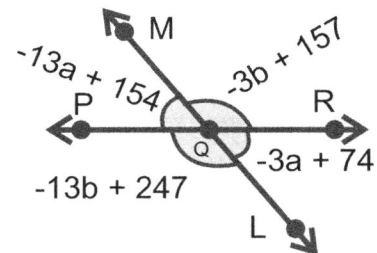

-13a + 154
-3b + 157
-13b + 247
-3a + 74

32) Find the value of a and b.
Angle PQR is 180^0.

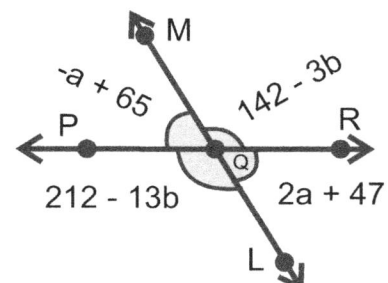

-a + 65
142 - 3b
212 - 13b
2a + 47

www.math-knots.com | www.a4ace.com

33) Find the value of a and b.
Angle PQR is 180^0.

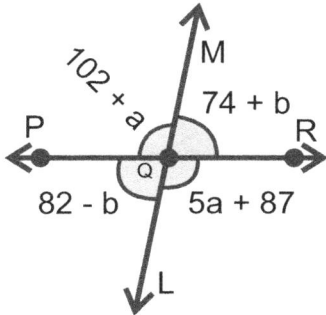

$102 + a$ M $74 + b$
P R
Q
$82 - b$ $5a + 87$
L

37) Find the value of a and b.
Angle PQR is 180^0.

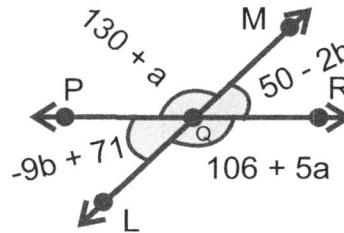

$130 + a$ M $50 - 2b$
P R
Q
$-9b + 71$ $106 + 5a$
L

34) Find the value of a and b.
Angle PQR is 180^0.

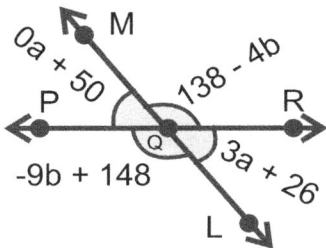

$0a + 50$ M $138 - 4b$
P R
Q
$-9b + 148$ $3a + 26$
L

38) Find the value of a and b.
Angle XQR is 180^0.

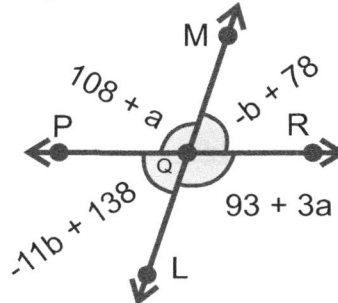

$108 + a$ M $-b + 78$
P R
Q
$-11b + 138$ $93 + 3a$
L

35) Find the value of a and b.
Angle PQR is 180^0.

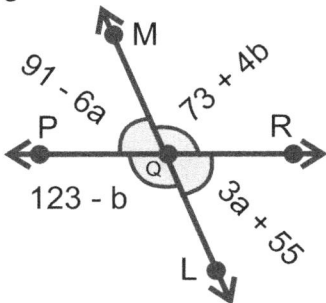

$91 - 6a$ M $73 + 4b$
P R
Q
$123 - b$ $3a + 55$
L

39) Find the value of a and b.
Angle PQR is 180^0.

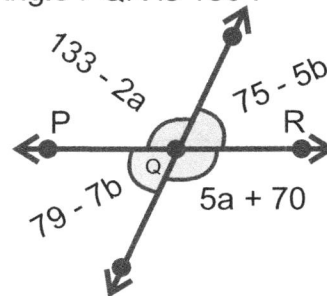

$133 - 2a$ $75 - 5b$
P R
Q
$79 - 7b$ $5a + 70$
L

36) Find the value of a and b.
Angle PQR is 180^0.

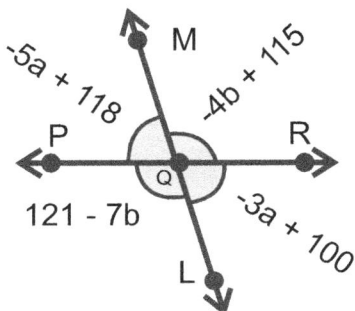

$-5a + 118$ M $-4b + 115$
P R
Q
$121 - 7b$ $-3a + 100$
L

40) Find the value of a and b.
Angle PQR is 180^0.

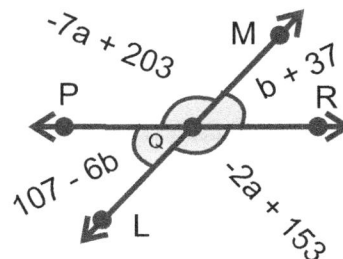

$-7a + 203$ M $b + 37$
P R
Q
$107 - 6b$ $-2a + 153$
L

www.math-knots.com | www.a4ace.com

41) Find the value of A in the set of supplementary angles

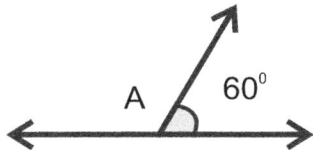

42) Find the value of A in the set of supplementary angles

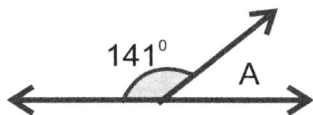

43) Find the value of A in the set of supplementary angles

44) Find the value of A in the set of supplementary angles

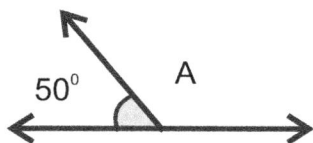

45) Find the value of A in the set of supplementary angles

46) Find the value of A in the set of supplementary angles

47) Find the value of A in the set of supplementary angles

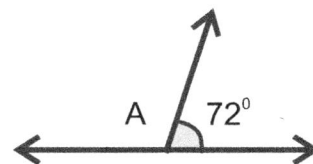

48) Find the value of A in the set of supplementary angles

www.math-knots.com | www.a4ace.com

49) Find the value of A in the set of supplementary angles

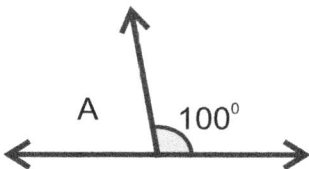

A 100^0

50) Find the value of A in the set of supplementary angles

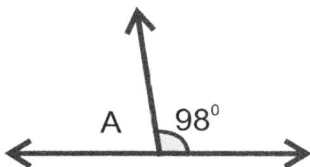

A 98^0

51) Find the value of A in the set of supplementary angles

160^0
A

52) Find the value of A in the set of supplementary angles

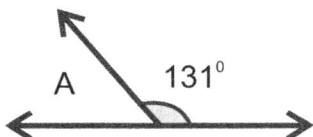

A 131^0

53) Find the value of A in the set of supplementary angles

23^0 A

54) Find the value of A in the set of supplementary angles

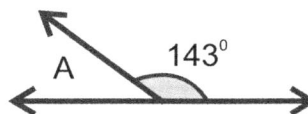

A 143^0

55) Find the value of A in the set of supplementary angles

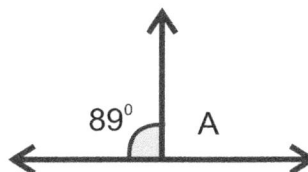

89^0 A

56) Find the value of A in the set of supplementary angles

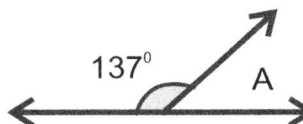

137^0 A

www.math-knots.com | www.a4ace.com

57) Find the value of A in the set of supplementary angles

147^0

A

58) Find the value of A in the set of supplementary angles

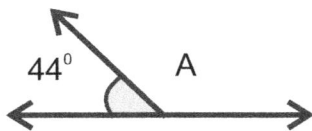

44^0 A

59) Find the value of A in the set of supplementary angles

A 23^0

60) Find the value of A in the set of supplementary angles

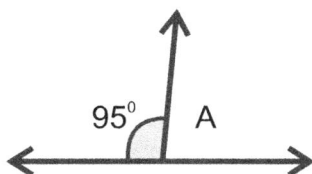

95^0 A

61) Find the value of A in the set of supplementary angles

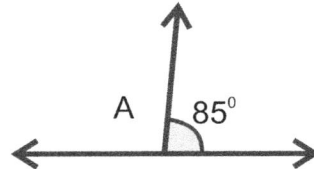

A 85^0

62) Find the value of A in the set of supplementary angles

A 21^0

63) Find the value of A in the set of supplementary angles

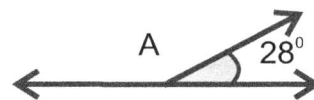

A 28^0

64) Find the value of A in the set of supplementary angles

A 43^0

       www.math-knots.com | www.a4ace.com

65) Find the value of A in the set of supplementary angles

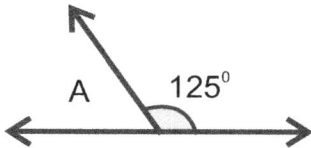

A 125^0

66) Find the value of A in the set of supplementary angles

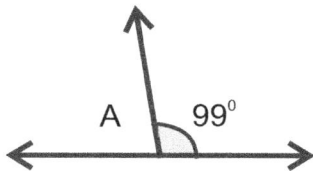

A 99^0

67) Find the value of A in the set of supplementary angles

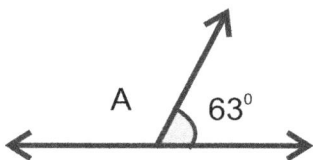

A 63^0

68) Find the value of A in the set of supplementary angles

A 40^0

69) Find the value of A in the set of supplementary angles

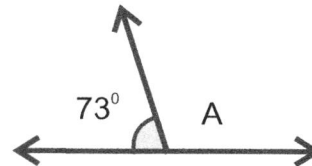

73^0 A

70) Find the value of A in the set of supplementary angles

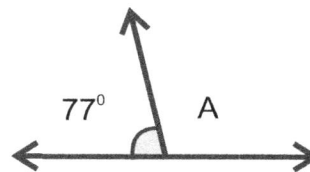

77^0 A

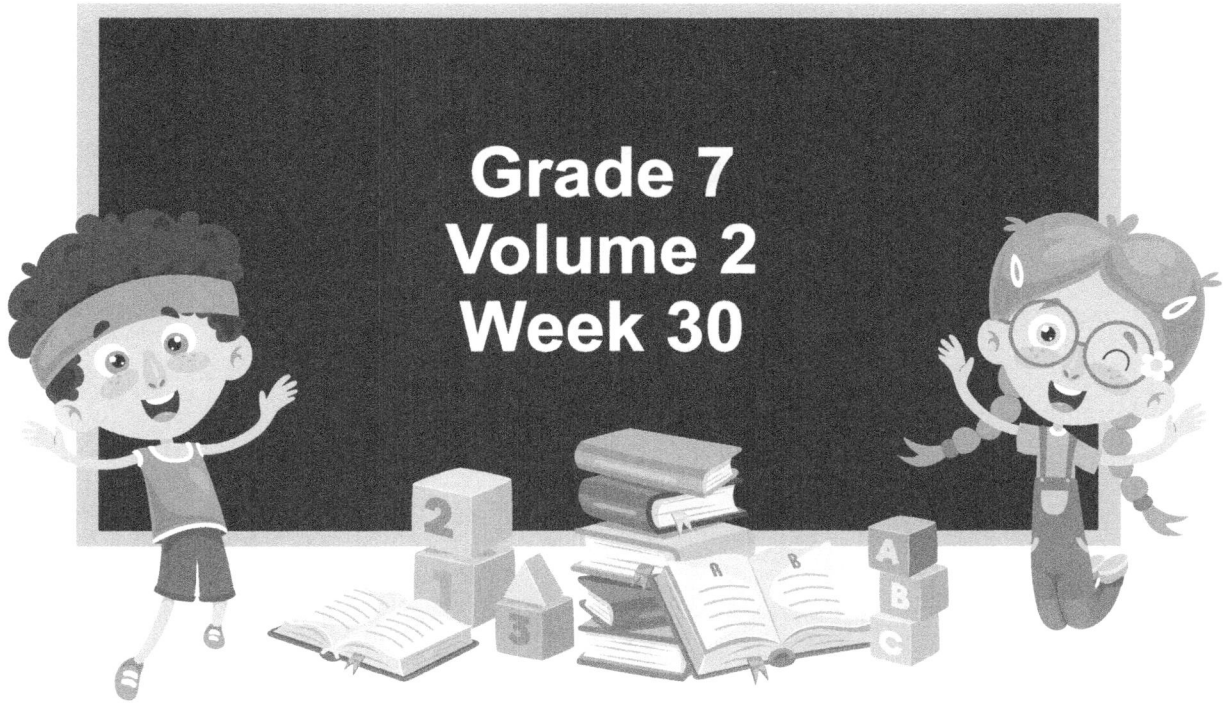

Grade 7
Volume 2
Week 30

240   www.math-knots.com | www.a4ace.com

1) Identify the angle relationship in the figure below

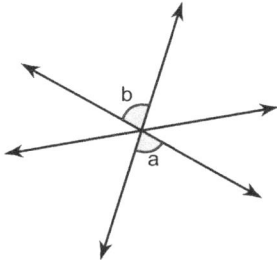

A) adjacent   B) supplementary

C) vertical   D) corresponding

2) Identify the angle relationship in the figure below

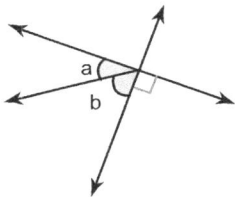

A) alternate exterior

B) corresponding

C) vertical

D) complementary

3) Identify the angle relationship in the figure below

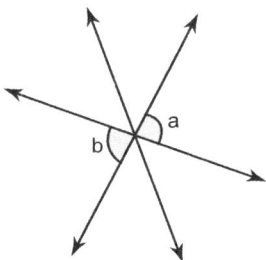

A) alternate exterior

B) adjacent

C) vertical

D) complementary

4) Identify the angle relationship in the figure below

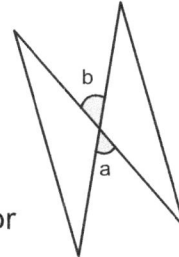

A) alternate exterior

B) adjacent

C) alternate interior

D) vertical

5) Identify the angle relationship in the figure below

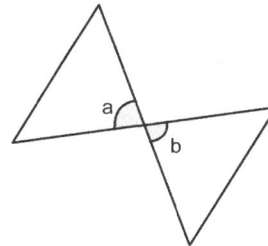

A) corresponding   B) adjacent

C) complementary   D) vertical

6) Identify the angle relationship in the figure below

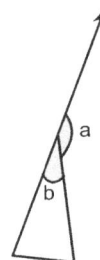

A) corresponding

B) alternate interior

C) complementary

D) supplementary

www.math-knots.com | www.a4ace.com

7) Identify the angle relationship in the figure below

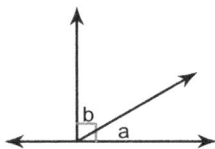

A) complementary

B) supplementary

C) alternate exterior

D) corresponding

8) Identify the angle relationship in the figure below

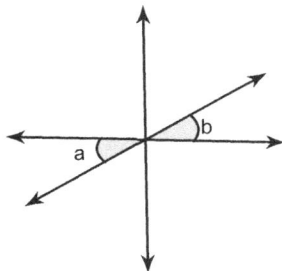

A) adjacent

B) vertical

C) corresponding

D) alternate exterior

9) Identify the angle relationship in the figure below

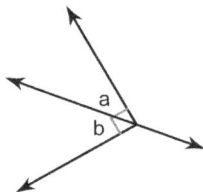

A) alternate exterior

B) complementary

C) corresponding

D) vertical

10) Identify the angle relationship in the figure below

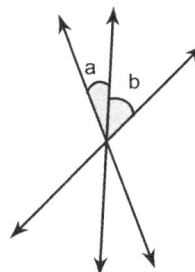

A) adjacent

B) alternate exterior

C) alternate interior

D) supplementary

11) Identify the angle relationship in the figure below

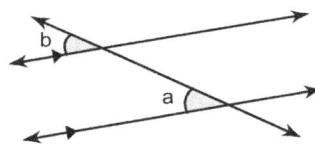

A) supplementary

B) adjacent

C) corresponding

D) complementary

12) Identify the angle relationship in the figure below

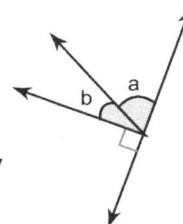

A) complementary

B) supplementary

C) alternate interior

D) alternate exterior

13) Identify the angle relationship in the figure below

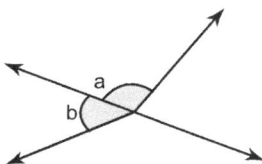

A) alternate exterior

B) adjacent

C) alternate interior

D) vertical

14) Identify the angle relationship in the figure below

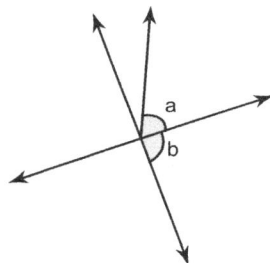

A) alternate interior

B) supplementary

C) adjacent

D) vertical

15) Identify the angle relationship in the figure below

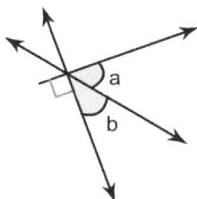

A) complementary

B) alternate exterior

C) corresponding

D) alternate interior

16) Identify the angle relationship in the figure below

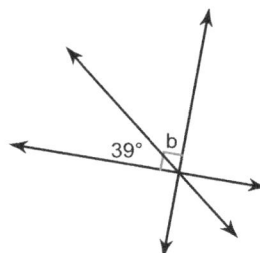

A) 51°   B) 39°

C) 129°   D) 43°

17) Identify the angle relationship in the figure below

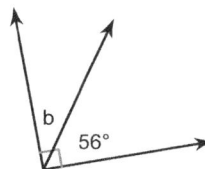

A) 34°   B) 124°

C) 146°   D) 56°

18) Identify the angle relationship in the figure below

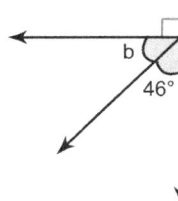

A) 46°   B) 134°

C) 44°   D) 136°

                   www.math-knots.com | www.a4ace.com

19) Find the measurement of angle b.

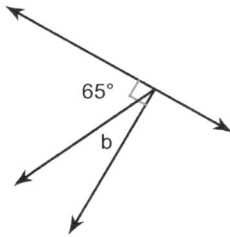

A) 25°   B) 65°

C) 67°   D) 45°

20) Find the measurement of angle b.

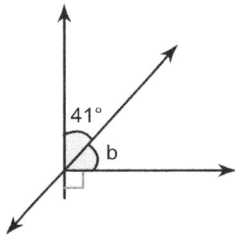

A) 111°   B) 131°

C) 49°   D) 21°

21) Find the measurement of angle b.

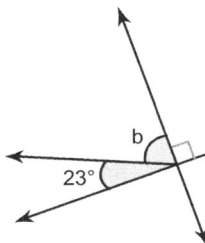

A) 157°   B) 23°

C) 113°   D) 67°

22) Find the measurement of angle b.

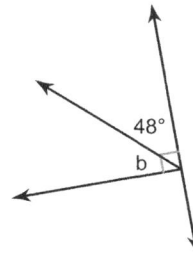

A) 42°   B) 138°

C) 48°   D) 132°

23) Find the measurement of angle b.

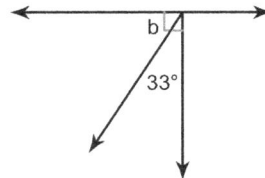

A) 149°   B) 33°

C) 57°   D) 123°

24) Find the measurement of angle b.

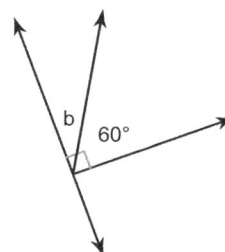

A) 30°   B) 82°

C) 39°   D) 141°

www.math-knots.com | www.a4ace.com

25) Find the measurement of angle b.

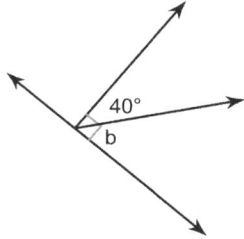

A) 63°   B) 50°

C) 40°   D) 140°

28) Find the measurement of angle b.

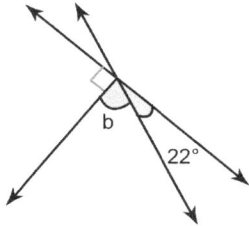

A) 29°   B) 151°

C) 61°   D) 119°

26) Find the measurement of angle b.

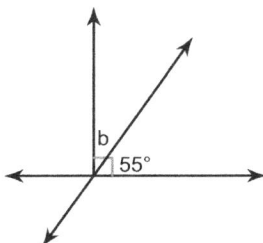

A) 112°   B) 22°

C) 68°   D) 158°

29) Find the measurement of angle b.

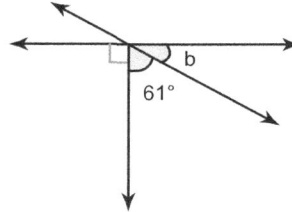

A) 64°   B) 26°

C) 154°   D) 116°

27) Find the measurement of angle b.

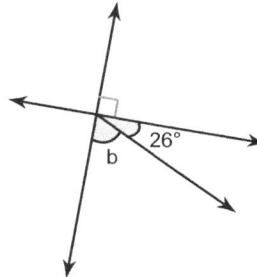

A) 35°   B) 66°

C) 146°   D) 24°

30) Find the measurement of angle b.

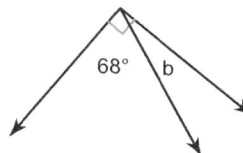

A) 68°   B) 22°

C) 158°   D) 112°

31) Find the measurement of angle b.

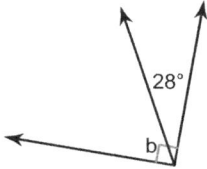

A) 62°   B) 148°

C) 28°   D) 152°

34) Find the measurement of angle b.

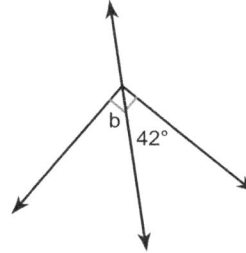

A) 132°   B) 48°

C) 5°   D) 95°

32) Find the measurement of angle b.

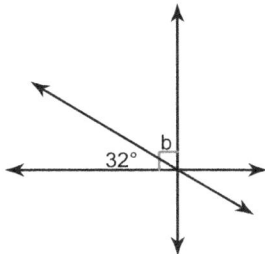

A) 122°   B) 32°

C) 58°   D) 148°

35) Find the measurement of angle b.

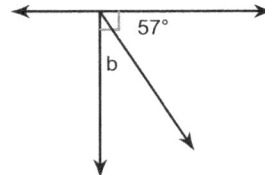

A) 72°   B) 33°

C) 18°   D) 162°

33) Find the measurement of angle b.

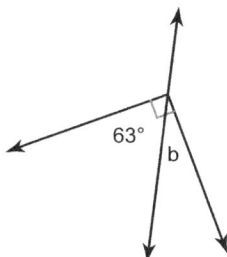

A) 63°   B) 27°

C) 117°   D) 153°

36) Find the measurement of angle b.

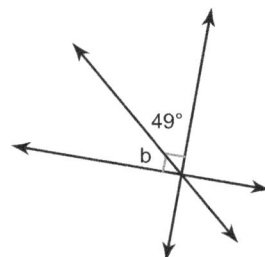

A) 41°   B) 139°

C) 49°   D) 98°

246

37) Find the measurement of angle b.

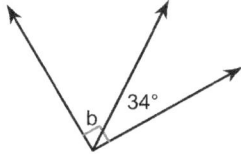

A) 34°   B) 146°

C) 56°   D) 124°

40) Find the measurement of angle b.

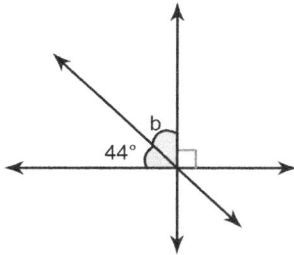

A) 54°   B) 63°

C) 126°   D) 36°

38) Find the measurement of angle b.

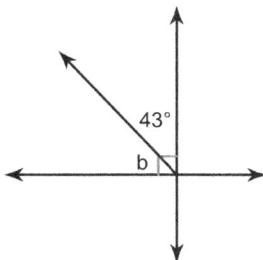

A) 46°   B) 44°

C) 7°   D) 97°

41) Find the measurement of angle b.

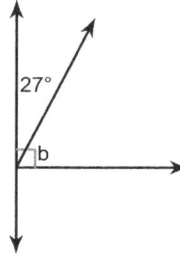

A) 19°   B) 36°

C) 71°   D) 161°

39) Find the measurement of angle b.

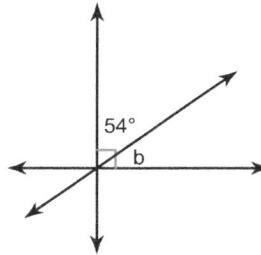

A) 43°   B) 62°

C) 162°   D) 47°

42) Find the measurement of angle b.

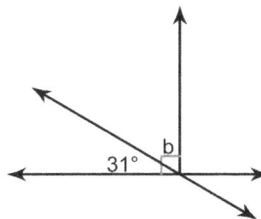

A) 59°   B) 149°

C) 121°   D) 31°

www.math-knots.com | www.a4ace.com

43) Find the measurement of angle b.

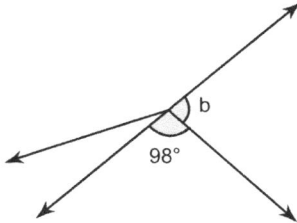

A) 154°   B) 26°

C) 8°   D) 82°

44) Find the measurement of angle b.

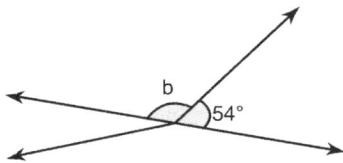

A) 100°   B) 80°

C) 36°   D) 126°

45) Find the measurement of angle b.

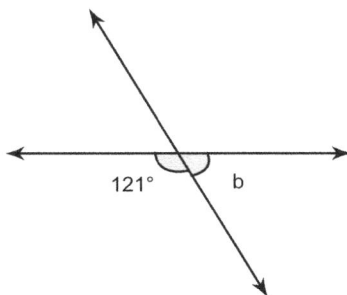

A) 75°   B) 121°

C) 59°   D) 35°

46) Find the measurement of angle b.

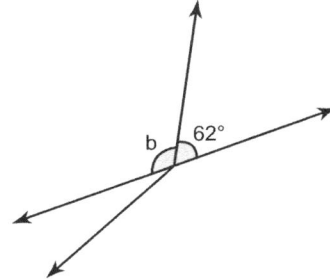

A) 62°   B) 28°

C) 118°   D) 78°

47) Find the measurement of angle b.

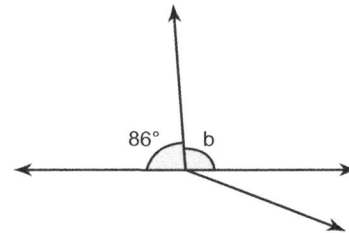

A) 86°   B) 142°

C) 4°   D) 94°

48) Find the measurement of angle b.

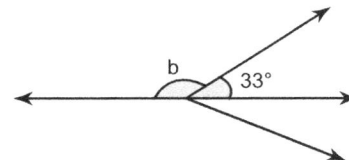

A) 123°   B) 124°

C) 57°   D) 147°

49) Find the measurement of angle b.

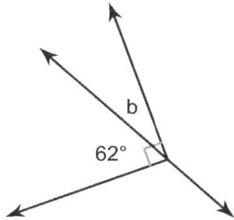

A) 28°   B) 62°

C) 152°   D) 150°

50) Find the measurement of angle b.

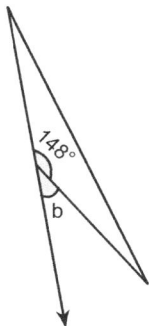

A) 145°   B) 32°

C) 55°   D) 35°

51) Find the measurement of angle b.

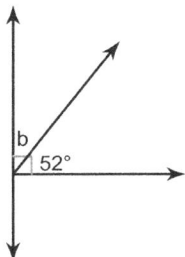

A) 38°   B) 128°

C) 52°   D) 142°

52) Find the measurement of angle b.

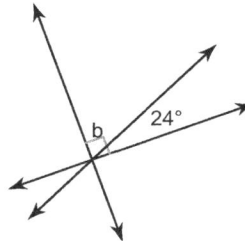

A) 66°   B) 24°

C) 156°   D) 114°

53) Find the measurement of angle b.

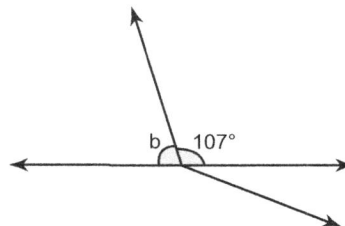

A) 73°   B) 54°

C) 102°   D) 36°

54) Find the measurement of angle b.

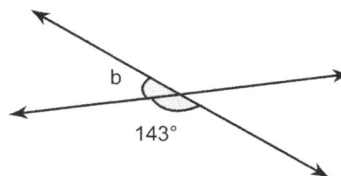

A) 53°   B) 37°

C) 143°   D) 127°

55) Find the measurement of angle b.

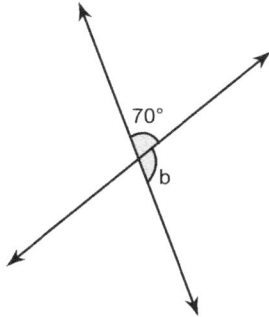

A) 86°   B) 4°

C) 110°   D) 70°

56) Find the measurement of angle b.

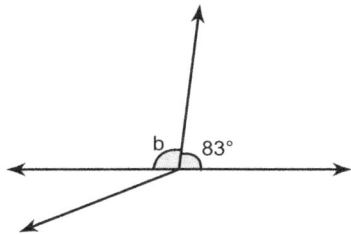

A) 7°   B) 173°

C) 97°   D) 83°

57) Find the measurement of angle b.

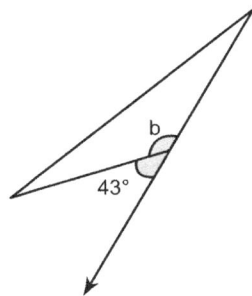

A) 137°   B) 47°

C) 43°   D) 133°

58) Find the measurement of angle b.

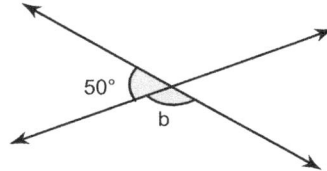

A) 50°   B) 51°

C) 130°   D) 141°

59) Find the measurement of angle b.

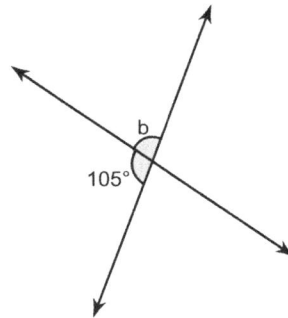

A) 15°   B) 75°

C) 105°   D) 165°

60) Find the measurement of angle b.

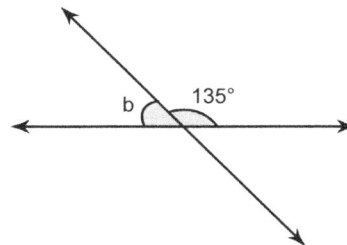

A) 13°   B) 135°

C) 77°   D) 45°

 www.math-knots.com | www.a4ace.com

61) Find the measurement of angle b.

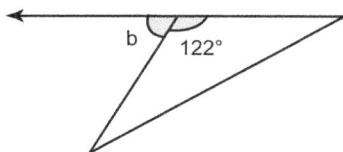

A) 148°   B) 45°

C) 32°   D) 58°

62) Find the measurement of angle b.

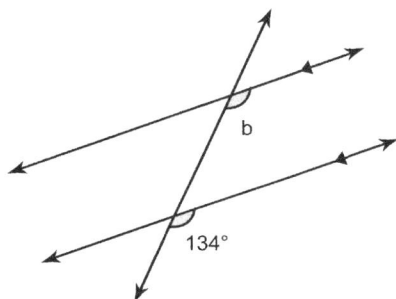

A) 134°   B) 64°

C) 131°   D) 49°

63) Find the measurement of angle b.

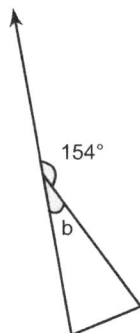

A) 64°   B) 26°

C) 97°   D) 116°

64) Find the measurement of angle b.

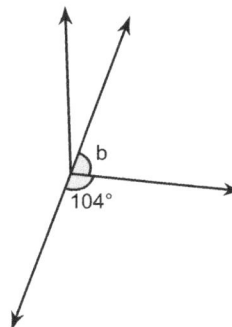

A) 14°   B) 66°

C) 166°   D) 76°

65) Find the measurement of angle b.

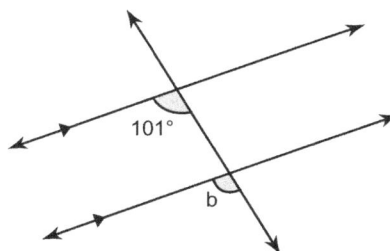

A) 79°   B) 97°

C) 7°   D) 101°

66) Find the measurement of angle b.

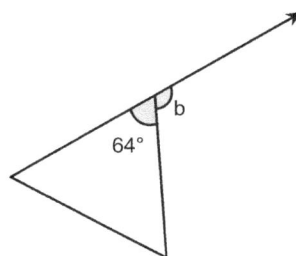

A) 154°   B) 64°

C) 26°   D) 116°

www.math-knots.com | www.a4ace.com

67) Find the measurement of angle b.

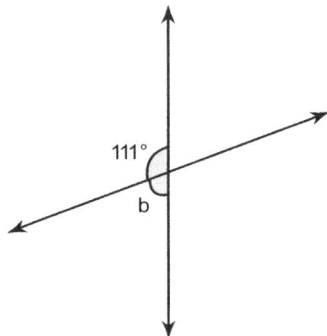

A) 69°   B) 41°

C) 21°   D) 159°

68) Find the measurement of angle b.

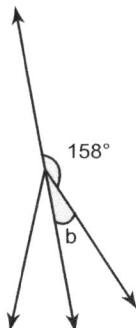

A) 22°   B) 158°

C) 68°   D) 114°

69) Find the measurement of angle b.

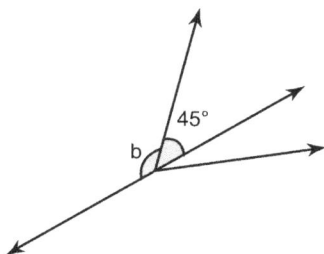

A) 45°   B) 135°

C) 71°   D) 109°

70) Find the measurement of angle b.

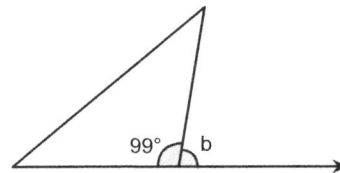

A) 81°   B) 46°

C) 134°   D) 99°

71) Find the measurement of angle b.

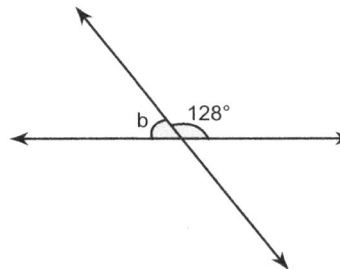

A) 52°   B) 78°

C) 168°   D) 12°

72) Find the measurement of angle b.

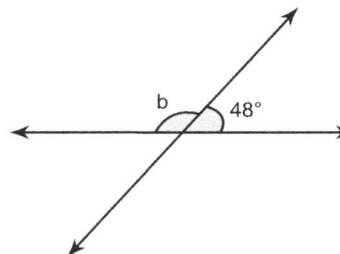

A) 5°   B) 85°

C) 132°   D) 48°

73) Find the measurement of angle b.

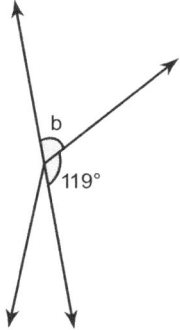

A) 102°　　B) 61°

C) 119°　　D) 29°

74) Find the measurement of angle b.

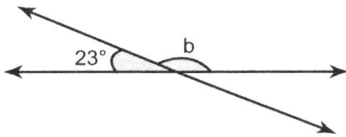

A) 39°　　B) 157°

C) 108°　　D) 67°

75) Find the measurement of angle b.

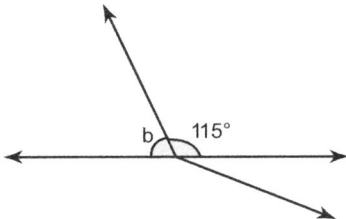

A) 22°　　B) 115°

C) 25°　　D) 65°

76) Find the measurement of angle b.

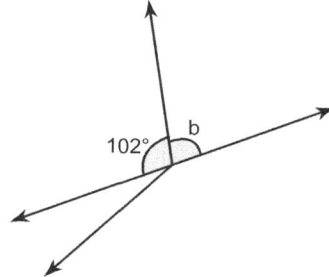

A) 78°　　B) 12°

C) 85°　　D) 95°

77) Find the measurement of angle b.

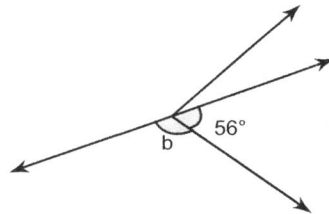

A) 120°　　B) 56°

C) 124°　　D) 34°

78) Find the measurement of angle b.

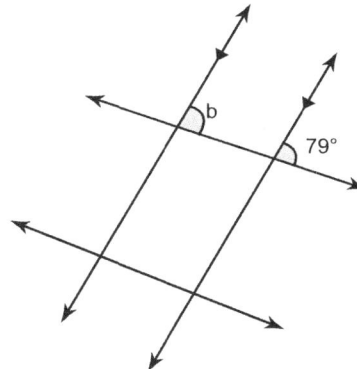

A) 169°　　B) 11°

C) 101°　　D) 79°

　　253

79) Find the measurement of angle b.

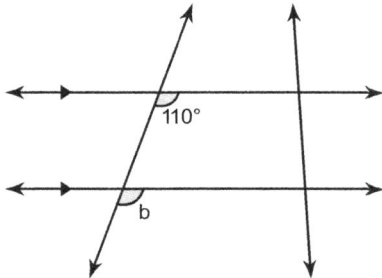

A) 126°   B) 110°

C) 61°   D) 54°

81) Find the measurement of angle b.

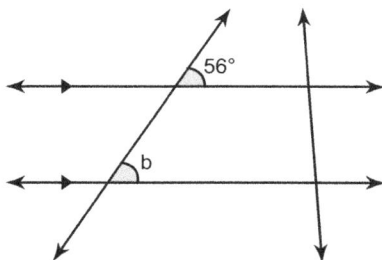

A) 148°   B) 58°

C) 32°   D) 122°

80) Find the measurement of angle b.

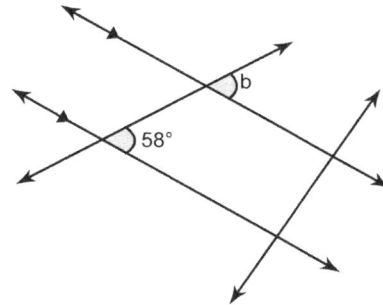

A) 158°   B) 56°

C) 124°   D) 119°

82) Find the measurement of angle b.

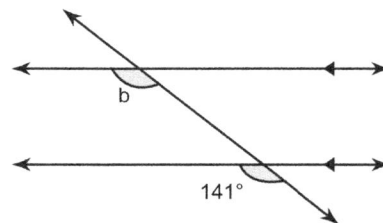

A) 39°   B) 141°

C) 152°   D) 51°

83) Find the measurement of angle b.

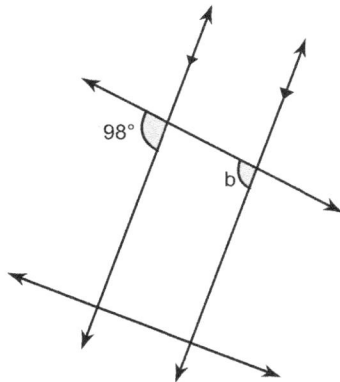

A) 103°   B) 77°

C) 8°   D) 98°

85) Find the measurement of angle b.

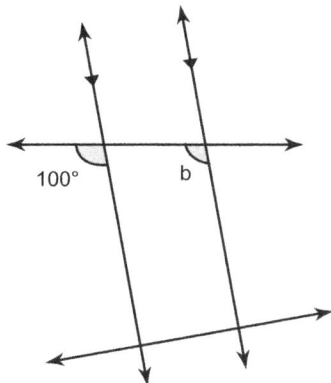

A) 68°   B) 158°

C) 22°   D) 112°

84) Find the measurement of angle b.

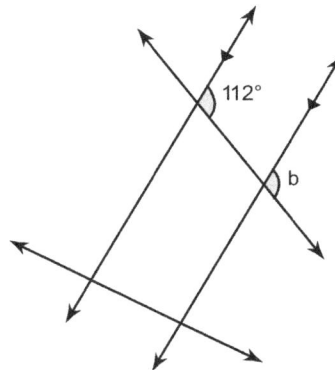

A) 50°   B) 127°

C) 156°   D) 100°

86) Find the measurement of angle b.

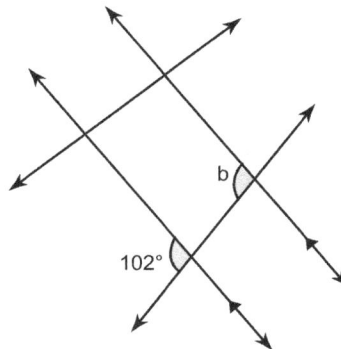

A) 102°   B) 78°

C) 168°   D) 12°

87) Find the measurement of angle b.

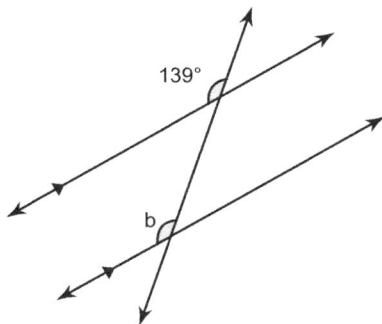

A) 139°   B) 17°

C) 163°   D) 73°

89) Find the measurement of angle b.

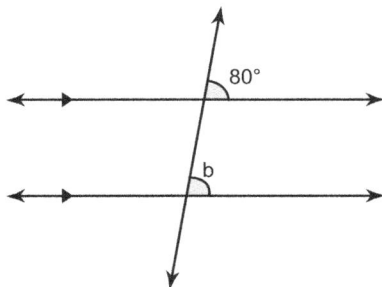

A) 87°   B) 3°

C) 93°   D) 106°

88) Find the measurement of angle b.

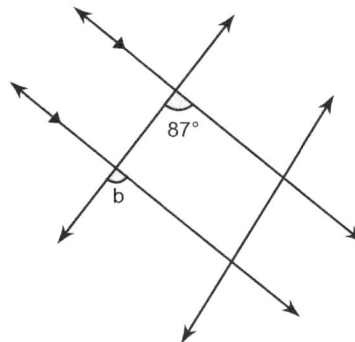

A) 80°   B) 100°

C) 10°   D) 170°

90) Find the measurement of angle b.

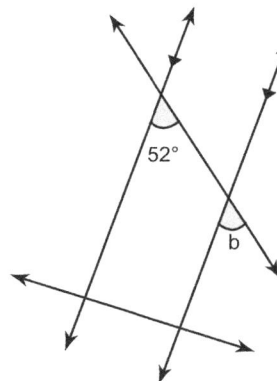

A) 149°   B) 52°

C) 128°   D) 129°

91) Find the measurement of angle b.

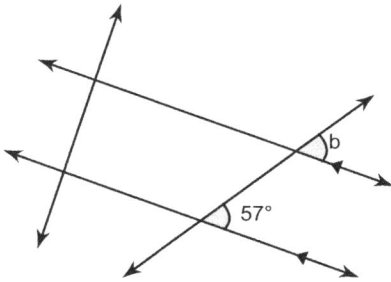

A) 88°   B) 29°

C) 57°   D) 151°

93) Find the measurement of angle b.

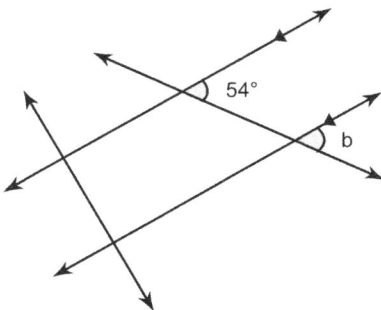

A) 2°   B) 88°

C) 126°   D) 54°

92) Find the measurement of angle b.

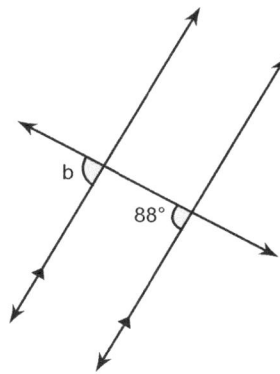

A) 54°   B) 41°

C) 126°   D) 139°

94) Find the measurement of angle b.

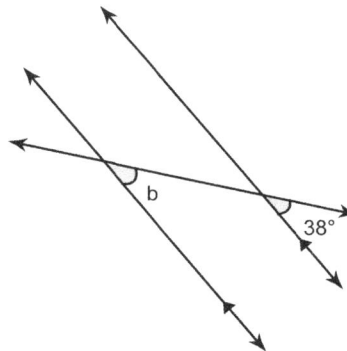

A) 142°   B) 52°

C) 127°   D) 38°

258   www.math-knots.com | www.a4ace.com

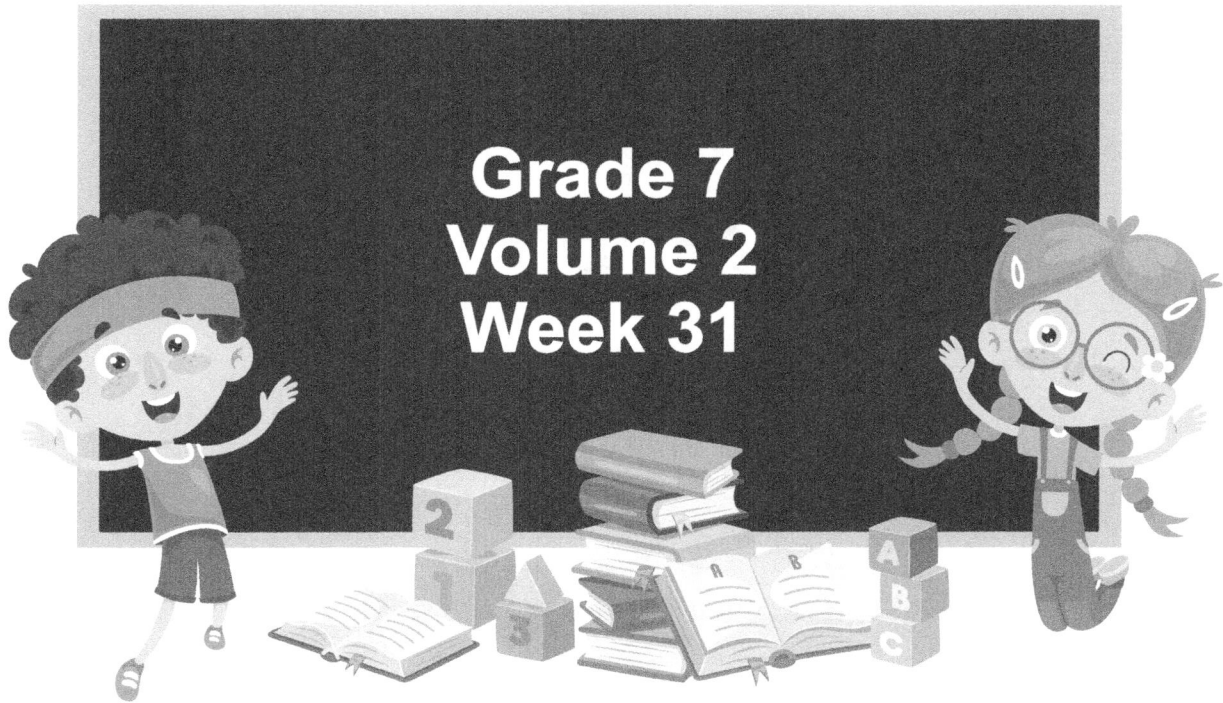

Grade 7
Volume 2
Week 31

1) Find the measurement of angle b.

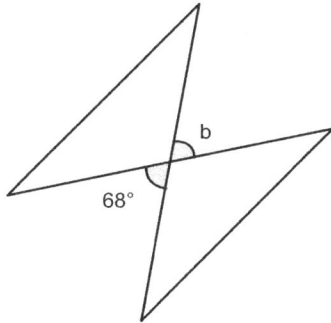

A) 22°   B) 158°

C) 68°   D) 86°

2) Find the measurement of angle b.

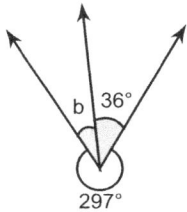

A) 153°   B) 30°

C) 63°   D) 27°

3) Find the measurement of angle b.

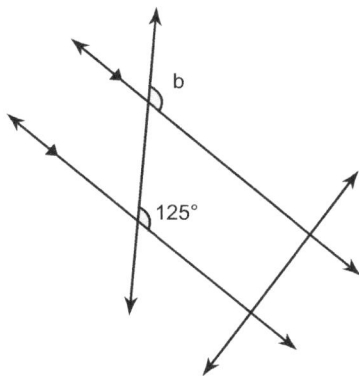

A) 142°   B) 52°

C) 128°   D) 125°

4) Find the measurement of angle b.

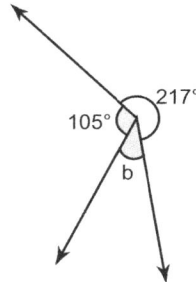

A) 151°   B) 61°

C) 38°   D) 29°

5) Find the measurement of angle b.

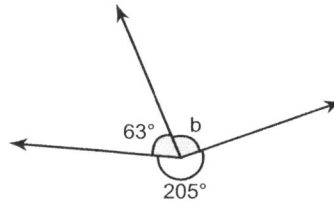

A) 88°   B) 2°

C) 178°   D) 92°

6) Find the measurement of angle b.

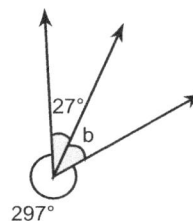

A) 36°   B) 62°

C) 28°   D) 144°

7) Find the measurement of angle b.

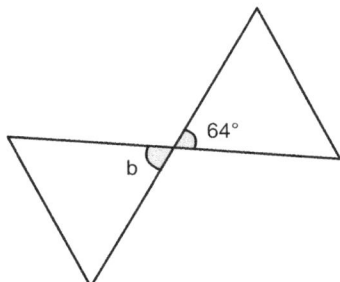

A) 99°   B) 154°

C) 64°   D) 26°

8) Find the measurement of angle b.

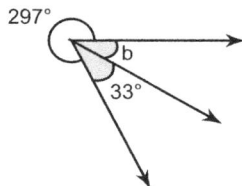

A) 109°   B) 30°

C) 71°   D) 60°

9) Find the measurement of angle b.

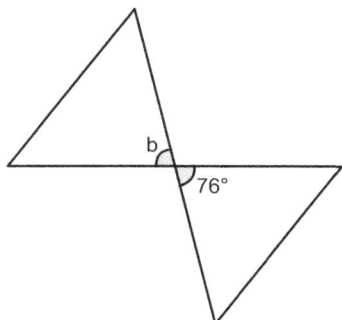

A) 31°   B) 104°

C) 121°   D) 76°

10) Find the measurement of angle b.

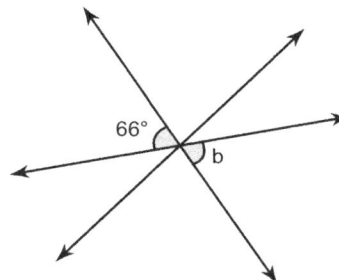

A) 142°   B) 24°

C) 38°   D) 66°

11) Find the measurement of angle b.

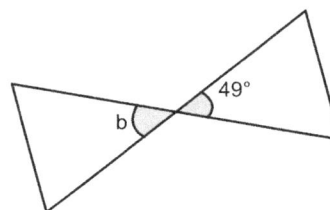

A) 41°   B) 131°

C) 139°   D) 49°

12) Find the measurement of angle b.

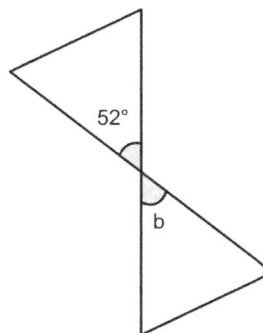

A) 52°   B) 89°

C) 155°   D) 38°

         www.math-knots.com | www.a4ace.com

13) Find the measurement of angle b.

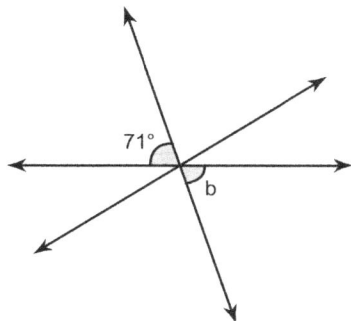

A) 17°   B) 71°

C) 156°   D) 107°

14) Find the measurement of angle b.

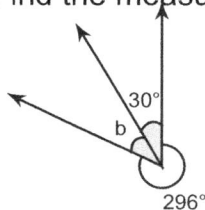

A) 146°   B) 34°

C) 124°   D) 56°

15) Find the measurement of angle b.

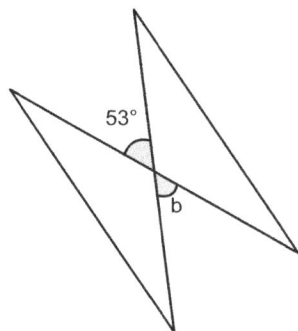

A) 53°   B) 28°

C) 152°   D) 75°

16) Find the measurement of angle b.

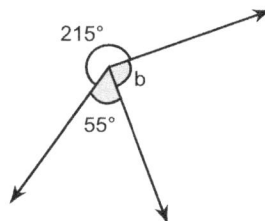

A) 59°   B) 90°

C) 149°   D) 31°

17) Find the measurement of angle b.

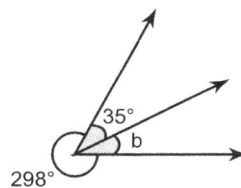

A) 23°   B) 63°

C) 27°   D) 117°

18) Find the measurement of angle b.

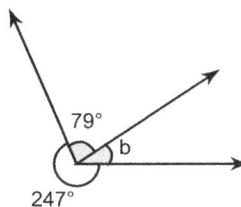

A) 56°   B) 146°

C) 34°   D) 116°

           www.math-knots.com | www.a4ace.com

19) Find the measurement of angle b.

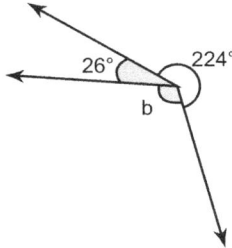

A) 70°   B) 22°

C) 20°   D) 110°

20) Find the measurement of angle b.

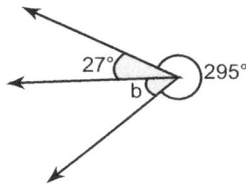

A) 45°   B) 135°

C) 88°   D) 38°

21) Find the measurement of angle b.

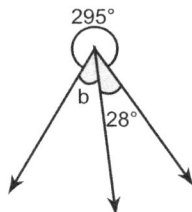

A) 37°   B) 143°

C) 137°   D) 43°

22) Find the measurement of angle b.

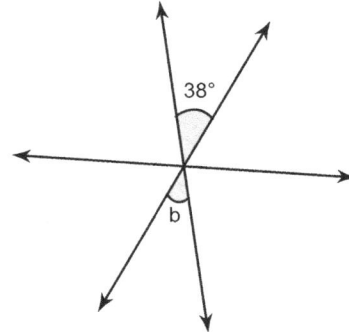

A) 38°   B) 17°

C) 81°   D) 163°

23) Find the measurement of angle b.

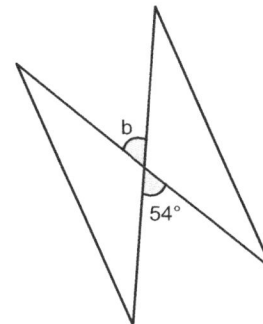

A) 97°   B) 144°

C) 54°   D) 36°

24) Find the measurement of angle b.

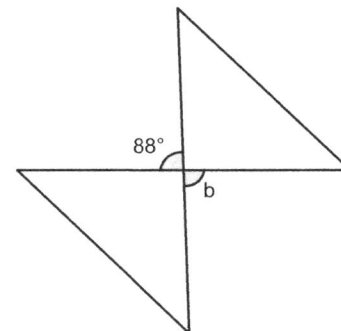

A) 88°   B) 2°

C) 178°   D) 92°

www.math-knots.com | www.a4ace.com

25) Find the measurement of angle b.

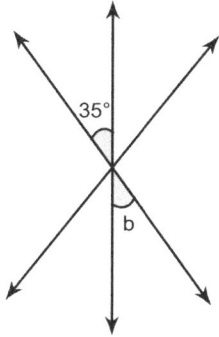

A) 145°   B) 113°

C) 55°   D) 35°

26) Find the measurement of angle b.

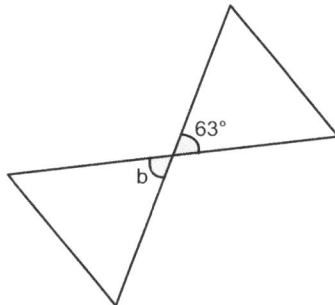

A) 27°   B) 153°

C) 34°   D) 63°

27) Find the measurement of angle b.

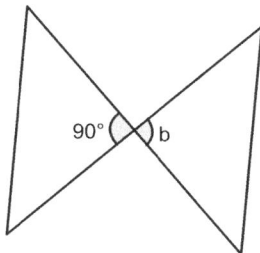

A) 23°   B) 90°

C) 67°   D) 113°

28) Find the measurement of angle b.

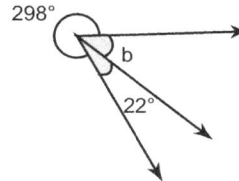

A) 50°   B) 0°

C) 90°   D) 40°

29) Find the measurement of angle b.

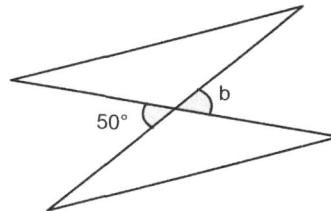

A) 50°   B) 164°

C) 106°   D) 74°

30) Find the measurement of angle b.

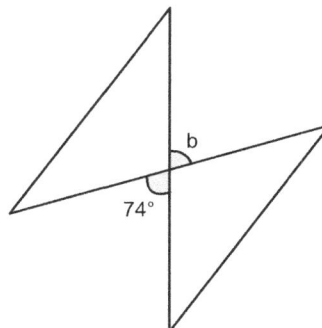

A) 83°   B) 97°

C) 74°   D) 7°

www.math-knots.com | www.a4ace.com

31) Find the measurement of angle b.

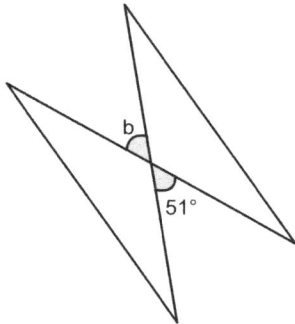

A) 51°   B) 141°

C) 155°   D) 39°

32) Find the measurement of angle b.

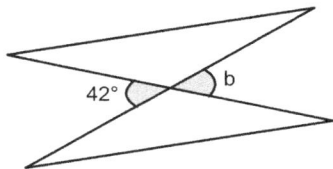

A) 80°   B) 170°

C) 42°   D) 10°

33) Find the measurement of angle b.

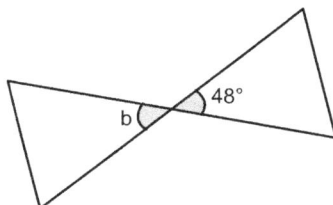

A) 158°   B) 22°

C) 48°   D) 112°

34) Find the measurement of angle b.

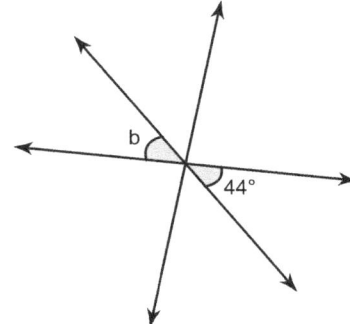

A) 44°   B) 132°

C) 134°   D) 46°

35) Find the measurement of angle b.

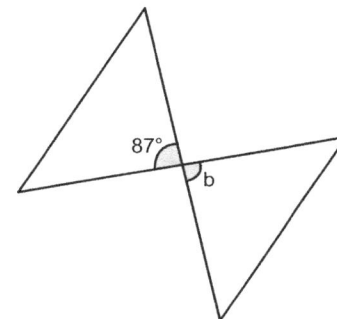

A) 87°   B) 44°

C) 3°   D) 177°

36) Find the measurement of angle b.

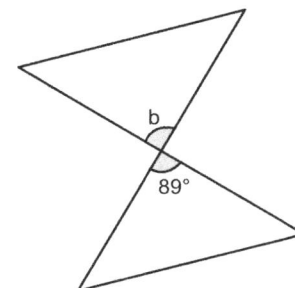

A) 1°   B) 89°

C) 91°   D) 179°

www.math-knots.com | www.a4ace.com

37) Find the measurement of angle b.

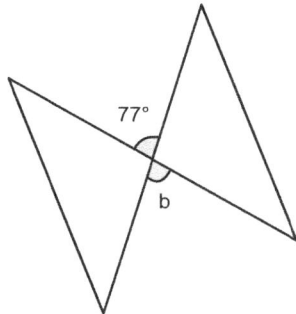

A) 72°   B) 108°

C) 77°   D) 18°

38) Find the measurement of angle b.

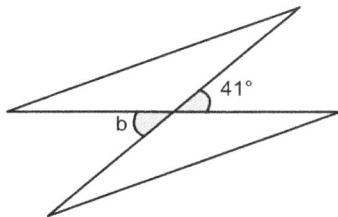

A) 107°   B) 49°

C) 139°   D) 41°

39) Find the measurement of angle b.

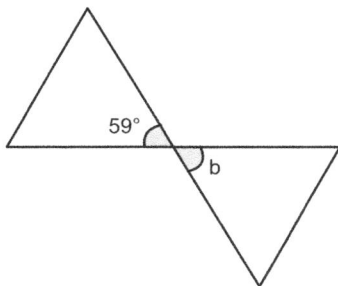

A) 50°   B) 59°

C) 91°   D) 40°

40) Find the measurement of angle b.

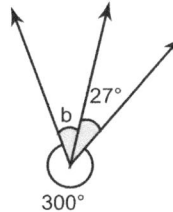

A) 80°   B) 116°

C) 147°   D) 33°

41) Find the measurement of angle b.

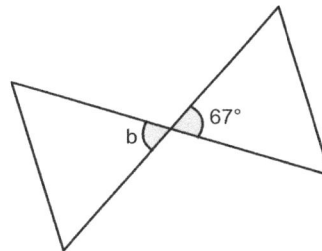

A) 67°   B) 23°

C) 113°   D) 157°

www.math-knots.com | www.a4ace.com

42) Find the value of x.

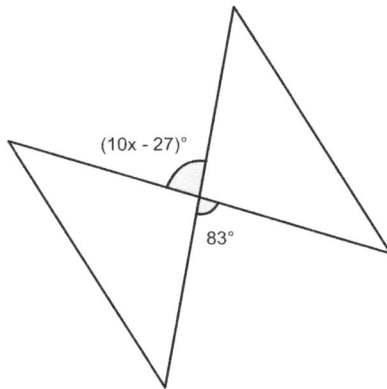

(10x - 27)°

83°

A) 54   B) 40

C) 11   D) 102

43) Find the value of x.

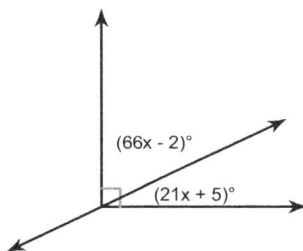

(66x - 2)°

(21x + 5)°

A) 1   B) -2

C) 11   D) -1

44) Find the value of x.

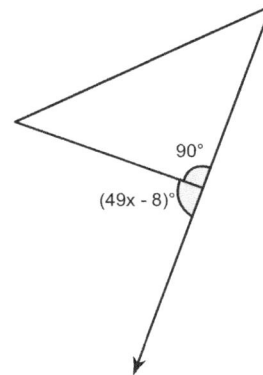

90°

(49x - 8)°

A) 35   B) -8

C) 2   D) -31

45) Find the value of x.

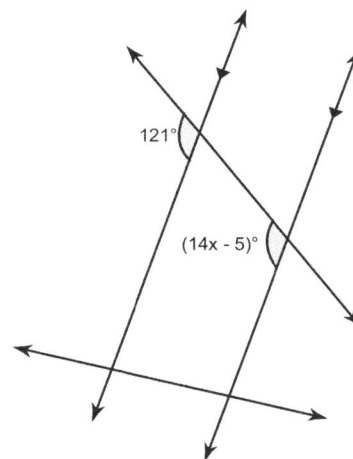

121°

(14x - 5)°

A) 8   B) 9

C) 40   D) 53

 www.math-knots.com | www.a4ace.com

46) Find the value of x.

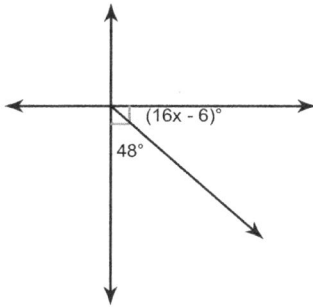

(16x - 6)°
48°

A) 41   B) 3

C) 53   D) 7

47) Find the value of x.

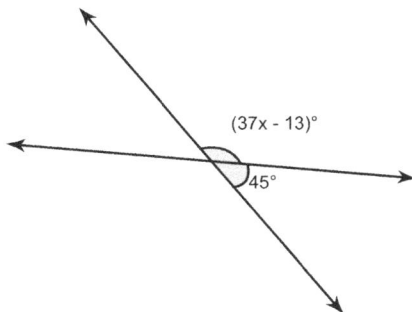

(37x - 13)°
45°

A) -2   B) 4

C) -32   D) -40

48) Find the value of x.

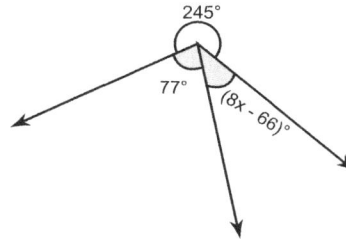

245°
77°
(8x - 66)°

A) 22   B) 13

C) 62   D) 21

49) Find the value of x.

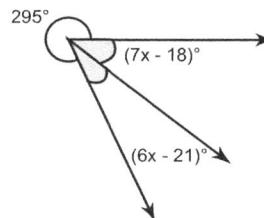

295°
(7x - 18)°
(6x - 21)°

A) 6   B) 43

C) 8   D) -7

50) Find the value of x.

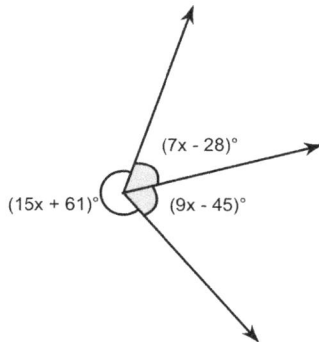

A) -52   B) -29

C) -10   D) 12

52) Find the value of x.

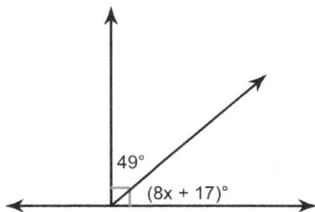

A) -29   B) -77

C) 6   D) -89

51) Find the value of x.

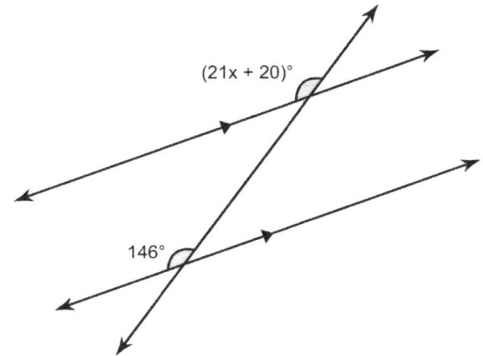

A) 44   B) 28

C) 14   D) 3

53) Find the value of x.

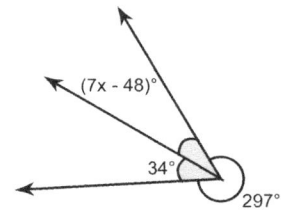

A) 11   B) -33

C) -13   D) -45

54) Find the value of x.

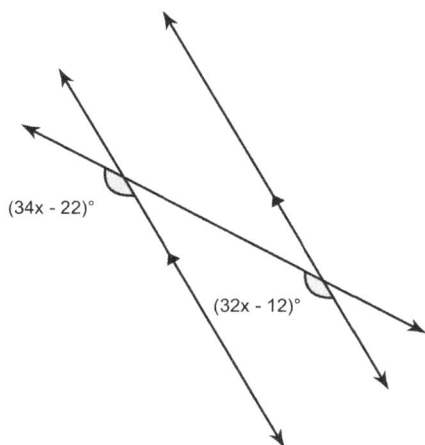

(34x - 22)°

(32x - 12)°

A) 5   B) 102

C) 52   D) 64

55) Find the value of x.

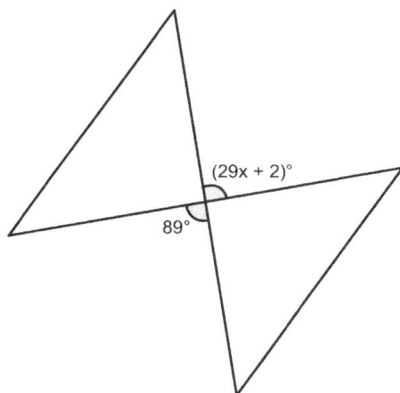

(29x + 2)°

89°

A) 110   B) 50

C) 88   D) 3

56) Find the value of x.

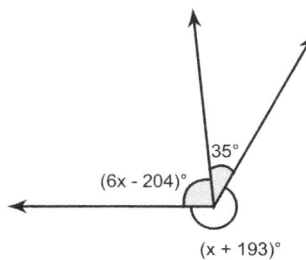

35°

(6x - 204)°

(x + 193)°

A) 33   B) 84

C) 64   D) 48

57) Find the value of x.

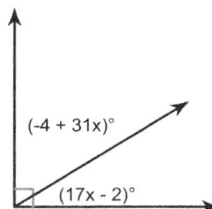

(-4 + 31x)°

(17x - 2)°

A) 2   B) 38

C) 33   D) 47

www.math-knots.com | www.a4ace.com

58) Find the value of x.

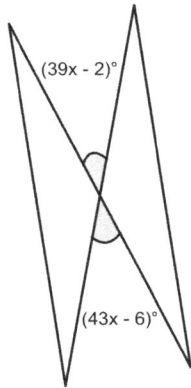

(39x - 2)°

(43x - 6)°

A) 1   B) 63

C) 78   D) 18

60) Find the value of x.

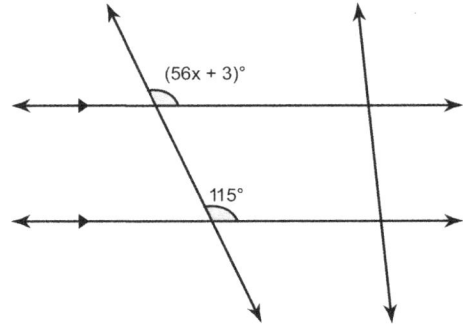

(56x + 3)°

115°

A) -108   B) -19

C) 2   D) -63

59) Find the value of x.

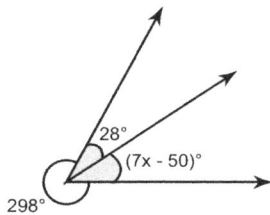

28°

(7x - 50)°

298°

A) 69   B) 41

C) 12   D) 13

61) Find the value of x.

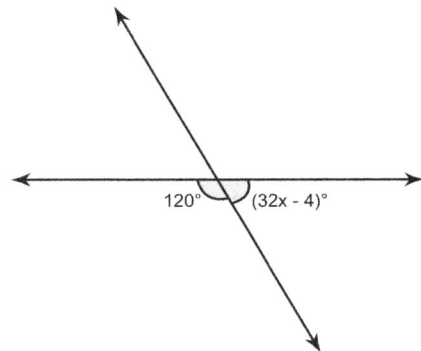

120°   (32x - 4)°

A) 22   B) 2

C) -19   D) 41

www.math-knots.com | www.a4ace.com

62) Find the value of x.

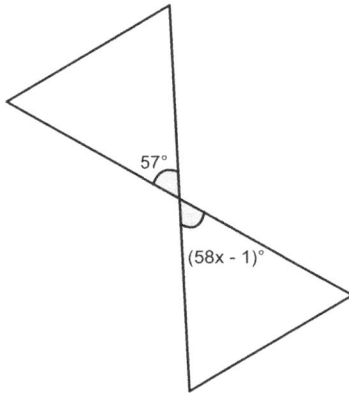

57°

(58x - 1)°

A) 26   B) 1

C) 20   D) 22

63) Find the value of x.

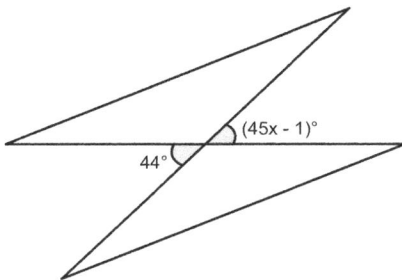

(45x - 1)°

44°

A) -9   B) 48

C) 1   D) 20

64) Find the value of x.

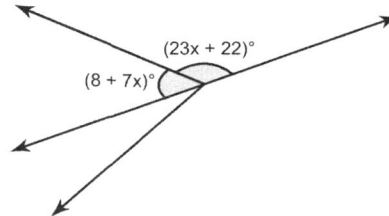

(23x + 22)°

(8 + 7x)°

A) 33   B) 101

C) 5   D) 72

65) Find the value of x.

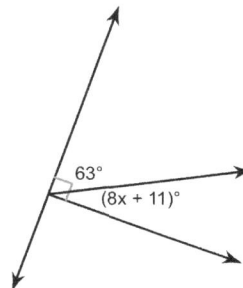

63°

(8x + 11)°

A) 2   B) -34

C) -31   D) -33

66) Find the value of x.

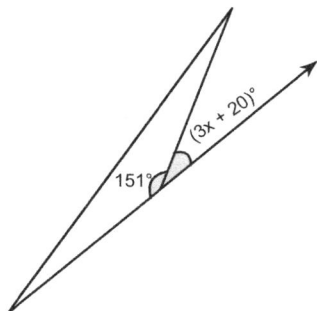

A) 16   B) -6

C) 28   D) 3

67) Find the value of x.

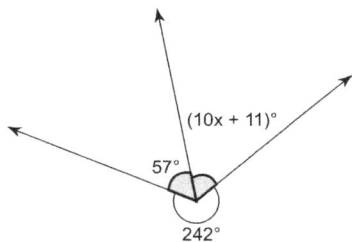

A) -80   B) -33

C) -45   D) 5

68) Find the value of x.

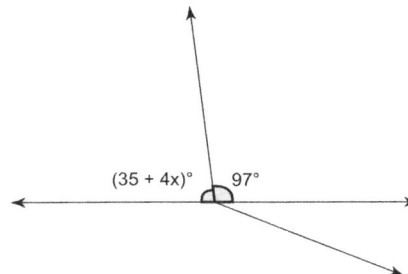

A) -2   B) 13

C) 12   D) -24

69) Find the value of x.

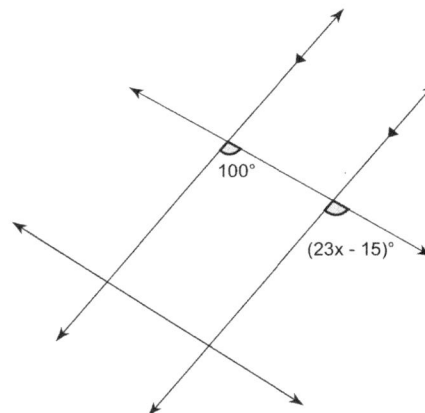

A) 5   B) -5

C) 8   D) 7

70) Find the value of x.

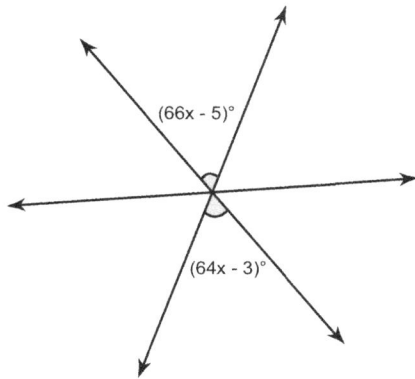

$(66x - 5)°$

$(64x - 3)°$

A) 1 B) 93

C) 87 D) 44

71) Find the value of x.

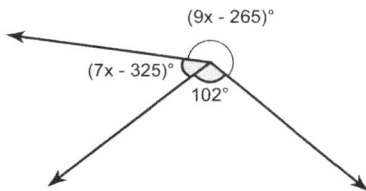

$(9x - 265)°$

$(7x - 325)°$

$102°$

A) 64 B) 53

C) 77 D) 29

72) Find the value of x.

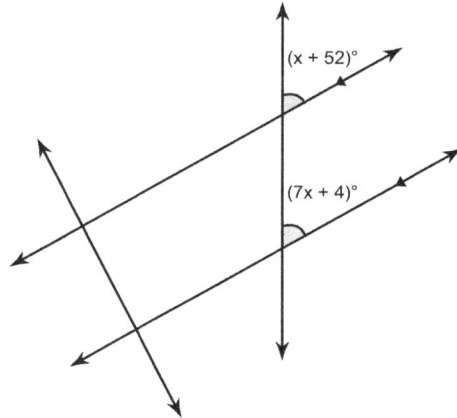

$(x + 52)°$

$(7x + 4)°$

A) 26 B) 86

C) 8 D) 53

73) Find the value of x.

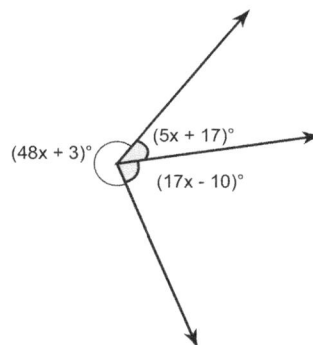

$(48x + 3)°$

$(5x + 17)°$

$(17x - 10)°$

A) 5 B) -40

C) -49 D) -79

74) Find the value of x.

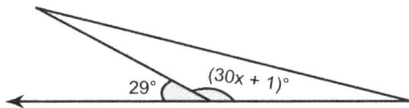

29° (30x + 1)°

A) 5   B) 81

C) 89   D) 51

75) Find the value of x.

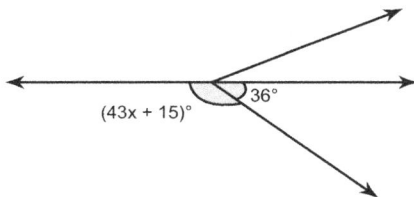

(43x + 15)°   36°

A) 43   B) 3

C) 7   D) 4

76) Find the value of x.

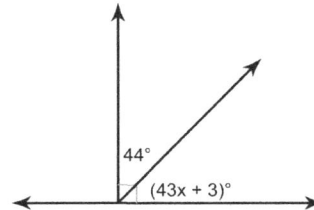

44°
(43x + 3)°

A) 1   B) 36

C) 64   D) 82

77) Find the value of x.

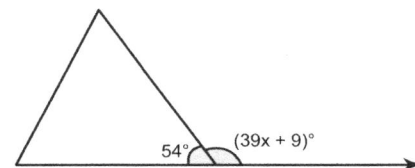

54°   (39x + 9)°

A) 3   B) -40

C) -60   D) -27

276

78) Find the value of x.

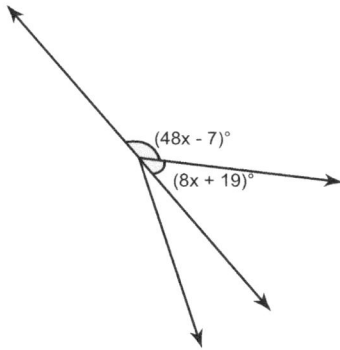

(48x - 7)°
(8x + 19)°

A) 16   B) 56

C) -14   D) 3

80) Find the value of x.

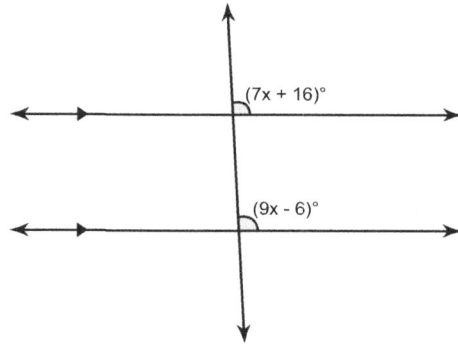

(7x + 16)°
(9x - 6)°

A) 11   B) 24

C) -11   D) -15

79) Find the value of x.

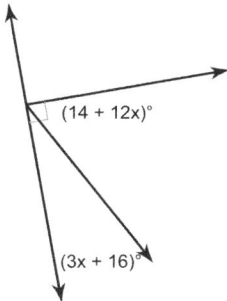

(14 + 12x)°
(3x + 16)°

A) 38   B) 48

C) 4   D) -6

81) Find the value of x.

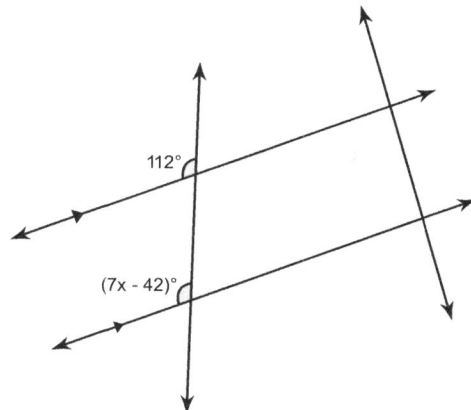

112°
(7x - 42)°

A) 22   B) -82

C) -62   D) -19

277   www.math-knots.com | www.a4ace.com

82) Find the value of x.

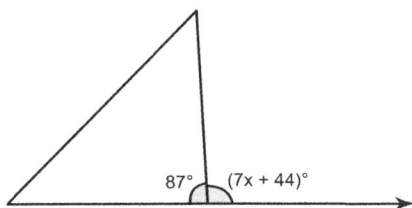

A) 7   B) -3

C) -8   D) -23

83) Find the value of x.

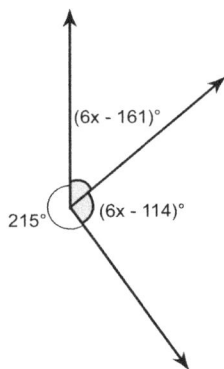

A) 71   B) 108

C) 48   D) 35

84) Find the value of x.

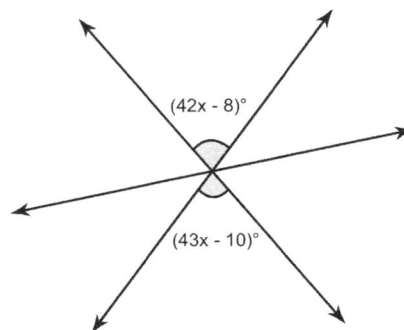

A) -36   B) 2

C) -39   D) -31

85) Find the value of x.

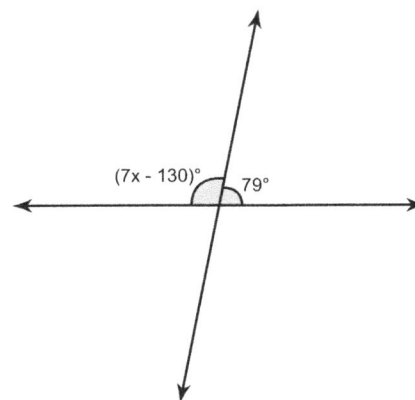

A) -7   B) 40

C) 80   D) 33

 www.math-knots.com | www.a4ace.com

86) Find the value of x.

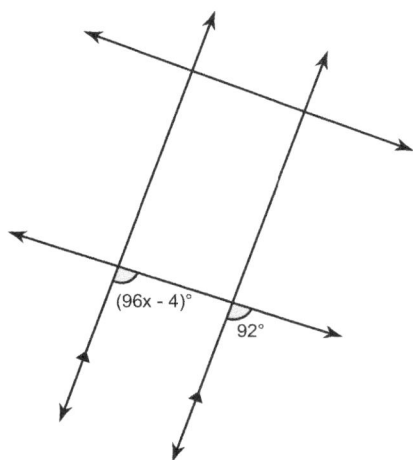

(96x - 4)°
92°

A) -14   B) -39

C) -62   D) 1

87) Find the value of x.

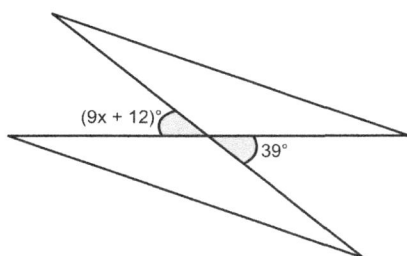

(9x + 12)°
39°

A) 3   B) 37

C) 13   D) 23

88) Find the value of x.

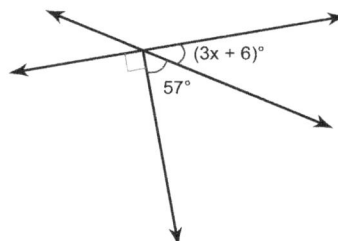

(3x + 6)°
57°

A) 33   B) 6

C) -35   D) 9

89) Find the value of x.

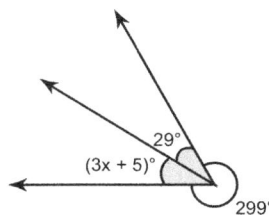

29°
(3x + 5)°
299°

A) 12   B) 9

C) -12   D) 18

90) Find the value of x.

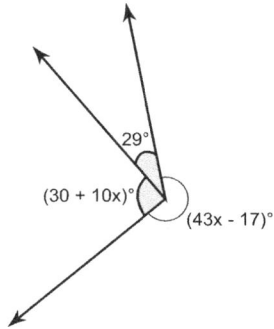

29°

(30 + 10x)°

(43x - 17)°

A) 25   B) -63

C) -20   D) 6

92) Find the value of x.

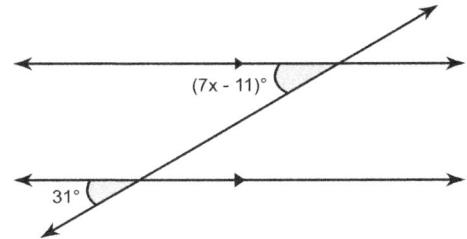

(7x - 11)°

31°

A) -31   B) -25

C) 3   D) 6

91) Find the value of x.

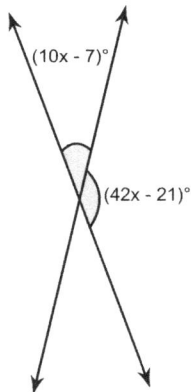

(10x - 7)°

(42x - 21)°

A) 20   B) -2

C) 16   D) 4

93) Find the value of x.

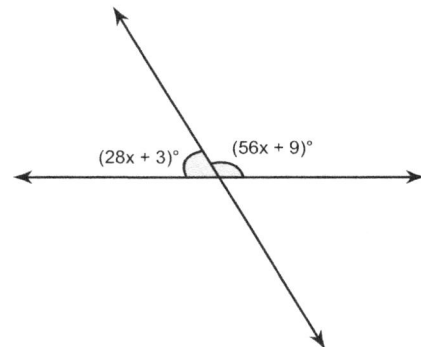

(28x + 3)°   (56x + 9)°

A) 15   B) 49

C) -18   D) 2

94) Find the value of x.

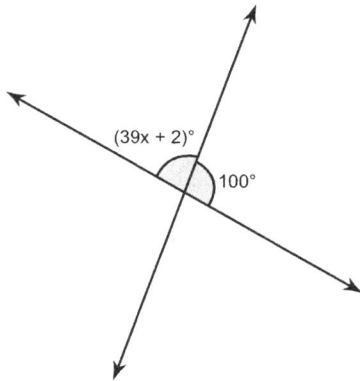

(39x + 2)°
100°

A) -45   B) -3

C) 2   D) 8

95) Find the value of x.

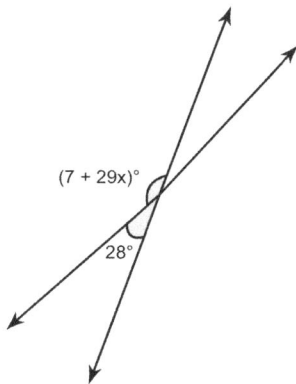

(7 + 29x)°
28°

A) -23   B) 5

C) 18   D) -19

96) Find the value of x.

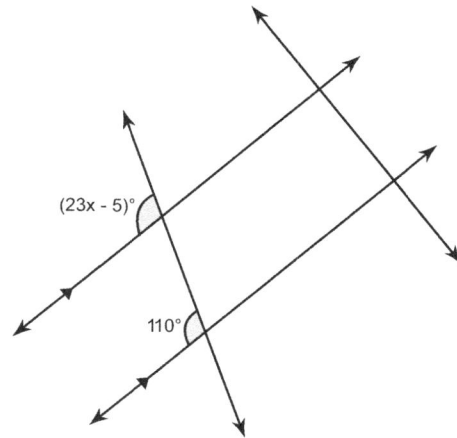

(23x - 5)°
110°

A) 39   B) -9

C) 5   D) 29

97) Find the value of x.

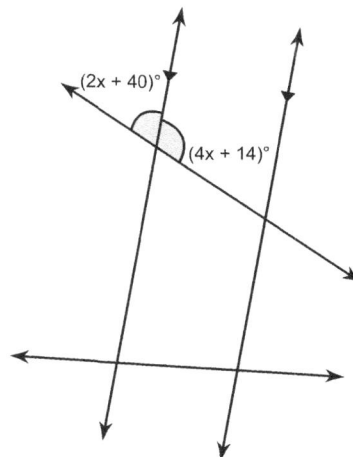

(2x + 40)°
(4x + 14)°

A) 22   B) 15

C) 5   D) 13

www.math-knots.com | www.a4ace.com

98) Find the value of x.

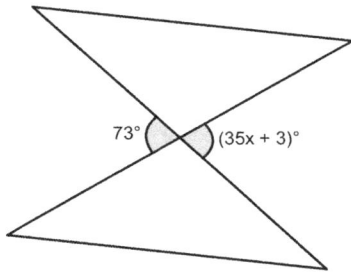

73° (35x + 3)°

A) -35   B) 2

C) -34   D) -68

100) Find the value of x.

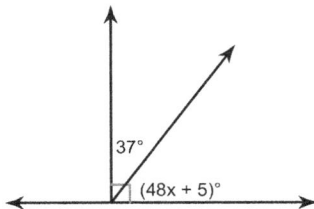

112° (7x + 33)°

A) -28   B) 5

C) -73   D) 20

99) Find the value of x.

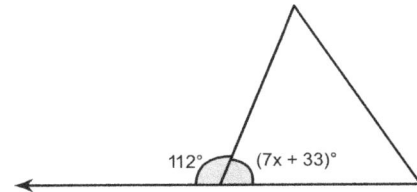

37°
(48x + 5)°

A) 1   B) 48

C) 20   D) 35

101) Find the value of x.

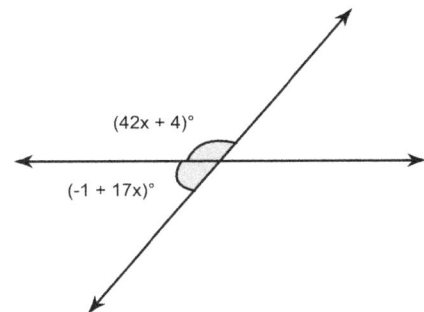

(42x + 4)°
(-1 + 17x)°

A) -33   B) -3

C) 3   D) -29

                   www.math-knots.com | www.a4ace.com

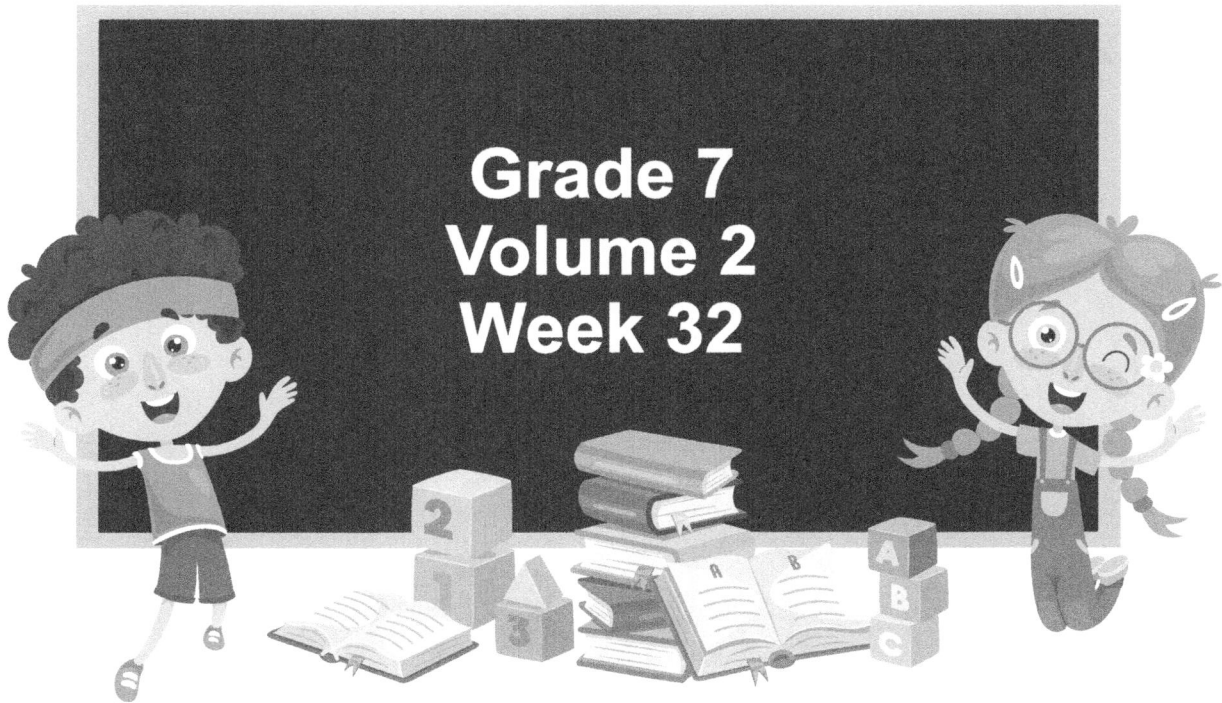

Grade 7
Volume 2
Week 32

www.math-knots.com | www.a4ace.com

1) Find the measure of angle b
   from the below figure

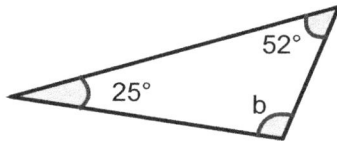

A) 85°   B) 103°

C) 95°   D) 79°

2) Find the measure of angle b
   from the below figure

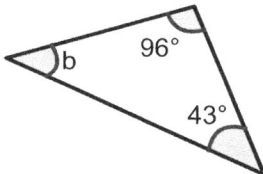

A) 60°   B) 41°

C) 55°   D) 49°

3) Find the measure of angle b
   from the below figure

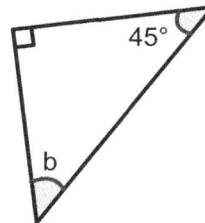

A) 58°   B) 39°

C) 45°   D) 49°

4) Find the measure of angle b
   from the below figure

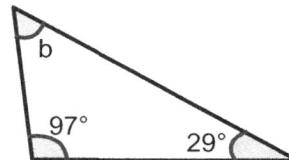

A) 57°   B) 64°

C) 54°   D) 66°

         www.math-knots.com | www.a4ace.com

5) Find the measure of angle b
from the below figure

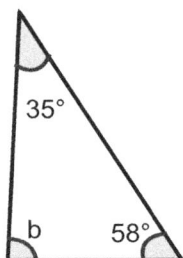

A) 94°   B) 87°

C) 82°   D) 92°

6) Find the measure of angle b
from the below figure

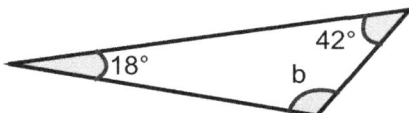

A) 120°   B) 114°

C) 124°   D) 116°

7) Find the measure of angle b
from the below figure

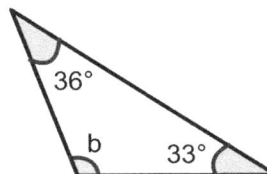

A) 111°   B) 118°

C) 112°   D) 106°

8) Find the measure of angle b
from the below figure

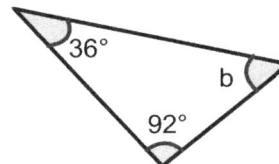

A) 52°   B) 62°

C) 45°   D) 54°

www.math-knots.com | www.a4ace.com

9) Find the measure of angle b
   from the below figure

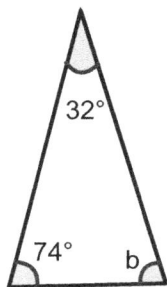

A) 79°   B) 69°

C) 74°   D) 87°

11) Find the measure of angle b
    from the below figure

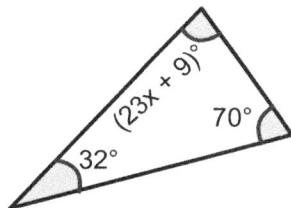

A) 97°   B) 107°

C) 94°   D) 89°

10) Find the measure of x from the
    below figure

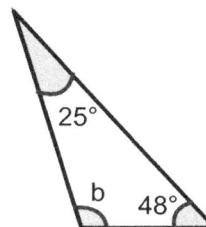

A) 17   B) 8

C) 2   D) 3

12) Find the measure of x from the
    below figure

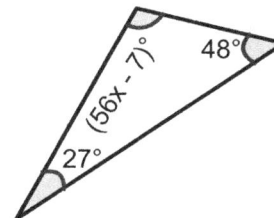

A) 2   B) 5

C) 9   D) 4

www.math-knots.com | www.a4ace.com

13) Find the measure of x from the below figure

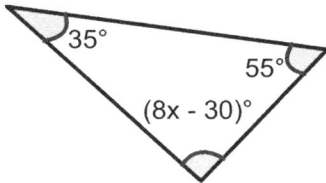

35°

55°

(8x - 30)°

A) 19   B) 14

C) 9   D) 15

15) Find the measure of x from the below figure

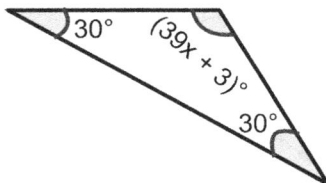

32°   122°

(30x - 4)°

A) 13   B) 23

C) 1   D) 6

14) Find the measure of x from the below figure

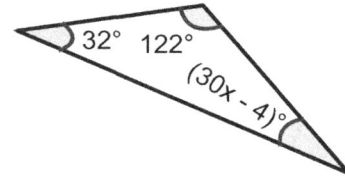

30°   (39x + 3)°

30°

A) 8   B) 10

C) 3   D) 18

16) Find the measure of x from the below figure

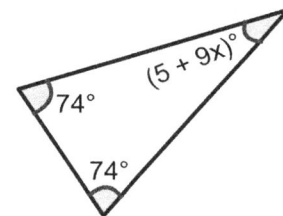

(5 + 9x)°

74°

74°

A) 18   B) 12

C) 3   D) 10

17) Find the measure of x from the below figure

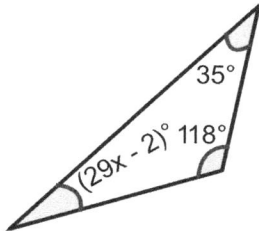

A) 11   B) 20

C) 30   D) 1

18) Find the measure of x from the below figure

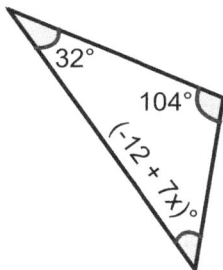

A) 8   B) 3

C) 15   D) 6

19) Find the measure of x from the below figure

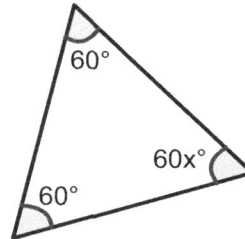

A) 6   B) 12

C) 1   D) 4

20) Find the measure of x from the below figure

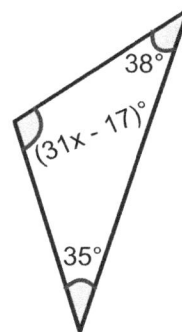

A) 1   B) 7

C) 4   D) 2

www.math-knots.com | www.a4ace.com

21) Find the measure of angle b
from the below figure

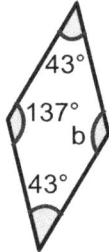

A) 137°   B) 146°

C) 151°   D) 160°

23) Find the measure of angle b
from the below figure

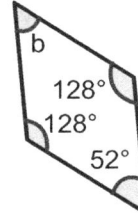

A) 57°   B) 40°

C) 48°   D) 52°

22) Find the measure of angle b
from the below figure

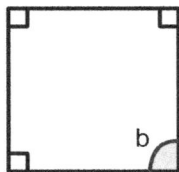

A) 81°   B) 76°

C) 90°   D) 85°

24) Find the measure of angle b
from the below figure

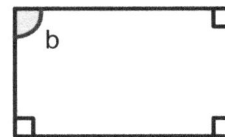

A) 96°   B) 77°

C) 86°   D) 90°

25) Find the measure of angle b
from the below figure

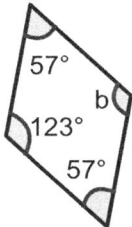

A) 123°   B) 116°

C) 107°   D) 114°

27) Find the measure of angle b
from the below figure

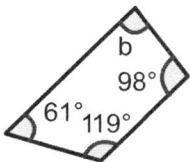

A) 145°   B) 144°

C) 136°   D) 154°

26) Find the measure of angle b
from the below figure

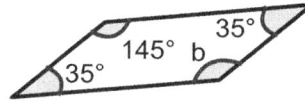

A) 82°   B) 73°

C) 79°   D) 84°

28) Find the measure of angle b
from the below figure

A) 141°   B) 151°

C) 160°   D) 146°

www.math-knots.com | www.a4ace.com

29) Find the measure of angle b
from the below figure

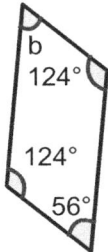

A) 47°   B) 58°

C) 52°   D) 56°

31) Find the measure of angle b
from the below figure

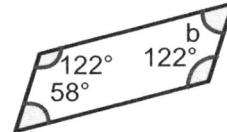

A) 52°   B) 59°

C) 68°   D) 58°

30) Find the measure of x from the
below figure

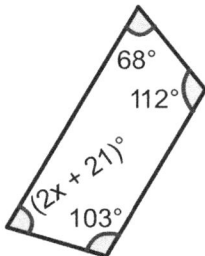

A) 18   B) 23

C) 28   D) 33

32) Find the measure of x from the
below figure

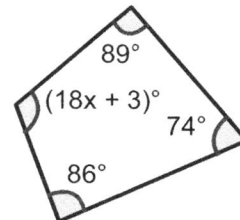

A) -1   B) 3

C) 6   D) 8

33) Find the measure of x from the below figure

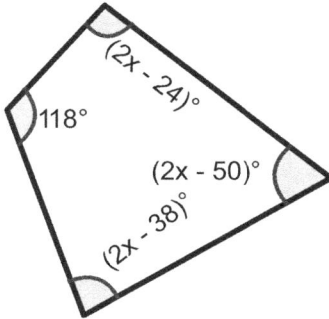

A) 69   B) 71

C) 59   D) 64

34) Find the measure of x from the below figure

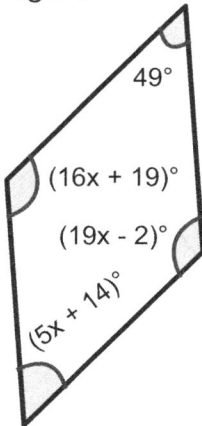

A) 12   B) 7

C) 3   D) 13

35) Find the measure of x from the below figure

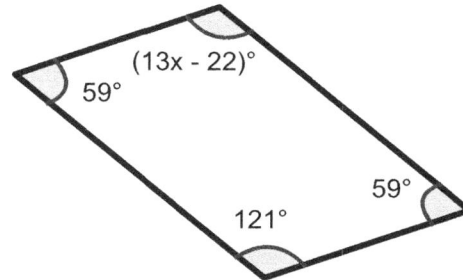

A) 11   B) -3

C) 2   D) 6

36) Find the measure of x from the below figure

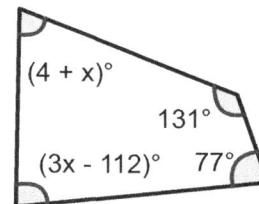

A) 79   B) 72

C) 80   D) 65

www.math-knots.com | www.a4ace.com

37) Find the measure of x from the below figure

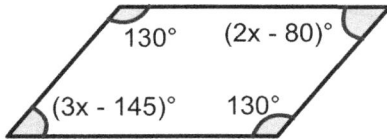

A) 67   B) 57

C) 58   D) 65

39) Find the measure of x from the below figure

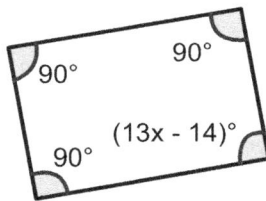

A) 6   B) 1

C) 13   D) 8

38) Find the measure of x from the below figure

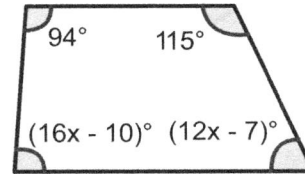

A) 3   B) 8

C) -6   D) 1

40) Find the measure of x from the below figure

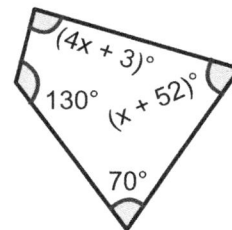

A) 29   B) 21

C) 24   D) 34

41) A rectangluar pyramid of height 7 cm measuring 5 cm and 10 cm along the base. Find the volume.

   A) 93.76 cm³   B) 167.15 cm³

   C) 116.67 cm³   D) 350 cm³

42) A square prism measuring 16 km along each edge of the base and 8 km tall. Find the volume.

   A) 2059 km³   B) 2048 km³

   C) 2279 km³   D) 1428 km³

43) A square prism measuring 15 cm along each edge of the base and 17 cm tall. Find the volume.

   A) 5724 cm³   B) 3825 cm³

   C) 3746 cm³   D) 5624 cm³

44) A square prism measuring 17 in along each edge of the base and 11 in tall. Find the volume.

   A) 3499 in³   B) 3167 in³

   C) 3223 in³   D) 3179 in³

45) A square pyramid measuring 7 yd along each edge of the base with a height of 10 yd. Find the volume.

   A) 131.68 yd³   B) 165.63 yd³

   C) 163.33 yd³   D) 490 yd³

46) A rectangular prism measuring 20 mi and 9 mi along the base and 17 mi tall. Find the volume.

   A) 1837 mi³   B) 1641 mi³

   C) 3060 mi³   D) 2884 mi³

47) A square prism measuring 18 m along each edge of the base and 17 m tall. Find the volume.

   A) 5148 m³   B) 7878 m³

   C) 5417 m³   D) 5508 m³

48) A square prism measuring 5 m along each edge of the base and 2 m tall. Find the volume.

   A) 73 m³   B) 47 m³

   C) 61 m³   D) 50 m³

www.math-knots.com | www.a4ace.com

49) A square pyramid measuring 14 in along each edge of the base with a height of 18 in. Find the volume.

A) 1674 in³   B) 1176 in³

C) 969 in³   D) 3528 in³

50) A square prism measuring 8 yd along each edge of the base and 7 yd tall. Find the volume.

A) 448 yd³   B) 413 yd³

C) 408 yd³   D) 552 yd³

51) A rectangular prism measuring 13 in and 14 in along the base and 10 in tall. Find the volume.

A) 2275 in³   B) 1257 in³

C) 2527 in³   D) 1820 in³

52) A square prism measuring 10 m along each edge of the base and 7 m tall. Find the volume.

A) 700 m³   B) 357 m³

C) 617 m³   D) 831 m³

53) A rectangluar pyramid of height 10 mi measuring 5 mi and 6 mi along the base. Find the volume.

A) 300 mi³   B) 123 mi³

C) 147 mi³   D) 100 mi³

54) A square prism measuring 4 m along each edge of the base and 7 m tall. Find the volume.

A) 119 m³   B) 110 m³

C) 85 m³   D) 112 m³

55) A rectangluar pyramid of height 12 mi measuring 11 mi and 18 mi along the base. Find the volume.

A) 1056 mi³   B) 513 mi³

C) 2376 mi³   D) 792 mi³

56) A rectangular prism measuring 29 yd and 23 yd along the base and 20 yd tall. Find the surface area.

A) 3268 yd²   B) 2747 yd²

C) 3414 yd²   D) 2796 yd²

57) A rectangular prism measuring 8 mi and 17 mi along the base and 15 mi tall. Find the surface area.

A) 1022 mi²   B) 886 mi²

C) 1312 mi²   D) 1417 mi²

58) A rectangular pyramid measuring 14 km and 18 km along the base, with slant heights of 31.3 km and 30.8 km, respectively. Find the surface area.

A) 1244.6 km²   B) 1455.4 km²

C) 1735.4 km²   D) 1057.3 km²

59) A rectangular prism measuring 20 m and 22 m along the base and 4 m tall. Find the surface area.

A) 1498 m²   B) 1216 m²

C) 776 m²   D) 1298 m²

60) A rectangular pyramid measuring 9 km and 12 km along the base, with slant heights of 16.2 km and 15.7 km, respectively. Find the surface area.

A) 414.5 km²   B) 442.2 km²

C) 435.4 km²   D) 238.4 km²

61) A square prism measuring 28 km along each edge of the base and 27 km tall. Find the surface area.

A) 3886 km²   B) 4592 km²

C) 3808 km²   D) 4388 km²

62) A square prism measuring 28 yd along each edge of the base and 2 yd tall. Find the surface area.

A) 2412 yd²   B) 1008 yd²

C) 1761 yd²   D) 1792 yd²

63) A rectangular pyramid measuring 10 ft and 22 ft along the base, with slant heights of 28.2 ft and 26.5 ft, respectively. Find the surface area.

A) 1085 ft²   B) 1168 ft²

C) 1067 ft²   D) 1540 ft²

64) rectangular prism measuring 16 m and 20 m along the base and 11 m tall. Find the surface area.

A) 1188 m²   B) 1112 m²

C) 1703 m²   D) 1432 m²

65) A square prism measuring 6 in along each edge of the base and 11 in tall. Find the surface area.

A) 378 in²   B) 300 in²

C) 173 in²   D) 336 in²

66) A square prism measuring 2 m along each edge of the base and 3 m tall. Find the surface area.

A) 32 m²   B) 22 m²

C) 17 m²   D) 28 m²

67) A rectangular prism measuring 28 cm and 27 cm along the base and 6 cm tall. Find the surface area.

A) 1921 cm²   B) 2172 cm²

C) 1416 cm²   D) 2783 cm²

68) A square prism measuring 15 ft along each edge of the base and 5 ft tall. Find the surface area.

A) 849 ft²   B) 750 ft²

C) 525 ft²   D) 1006 ft²

69) A rectangular pyramid measuring 26 m and 29 m along the base, with slant heights of 31.5 m and 30.9 m, respectively. Find the surface area.

A) 1525.5 m²   B) 2353.3 m²

C) 2201.6 m²   D) 2469.1 m²

70) A square prism measuring 29 yd along each edge of the base and 10 yd tall. Find the surface area.

A) 2001 yd²   *B) 2842 yd²

C) 2534 yd²   D) 1868 yd²

71) State if the below three numbers can be the measures of the sides of a triangle.

42, 37, 27

72) State if the below three numbers can be the measures of the sides of a triangle.

13, 50, 34

73) State if the below three numbers can be the measures of the sides of a triangle. 43, 25, 70

74) State if the below three numbers can be the measures of the sides of a triangle. 12, 43, 31

75) State if the below three numbers can be the measures of the sides of a triangle. 50, 31, 49

76) Find the value of x

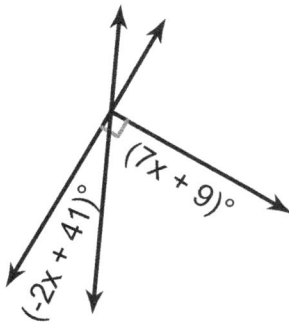

A) -8   B) 41

C) 39   D) 8

77) Find the value of x

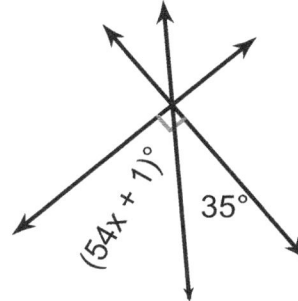

A) 1   B) 59

C) 41   D) -6

78) Find the value of x

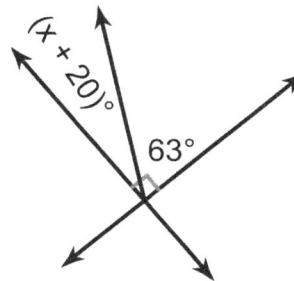

A) -23   B) 7

C) -21   D) 17

79) Find the value of x

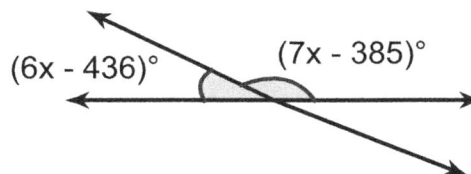

A) 77   B) 42

C) 27   D) 72

www.math-knots.com | www.a4ace.com

80) Two sides of a triangle have following measures. Find the range of possible measures for the third side

16, 15

A) 2 < x < 31   B) 2 < x < 28

C) 1 < x < 30   D) 1 < x < 31

81) Two sides of a triangle have following measures. Find the range of possible measures for the third side

23, 19

A) 4 < x < 39   B) 4 < x < 41

C) 5 < x < 41   D) 4 < x < 42

82) Two sides of a triangle have following measures. Find the range of possible measures for the third side

15, 21

A) 6 < x < 35   B) 6 < x < 36

C) 6 < x < 34   D) 9 < x < 35

83) Two sides of a triangle have following measures. Find the range of possible measures for the third side

21, 17

A) 4 < x < 38   B) 6 < x < 37

C) 4 < x < 34   D) 5 < x < 37

84) Two sides of a triangle have following measures. Find the range of possible measures for the third side

23, 15

A) 8 < x < 37   B) 9 < x < 37

C) 8 < x < 35   D) 8 < x < 38

85) Find the area of the circle given radius is 13.7 mi. Round your answer to the nearest tenth (Use π = 3.14)

86) Find the area of the circle given diameter is 55 m. Round your answer to the nearest tenth (Use π = 3.14)

A) 3846.4 m²   B) 972.6 m²

C) 961.6 m²   D) 1040.1 m²

87) Find the area of the circle given circumference is 62.8 m. Round your answer to the nearest tenth (Use π = 3.14)

A) 314 m²   B) 379.9 m²

C) 78.5 m²   D) 373.1 m²

88) Find the area of the circle given circumference is 85.4 mi. Round your answer to the nearest tenth (Use ∏ = 3.14)

A) 615.4 mi²   B) 42.7 mi²

C) 624.2 mi²   D) 580.7 mi²

89) Find the area of the circle given radius is 6 in. Round your answer to the nearest tenth (Use ∏ = 3.14)

65.6 km

90) Find the area of the circle given diameter is 65.6 km. Round your answer to the nearest tenth (Use ∏ = 3.14)

A) 3378.1 km²   B) 103 km²

C) 844.5 km²   D) 3544.9 km²

91) Find the area of the circle given circumference is 50.2 km. Round your answer to the nearest tenth (Use ∏ = 3.14)

A) 25.1 km²   B) 242.8 km²

C) 210.8 km²   D) 200.6 km²

92) Find the area of the circle given circumference is 94.2 in. Round your answer to the nearest tenth (Use ∏ = 3.14)

A) 783.9in²   B) 754.4 in²

C) 706.5 in²   D) 764.2 in²

93) Find the area of the circle given circumference is 106.8 cm. Round your answer to the nearest tenth (Use ∏ = 3.14)

A) 908.1 cm²   B) 918.8 cm²

C) 53.4 cm²   D) 3632.4 cm²

530.7 cm²

94) Find the circumference of the circle given area is 50.2 km. Round your answer to the nearest tenth (Use ∏ = 3.14)

A) 81.6 cm   B) 82.9 cm

C) 82.2 cm   D) 22.6 cm

95) Find the circumference of the circle given area is 2826cm². Round your answer to the nearest tenth (Use ∏ = 3.14)

A) 376.8 cm   B) 188.4 cm

C) 34.4 cm   D) 94.2 cm

96) Find the circumference of the circle given area is 28.3 cm². Round your answer to the nearest tenth (Use ∏ = 3.14)

A) 10.9cm   B) 18.9cm

C) 20.2cm   D) 56.9cm

97) Find the circumference of the circle given area is 7234.6 m². Round your answer to the nearest tenth (Use ∏ = 3.14)

A) 14465.3m   B) 303.3m

C) 150.7m   D) 301.4m

98) Find the diameter of the circle given circumference is 81.6 mi. Round your answer to the nearest tenth (Use ∏ = 3.14)

A) 26 mi   B) 26.6mi

C) 27.8mi   D) 13 mi

99) Find the diameter of the circle given circumference is 18.8 mi. Round your answer to the nearest tenth (Use ∏ = 3.14)

A) 6.4 mi   B) 6 mi

C) 3.5 mi   D) 18 mi

100) Find the diameter of the circle given circumference is 52.1 m. Round your answer to the nearest tenth (Use ∏ = 3.14)

A) 17.4m   B) 17.8m

C) 16.6m   D) 8.3m

101) Find the diameter of the circle given circumference is 12.6 cm. Round your answer to the nearest tenth (Use ∏ = 3.14)

A) 4 cm   B) 2 cm

C) 8 cm   D) 4.4cm

102) Find the diameter of the circle given circumference is 244.9 ft. Round your answer to the nearest tenth (Use ∏ = 3.14)

A) 78.2ft   B) 78 ft

C) 39 ft   D) 79.6ft

103) Find the radius of the circle given area is 5805.9 m². Round your answer to the nearest tenth (Use ∏ = 3.14)

A) 43.1m   B) 6.6m

C) 43 m   D) 43.5m

104) Identify the angle relationship between angle a and angle b

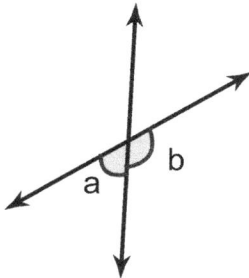

A) alternate interior

B) alternate exterior

C) vertical

D) supplementary

105) Identify the angle relationship between angle a and angle b

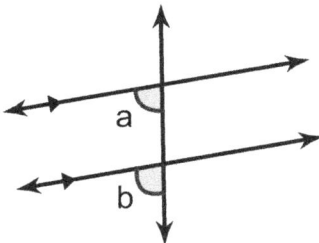

A) vertical

B) supplementary

C) corresponding

D) complementary

106) Identify the angle relationship between angle a and angle b

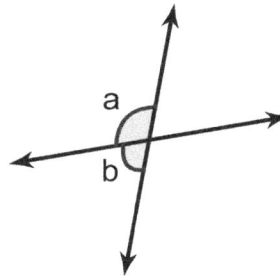

A) vertical

B) complementary

C) corresponding

D) supplementary

107) Identify the angle relationship between angle a and angle b

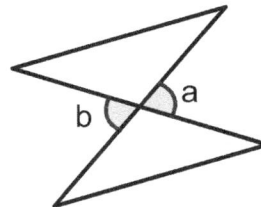

A) supplementary

B) adjacent

C) alternate interior

D) vertical

108) Identify the angle relationship between angle a and angle b

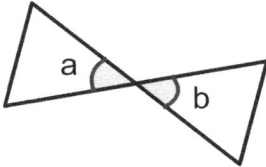

A) corresponding

B) alternate exterior

C) alternate interior

D) vertical

109) Identify the angle relationship between angle a and angle b

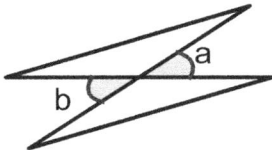

A) supplementary

B) vertical

C) alternate exterior

D) alternate interior

110) Identify the angle relationship between angle a and angle b

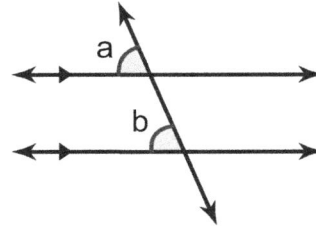

A) corresponding

B) alternate interior

C) alternate exterior

D) supplementary

111) Identify the angle relationship between angle a and angle b

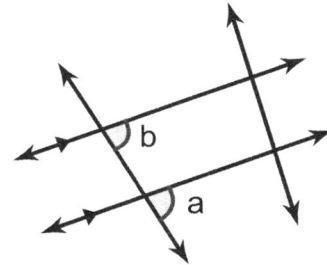

A) corresponding

B) adjacent

C) vertical

D) alternate exterior

www.math-knots.com | www.a4ace.com

112) Find the measure of angle b

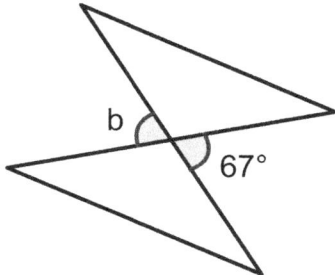

A) 23°   B) 67°

C) 113°   D) 157°

113) Find the measure of angle b

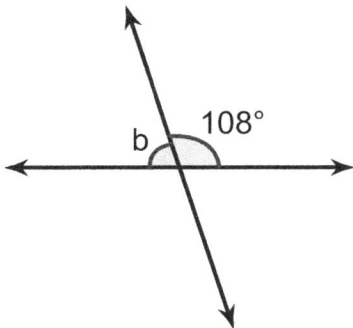

A) 72°   B) 55°

C) 125°   D) 18°

114) Find the measure of angle b

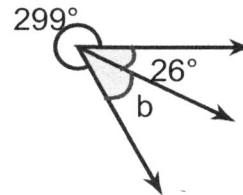

A) 35°   B) 52°

C) 145°   D) 55°

115) Find the measure of angle b

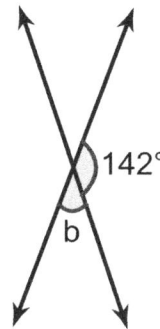

A) 47°   B) 43°

C) 133°   D) 38°

116) Find the measure of angle b

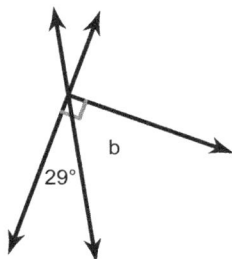

A) 29°   B) 119°

C) 61°   D) 93°

118) Find the measure of angle b

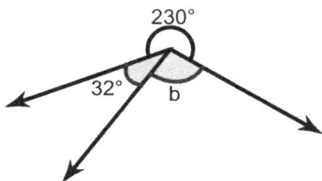

A) 116°   B) 154°

C) 64°   D) 26°

117) Find the measure of angle b

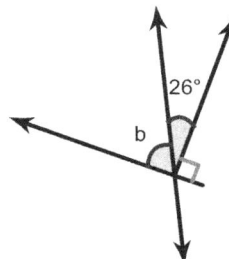

A) 98°   B) 77°

C) 82°   D) 8°

119) Find the measure of angle b

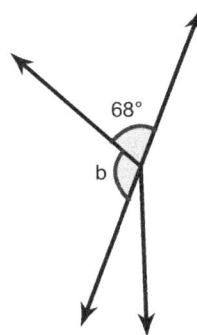

A) 112°   B) 68°

C) 109°   D) 22°

120) Find the measure of angle b

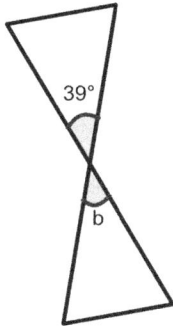

A) 72°   B) 39°

C) 74°   D) 146°

121) Find the measure of angle b

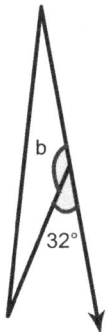

A) 58°   B) 89°

C) 32°   D) 148°

122) Find the measure of angle b

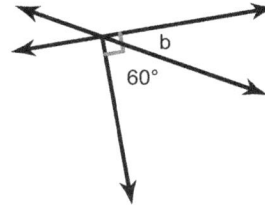

A) 33°   B) 150°

C) 60°   D) 30°

123) Find the measure of angle b

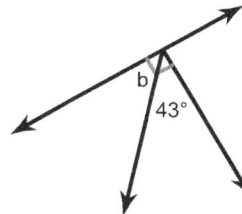

A) 133°   B) 47°

C) 136°   D) 46°

124) Find the measure of angle b

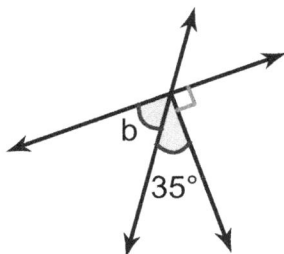

A) 35°   B) 55°

C) 145°   D) 125°

126) Find the measure of angle b

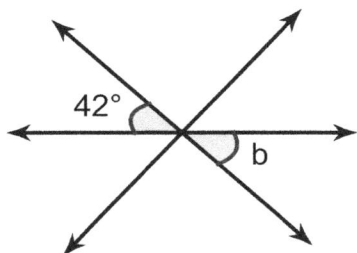

A) 86°   B) 94°

C) 101°   D) 4°

125) Find the measure of angle b

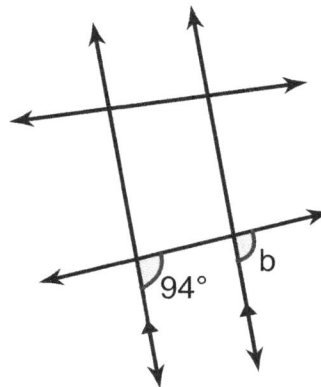

A) 44°   B) 42°

C) 136°   D) 46°

127) Find the measure of angle b

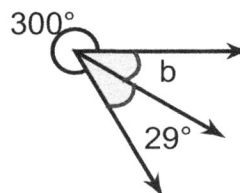

A) 149°   B) 31°

C) 59°   D) 121°

               www.math-knots.com | www.a4ace.com

128) Find the measure of angle b

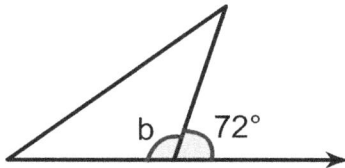

A) 18°   B) 162°

C) 72°   D) 108°

130) Find the measure of angle b

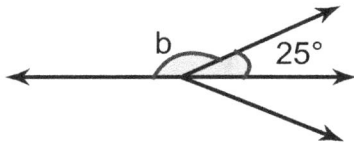

A) 149°   B) 16°

C) 31°   D) 74°

129) Find the measure of angle b

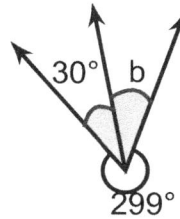

A) 65°   B) 115°

C) 25°   D) 155°

131) Find the measure of angle b

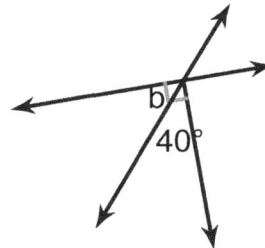

A) 50°   B) 22°

C) 40°   D) 158°

www.math-knots.com | www.a4ace.com

132) Find the measure of angle b

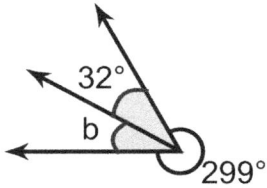

32°

b

299°

A) 29°   B) 119°

C) 61°   D) 151°

134) Find the measure of angle b

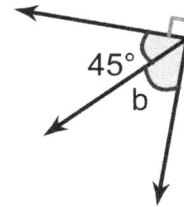

45°

b

A) 55°   B) 45°

C) 135°   D) 35°

133) Find the measure of angle b

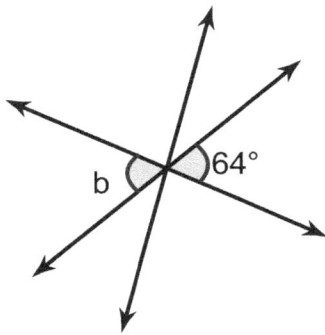

b   64°

A) 111°   B) 98°

C) 26°   D) 64°

135) Find the measure of angle b

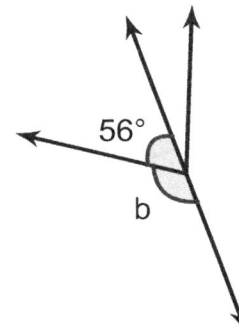

56°

b

A) 124°   B) 146°

C) 34°   D) 56°

                   www.math-knots.com | www.a4ace.com

136) Find the measure of angle b

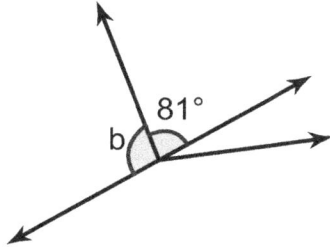

A) 99°   B) 9°

C) 171°   D) 81°

138) Find the measure of angle b

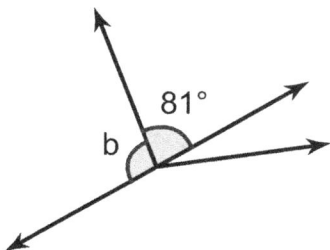

A) 65°   B) 96°

C) 84°   D) 155°

137) Find the measure of angle b

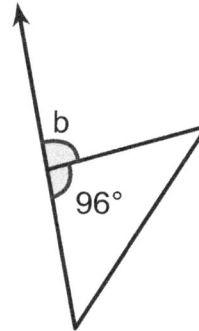

A) 99°   B) 9°

C) 171°   D) 81°

139) Find the measure of angle b

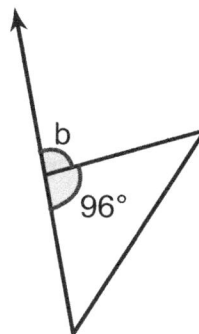

A) 65°   B) 96°

C) 84°   D) 155°

140) Find the measure of angle b

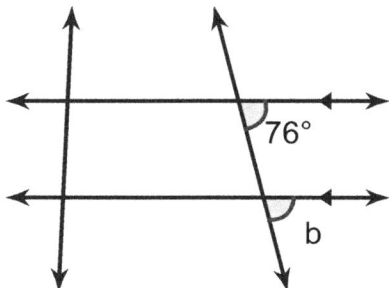

A) 14°   B) 82°

C) 76°   D) 98°

142) Find the measure of angle b

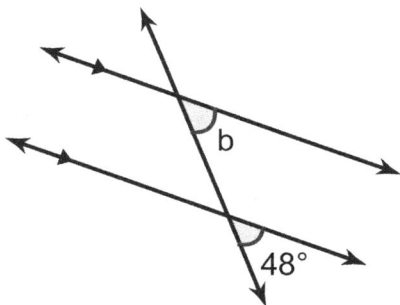

A) 1°   B) 179°

C) 89°   D) 91°

141) Find the measure of angle b

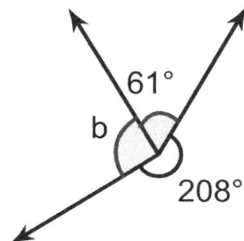

A) 48°   B) 42°

C) 132°   D) 142°

143) Find the measure of angle b

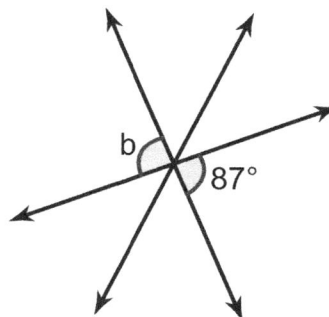

A) 87°   B) 16°

C) 164°   D) 3°

144) Find the value of x

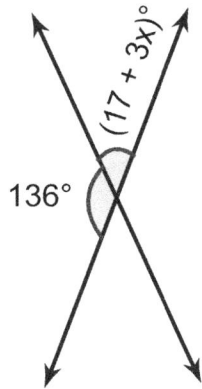

A) -32   B) 9

C) 8   D) 13

145) Find the value of x

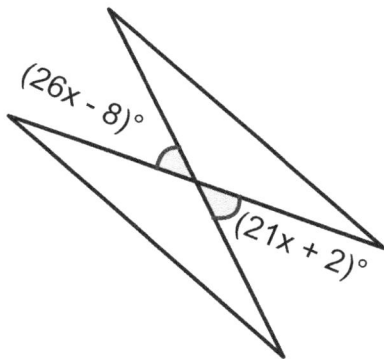

A) -6   B) 48

C) 2   D) 18

146) Find the value of x

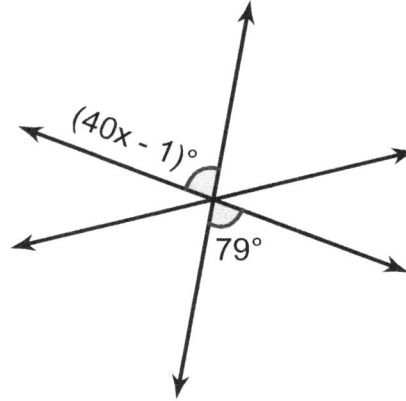

A) 2   B) -40

C) -76   D) -41

147) Find the value of x

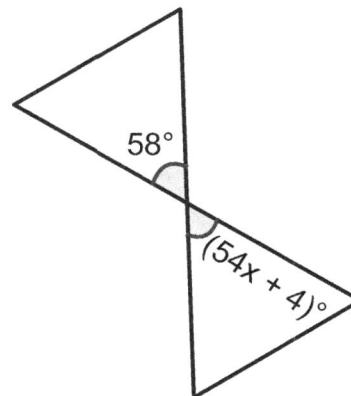

A) -1   B) 14

C) 1   D) 33

148) Find the value of x

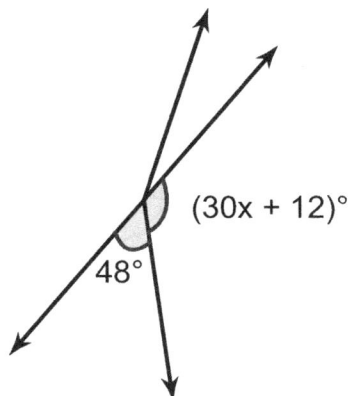

(30x + 12)°

48°

A) -24   B) 24

C) -7   D) 4

149) Find the value of x

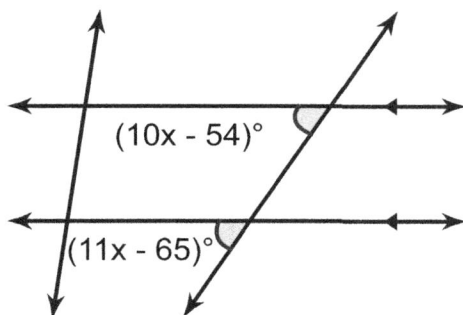

(10x - 54)°

(11x - 65)°

A) -22   B) -16

C) 11   D) -70

150) Find the value of x

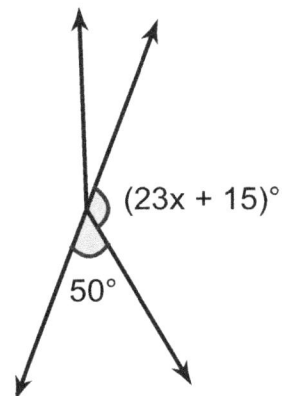

(23x + 15)°

50°

A) 46   B) 19

C) 5   D) 25

151) Find the value of x

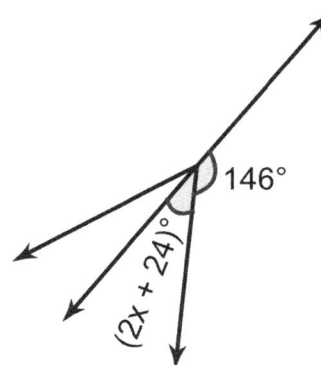

146°

(2x + 24)°

A) -27   B) -71

C) -70   D) 5

www.math-knots.com | www.a4ace.com

152) Find the value of x

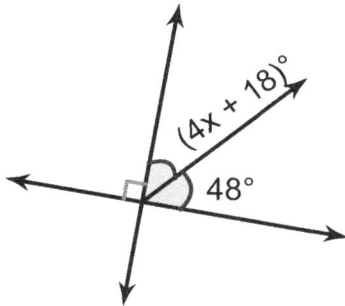

(4x + 18)°

48°

A) -5   B) 19

C) 6   D) -50

154) Find the value of x

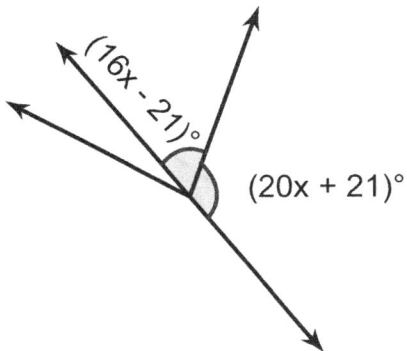

(60x - 2)°

32°

A) -37   B) 1

C) -14   D) 6

153) Find the value of x

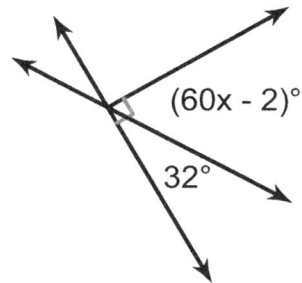

(16x - 21)°

(20x + 21)°

A) 3   B) 12

C) 5   D) 30

155) Find the value of x

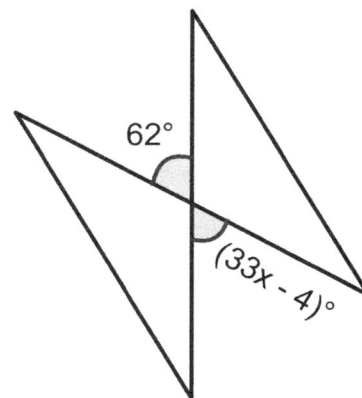

62°

(33x - 4)°

A) 2   B) 3

C) 12   D) 8

       www.math-knots.com | www.a4ace.com

156) Find the value of x

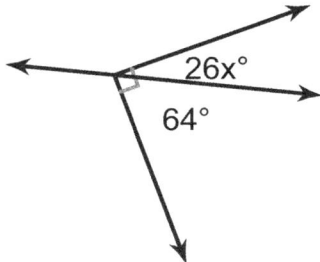

26x°
64°

A) 1 B) -30

C) -78 D) -83

157) Find the value of x

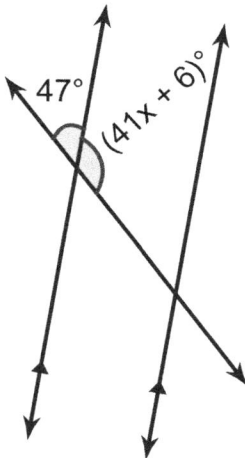

47°
(41x + 6)°

A) -4 B) -35

C) 29 D) 1

158) Find the value of x

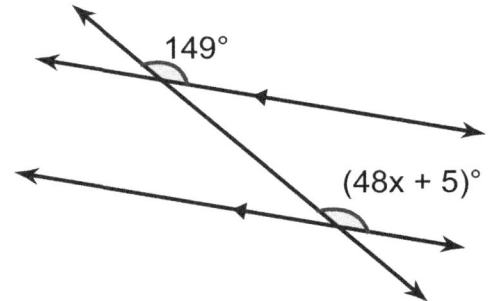

149°
(48x + 5)°

A) -14 B) 32

C) 3 D) -36

159) Find the value of x

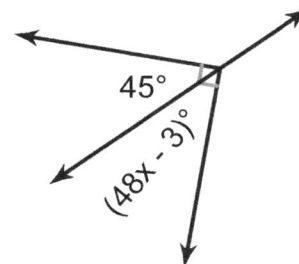

45°
(48x - 3)°

A) -47 B) -29

C) 1 D) -30

160) Find the value of x

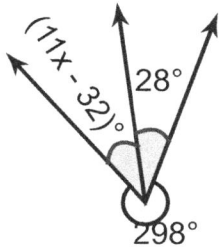

A) 51 B) 97

C) 6 D) 108

161) Find the value of x

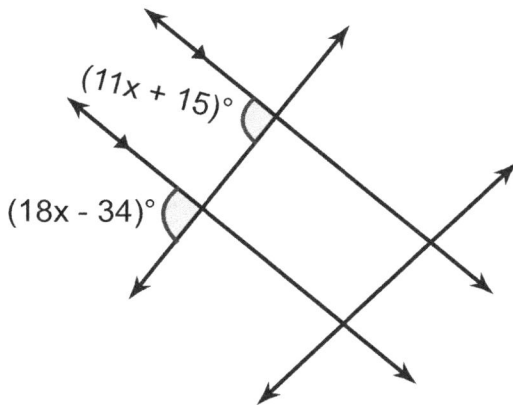

A) 54 B) 46

C) 42 D) 7

162) Find the value of x

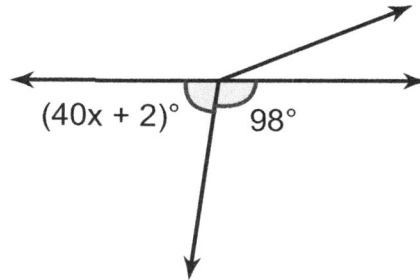

A) 2 B) 32

C) 49 D) 5

163) Find the value of x

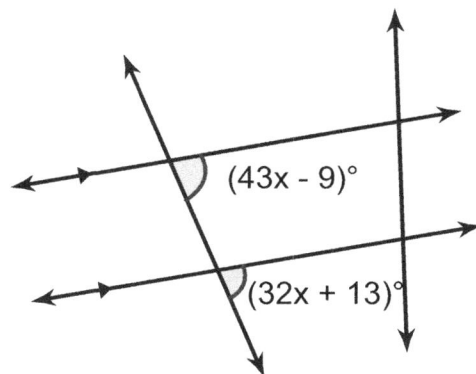

A) 2 B) 91

C) 43 D) 21

164) Find the value of x

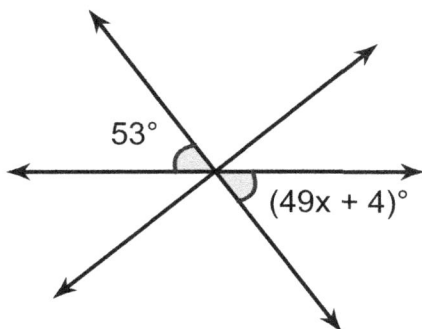

A) 66   B) 3

C) 1   D) 31

165) Find the value of x

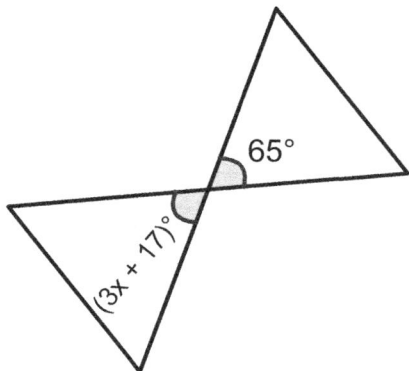

A) 16   B) 85

C) 77   D) 34

166) Find the value of x

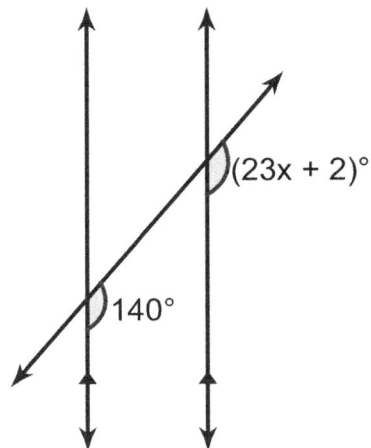

A) 54   B) 10

C) 15   D) 6

167) Find the value of x

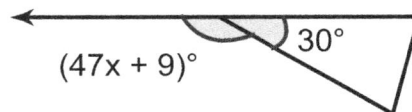

A) -76   B) -100

C) -37   D) 3

     318

168) Find the value of x

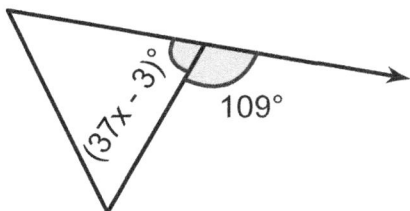

(37x − 3)° 109°

A) 2   B) 39

C) 84   D) 94

169) Find the value of x

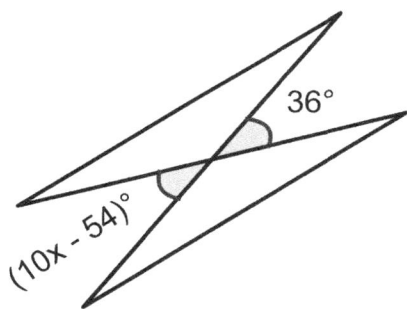

36°

(10x − 54)°

A) 24   B) -15

C) -18   D) 9

170) Find the radius of the circle given area is 2255.3 cm². Round your answer to the nearest tenth (Use ∏ = 3.14)

A) 27.3 cm   B) 27.8 cm

C) 26.8 cm   D) 27 cm

171) Find the radius of the circle given area is 4775.9 in². Round your answer to the nearest tenth (Use ∏ = 3.14)

A) 19.5 in   B) 39.5 in

C) 1521 in   D) 39 in

172) Find the radius of the circle given area is 530.7 m². Round your answer to the nearest tenth (Use ∏ = 3.14)

A) 13 m   B) 13.3 m

C) 6.5 m   D) 3.6 m

173) Find the radius of the circle given area is 7539.1 ft². Round your answer to the nearest tenth (Use ∏ = 3.14)

A) 7 ft   B) 49 ft

C) 49.1 ft   D) 2401 ft

174) Find the radius of the circle given area is 4137.5 mi². Round your answer to the nearest tenth (Use ∏ = 3.14)

A) 36.3 mi   B) 6 mi

C) 18.2 mi   D) 36.6 mi

www.math-knots.com | www.a4ace.com

Grade 7
Volume 2
Week 33

1) MK Academy principal wants to see which subject the 1021 students in his school liked best.

   Which choice **best** represents a sample?

   A. All the students in the school.

   B. The students in 6th grade.

   C. The first 125 students who come into the school.

   D. The students making a A in math.

2) A super gaming website wanted to find out which console its visitors owned.

   Which choice **best** represents a sample?

   A. All of the website visitors.

   B. Visitors over age of 22.

   C. Visitors with an 'd' in their user name.

   D. Visitors to the 3DS section.

3) A yummy restaurant chain wanted to find out the customer experience in their stores.

   Which choice **best** represents a population?

   A. Every 34th customer.

   B. 301 customers who filled out complaint cards.

   C. All of the people who ate at the store.

   D. 422 customers who spent more than $30.

4) Before a nation wide election, a polling place was trying to see who would win. Which choice **best** represents a sample?

   A. All voters.

   B. A selection of male voters.

   C. A selection of votes from one part of the nation.

   D. A selection of voters from all over the nation.

5) MK Academy students set up online survey to see if people in their state thought the pollution was too high.

   Which choice **best** represents a population?

   A. Every person who owns more than 5 cars.

   B. Every person in the state.

   C. A selection of people from each neighborhood in the state.

   D. A selection of people who live in small towns.

6) A musician wanted to see people's opinion on last released album of his songs.

   Which choice **best** represents a sample?

   A. Every person from age 5 - 10 who bought the album.

   B. Every person who bought the album.

   C. 146 girls who bought the album.

   D. A selection of 9,514 people who bought the album.

7) City mayor wanted to survey on people's opinion on his leadership of doing the best for the city

Which choice **best** represents a sample?

A. The residents of the town.

B. The people who voted for the mayor.

C. 500 unemployed voters.

D. The residents of 8 different neighborhoods.

8) Cool beverage company took a survey on their new released logo.

Which choice **best** represents a population?

A. 280 male and female employees

B. 1,012 children age 5 - 10

C. A selection of shoppers from different states.

D. Every person in the United States.

9) A toy store owner tracking how much kids spend each month on toys.
Which choice **best** represents a sample?

A. 80 boys age 7 - 13

B. All of the kids who buy toys.

C. 424 rich kids.

D. 630 kids from age 8 to 16.

10) A pop singer wanted to take a pole of opinions on his latest video album.

Which choice **best** represents a population?

A. Every person who bought the album.

B. Every person from age 3 - 9 who bought the album.

C. A selection of 5,250 people who bought the album.

D. 980 girls who bought the album.

11) A fast food restaurant chain wants to know the customers dining experience.

Which choice **best** represents a population?

A. Every 100th customer.

B. All of the people who ate at the store.

C. 330 customers who spent more than 25.

D. 532 customers who filled out complaint cards.

12) MK Academy students set up an online poll to reduce the carbon fuels.

Which choice **best** represents a sample?

A. A selection of people from each neighborhood in the state.

B. Every person who sent in a complaint about pollution.

C. Every person in the state.

D. A selection of people who live in dirty neighborhoods.

13) Joe the carpenter has accumulated a large collection of nails, screws and bolts, which he had randomly thrown together into a bucket. Later he wanted to estimate how many of each he had. To do this he grabbed a handful from the bucket. His results are shown below.

Sample	1	2	3	4	5
Nails	29	30	28	31	28
Screws	28	32	28	32	29
Bolts	29	32	28	28	29

Based on the information presented can you infer anything about the relationship between the number of nails, screws and bolts in the bucket?

14) In order to determine which type of sweets Tom should keep the most of in his shop a baker logged every 5th customers order. His findings are shown below:

Sample	1	2	3	4	5
Cookies	23	24	22	22	24
Brownies	32	29	32	28	31
Cupcakes	11	16	13	12	15

Based on the information presented what can you infer about which type he should stock?

15) Ron pizzeria owner was trying to determine which types of meat he should stock the most of for his new store. To do this he asked several pizza eaters what their favorite toppings were. His results are shown below:

Sample	1	2	3	4	5	6	7
Pepperoni	4	5	3	5	6	3	6
Tomatoes	4	3	2	3	6	2	5
Olives	2	6	4	2	5	6	2

Based on the information presented what can you infer about which type of meat he should stock?

16) In order to determine which type of sweets Henry should keep the most in his shop a baker logged every 10th customers order. His findings are shown below:

Sample	1	2	3	4	5
Cookies	51	52	51	52	53
Brownies	41	42	44	41	43
Cupcakes	62	61	60	62	62

Based on the information presented what can you infer about which type he should stock?

17) At the football game a vendor was trying to determine if Coke or Pepsi sold better. To do this he asked several rows of attendees which flavor they bought. His results are shown below:

Sample	1	2
Coke	4	5
Pepsi	5	2

Based on the information presented what can you infer about the types of soda sold?

18) A dentists was trying to determine if more boys or girls had cavities. He checked the visits from the last month and his results are shown below:

Sample	1	2	3	4	5	6
Boys	51	49	51	50	48	51
Girls	40	41	44	44	43	40

Based on the information presented what can you infer about who had cavities?

19) In a library there was a donation box for books. A librarian wanted to estimate how many fiction and how many non-fiction books were in the box so she pulled out a sample. The results are shown below:

Sample	1	2	3	4	5	6	7
Fiction	22	21	20	21	23	20	22
Non-fiction	30	31	30	29	28	30	28

Based on the information presented can you infer anything about the types of books donated?

20) During a class election a teacher wanted to predict who would win. To do this she took a sample of students from each class and asked who they would vote for. The results are shown below:

Sample	1	2	3	4	5	6	7	8
Candidate A	59	61	61	62	59	62	61	59
Candidate B	51	54	52	52	51	51	52	50

Based on the information presented can you infer anything about who will win the election?

21) In a lake there are 3 types of fish: minnows, goldfish and sunfish. A fisherman wanted to estimate how many of each type there were. He scooped up several nets full and recorded his results (shown below).

Sample	1	2	3	4	5	6	7	8
Minnows	2	1	4	5	5	4	3	1
Goldfish	2	5	5	5	5	3	3	5
Sunfish	3	3	1	3	4	3	1	3

Based on the information presented can you infer anything about the number of different types of fish in the lake?

www.math-knots.com | www.a4ace.com

22) Two rooms in a house need to be painted. Each room can be painted either white or yellow. Write the sample space in notation.

   A) {(W, W), (W, Y),
       (Y, W), (Y, Y)}

   B) {(W, W), (Y, Y)}

   C) {(W, W), (W, Y)}

   D) {(W, W), (Y, W)}

23) A new car is available in a sedan model and a Luxury model. It is available in red, white, and green. Write the sample space in notation.

   A) {(S, R), (S, W), (S, G)}

   B) {(R, R), (R, W), (R, G),
      (W, R), (W, W), (W, G),
      (G, R), (G, W), (G, G)}

   C) {(S, R), (H, R)}

   D) {(S, R), (S, W), (S, G),
      (H, R), (H, W), (H, G)}

24) An ice cream stand offers single-scoop waffle-cones or bowls. Four flavors are available: strawberry, chocolate, vanilla, and mango. Write the sample space in notation.

   A) {(W, S), (W, C), (W, V), (W, M)}

   B) {(W, S), (B, S)}

   C) {(S, S), (S, C), (S, V), (S, M),
      (C, S), (C, C), (C, V), (C, M),
      (V, S), (V, C), (V, V), (V, M),
      (M, S), (M, C), (M, V), (M, M)}

   D) {(W, S), (W, C), (W, V), (W, M),
      (B, S), (B, C), (B, V), (B, M)}

25) When a button is pressed, a computer program outputs a random odd number greater than 1 and less than 9. You press the button twice. Write the sample space in notation.

   A) {(3, 3), (5, 3), (7, 3)}

   B) {(3, 3), (3, 5), (3, 7),
      (5, 3), (5, 5), (5, 7),
      (7, 3), (7, 5), (7, 7)}

   C) {(3, 5, 7, 3, 5, 7)}

   D) {(3, 3), (3, 5), (3, 7)}

26) A spinner can land on either white or black. You flip a coin and then spin the spinner. Write the sample space in notation.

   A) {(H, W), (H, B),
      (T, R), (T, B)}

   B) {(H, W), (T, W)}

   C) {(W, W), (W, B),
      (B, W), (B, B)}

   D) {(H, W), (H, B)}

27) A sandwich shop has three types of sandwiches: vegetable, turkey, and chicken. Each sandwich can be ordered with white bread or multi-grain bread. Write the sample space in notation.

   A) {(V, W), (T, W), (C, W)}

   B) {(W, W), (W, M),
      (M, W), (M, M)}

   C) {(V, W), (V, M),
      (T, W), (T, M),
      (C, W), (C, M)}

   D) {(V, V), (V, T), (V, C),
      (T, V), (T, T), (T, C),
      (C, V), (C, T), (C, C)}

www.math-knots.com | www.a4ace.com

28) A new car is available in a SUV model and a Truck model. It is available in red, white, and green. Write the sample space in notation.

A) {(R, R), (R, W), (R, G),

(W, R), (W, W), (W, G),

(G, R), (G, W), (G, G)}

B) {(S, R), (S, W), (S, G),
(T, R), (T, W), (T, G)}

C) {(S, R), (S, W), (S, G)}

D) {(S, R), (T, R)}

29) A spinner can land on either white, silver, green, yellow, purple, or orange. You flip a coin and then spin the spinner. Write the sample space in notation.

A) {(H, W), (H, S), (H, G), (H, Y), (H, P), (H, O),

(T, R), (T, B), (T, G), (T, Y), (T, P), (T, O)}

B) {(H, W), (T, W)}

C) {(H, H), (H, T),
(T, H), (T, T)}

D) {(W, W), (W, S), (W, G), (W, Y), (W, P), (W, O),

(S, W), (S, S), (S, G), (S, Y), (S, P), (S, O),

(G, W), (G, S), (G, G), (G, Y), (G, P), (G, O),

(Y, W), (Y, S), (Y, G), (Y, Y), (Y, P), (Y, O),

(P, W), (P, S), (P, G), (P, Y), (P, P), (P, O),

(O, W), (O, S), (O, G), (O, Y), (O, P), (O, O)}

30) There is one quarter, one dime, and one nickel in your pocket. You randomly pick a coin from your pocket and place it on the counter. Then you pick a second coin from your pocket.

A) {(Q, Q), (Q, D), (Q, N),
(D, Q), (D, D), (D, N),
(N, Q), (N, D), (N, N)}

B) {(Q, D), (Q, N),
(D, Q), (D, N),
(N, Q), (N, D)}

C) {(Q, Q), (D, D), (N, N)}

D) {(Q, Q), (D, Q), (N, Q)}

31) A basket contains one apple, one peach, and one orange. You randomly pick a piece of fruit to eat. Then you pick another piece to eat later

A) {(A, A), (A, P), (A, O)}

B) {(A, P), (A, O),

(P, A), (P, O),

(O, A), (O, P)}

C) {(A, A), (A, P), (A, O),

(P, A), (P, P), (P, O),

(O, A), (O, P), (O, O)}

D) {(A, A), (P, P), (O, O)}

32) An ice cream stand offers single-scoop waffle-cones or bowls. Four flavors are available: Orange, chocolate, vanilla, and mango. Write the sample space in notation.

A) {(W, O), (W, C), (W, V), (W, M),

(B, O), (B, C), (B, V), (B, M)}

B) {(O, O), (O, C), (O, V), (O, M),

(C, S), (C, C), (C, V), (C, M),

(V, O), (V, C), (V, V), (V, M),

(M, O), (M, C), (M, V), (M, M)}

C) {(W, W), (W, B),

(B, W), (B, B)}

D) {(W, S), (W, C), (W, V), (W, M)}

33) Tony flip a coin and then roll a six-sided die. Write the sample space in notation.
A) {(H, 1), (T, 1)}

B) {(H, 1), (H, 2), (H, 3), (H, 4), (H, 5), (H, 6),

(T, 1), (T, 2), (T, 3), (T, 4), (T, 5), (T, 6)}

C) {(H, 1), (H, 2), (H, 3), (H, 4), (H, 5), (H, 6)}

D) {(H, H), (H, T),

(T, H), (T, T)}

34) A spinner can land on either yellow or violet. Ben flips a coin and then spins the spinner. Write the sample space in notation.

A) {(H, H), (H, T),
(T, H), (T, T)}

B) {(H, Y), (T, Y)}

C) {(H, Y), (H, V),
(T, Y), (T, V)}

D) {(H, Y), (H, V)}

35) A new car is available in a wagon model and a cooper model. It is available in red, white, and green. Write the sample space in notation.

A) {(W, R), (W, W), (W, G)}

B) {(S, R), (C, R)}

C) {(W, R), (W, W), (W, G),
(C, R), (C, W), (C, G)}

D) {(R, R), (R, W), (R, G),
(W, R), (W, W), (W, G),

(G, R), (G, W), (G, G)}

36) A new car is available in a sedan model and a Wagon model. It is available in red, white, green, and black. Write the sample space in notation.

A) {(S, R), (H, R)}

B) {(S, R), (S, W), (S, G), (S, B),
(W, R), (W, W), (W, G), (W, B)}

C) {(R, R), (R, W), (R, G), (R, B),
(W, R), (W, W), (W, G), (W, B),
(G, R), (G, W), (G, G), (G, B),
(B, R), (B, W), (B, G), (B, B)}

D) {(S, R), (S, W), (S, G), (S, B)}

37) Olivia flips a coin twice. Write the sample space in notation.

A) {(H, H), (T, T)}

B) {(H, T, H, T)}

C) {(H, H), (H, T),
(T, H), (T, T)}

D) {(H, H), (H, T)}

38) A basket contains two apples and a peach. You randomly pick a piece of fruit to eat. Then you pick another piece to eat later. Write the sample space in notation.

   A) $\{(A_1, A_2), (A_1, P),$
   $(A_2, A_1), (A_2, P),$
   $(P, A_1), (P, A_2)\}$

   B) $\{(A_1, A_1), (A_2, A_1), (P, A_1)\}$

   C) $\{(A_1, A_1), (A_1, A_2), (A_1, P),$
   $(A_2, A_1), (A_2, A_2), (A_2, P),$
   $(P, A_1), (P, A_2), (P, P)\}$

   D) $\{(A_1, A_1), (A_1, A_2), (A_1, P)\}$

39) A soccer player takes two penalty kicks in a game. Each attempt results in a goal or a miss. Write the sample space in notation.

   A) $\{(G, G), (M, M)\}$

   B) $\{(G, G), (M, G)\}$

   C) $\{(G, G), (G, M)\}$

   D) $\{(G, G), (G, M),$
   $(M, G), (M, M)\}$

40) An ice cream stand offers single-scoopwaffle-cones or bowls. Four flavors are available: orange, chocolate, vanilla, and mint chocolate chip. Write the sample space in notation.

   A) $\{(W, W), (W, B),$
   $(B, W), (B, B)\}$

   B) $\{(W, O), (W, C), (W, V), (W, M),$
   $(B, O), (B, C), (B, V), (B, M)\}$

   C) $\{(O, O), (S, C), (O, V), (O, M),$
   $(C, O), (C, C), (C, V), (C, M),$
   $(V, O), (V, C), (V, V), (V, M),$
   $(M, O), (M, C), (M, V), (M, M)\}$

   D) $\{(W, O), (B, O)\}$

41) A new car is available in a sedan model and a hatchback model. It is available in red, white, green, and black. Write the sample space in notation.

   A) $\{(S, S), (S, H),$
   $(H, S), (H, H)\}$

   B) $\{(S, R), (S, W), (S, G), (S, B)\}$

   C) $\{(R, R), (R, W), (R, G), (R, B),$
   $(W, R), (W, W), (W, G), (W, B),$
   $(G, R), (G, W), (G, G), (G, B),$
   $(B, R), (B, W), (B, G), (B, B)\}$

   D) $\{(S, R), (S, W), (S, G), (S, B),$
   $(H, R), (H, W), (H, G), (H, B)\}$

42) The band must decide when to meet for a practice. The possible days are Tuesday Wednesday, or Thursday. The possible times are 5 or 6 p.m. Write the sample space in notation.

   A) $\{(T, 5), (W, 5), (R, 5)\}$

   B) $\{(T, 5), (T, 6),$
   $(W, 5), (W, 6),$
   $(R, 5), (R, 6)\}$

   C) $\{(5, 5), (5, 6),$
   $(6, 5), (6, 6)\}$

   D) $\{(T, 3), (T, 6)\}$

43) A softball player bats twice in a game. Each at-bat results in an out, getting on base, or hitting a home run. Write the sample space in notation.

   A) $\{(O, O), (B, B), (H, H)\}$

   B) $\{(O, B, H, O, B, H)\}$

   C) $\{(O, O), (O, B), (O, H),$
   $(B, O), (B, B), (B, H),$
   $(H, O), (H, B), (H, H)\}$

   D) $\{(O, O), (O, B), (O, H)\}$

44) Yummy sandwich shop has four types of sandwiches: ham, turkey, cheese, and PB&J. Each sandwich can be ordered with white bread or multi-grain bread. Write the sample space in notation.

A) {(H, W), (T, W), (C, W), (P, W)}

B) {(H, W), (H, M),
(T, W), (T, M),
(C, W), (C, M),
(P, W), (P, M)}

C) {(H, W), (H, M)}

D) {(H, H), (H, T), (H, C), (H, P),
(T, H), (T, T), (T, C), (T, P),
(C, H), (C, T), (C, C), (C, P,
(P, H), (P, T), (P, C), (P, P)}

45) Ian flips a coin and then rolls a six sided die. Write the sample space in notation.

A) {(H, 1), (H, 2), (H, 3), (H, 4), (H, 5), (H, 6),
(T, 1), (T, 2), (T, 3), (T, 4), (T, 5), (T, 6)}

B) {(H, H), (H, T),
(T, H), (T, T)}

C) {(1, 1), (1, 2), (1, 3), (1, 4), (1, 5), (1, 6),
(2, 1), (2, 2), (2, 3), (2, 4), (2, 5), (2, 6),
(3, 1), (3, 2), (3, 3), (3, 4), (3, 5), (3, 6),
(4, 1), (4, 2), (4, 3), (4, 4),(4, 5), (4, 6),
(5, 1), (5, 2), (5, 3), (5, 4), (5, 5), (5, 6),
(6, 1), (6, 2), (6, 3), (6, 4), (6, 5), (6, 6)}

D) {(H, 1), (T, 1)}

46) When a button is pressed, a computer program outputs a random even number greater than 0 and less than 8. Chris press the button twice. Write the sample space in notation.

A) {(2, 4, 6, 2, 4, 6)}

B) {(2, 2), (2, 4), (2, 6),
(4, 2), (4, 4), (4, 6),
(6, 2), (6, 4), (6, 6)}

C) {(2, 2), (4, 4), (6, 6)}

D) {(2, 2), (2, 4), (2, 6)}

47) A fine jewelry store sells gold and platinum rings. Each ring is fitted with a ruby, sapphire, emerald, or diamond gemstone. Write the sample space in notation.

A) {(G, R), (P, R)}

B) {(G, R), (G, S), (G, E), (G, D)}

C) {(G, R), (G, S), (G, E), (G, D),
(P, R), (P, S), (P, E), (P, D)}

D) {(R, R), (R, S), (R, E), (R, D),
(S, R), (S, S), (S, E), (S, D),
(E, R), (E, S), (E, E), (E, D),
(D, R), (D, S), (D, E), (D, D)}

48) A bag contains one red marble and two green marbles. Rosy randomly picks a marble and keeps it to play with. Then her friend picks a marble from the bag. Write the sample space in notation.

A) $\{(R, R), (R, G_1), (R, G_2)\}$

B) $\{(R, R), (R, G_1), (R, G_2),$
$(G_1, R), (G_1, G_1), (G_1, G_2),$
$(G_2, R), (G_2, G_1), (G_2, G_2)\}$

C) $\{(R, R), (G_1, R), (G_2, R)\}$

D) $\{(R, G_1), (R, G_2),$
$(G_1, R), (G1, G_2),$
$(G_2, R), (G_2, G_1)\}$

49) A sandwich shop has four types of sandwiches: ham, turkey, vegetable, and PB&J. Each sandwich can be ordered with white bread, multi-grain bread, or rye bread. Write the sample space in notation.

A) $\{(H, H), (H, T), (H, V), (H, P),$

$(T, H), (T, T), (T, V), (T, P),$

$(V, H), (V, T), (V, V), (V, P),$

$(P, H), (P, T), (P, V), (P, P)\}$

B) $\{(H, W), (T, W), (V, W), (P, W)\}$

C) $\{(W, W), (W, M), (W, R),$

$(M, W), (M, M), (M, R),$

$(R, W), (R, M), (R, R)\}$

D) $\{(H, W), (H, M), (H, R),$

$(T, W), (T, M), (T, R),$

$(V, W), (V, M), (V, R),$

$(P, W), (P, M), (P, R)\}$

50) There are two boys and a girl on a trivia team. Two questions remain. One team member is randomly picked to answer the first question and a different member is picked to answer the second question. Write the sample space in notation.

A) $\{(B_1, B_1), (B_1, B_2), (B_1, G),$
$(B_2, B_1), (B_2, B_2), (B_2, G),$
$(G, B_1), (G, B_2), (G, G)\}$

B) $\{(B_1, B_2), (B_1, G),$
$(B_2, B_1), (B_2, G),$
$(G, B_1), (G, B_2)\}$

C) $\{(B_1, B_1), (B_1, B_2), (B_1, G)\}$

D) $\{(B_1, B_1), (B_2, B_2), (G, G)\}$

51) There are two dimes and a nickel in Mary's pocket. She randomly picks a coin from her pocket and places it on the counter. Then she picks a second coin from her pocket. Write the sample space in notation.

A) $\{(D_1, D_2), (D_1, N),$

$(D_2, D_1), (D_2, N),$

$(N, D_1), (N, D_2)\}$

B) $\{(D_1, D_1), (D_1, D_2), (D_1, N),$

$(D_2, D_1), (D_2, D_2), (D_2, N),$

$(N, D_1), (N, D_2), (N, N)\}$

C) $\{(D_1, D_1), (D_1, D_2), (D_1, N)\}$

D) $\{(D_1, D_1), (D_2, D_1), (N, D_1)\}$

www.math-knots.com | www.a4ace.com

52) The chess club must decide when to meet for a practice. The possible days are Tuesday, Wednesday , or Thursday. The possible times are 4 or 5 p.m. Write the sample space in notation.

A) {(T, T), (T, W), (T, R),

(W, T), (W, W), (W, R),

(R, T), (R, W), (R, R)}

B) {(4, 4), (4, 5),

(5, 4), (5, 5)}

C) {(T, 4), (W, 4), (R, 4)}

D) {(T, 4), (T, 5),

(W, 4), (W, 5),

(R, 4), (R, 5)}

53) A room in a house needs to be painted. The room can be painted white, yellow, or pink. Find the number of possible ways.

A) 6   B) 4   C) 3   D) 1

54) A jewelry store sells rings with either a ruby, sapphire, or emerald gemstone. Find the number of possible ways.

A) 0   B) 2   C) 3   D) 6

55) A bagel shop has three types of bagels: plain, onion, and raisin. Find the number of possible ways.

A) 3   B) 1   C) 2   D) 8

56) There are two girls and a boy on a trivia team. One team member is randomly picked to answer a question. Find the number of possible ways.

A) 4   B) 3   C) 1   D) 5

57) A room in a house needs to be painted. The room can be painted white, yellow, or pink. Find the number of possible ways.

A) 3   B) 6   C) 8   D) 1

58) A coffee shop offers French roast, Italian roast, and American roast coffee. Find the number of possible ways.

A) 2   B) 3   C) 1   D) 6

59) There is one quarter, one dime, and one nickel in your pocket. You randomly pick a coin. Find the number of possible ways.

A) 8   B) 3   C) 0   D) 1

60) An ice cream stand offers three flavors: strawberry, chocolate, and vanilla. Find the number of possible ways.

A) 5   B) 8   C) 7   D) 3

               www.math-knots.com | www.a4ace.com

61) A bag contains three real diamonds and two fake diamonds. You randomly pick a diamond. Find the number of possible ways.

A) 3   B) 5   C) 8   D) 0

62) A coffee shop offers French roast, Italian roast, and American roast coffee. Find the number of possible ways.

A) 4   B) 3   C) 2   D) 8

63) A new car is available in red, white, green, and black. Find the number of possible ways.

A) 5   B) 1   C) 6   D) 4

64) When a button is pressed, a computer program outputs a random even number greater than 0 and less than 12. Rik presses the button once. Find the number of possible ways.

A) 5   B) 4   C) 10   D) 0

65) A new car is available in red, green, and black. Find the number of possible ways.

A) 1   B) 5   C) 6   D) 4

66) The chess club must decide when to meet for a practice. The possible days are Tuesday or Wednesday. Find the number of possible ways.

A) 0   B) 7   C) 2   D) 1

67) A new car is available in red, white, and green. Find the number of possible ways.

A) 2   *B) 3   C) 0   D) 7

68) A new car is available in red, white, green, and black. Find the number of possible ways.

A) 7   B) 3   C) 6   *D) 4

79) When a button is pressed, a computer program outputs a random even number greater than 10 and less than 20. Lola press the button once. Find the number of possible ways.

A) 6   B) 9   C) 3   D) 5

70) A basket contains two apples and three peaches. Mary randomly picks a piece of fruit. Find the number of possible ways.

A) 3   B) 8   C) 6   D) 5

71) There are two girls and a boy on a trivia team. One team member is randomly picked to answer a question. Find the number of possible ways.

A) 6   B) 5   C) 4   D) 3

72) The chess club must decide when to meet for a practice. The possible days are Tuesday or Wednesday. Find the number of possible ways.

A) 4   B) 2   C) 5   D) 3

73) A spinner can land on either red, blue, or green. You spin once. Find the number of possible ways.

A) 3   B) 1   C) 2   D) 0

74) A soccer player takes a penalty kick. The attempt can result in a goal or a miss. Find the number of possible ways.

A) 1   B) 7   C) 0   D) 2

75) When a button is pressed, a computer program outputs a random even number greater than 50 and less than 65. Rack presses the button once. Find the number of possible ways.

A) 7   B) 4   C) 10   D) 9

76) There are two dimes and a nickel in your pocket. Ben randomly picks a coin. Find the number of possible ways.

A) 6   B) 0   C) 8   D) 3

77) The chess club must decide when to meet for a practice. The possible days are Tuesday, Wednesday, or Thursday. Find the number of possible ways.

A) 0   B) 2   C) 1   D) 3

78) A bag contains one red marble, one green marble, and one blue marble. Dan randomly picks a marble. Find the number of possible ways.

A) 3   B) 1   C) 2   D) 5

79) A room in a house needs to be painted. The room can be painted either white or yellow. Find the number of possible ways.

A) 6   B) 5   C) 2   D) 4

80) A sandwich shop has three types of sandwiches: ham, turkey, and chicken. Find the number of possible ways.

A) 0   B) 3   C) 6   D) 8

81) When a button is pressed, a computer program outputs a random odd number greater than 1 and less than 13. Tara presses the button once. Find the number of possible ways.

A) 2   B) 3   C) 7   D) 5

82) A sandwich shop has four types of sandwiches: ham, turkey, chicken, and PB&J. Find the number of possible ways.

A) 4   B) 7   C) 3   D) 2

83) A spinner can land on either red or blue. Kate spins it once. Find the number of possible ways.

A) 1   B) 2   C) 6   D) 0

www.math-knots.com | www.a4ace.com

84) A bag contains two red marbles and three blue marbles. Gary randomly picks a marble. Find the number of possible ways.

A) 0   B) 4   C) 10   D) 5

85) A spinner can land on either red, blue, or green. Fiona spins it once. Find the number of possible ways.

A) 5   B) 8   C) 3   D) 2

86) The chess club must decide when to meet for a practice. The possible times are 3, 4, or 5 p.m. Find the number of possible ways.

A) 4   B) 3   C) 6   D) 2

87) The band must decide when to meet for a practice. The possible times are 3, 4, or 5 p.m. Find the number of possible ways.

A) 0   B) 5   C) 3   D) 1

88) A sandwich shop has four types of sandwiches: ham, turkey, chicken, and PB&J. Find the number of possible ways.

A) 5   B) 9   C) 4   D) 3

89) A basketball player attempts a shot that can result in a score or a miss. Find the number of possible ways.

A) 2   B) 4   C) 1   D) 5

90) A hot dog stand offers both small and large hot dogs. Find the number of possible ways.

A) 1   B) 6   C) 2   D) 4

91) A pizza stand offers hand-tossed, pan, and thin-crust pizza. Find the number of possible ways.

A) 3   B) 1   C) 7   D) 8

92) There are two dimes and a nickel in your pocket. Amy randomly picks a coin. Find the number of possible ways.

A) 7   B) 2   C) 3   D) 0

93) A pizza stand offers hand-tossed, pan, and thin-crust pizza. Find the number of possible ways.

A) 3   B) 5   C) 4   D) 1

94) There is one quarter, one dime, and one nickel in her pocket. Sara randomly picks a coin. Find the number of possible ways.

A) 1   B) 0   C) 6   D) 3

95) The band must decide when to meet for a practice. The possible days are Tuesday, Wednesday , or Thursday. Find the number of possible ways.

A) 1   B) 2   C) 3   D) 4

96) A pizza stand offers hand-tossed, pan, and thin-crust pizza. Find the number of possible ways.

   A) 1   B) 4   C) 3   D) 7

97) A football player attempts a pass in overtime. The pass attempt can result in a completion, an incompletion, or a turnover. Find the number of possible ways.

   A) 6   B) 2   C) 3   D) 7

98) The chess club must decide when to meet for a practice. The possible days are Tuesday or Wednesday. Find the number of possible ways.

   A) 5   B) 7   C) 2   D) 0

99) A bag contains one red marble, one green marble, and one blue marble. Julia randomly picks a marble. Find the number of possible ways.

   A) 8   B) 3   C) 1   D) 7

100) A basket contains two apples and three peaches. Ron randomly picks a piece of fruit. Find the number of possible ways.

   A) 0   B) 4   C) 5   D) 3

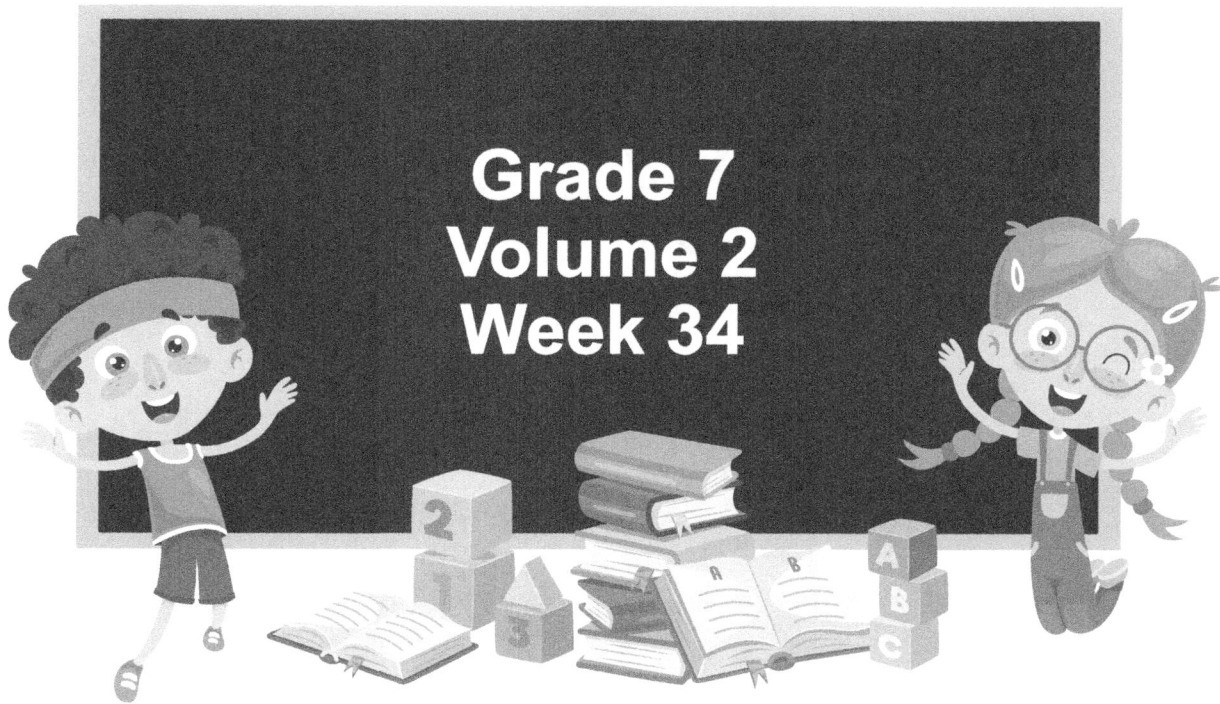

Grade 7
Volume 2
Week 34

340   www.math-knots.com | www.a4ace.com

Sally spins the below spinner. Find the below probability of each spin as a fraction in simplified form.

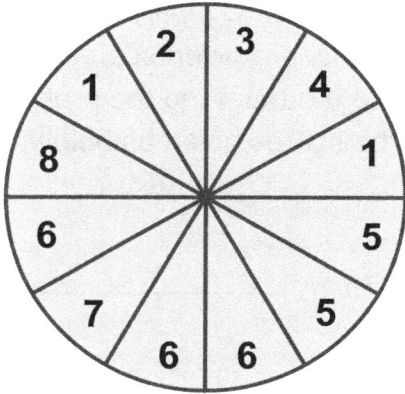

1. P(1) = _____

2. P(5 or 6) =_____

3. P(number > 2) =_____

4. P(composite number) = _____

5. P(7) = _____

6. P(odd number) = _____

7. P(number < 5) = _____

8. P(prime number) = _____

Jolly throws a dart at the game board. Find the probability of each throw in the simplified form

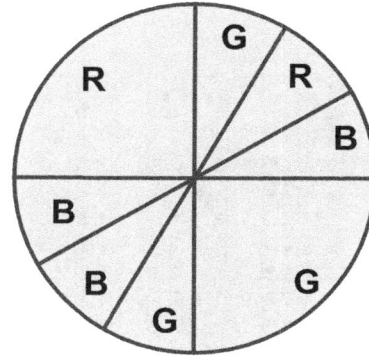

9. P(R) = _____

10. P(R,B or G) = _____

11. P(R or G) = _____

12. P(G or B) = _____

13. P(not R) = _____

14. P(not R or G) = _____

Jack and Jill are playing a board game using two dice. Find the probability of each role as a fraction in simplified form.

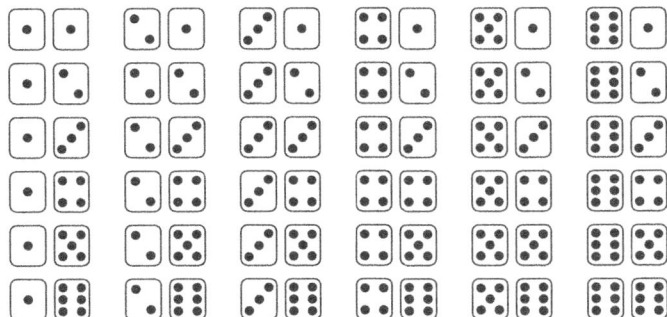

Grade 8 class math quiz scores are recorded as below at MK Academy class, there were eight "A's", fourteen "B's", seven "C's", and two "D's". Students are given score sheets in random order. Find the probability of the scores given as below.

15. P(sum of 3) = _____

16. P(sum less than 10) = _____

17. P(sum greater than 1) = _____

18. P(sum that is even) = _____

19. P(sum of 10) = _____

20. P(sum greater than 3) = _____

21. P(sum of 8) = _____

22. P(sum that is odd) = _____

23. P(A) = _____

24. P(C or D) = _____

25. P(A,B or C) = _____

26. P(A or B) = _____

27. P(not an A) = _____

28. P(not a D) = _____

www.math-knots.com | www.a4ace.com

Bella and Stella are playing a letter game with a cube with each side marked as P,Q, R,S,T and U. Find the probability of each of the below events as a fraction in simplified form

29. P(P) = _____

30. P(Q) = _____

31. P(P,Q or R) = _____

32. P(not P) = _____

33. P(Q or R) = _____

34. P(Q,R,S or T) = _____

35. If you roll a vowel, you win. If Bella rolls a consonant she wins. Is this a fair game?

Chris is playing a board game with his brother. Find the probabilities of each role of the dice as a fraction in simplified form for the below.

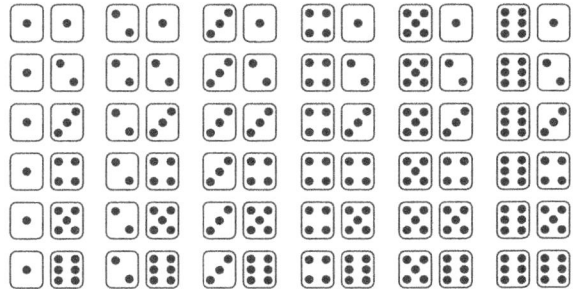

36. P(sum of 4) = _____

37. P(sum of 5) = _____

38. P(4 on both cubes) = _____

39. P(sum of 11) = _____

40. P(same number on both cubes) = _____

41. P(sum less than 20) = _____

The below table shows the 7th grade math quiz scores.

42. What is the probability that Harry earned higher than a "D" on the quiz ?

Letter Grade	Number of students
A	10
B	18
C	14
D	8
F	0

Ron has a bag of balls with 2 blue balls, 3 pink balls, 2 yellow balls and 1 green ball. Every time he chooses a ball, he will replace it. Find each of the probabilities of the below. Express as fractions in simplified form.

43. P(green, then pink) = _____

44. P(pink then green) = _____

45. P(two blues) = _____

46. P(two greens) = _____

47. P(blue then yellow) = _____

48. P(yellow then pink) = _____

49. P(two yellows) = _____

50. P(pink, yellow then blue) = _____

John has a bag of cubes. There are 2 blue cubes, 3 orange cubes, 2 yellow cubes and 1 green cube. Every time he chooses a cube, he will keep it aside. Find the probability of the below. Express the answers as fractions in simplest form.

51. P(green, then orange) = _____

52. P(blue then yellow) = _____

53. P(two blues) = _____

54. P(two yellows) = _____

55. P(orange then green) = _____

56. P(yellow then orange) = _____

57. P(two greens) = _____

58. P(orange, yellow then blue) = _____

Identify the below as independent or dependent events

59. rolling a number cube and spinning a four-part spinner

60. choosing a jellybean, eating it and then choosing another jellybean.

61. tossing two coins

62. picking a club or a heart from a set of cards, putting it back and then a picking a jack

63. spinning a four-part spinner and landing on a 2, then spinning again and landing on a 4.

64. A nationwide poll found that 3 of 5 voters planned to vote for John. Jack and Mary voted. What is the probability that both voted for John?

65. Lola rolled a 6-sided die and flip a coin. What is the probability of getting an even number on the die and heads on the coin?

66. A jar of jellybeans has 6 blue, 2 orange, and 8 red jellybeans. Olivia choose 1 jellybean, eat it, and then choose another. What is the probability that you choose 2 blue jellybeans?

67. Tara the Magical Tarot Reader has picked two cards from her standard deck of playing cards. What is the probability that both cards she chose will be a club?

68. A bag contains 3 pennies, 2 nickels, and 4 dimes.If you select 3 coins, without replacing them, what is the probability that Tom will pick 3 pennies in a row?

                   www.math-knots.com | www.a4ace.com

A number cube is rolled and the spinner spun. Find the probability for each of the below

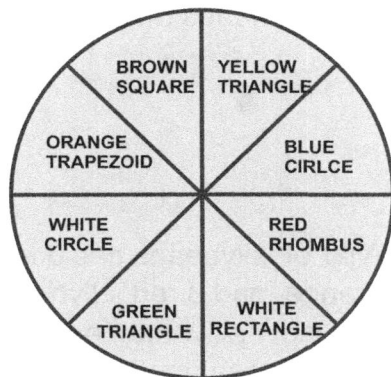

69. P(green triangle) = _____

70. P(a quadrilateral) = _____

71. P(an odd number) = _____

72. P(a circle and a parallelogram) = _____

There are 10 yellow marbles, 1 blue marble, 7 white marbles and 6 red marbles in a bag. Once a marble is drawn, it is not replaced. Find the probability of each outcome.

73. P(a blue then a white marble)

74. P(a red then a yellow marble)

75. P(two green marbles in a row)

76. P(a blue then a red marble)

77) Bella has colored cards that are the same size and shape. The probability of randomly selecting a blue card is 20%. The probability of randomly selecting a gold card is 30%. What is the probability Stella will randomly select a card that is not blue, replace it, then randomly select a card that is gold?

78) Lilly has 6 blue clips, 9 gold clips and 10 orange clips that are the same size and shape. What is the probability that Lilly will randomly select an orange clip, not replace it, then randomly select a blue clip?

79) A box contains 16 new batteries and 4 used batteries. Each battery is the same size and shape. Oliver will randomly select 2 batteries from the box without replacement. What is the probability Oliver will select two new batteries?

80) Two fair coins are flipped at the same time. What is the probability that both display tails?

81) The circle graph shows the probability of drawing different colored marbles out of a bag. What is the probability that a blue marble is selected, replaced and then a green marble is selected ?

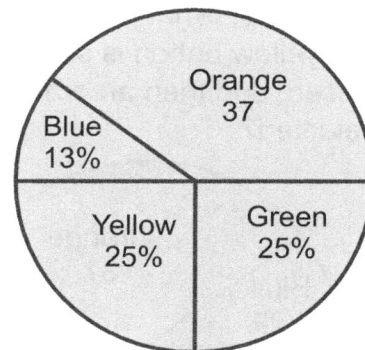

82) Zara has a bag of same-sized animal cookies. There are 9 star cookies, 5 square cookies, 3 round cookies and 9 moon cookies. Zara chooses two cookies random, what is the probability that Zara chooses a round first, eats it and then selects a cookie that is not a moon?

www.math-knots.com | www.a4ace.com

83) A coin is flipped three times. What is the probability that it lands on tails all three times?

A standard deck of 52 cards has 4 suits: hearts, diamonds, spades clubs. Each suit has 13 cards. Write each probability as a fraction in simplest form.

86) What is the probability of drawing a king from a deck of cards, putting it back in the deck, shuffling the deck, and then drawing a queen?

84) A circle graph shows the probability of drawing different color buttons out of a bag. What is the probability that a yellow button is selected, replaced, and then an orange button is selected?

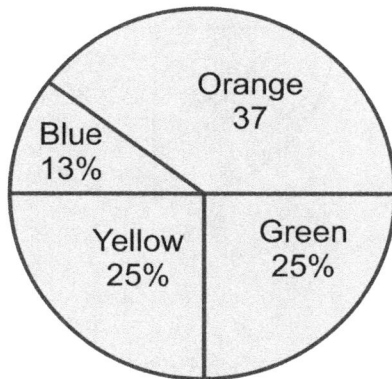

87) What is the probability of drawing a king from a deck of cards, putting it back in the deck, shuffling the deck, and then drawing a jack?

85) There are 3 red chips and 5 white chips in a bag. If 2 chips are drawn, without replacement, what is the probability that both chips will be white?

88) What is the probability of drawing a black card from a deck of cards, putting it aside, and then drawing a red card?

89) What is the probability of flipping heads on a coin and then flipping tails?

90) Mary has a bag of 10 marbles. Four are red and six are blue. What is the probability of drawing a blue marble, putting it aside, and then drawing a red marble?

91) Violet has a bag of 10 marbles. Four are red and six are blue. What is the probability of drawing a red marble, putting it aside, and then drawing a red marble?

92) What is the probability of drawing the queen of hearts from a deck of cards, putting it back in the deck, shufling the deck, and then drawing the same card again?

93) What is the probability of drawing a king from a deck of cards, putting it aside and then drawing another king?

94) What is the probability of rolling a 3 on a number cube and then flipping heads on a coin?

95) Each letter in the word MATH is written on a card and put into a bag. What is the probability of drawing the A, putting it aside, and then drawing the H?

96) Henry has a bag of 10 marbles. Four are red and six are blue. What is the probability of drawing a red marble, putting it aside, and then drawing another red marble?

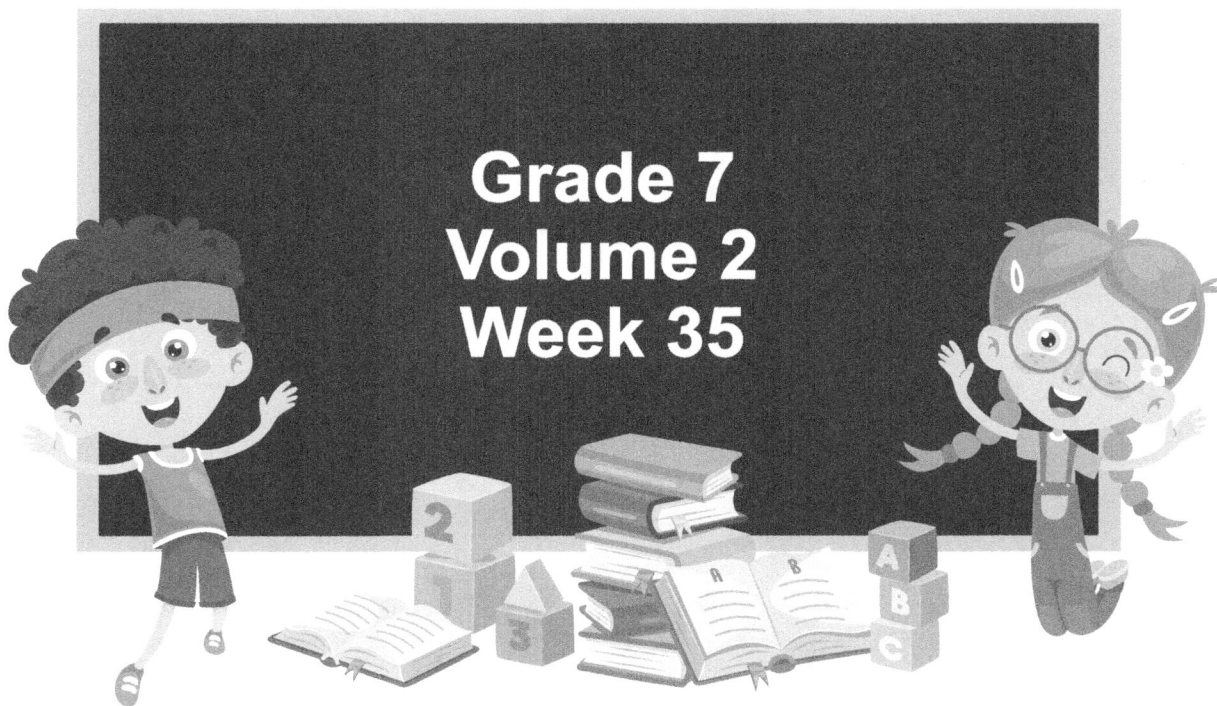

Grade 7
Volume 2
Week 35

| 45 , 90 , 36 , 45 , 36 , 45 , 91 , 34 , 54 |

1. Find the Range for the above data

2. Find the Mode for the above data

| 105 , 21 , 22 , 80 , 45 , 20 , 90 , 54 , 22 |

3. Find the Range for the above data

4. Find the Mode for the above data

| 76 , 65 , 68 , 72 , 43 , 68 , 65 , 68 , 56 |

5. Find the Range for the above data

6. Find the Mode for the above data

| 120 , 60 , 40 , 90 , 40 , 60 , 110 , 80 , 60 |

7. Find the Range for the above data

8. Find the Mode for the above data

| 35 , 45 , 63 , 74 , 19 , 29 , 95 , 63 , 62 |

9. Find the Range for the above data

10. Find the Mode for the above data

| 91 , 99 , 110 , 85 , 91 , 84 , 6 , 91 , 99 |

11. Find the Range for the above data

12. Find the Mode for the above data

| 48 , 36 , 25 , 45 , 8 , 40 , 45 , 46 , 50 | | 30 , 48 , 24 , 48 , 24 , 35 , 24 |

13. Find the Range for the above data

19. Find the Range for the above data

14. Find the Mode for the above data

20. Find the Mode for the above data

| 18 , 19 , 20 , 18 , 17 , 13 , 17 , 16 , 18 , 11 | | 14 , 28 , 30 , 28 , 25 , 16 , 19 |

15. Find the Range for the above data

21. Find the Range for the above data

16. Find the Mode for the above data

22. Find the Mode for the above data

| 54 , 84 , 90 , 70 , 56 , 70 , 78 , 80 | | 12 , 15 , 10 , 18 , 19 , 21 , 12 |

23. Find the Range for the above data

17. Find the Range for the above data

24. Find the Median for the above data

18. Find the Mode for the above data

25. Find the Mode for the above data

www.math-knots.com | www.a4ace.com

| 21 , 24 , 19 , 19 , 21 , 24 , 19 |

26. Find the Range for the above data

27. Find the Median for the above data

28. Find the Mode for the above data

| 25 , 30 , 35 , 23 , 23 , 27 , 23 |

29. Find the Range for the above data

30. Find the Median for the above data

31. Find the Mode for the above data

| 18 , 16 , 20 , 14 , 12 , 18 |

32. Find the Range for the above data

33. Find the Median for the above data

34. Find the Mode for the above data

| 44 , 40 , 44 , 38 , 40 , 44 |

35. Find the Range for the above data

36. Find the Median for the above data

37. Find the Mode for the above data

| 13, 14, 12, 12, 14, 9, 12 |

38. Find the Range for the above data

39. Find the Median for the above data

40. Find the Mode for the above data

| 15 , 20 , 15 , 18 , 17 , 19 , 15 |

41. Find the Range for the above data

42. Find the Median for the above data

43. Find the Mode for the above data

355   www.math-knots.com | www.a4ace.com

11 , 15 , 9 , 15 , 16 , 17 , 11 , 9 , 9

44. Find the Range for the above data

45. Find the Median for the above data

46. Find the Mode for the above data

Bella has 24 yellow candies, 20 blue candies, 18 green candies, 24 purple candies, 16 red candies and 15 orange candies.

47. Find the Range for the above data

48. Find the Median for the above data

49. Find the Mode for the above data

Lola sold the following ice cream flavors: 36 strawberry, 38 chocolate, 40 vanilla, 30 mango, 34 caramel, 40 green tea.

50. Find the Range for the above data

51. Find the Median for the above data

52. Find the Mode for the above data

53. Beth received a score of 97, 90, 95 on her first three math exams. Find her average score.

54. The school listed the number of students from Grade 1 to Grade 5: 36, 50, 44, 30 and 40 . Find the mean number of students in each grade.

55. The coffee shop recorded the number of cups they sold each day for 1 week: 15, 18, 17, 16, 20, 35, 40. Find the average of the number of cups of coffee sold each day.

15 , 14 , 10

56. Find the Mean for the above data

www.math-knots.com | www.a4ace.com

7 , 18 , 9 , 11 , 12 , 15

57. Find the Mean for the above data

24 , 10 , 20 , 17 , 18 , 19

58. Find the Mean for the above data

14 , 9 , 21 , 18 , 18

59. Find the Mean for the above data

33 , 34 , 40 , 45

60. Find the Mean for the above data

1 , 3 , 4 , 5 , 6 , 8 , 9 , 10 , 4 , 8

61. Find the Mean for the above data

Class interval	10-15	15-20	20-25	25-30	30-35
Frequency	5	15	10	3	7

62. The upper limit in the third class interval is

A) 15   B) 20

C) 25   D) 30

63) The size of the class interval for the above distribution is

A) 10   B) 5

C) 20   D) 25

64) Which class interval has the highest frequency?

A) 10–15   B) 20–25

C) 15–20   D) 30–35

357

65) The arithmetic mean of 13 observations is calculated as 43. But, this is because the observation 87 is misread as 35. The correct mean is

A) 35

B) 47

C) 49

D) 52

66) If the mode of observations 4, 3, 2, 5, 2, 1, 2 and x is x, then find their mean.

A) 2.5

B) 2.625

C) 2.750

D) 2.225

67) The mean marks obtained in mathematics, physical science and social studies in a class of certain strength is 70, 65 and 75 respectively. The total marks scored by all the students in the above subjects is 7350. Find the strength of the class.

A) 35

B) 40

C) 45

D) 50

68) Which of the following values can be the median of the series 5, 12, 13, 14, x, 18 and 6?

A) 6

B) 14

C) 12.5

D) 18

69) The price of an article increases every year by 10%. Find the mean percentage increase per year in the price of the article for the next two years.

A) 10

B) 11

C) 10.5

D) None of these

70) On an average, there are 100 A.T.Ms per district in a state which has 15 districts. If all the 420 A.T.Ms located in 3 districts are closed down, then find the mean (average number) of the A.T.Ms in the remaining districts.

A) 95

B) 90

C) 98

D) 80

71) The mean of n observations is 25. If 2 is subtracted from each observation and the resulting numbers are each multiplied by 10, then the mean of the new observations is

A) 230

B) 248

C) 250

D) 238

72) The mean of x observations is 10 and that of y observations is 60. If the total number of observations is 25, and their combined mean is 30, then find the values of x and y.

A) x = 15, y = 10

B) x = 10, y = 15

C) x = 12, y = 13

D) None of these

73) In a three-digit number, the hundreds digit is x, tens digit is 2x and units digit is 3x. The mean of the digits can be

A) 2

B) 4

C) 6

D) None of these

74) The median of 20 observations is 53. If the first two observations and the last two observations are excluded, then the median of the observations is

A) 35

B) 53

C) 46

D) 59

75) The arithmetic mean of 12 observations is 25. The arithmetic mean remains unaltered, even after including one more observation. Find the included observation

A) 25

B) 30

C) 18

D) 36

76) The lowest score and the range of a frequency distribution are 3.9 and 2.1 respectively. Find the highest score.

A) 3.9

B) 6

C) 2.1

D) 1.8

77) For the below distribution, if mean is 12, then find p.

f	2	4	6	8
x	3	1.5	p	4.5

A) 24

B) 28

C) 32

D) 36

78) The arithmetic mean of the first five observations is 16 and that of next three observations is 8. Find the arithmetic mean of all the eight observations.

A) 10

B) 11

C) 12

D) 13

79) A set of numbers contain four 5's, six 4's, five 7's, four 8's and three 9's. What is the mode of the set of numbers?

A) 7

B) 4

C) 8

D) 9

80) The median of prime numbers from 1 to 50 is

   A) 17

   B) 19

   C) 23

   D) 29

81) The median of first 10 composite numbers is

   A) 10

   B) 11

   C) 12

   D) 13

82) The range of the data 10, 9, 20, 15, 19, 7, 22, 16, 15 and 19 is

   A) 20

   B) 15

   C) 19

   D) 13

83) The arithmetic mean of 10 observations is 20. If 5 is added to each observation, then the arithmetic mean of the new set of observations is

   A) 20

   B) 25

   C) 15

   D) 30

84) If the arithmetic mean of the observations 240, 233, 250, 289, 248 is 252, then the arithmetic mean of the observations 699, 867, 750, 744, 720 is

   A) 672

   B) 254

   C) 756

   D) 867

85) If the arithmetic mean and median of a distribution are 20 and 30 respectively, then its mode is

   A) 50

   B) 60

   C) 40

   D) 10

86) The median of 9 observations is 21. If the observations 18 and 26 are included, then the median of new observations is

   A) 21

   B) 18

   C) 26

   D) Cannot be determined

87) The mode of a distribution is 7. If each observation is increased by 7, then the mode of the new distribution is

   A) 0

   B) 7

   C) 14

   D) 1

www.math-knots.com | www.a4ace.com

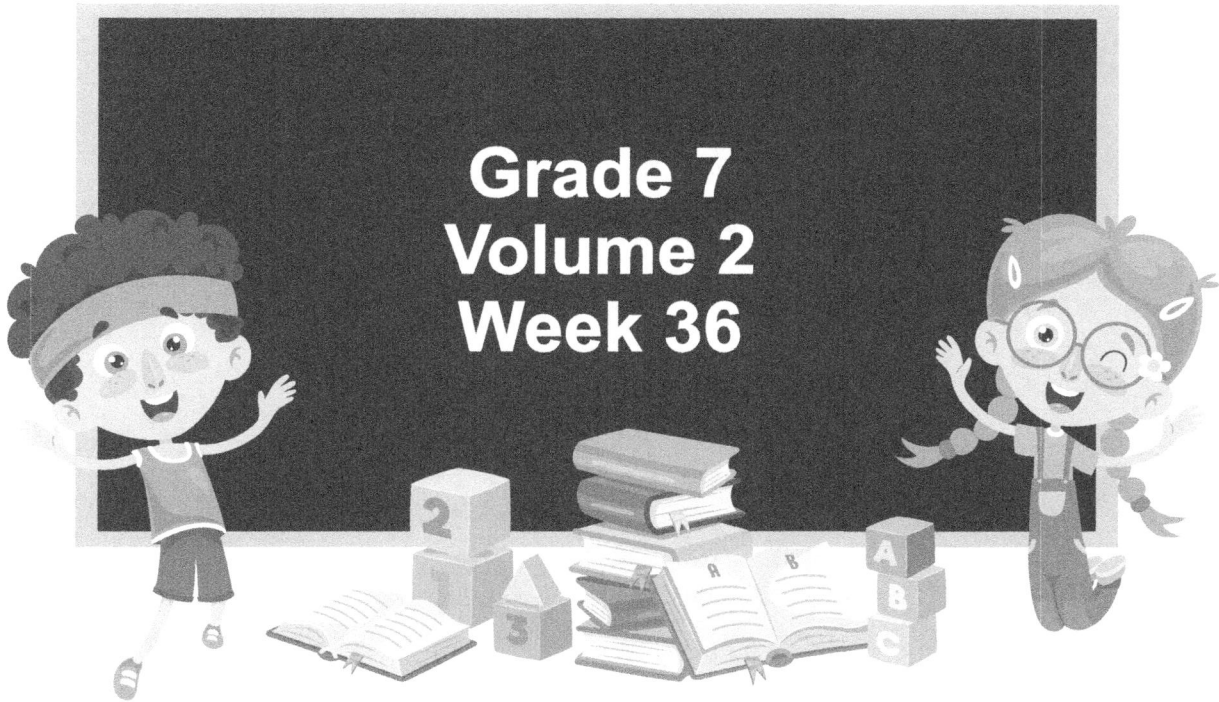

Grade 7
Volume 2
Week 36

www.math-knots.com | www.a4ace.com

1) Draw a box and whisker plot for the below data set

30	45.1	28.6	38.9	34.7
27.9	25	33.6	38.4	25
23.6	20.8	32.6	45.8	28.5
36				

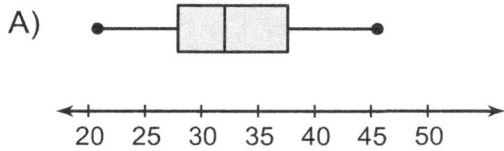

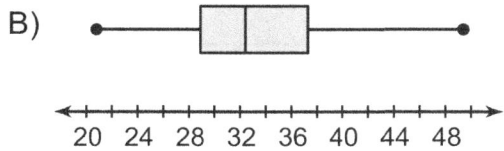

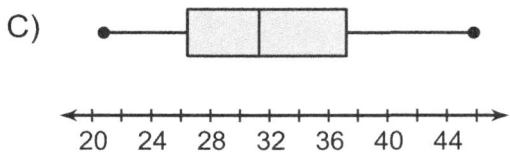

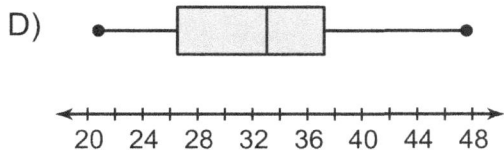

A)

B)

C)

D)

2) Draw a box and whisker plot for the below data set

5	5	4	6	7	5	6	7
7	7	7	4	4	6	4	

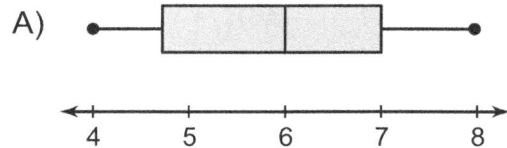

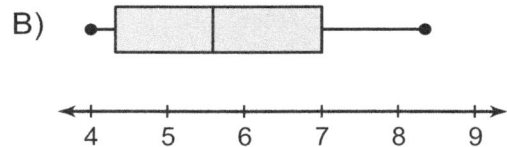

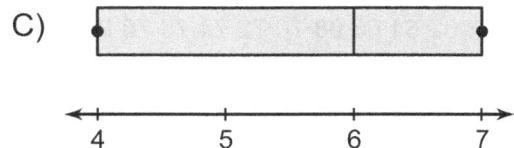

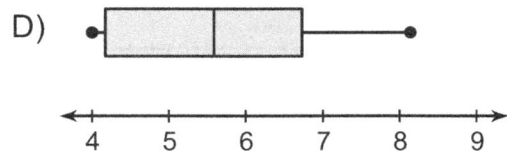

A)

B)

C)

D)

3) Draw a box and whisker plot for the below data set

73	70	73	69	69	74	67
65	73	70	67	62	79	73
77	69	71				

A)

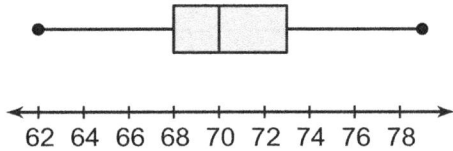

```
62 64 66 68 70 72 74 76 78
```

B)

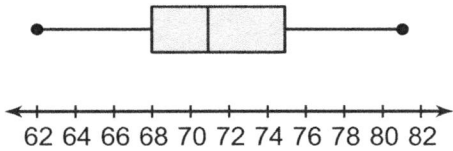

```
62 64 66 68 70 72 74 76 78 80 82
```

C)

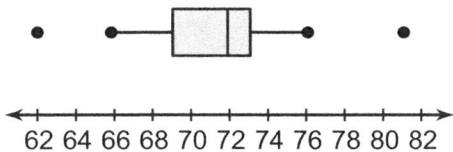

```
62 64 66 68 70 72 74 76 78 80 82
```

D)

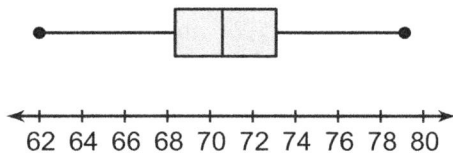

```
62 64 66 68 70 72 74 76 78 80
```

4) Draw a box and whisker plot for the below data set

177	186	178	178	177	181
180	178	176	173	183	174
170	179	175			

A)

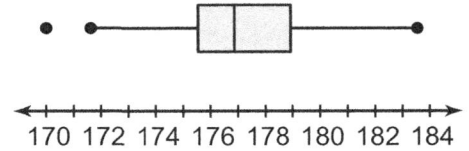

```
170 172 174 176 178 180 182 184
```

B)

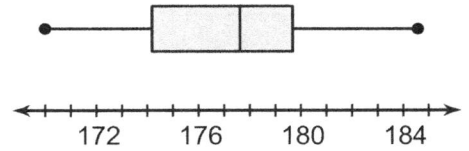

```
172    176    180    184
```

C)

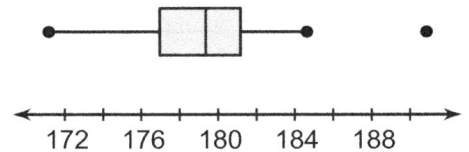

```
172    176    180    184    188
```

D)

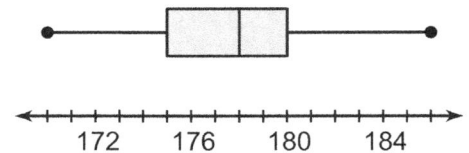

```
172    176    180    184
```

5) Draw a box and whisker plot for the below data set

50	46	49	52	41	45	56
44	50	38	44	55	44	51
40	50	39				

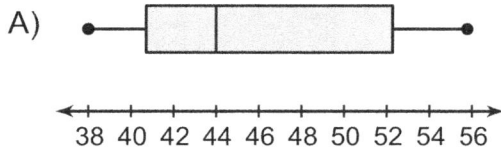

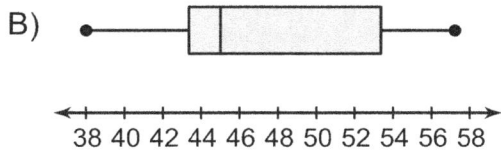

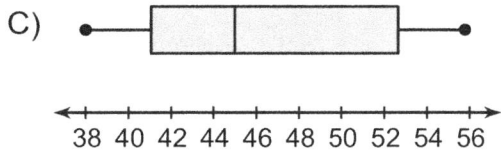

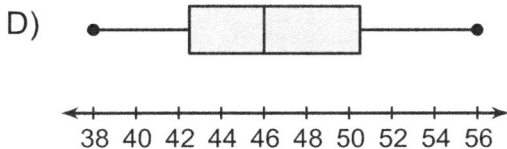

A)

38 40 42 44 46 48 50 52 54 56

B)

38 40 42 44 46 48 50 52 54 56 58

C)

38 40 42 44 46 48 50 52 54 56

D)

38 40 42 44 46 48 50 52 54 56

6) Draw a box and whisker plot for the below data set

39	37	52	42	49	40	36
51	48	52	54	50	56	50
47	47	50				

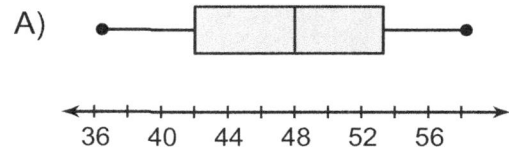

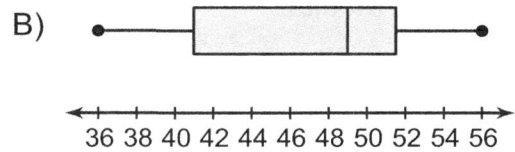

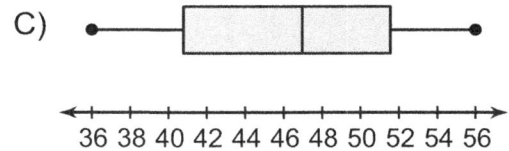

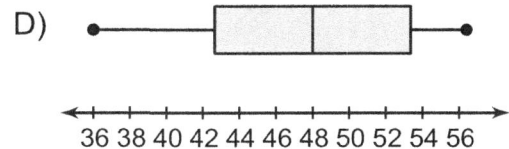

A)

36   40   44   48   52   56

B)

36 38 40 42 44 46 48 50 52 54 56

C)

36 38 40 42 44 46 48 50 52 54 56

D)

36 38 40 42 44 46 48 50 52 54 56

28.2	40.4	24.7	33	20.1
33.5	48	34.9	22.2	37
39.9	28.6	25.9	30.3	32.1
34.9				

34,800	17,900	12,550	7,750
26,400	13,650	11,950	9,950
17,400	14,600	9,800	40,950
17,900	6,500	22,150	

Based on the above data answer the questions 7 - 13

Based on the above data answer the questions 14 - 20

7) Find the mode

8) Find the median

9) Find the mean

10) Find the range

11) Find the lower quartile

12) Find the upper quartile

13) Find the inter quartile range

14) Find the mode

15) Find the median

16) Find the mean

17) Find the range

18) Find the lower quartile

19) Find the upper quartile

20) Find the inter quartile range

| 5 | 6 | 7 | 4 | 7 | 4 | 7 | 7 |
| 7 | 6 | 7 | 4 | 7 | 5 | 5 | 7 |

Based on the above data answer the questions 21 - 27

8.5	10	8	12	7.5	10	7
8	10	8	7.5	8.5	8	7
6	8	8				

Based on the above data answer the questions 28 - 34

21) Find the mode

22) Find the median

23) Find the mean

24) Find the range

25) Find the lower quartile

26) Find the upper quartile

27) Find the inter quartile range

28) Find the mode

29) Find the median

30) Find the mean

31) Find the range

32) Find the lower quartile

33) Find the upper quartile

34) Find the inter quartile range

9	6.5	8	7	8.5	6.5
5.5	8	7	5.5	6.5	8
8	6	4.5	8.5		

Based on the above data answer the questions 35 - 41

Percent	Frequency
0	3
4	2
4.23	1
4.7	1
5.6	1
6	4
6.25	2
7	2

Based on the above data answer the questions 42 - 48

35) Find the mode

36) Find the median

37) Find the mean

38) Find the range

39) Find the lower quartile

40) Find the upper quartile

41) Find the inter quartile range

42) Find the mode

43) Find the median

44) Find the mean

45) Find the range

46) Find the lower quartile

47) Find the upper quartile

48) Find the inter quartile range

www.math-knots.com | www.a4ace.com

Age	Frequency
11	1
13	4
14	2
16	1
17	2
18	1
19	3
20	3

Based on the above data answer the questions 49 - 55

49) Find the mode

50) Find the median

51) Find the mean

52) Find the range

53) Find the lower quartile

54) Find the upper quartile

55) Find the inter quartile range

Goals	Frequency
3	5
5	6
6	2
7	3

Based on the above data answer the questions 56 - 62

56) Find the mode

57) Find the median

58) Find the mean

59) Find the range

60) Find the lower quartile

61) Find the upper quartile

62) Find the inter quartile range

# Awards	Frequency
2	1
3	3
4	3
5	5
6	1
7	1
8	3

Based on the above data answer the questions 63 - 79

63) Find the mode

64) Find the median

65) Find the mean

66) Find the range

67) Find the lower quartile

68) Find the upper quartile

69) Find the inter quartile range

70) Draw a box and whisper plot for the below given data

30,810	65,020	51,570	63,060
63,130	45,370	39,960	27,820
52,280	49,230	26,030	42,190
50,260	29,420	55,150	

71) Draw a box and whisper plot for the below given data

124	112	62	56	82	156
92	73	149	126	89	91
155	91	96	140	134	

72) Draw a box and whisper plot for the below given data

11	7	12	7	5	2	9	3
15	3	13	2	12	8	2	

73) Draw a box and whisper plot for the below given data

53	41	33	57	39	40	54
55	50	44	45	38	38	52
48						

www.math-knots.com | www.a4ace.com

74) Draw a box and whisper plot for the below given data

28.8	23.6	27.6	5	17.2
35	15.2	46.6	20	69.6
12.2	27.6	14.6	28.2	12.2

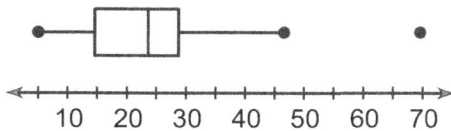

77) Draw a box and whisper plot for the below given data

38	46	48	52	43	50	53
47	52	51	53	56	46	51
48	46	47				

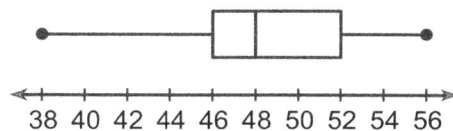

75) Draw a box and whisper plot for the below given data

76,200	52,350	51,250	66,760
54,810	75,170	55,300	56,210
86,100	80,370	41,280	57,630
56,350	53,220	52,270	

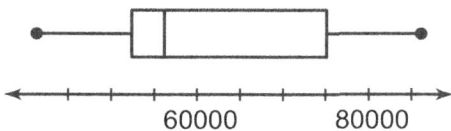

78) Draw a box and whisper plot for the below given data

75,230	49,220	53,190	55,930
72,020	51,520	45,050	38,090
35,180	43,520	40,650	45,730
34,050	41,530	60,800	

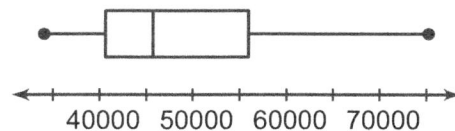

76) Draw a box and whisper plot for the below given data

24,400	11,800	20,100	38,800
35,050	27,550	27,150	11,050
19,150	18,850	13,800	19,700
36,050	17,950	24,150	18,850
36,750			

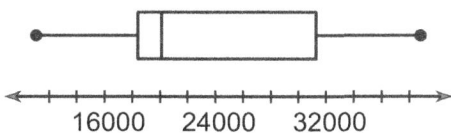

79) Draw a box and whisper plot for the below given data

430,100	427,200	424,700	437,400
410,200	415,800	423,800	414,100
402,600	430,000	423,200	409,100
420,200	398,300	398,300	

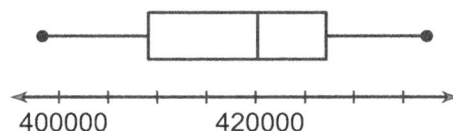

www.math-knots.com | www.a4ace.com

6	9	4	4	12	3	4	3
7	7	8	12	13	6	3	3

43	43	52	52	43	50	51
46	46	49	41	44	44	42
53	49					

Based on the above data answer the questions 80 - 86

Based on the above data answer the questions 87 - 93

80) Find the mode

87) Find the mode

81) Find the median

88) Find the median

82) Find the mean

89) Find the mean

83) Find the range

90) Find the range

84) Find the lower quartile

91) Find the lower quartile

85) Find the upper quartile

92) Find the upper quartile

86) Find the inter quartile range

93) Find the inter quartile range

www.math-knots.com | www.a4ace.com

69	45	133	124	49	109
116	118	155	145	70	66
41	80	124	58		

Based on the above data answer the questions 94 - 100

94) Find the mode

95) Find the median

96) Find the mean

97) Find the range

98) Find the lower quartile

99) Find the upper quartile

100) Find the inter quartile range

8	15	8	5	6	5	2
18	20	9	8	14	5	6
6	8					

Based on the above data answer the questions 101 - 107

101) Find the mode

102) Find the median

103) Find the mean

104) Find the range

105) Find the lower quartile

106) Find the upper quartile

107) Find the inter quartile range

| 3 | 4 | 5 | 1 | 2 | 2 | 2 | 2 |
| 3 | 6 | 2 | 5 | 3 | 4 | 3 | 2 |

Based on the above data answer the questions 108 - 114

108) Find the mode

109) Find the median

110) Find the mean

111) Find the range

112) Find the lower quartile

113) Find the upper quartile

114) Find the inter quartile range

| 2 | 4 | 2 | 3 | 4 | 2 | 2 | 3 |
| 4 | 2 | 1 | 1 | 2 | 3 | 1 | 4 |

Based on the above data answer the questions 115 - 121

115) Find the mode

116) Find the median

117) Find the mean

118) Find the range

119) Find the lower quartile

120) Find the upper quartile

121) Find the inter quartile range

17	14	17	16	17	15	13
13	18	22	18	18	16	14
15						

Based on the above data answer the questions 122 - 128

122) Find the mode

123) Find the median

124) Find the mean

125) Find the range

126) Find the lower quartile

127) Find the upper quartile

128) Find the inter quartile range

1,290	1,650	1,730	1,075	1,525
1,500	1,055	1,525	1,655	1,360
1,450	1,625	1,485	1,035	900
1,675				

Based on the above data answer the questions 129 - 135

129) Find the mode

130) Find the median

131) Find the mean

132) Find the range

133) Find the lower quartile

134) Find the upper quartile

135) Find the inter quartile range

| 6 | 2 | 3 | 3 | 3 | 3 | 2 | 3 |
| 2 | 5 | 2 | 2 | 3 | 1 | 5 | 1 |

Based on the above data answer the
questions 136 - 142

136) Find the mode

137) Find the median

138) Find the mean

139) Find the range

140) Find the lower quartile

141) Find the upper quartile

142) Find the inter quartile range

13	15	17	21	21	13	19
22	15	17	15	21	16	16
15	14					

Based on the above data answer the
questions 143 - 149

143) Find the mode

144) Find the median

145) Find the mean

146) Find the range

147) Find the lower quartile

148) Find the upper quartile

149) Find the inter quartile range

5	4	6	7	7	7	6	7
6	7	5	7	7	7	6	7
5							

Based on the above data answer the
questions 150 - 156

150) Find the mode

151) Find the median

152) Find the mean

153) Find the range

154) Find the lower quartile

155) Find the upper quartile

156) Find the inter quartile range

72	77	75	69	66	64	68
75	74	75	61	73	73	75
69	72					

Based on the above data answer the
questions 157 - 163

157) Find the mode

158) Find the median

159) Find the mean

160) Find the range

161) Find the lower quartile

162) Find the upper quartile

163) Find the inter quartile range

7.5	8	7.5	7.5	8	7.5
10	6	10.5	8.5	9	7
9	10	10			

Based on the above data answer the
questions 164 - 170

45	43	43	45	40	52	56
53	52	52	54	48	50	50
50	52	49				

Based on the above data answer the
questions 171 - 177

164) Find the mode

171) Find the mode

165) Find the median

172) Find the median

166) Find the mean

173) Find the mean

167) Find the range

174) Find the range

168) Find the lower quartile

175) Find the lower quartile

169) Find the upper quartile

176) Find the upper quartile

170) Find the inter quartile range

177) Find the inter quartile range

70	63	66	75	70	73	76
69	64	71	75	70	72	60
79	67					

6	7	4	6	6	7	7	5
7	5	7	6	5	4	7	6
6							

Based on the above data answer the
questions 178 - 184

Based on the above data answer the
questions 185 - 191

178) Find the mode

185) Find the mode

179) Find the median

186) Find the median

180) Find the mean

187) Find the mean

181) Find the range

188) Find the range

182) Find the lower quartile

189) Find the lower quartile

183) Find the upper quartile

190) Find the upper quartile

184) Find the inter quartile range

191) Find the inter quartile range

www.math-knots.com | www.a4ace.com

176	173	179	177	177	178
177	169	182	179	174	179
179	173	178	180		

4	6	5	7	7	4	7	6
7	6	7	7	6	4	7	

Based on the above data answer the questions 192 - 198

Based on the above data answer the questions 199 - 205

192) Find the mode

199) Find the mode

193) Find the median

200) Find the median

194) Find the mean

201) Find the mean

195) Find the range

202) Find the range

196) Find the lower quartile

203) Find the lower quartile

197) Find the upper quartile

204) Find the upper quartile

198) Find the inter quartile range

205) Find the inter quartile range

www.math-knots.com | www.a4ace.com

7.75	7	8.25	6	7.25	6
6	7.75	8.5	9.25	7	7
7.25	8	6.5	8.5	9	

Based on the above data answer the
questions 206 - 212

206) Find the mode

207) Find the median

208) Find the mean

209) Find the range

210) Find the lower quartile

211) Find the upper quartile

212) Find the inter quartile range

| 5 | 10 | 4 | 5 | 2 | 3 | 8 | 5 |
| 3 | 9 | 5 | 3 | 11 | 7 | 4 | 7 |

Based on the above data answer the
questions 213 - 219

213) Find the mode

214) Find the median

215) Find the mean

216) Find the range

217) Find the lower quartile

218) Find the upper quartile

219) Find the inter quartile range

www.math-knots.com | www.a4ace.com

6	3	7	3	10	5	3	5
8	9	7	5	5	7	5	3
5							

Based on the above data answer the
questions 220 - 226

220) Find the mode

221) Find the median

222) Find the mean

223) Find the range

224) Find the lower quartile

225) Find the upper quartile

226) Find the inter quartile range

7.5	10	9	6.5	7.5	9
9.5	8	5.5	6	9	6
9.5	7	9	8		

Based on the above data answer the
questions 227 - 233

227) Find the mode

228) Find the median

229) Find the mean

230) Find the range

231) Find the lower quartile

232) Find the upper quartile

233) Find the inter quartile range

10,950	6,800	9,700	15,050
21,200	18,450	8,050	26,850
8,750	18,950	27,350	18,800
8,750	6,950	21,750	12,300

Based on the above data answer the
questions 234 - 240

234) Find the mode

235) Find the median

236) Find the mean

237) Find the range

238) Find the lower quartile

239) Find the upper quartile

240) Find the inter quartile range

3	5	6	5	3	3	9	5
9	4	1	3	10	10	6	5
5							

Based on the above data answer the
questions 241 - 247

241) Find the mode

242) Find the median

243) Find the mean

244) Find the range

245) Find the lower quartile

246) Find the upper quartile

247) Find the inter quartile range

www.math-knots.com | www.a4ace.com

| 2 | 7 | 4 | 5 | 8 | 8 | 2 | 7 |
| 5 | 7 | 7 | 6 | 7 | 3 | 8 | |

| 8 | 6 | 6 | 11 | 5 | 6 | 9 | 5 |
| 3 | 6 | 5 | 5 | 9 | 5 | 4 | 7 |

Based on the above data answer the questions 248 - 254

Based on the above data answer the questions 255 - 261

248) Find the mode

255) Find the mode

249) Find the median

256) Find the median

250) Find the mean

257) Find the mean

251) Find the range

258) Find the range

252) Find the lower quartile

259) Find the lower quartile

253) Find the upper quartile

260) Find the upper quartile

254) Find the inter quartile range

261) Find the inter quartile range

www.math-knots.com | www.a4ace.com

7	7	5	4	5	4	5	6
4	5	6	7	6	7	7	7

Based on the above data answer the questions 262 - 268

5.5	5.75	6.25	7	7.75	7.5
6.5	7.5	6.75	5.75	6.5	7
6.5	7	7.25			

Based on the above data answer the questions 269 - 275

262) Find the mode

269) Find the mode

263) Find the median

270) Find the median

264) Find the mean

271) Find the mean

265) Find the range

272) Find the range

266) Find the lower quartile

273) Find the lower quartile

267) Find the upper quartile

274) Find the upper quartile

268) Find the inter quartile range

275) Find the inter quartile range

www.math-knots.com | www.a4ace.com

8.5	7	13	7	8	9	9
8.5	6	7	10	9	8	7.5
7.5	7					

Based on the above data answer the questions 276 - 282

276) Find the mode

277) Find the median

278) Find the mean

279) Find the range

280) Find the lower quartile

281) Find the upper quartile

282) Find the inter quartile range

46	55	50	53	43	50	57
46	51	39	42	58	37	44
45						

Based on the above data answer the questions 283 - 289

283) Find the mode

284) Find the median

285) Find the mean

286) Find the range

287) Find the lower quartile

288) Find the upper quartile

289) Find the inter quartile range

www.math-knots.com | www.a4ace.com

Size	Frequency
6	3
6.5	1
7.5	1
8	3
8.5	1
9	5
9.5	1
10	2

Based on the above data answer the
questions 290 - 296

290) Find the mode

291) Find the median

292) Find the mean

293) Find the range

294) Find the lower quartile

295) Find the upper quartile

296) Find the inter quartile range

Games	Frequency
4	4
5	3
6	2
7	7

Based on the above data answer the
questions 297 - 303

297) Find the mode

298) Find the median

299) Find the mean

300) Find the range

301) Find the lower quartile

302) Find the upper quartile

303) Find the inter quartile range

Age	Frequency
12	3
13	4
16	2
17	3
18	2
21	1
22	1

Based on the above data answer the questions 304 - 310

304) Find the mode

305) Find the median

306) Find the mean

307) Find the range

308) Find the lower quartile

309) Find the upper quartile

310) Find the inter quartile range

Age	Frequency
12	2
13	1
14	4
15	4
16	2
17	2
18	1
20	1

Based on the above data answer the questions 311 - 317

311) Find the mode

312) Find the median

313) Find the mean

314) Find the range

315) Find the lower quartile

316) Find the upper quartile

317) Find the inter quartile range

www.math-knots.com | www.a4ace.com

Percent	Frequency
4	2
5.125	1
5.5	2
6	4
6.25	1
6.35	1
6.5	2
7	2

Based on the above data answer the questions 318 - 324

318) Find the mode

319) Find the median

320) Find the mean

321) Find the range

322) Find the lower quartile

323) Find the upper quartile

324) Find the inter quartile range

Appearances	Frequency
1	3
2	4
3	1
4	2
7	1
8	3
9	1
17	1

Based on the above data answer the questions 325 - 331

325) Find the mode

326) Find the median

327) Find the mean

328) Find the range

329) Find the lower quartile

330) Find the upper quartile

331) Find the inter quartile range

www.math-knots.com | www.a4ace.com

Goals	Frequency
1	1
2	1
3	2
4	1
5	2
6	2
7	4
9	2
10	1
11	1

Based on the above data answer the questions 3332 - 338

332) Find the mode

333) Find the median

334) Find the mean

335) Find the range

336) Find the lower quartile

337) Find the upper quartile

338) Find the inter quartile range

Age	Frequency
13	3
14	1
15	3
16	4
17	2
18	3
20	1

Based on the above data answer the questions 339 - 345

339) Find the mode

340) Find the median

341) Find the mean

342) Find the range

343) Find the lower quartile

344) Find the upper quartile

345) Find the inter quartile range

# Words	Frequency
2	10
3	2
4	1
5	1
6	2

Based on the above data answer the questions 346 - 352

346) Find the mode

347) Find the median

348) Find the mean

349) Find the range

350) Find the lower quartile

351) Find the upper quartile

352) Find the inter quartile range

Games	Frequency
4	2
5	4
6	2
7	8

Based on the above data answer the questions 353 - 359

353) Find the mode

354) Find the median

355) Find the mean

356) Find the range

357) Find the lower quartile

358) Find the upper quartile

359) Find the inter quartile range

www.math-knots.com | www.a4ace.com

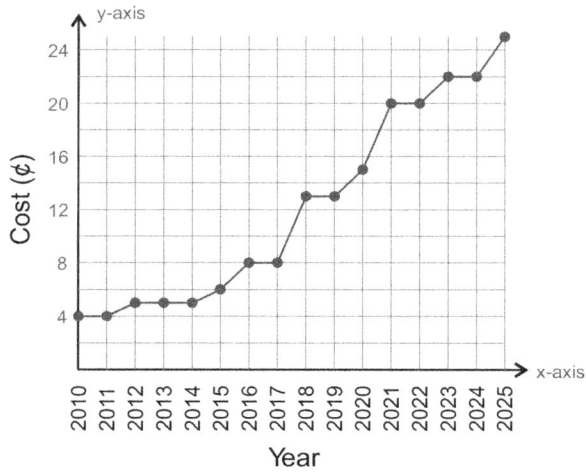

Based on the above data answer the questions 360 - 363

360) Find the mode

361) Find the median

362) Find the mean

363) Find the range

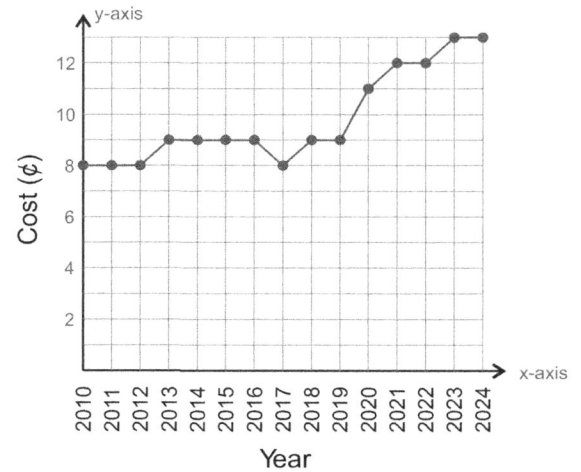

Based on the above data answer the questions 364 - 367

364) Find the mode

365) Find the median

366) Find the mean

367) Find the range

www.math-knots.com | www.a4ace.com

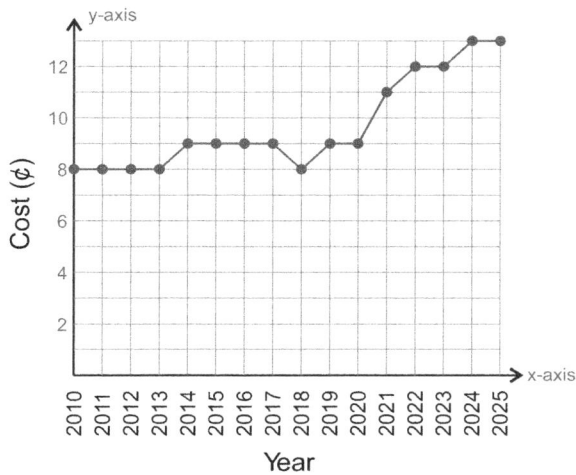

Based on the above data answer the questions 368 - 371

368) Find the mode

369) Find the median

370) Find the mean

371) Find the range

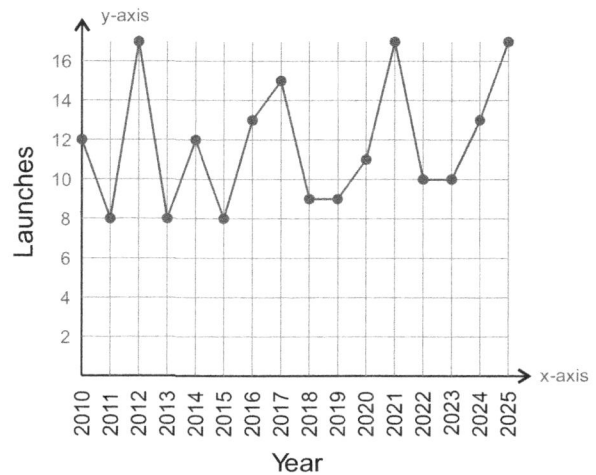

Based on the above data answer the questions 372 - 375

372) Find the mode

373) Find the median

374) Find the mean

375) Find the range

www.math-knots.com | www.a4ace.com

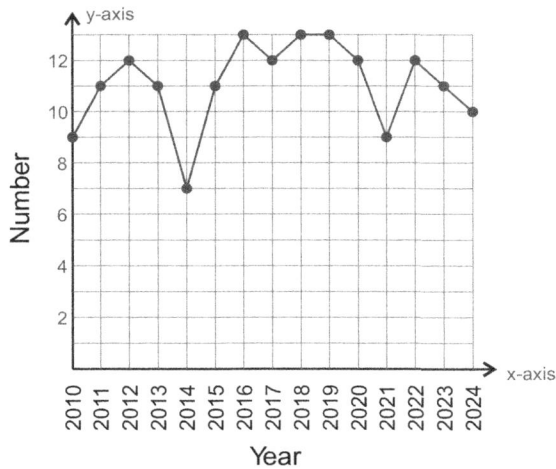

Based on the above data answer the questions 376 - 379

376) Find the mode

377) Find the median

378) Find the mean

379) Find the range

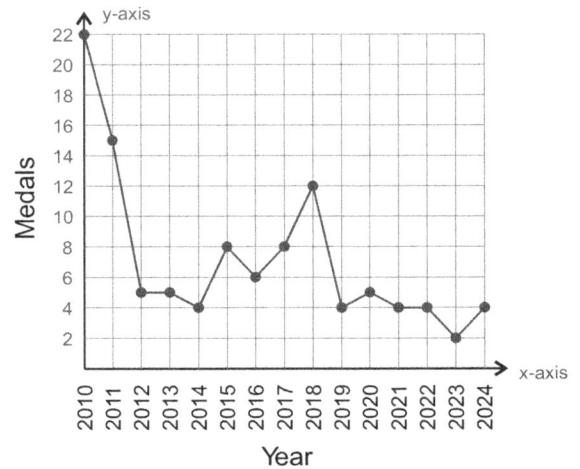

Based on the above data answer the questions 380 - 383

380) Find the mode

381) Find the median

382) Find the mean

383) Find the range

www.math-knots.com | www.a4ace.com

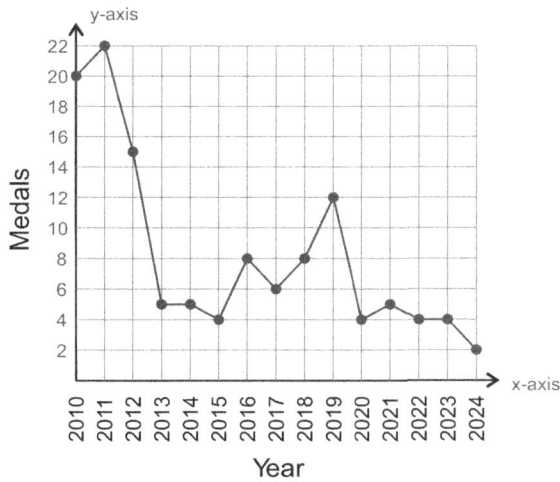

Based on the above data answer the
questions 384 - 387

384) Find the mode

385) Find the median

386) Find the mean

387) Find the range

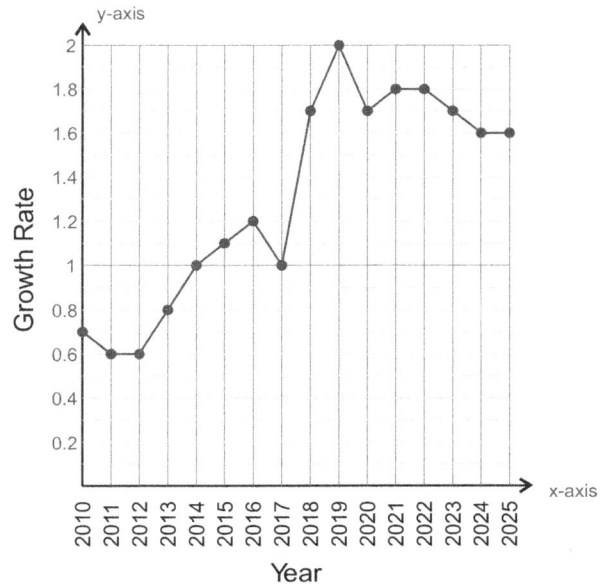

Based on the above data answer the
questions 388 - 391

388) Find the mode

389) Find the median

390) Find the mean

391) Find the range

Based on the above data answer the
questions 392 - 395

392) Find the mode

393) Find the median

394) Find the mean

395) Find the range

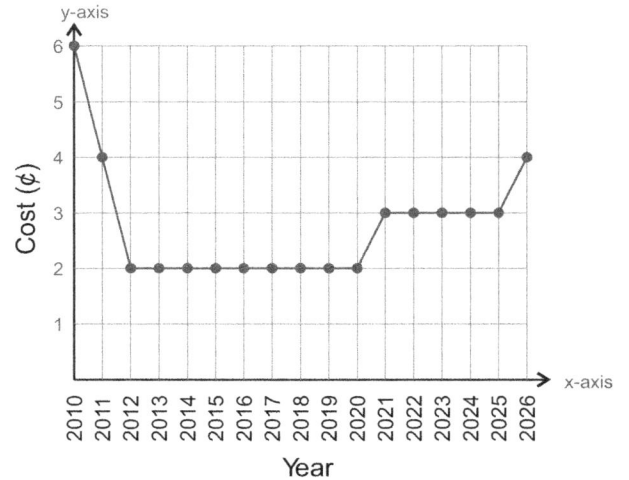

Based on the above data answer the
questions 396 - 399

396) Find the mode

397) Find the median

398) Find the mean

399) Find the range

2018

www.math-knots.com | www.a4ace.com

Grade 7
Volume 2
Answer Keys

	Week 19		Week 19		Week 19		Week 19		Week 19
1.	43	30.	-40	59.	-26	88.	4	117.	9
2.	16	31.	-48	60.	-29	89.	-46	118.	-14
3.	16	32.	-40	61.	-22	90.	-4	119.	1269
4.	23	33.	-7	62.	-14	91.	43	120.	888
5.	8	34.	-29	63.	20	92.	-529	121.	-31
6.	39	35.	-28	64.	-15	93.	230	122.	8
7.	-48	36.	-37	65.	27	94.	-40	123.	30
8.	-29	37.	46	66.	-23	95.	-38	124.	224
9.	-23	38.	-21	67.	9	96.	-1410	125.	-18
10.	17	39.	-25	68.	28	97.	-46	126.	-12
11.	-21	40.	42	69.	-22	98.	-35	127.	-46
12.	-46	41.	-43	70.	34	99.	41	128.	496
13.	-5	42.	47	71.	29	100.	-50	129.	1020
14.	-50	43.	-38	72.	5	101.	-1056	130.	29
15.	46	44.	-50	73.	48	102.	1620	131.	49
16.	16	45.	-18	74.	-5	103.	615	132.	-210
17.	8	46.	-37	75.	0	104.	-429	133.	40
18.	-14	47.	20	76.	-24	105.	47	134.	-35
19.	-34	48.	50	77.	21	106.	1554	135.	16
20.	38	49.	-18	78.	-43	107.	576	136.	-39
21.	-31	50.	48	79.	-25	108.	25	137.	-17
22.	27	51.	43	80.	14	109.	1296	138.	-16
23.	-45	52.	7	81.	28	110.	-4	139.	34,34
24.	34	53.	-40	82.	48	111.	-8	140.	5,-5
25.	-18	54.	-7	83.	-1020	112.	-1794	141.	2
26.	12	55.	16	84.	-47	113.	-30	142.	-225
27.	-17	56.	28	85.	32	114.	1131	143.	19,-19
28.	16	57.	1	86.	-486	115.	-2	144.	10,-10
29.	37	58.	31	87.	-70	116.	598	145.	28,-28

www.math-knots.com | www.a4ace.com

Week 19		**Week 20**

Week 19

146. 13,-13

147. 3,-3

148. 15,-15

149. 16,-16

150. 12,-12

151. 8,-8

152. 6,-6

153. 14,-14

154. 31,-31

155. 4,-4

156. 36,-36

157. 25,-25

158. 6,-6

159. 16,-16

160. 7,-7

161. 18,-18

162. 96,-96

163. 17,-17

164. 1,-1

165. 8,-8

166. 10,-10

167. 17,-17

168. 18,-18

169. 12,-12

170. 170,-170

Week 20

1.

2.

3.

4.

5.

6.

7.

8.

9.

10.

www.math-knots.com | www.a4ace.com

Grade 7

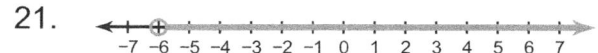
Vol 2
Answer
Key

Week 20

Week 20

11.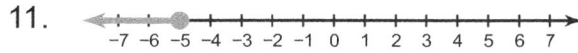

12.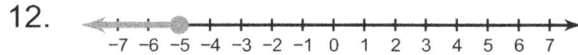

13.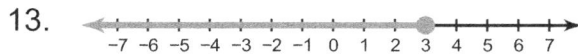

14.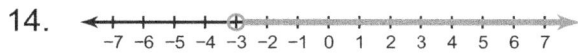

15.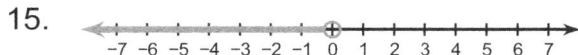

16.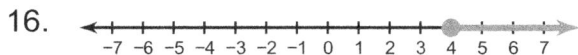

17.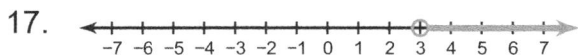

18.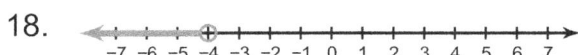

19.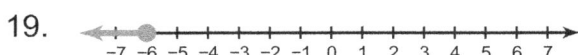

20.

21.

22.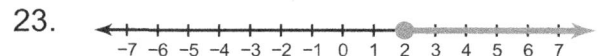

23.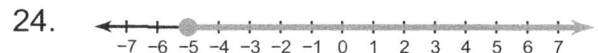

24.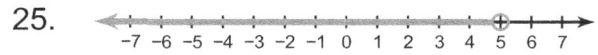

25.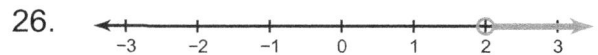

26.

27.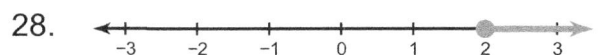

28.

29.

30.

www.math-knots.com | www.a4ace.com

Week 20

Week 20

31.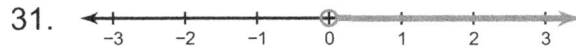

41.

32.

42.

33.

43.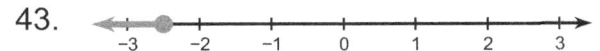

44. D

34.

45.

35.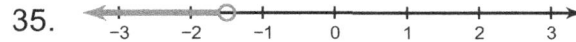

46.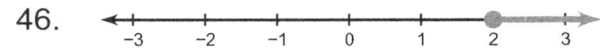

36.

47. D

48. A

49. B

37.

50. A

51. A

52. D

38.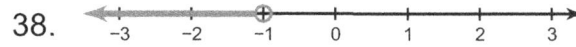

53. A

54. B

55. C

39.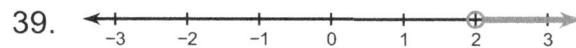

56. B

57. B

58. B

40.

www.math-knots.com | www.a4ace.com

Week 20		Week 20		Week 20		Week 21		Week 21	
59.	C	88.	B	117.	C	1.	D	30.	A
60.	D	89.	B	118.	A	2.	A	31.	D
61.	C	90.	D	119.	A	3.	A	32.	A
62.	A	91.	C	120.	C	4.	D	33.	B
63.	B	92.	A	121.	A	5.	D	34.	C
64.	B	93.	D	122.	D	6.	A	35.	B
65.	B	94.	C	123.	C	7.	C	36.	B
66.	A	95.	A	124.	B	8.	B	37.	A
67.	A	96.	A	125.	A	9.	C	38.	D
68.	B	97.	B	126.	D	10.	D	39.	A
69.	D	98.	C	127.	C	11.	D	40.	A
70.	D	99.	D	128.	D	12.	A	41.	A
71.	D	100.	A	129.	A	13.	A	42.	D
72.	A	101.	B	130.	D	14.	D	43.	B
73.	A	102.	D	131.	A	15.	D	44.	D
74.	C	103.	A	132.	B	16.	A	45.	C
75.	C	104.	B	133.	D	17.	C	46.	B
76.	B	105.	D	134.	C	18.	C	47.	C
77.	A	106.	D	135.	B	19.	C	48.	C
78.	A	107.	C	136.	A	20.	D	49.	C
79.	D	108.	A	137.	C	21.	C	50.	B
80.	C	109.	B	138.	B	22.	A	51.	B
81.	D	110.	A	139.	B	23.	D	52.	C
82.	C	111.	D	140.	D	24.	D	53.	D
83.	D	112.	D	141.	B	25.	A	54.	B
84.	A	113.	B	142.	C	26.	C	55.	B
85.	D	114.	C	143.	D	27.	A	56.	D
86.	C	115.	D	144.	C	28.	C	57.	A
87.	B	116.	C			29.	B	58.	D

Week 21		Week 21		Week 21		Week 22	
59.	D	88.	C	117.	A	1.	A
60.	B	89.	B	118.	D	2.	C
61.	A	90.	C	119.	B	3.	D
62.	A	91.	B	120.	B	4.	D
63.	A	92.	B	121.	A	5.	C
64.	C	93.	D			6.	D
65.	D	94.	A			7.	A
66.	B	95.	B			8.	B
67.	B	96.	B			9.	D
68.	B	97.	C			10.	C
69.	C	98.	B			11.	A
70.	B	99.	D			12.	B
71.	D	100.	B			13.	A
72.	D	101.	B			14.	B
73.	C	102.	C			15.	A
74.	B	103.	D			16.	D
75.	C	104.	C			17.	B
76.	C	105.	B			18.	B
77.	B	106.	A			19.	$n \leq 0$
78.	B	107.	D			20.	$x \geq -2$
79.	C	108.	B			21.	A
80.	B	109.	A			22.	A
81.	C	110.	B			23.	$x < -5$
82.	A	111.	B			24.	$p \geq 5$
83.	B	112.	A				
84.	D	113.	C				
85.	C	114.	D				
86.	A	115.	C				
87.	B	116.	C				

Week 22

25.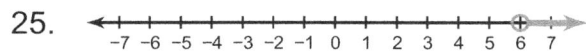

26.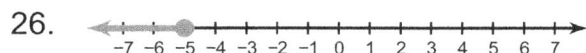

27.

28.

29.

30.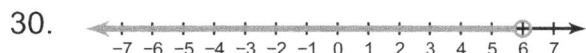

31.

32.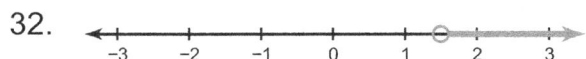

33.

34. D

35. B

Week 22

36. D

37.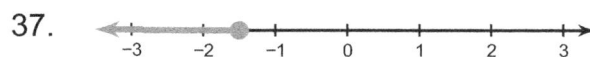

38. A

39. C

40. A

41. B

42. B

43. A

44. B

45. C

46. C

47. B

48. C

49. D

50. D

51. D

52. D

53. D

54. A

55. D

56. D

57. D

58. D

59. D

60. A

61. B

62. A

63. D

www.math-knots.com | www.a4ace.com

Week 22		**Week 23**		**Week 23**	
64.	B	1.	Yes	30.	A
65.	D	2.	Yes	31.	A
66.	C	3.	Yes	32.	D
67.	B	4.	No	33.	C
68.	D	5.	No	34.	B
69.	A	6.	Yes	35.	A
70.	D	7.	No	36.	D
71.	A	8.	Yes	37.	C
72.	D	9.	Yes	38.	A
73.	D	10.	No	39.	D
74.	B	11.	Yes	40.	A
75.	C	12.	No	41.	B
76.	A	13.	Yes	42.	D
77.	C	14.	Yes	43.	D
78.	C	15.	Yes	44.	A
		16.	Yes	45.	D
79.		17.	Yes	46.	B
		18.	Yes	47.	D
80.		19.	Yes	48.	A
		20.	Yes	49.	A
81.	D	21.	Yes	50.	A
82.	$x < 3$	22.	Yes	51.	B
		23.	No	52.	A
83.	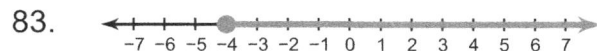	24.	No	53.	A
		25.	Yes	54.	B
84.		26.	A	55.	B
		27.	C	56.	A
		28.	A	57.	A
		29.	D	58.	A

www.math-knots.com | www.a4ace.com

Week 23

59.	B
60.	A
61.	D
62.	A
63.	A
64.	C
65.	A
66.	B
67.	C
68.	D
69.	C
70.	A
71.	D
72.	C
73.	D
74.	B
75.	D
76.	C
77.	D
78.	A
79.	A
80.	D
81.	B
82.	B
83.	A
84.	D
85.	C
86.	B
87.	B

Week 23

88.	C
89.	A
90.	B
91.	880 in
92.	1000 times
93.	28 ft.
94.	616 ft^2.
95.	154 inches^2
96.	132 in
97.	1386 inches^2.
98.	110 inches
99.	154 ft^2.
100.	10 inches.
101.	14 inches.
102.	Increased by four times
103.	3:4.
104.	25:36.
105.	154 inches^2.
106.	42 inches^2.
107.	3025 inches^2.
108.	176 ft^2.
109.	44 inches.
110.	346.5 inches^2.
111.	26.4 inches.
112.	55.44 inches^2.
113.	75.46 inches^2.
114.	98.56 inches^2.
115.	8.792 inches
116.	11.304 inches

Week 23

117.	15.7 inches.
118.	29.516 inches.
119.	16.328 inches.
120.	254.34 inches^2
121.	452.16 inches^2
122.	62.8 inches.
123.	25.12 inches.
124.	113.04 inches^2.
125.	6.3 inches.
126.	3.5 inches.
127.	5.6 inches.
128.	35 inches.
129.	10 inches.
130.	3.5 inches.
131.	4.9 inches.
132.	1.4 inches.
133.	15.4 inches.
134.	21 inches.
135.	30.144 inches.
136.	15.7 inches.
137.	12.56 inches
138.	43.96 inches.
139.	25.12 inches
140.	452.16 inches^2
141.	200.96 inches^2.
142.	94.985 inches^2
143.	706.5 inches^2
144.	615.44 inches^2.
145.	6 inches.

www.math-knots.com | www.a4ace.com

Week 23

146.	8 in
147.	4 in
148.	12 in
149.	12 in
150.	346.185 inches^2
151.	254.34 inches^2
152.	452.16 inches^2
153.	78.5 inches^2
154.	615.44 inches^2.
155.	21 in
156.	18 in
157.	24 in
158.	10 in
159.	28 in
160.	2 miles
161.	3,140 yards.
162.	33 yards.
163.	2352 revolutions.
164.	594 inches^2.
165.	392.5 inches^2.
166.	310.86 inches^2.
167.	706.5 inches^2.
168.	462 inches^2.
169.	$904.32.
170.	18.865 inches^2
171.	38.5 inches^2.
172.	55.44 inches^2
173.	5 : 1
174.	7 : 1

Week 23

175.	5 in
176.	16 in
177.	36 : 1.
178.	$866.64.
179.	71.5 inches^2.
180.	4 in
181.	6 in
182.	9 in
183.	21.98 cm.
184.	15.7 cm.
185.	25.12 cm.
186.	1760 m.
187.	154 m
188.	2750 m.
189.	19,800 m.
190.	379.94 cm^2
191.	530.66 cm^2.
192.	803.84 cm^2.
193.	1519.76 cm^2
194.	706.5 cm^2.
195.	314 cm^2.

Week 24

1.	1.26 sq.mi
2.	13.485 sq.ft
3.	7.65 sq.cm
4.	22.4 sq.ft
5.	33 sq.yd
6.	7.25 sq.yd
7.	32.8 sq.ft
8.	4.25 sq.in
9.	13.3 sq.yd
10.	16 sq.km
11.	144 sq.m
12.	30.25 sq.km
13.	36.5 sq.mi
14.	121 sq.cm
15.	132.25 sq.cm
16.	15.21 sq.ft
17.	4 sq.m
18.	2.89 sq.m
19.	42 sq.cm
20.	35.28 sq.mi
21.	10.89 sq.ft
22.	25 sq.m
23.	39.5 sq.in
24.	12.6 sq.in
25.	15 sq.in
26.	41.89 sq.m
27.	35.51 sq.in
28.	26.5 sq.mi
29.	16 sq.km

www.math-knots.com | www.a4ace.com

Week 24		Week 24		Week 24	
30.	20.54 sq.m	59.	25 π	88.	825 sq.yd
31.	14 sq.km	60.	144 π	89.	170.24 sq.cm
32.	40 sq.m	61.	12 π	90.	1314 sq.yd
33.	65.6 sq.mi	62.	24 π	91.	504 sq.yd
34.	91 sq.cm	63.	4 π	92.	138 sq.ft
35.	50 sq.mi	64.	16 π	93.	346.08 sq.cm
36.	30 sq.km	65.	6 π	94.	3780.6 sq.ft
37.	48 sq.yd	66.	10 π	95.	27.52 sq.yd
38.	9 sq.ft	67.	18 π	96.	55.04 sq.ft
39.	15.96 sq.m	68.	20 π	97.	580 sq.cm
40.	34.8 sq.m	69.	55.4 sq.cm	98.	42 sq.ft
41.	16.77 sq.mi	70.	14 π	99.	128 sq.units
42.	46.74 sq.in	71.	22 π	100.	265 sq.cm
43.	58.5 sq.km	72.	186.3 sq.cm	101.	55 sq.m
44.	8 sq.ft	73.	28.3 sq.ft	102.	75 sq.ft
45.	39.2 sq.m	74.	120.8 sq.yd	103.	23.2 sq.ft
46.	11 sq.m	75.	37.7 km	104.	52 sq.m
47.	49.2 sq.m	76.	21.2 sq.in	105.	27 sq.units
48.	11.52 sq.m	77.	44 cm	106.	51 sq.units
49.	36.48 sq.km	78.	33.9 yd	107.	27 sq.units
50.	36 π	79.	25.1 km	108.	28.5 sq.units
51.	4 π	80.	31.4 mi	109.	21 sq.units
52.	29.4 sq.in	81.	276 sq.m	110.	560 units
53.	9 π	82.	787.5 sq.cm	111.	59.12 m
54.	100 π	83.	520 sq.mm	112.	80 ft
55.	64 π	84.	627 sq.m	113.	74 cm
56.	49 π	85.	150 sq.m	114.	a) 400.96 m
57.	81 π	86.	344.52 sq.cm		b) 463.9 m
58.	121 π	87.	164.625 sq.cm		c) 62.8 m

Week 24		Week 25		Week 25		Week 25	
115.	113.04 m	1.	D	30.	D	59.	B
116.	100.48 m	2.	B	31.	A	60.	A
117.	43.96 cm	3.	C	32.	B	61.	D
118.	31.4 in	4.	D	33.	C	62.	A
119.	50.24 cm	5.	A	34.	D	63.	B
120.	56.52 cm	6.	A	35.	D	64.	C
121.	19.625 cm	7.	B	36.	C	65.	C
122.	62.8 m	8.	B	37.	C	66.	A
123.	113.04 ft	9.	C	38.	A	67.	C
124.	628 ft	10.	A	39.	C	68.	A
125.	1.91 cm	11.	A	40.	B	69.	B
126.	28.26 cm	12.	A	41.	C	70.	D
127.	3846.5 in	13.	D	42.	D	71.	D
128.	125286 sq. m	14.	A	43.	B	72.	C
129.	197.82 m	15.	D	44.	B	73.	B
130.	1884 m	16.	C	45.	A	74.	B
131.	50.24 cm	17.	B	46.	D	75.	D
		18.	D	47.	A	76.	D
		19.	A	48.	C	77.	A
		20.	B	49.	B	78.	B
		21.	A	50.	B	79.	A
		22.	B	51.	A	80.	C
		23.	A	52.	D	81.	C
		24.	B	53.	C	82.	A
		25.	D	54.	B	83.	D
		26.	D	55.	D	84.	D
		27.	A	56.	D	85.	D
		28.	A	57.	D	86.	A
		29.	B	58.	D	87.	A

Week 25		Week 25		Week 25	
88.	B	117.	C	144.	V = 8.54 cu.cm
89.	A	118.	C		SA = 80.45 sq.cm
90.	A	119.	C	145.	7.2 in
91.	A	120.	B	146.	9 in
92.	D	121.	C	147.	L = 13 in
93.	A	122.	C		SA = 422 sq.in
94.	D	123.	D	148.	3480 cu.in
95.	C	124.	C	149.	S = 4 m
96.	C	125.	A		SA = 96 sq.m
97.	A	126.	C	150.	1907.55 cu.in
98.	C	127.	B	151.	879.2 sq.in
99.	C	128.	C	152.	h = 40 ft
100.	D	129.	B	153.	375 sq.ft
101.	A	130.	B	154.	8 in
102.	D	131.	D	155.	L = 249.311
103.	D	132.	D		P = 1318
104.	C	133.	C		SA = 172023.9 sq.ft
105.	D	134.	D		
106.	A	135.	A		
107.	A	136.	A		
108.	A	137.	B		
109.	B	138.	C		
110.	C	139.	B		
111.	B	140.	D		
112.	D	141.	190.76 cu.cm		
113.	A	142.	1158.66 sq.in		
114.	B	143.	V = 4.71 cu.in		
115.	C		SA = 14.44 sq.in		
116.	D	144.	V = 4.71 cu.in		

Week 26		Week 26		Week 26		Week 26		Week 26	
1.	B	30.	B	59.	C	88.	B	117.	D
2.	D	31.	A	60.	B	89.	B	118.	B
3.	B	32.	D	61.	D	90.	A	119.	D
4.	C	33.	C	62.	B	91.	C	120.	A
5.	D	34.	D	63.	A	92.	D		
6.	A	35.	D	64.	A	93.	D		
7.	B	36.	D	65.	C	94.	B		
8.	C	37.	B	66.	A	95.	A		
9.	B	38.	A	67.	B	96.	D		
10.	D	39.	D	68.	D	97.	D		
11.	C	40.	B	69.	D	98.	B		
12.	C	41.	C	70.	A	99.	B		
13.	C	42.	C	71.	A	100.	A		
14.	D	43.	C	72.	C	101.	B		
15.	C	44.	C	73.	A	102.	A		
16.	D	45.	A	74.	B	103.	A		
17.	D	46.	D	75.	A	104.	A		
18.	C	47.	B	76.	C	105.	D		
19.	A	48.	D	77.	C	106.	A		
20.	D	49.	A	78.	D	107.	A		
21.	C	50.	D	79.	A	108.	B		
22.	D	51.	D	80.	B	109.	D		
23.	C	52.	B	81.	D	110.	C		
24.	B	53.	D	82.	B	111.	D		
25.	C	54.	C	83.	C	112.	C		
26.	C	55.	B	84.	A	113.	B		
27.	B	56.	D	85.	D	114.	D		
28.	C	57.	A	86.	D	115.	B		
29.	D	58.	D	87.	B	116.	C		

Week 27

1.	C
2.	D
3.	D
4.	B
5.	A
6.	D
7.	D
8.	B
9.	B
10.	A
11.	B
12.	A
13.	A
14.	A
15.	D
16.	A
17.	A
18.	B
19.	D
20.	C
21.	D
22.	C
23.	B
24.	D
25.	B
26.	C
27.	D
28.	B
29.	D

Week 27

30.	A
31.	angle
32.	vertex
33.	O
34.	Protractor
35.	degree
36.	Right angle
37.	acute
38.	$\angle$ DOC
39.	obtuse
40.	$\angle$ AOC
41.	90^0
42.	180^0
43.	60^0
44.	115^0
45.	$\angle x = 52^0$
46.	$\angle a = 115^0$
	$\angle b = 65^0$
	$\angle c = 115^0$
47.	$\angle x = 23^0$
	$\angle y = 90^0$
48.	$\angle t = 107^0$
49.	$\angle u = 36^0$
	$\angle v = 144^0$
	$\angle w = 36^0$
50.	$\angle d = 36^0$
51.	$\angle j = 100^0$
	$\angle k = 100^0$
	$\angle I = 80^0$

Week 27

52.	$\angle m = 52^0$
53.	$\angle p = 60^0$
	$\angle q = 30^0$
	$\angle r = 60^0$
54.	$\angle MTN = 30^0$
55.	$\angle MTP = 90^0$
56.	$\angle NTQ = 50^0$
57.	$\angle PTQ = 30^0$
58.	$\angle QTR = 35^0$
59.	$\angle RTS = 25^0$
60.	$\angle QTS = 60^0$
61.	$\angle OTR = 100^0$
62.	$\angle OTQ = 65^0$
63.	$\angle NTO = 25^0$
64.	$\angle NTQ = 90^0$
65.	$\angle MTO = 55^0$
66.	$\angle PTS = 90^0$
67.	$\angle MTS = 90^0$
68.	$\angle QTO = 65^0$
69.	$\angle NTR = 125^0$
70.	$\angle PTR = 65^0$

www.math-knots.com | www.a4ace.com

Grade 7

	Week 28		Week 28		Week 28		Week 28
1.	No	30.	No	59.	21^0	88.	77^0
2.	Yes	31.	Yes	60.	38^0	89.	30^0
3.	No	32.	No	61.	46^0	90.	74^0
4.	Yes	33.	No	62.	51^0	91.	96^0
5.	No	34.	No	63.	30^0	92.	111^0
6.	No	35.	Yes	64.	54^0	93.	151^0
7.	Yes	36.	No	65.	29^0	94.	
8.	Yes	37.	No	66.	66^0		
9.	Yes	38.	Yes	67.	45^0		
10.	No	39.	No	68.	41^0		
11.	Yes	40.	No	69.	67^0	95.	
12.	Yes	41.	Yes	70.	68^0		
13.	Yes	42.	Yes	71.	9^0		
14.	NO	43.	10^0	72.	151^0		
15.	Yes	44.	31^0	73.	33^0	96.	
16.	No	45.	30^0	74.	16^0		
17.	Yes	46.	33^0	75.	56^0		
18.	Yes	47.	47^0	76.	13^0		
19.	Yes	48.	63^0	77.	20^0	97.	
20.	Yes	49.	64^0	78.	62^0		
21.	No	50.	70^0	79.	22^0		
22.	Yes	51.	65^0	80.	45^0		
23.	Yes	52.	42^0	81.	58^0	98.	
24.	Yes	53.	35^0	82.	108^0		
25.	Yes	54.	22^0	83.	14^0		
26.	Yes	55.	50^0	84.	121^0		
27.	No	56.	56^0	85.	87^0	99.	
28.	No	57.	25^0	86.	55^0		
29.	Yes	58.	33^0	87.	85^0		

94.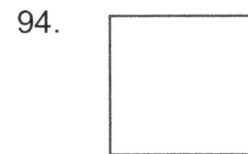

95.

96.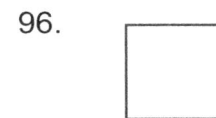

97.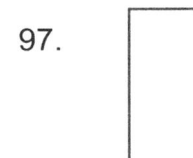

98.

99.

       www.math-knots.com | www.a4ace.com

Grade 7

Week 28

100.

101.

102.

103.

104.

105.

106.

Week 28

107.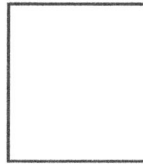

108.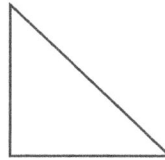

109.

110.

111.

112.

113.

Week 28

114.

115.

116.

117.

118.

119.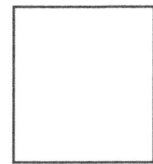

120.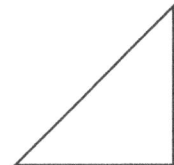

Week 29		Week 29		Week 29		Week 30	
1.	∟A = 120	15.	∟A = 44	42.	39^0	1.	C
	∟B = 60		∟B = 44	43.	27^0	2.	D
2.	∟X = 141	16.	∟X = 23	44.	130^0	3.	C
	∟Y = 141		∟Y = 157	45.	22^0	4.	D
3.	∟A = 153	17.	a = 10 & b = 3	46.	30^0	5.	D
	∟B = 153	18.	a = 2 & b = 3	47.	108^0	6.	D
4.	∟X = 130	19.	a = 8 & b = 3	48.	135^0	7.	A
	∟Y = 50	20.	a = 6 & b = 2	49.	80^0	8.	B
5.	∟A = 30	21.	a = 9 & b = 4	50.	82^0	9.	B
	∟B = 150	22.	a = 8 & b = 5	51.	20^0	10.	A
6.	∟X = 72	23.	a = 6 & b = 3	52.	49^0	11.	C
	∟Y = 72	24.	a = 2 & b = 5	53.	157^0	12.	A
7.	∟A = 135	25.	a = 7 & b = 7	54.	37^0	13.	B
	∟B = 45	26.	a = 6 & b = 3	55.	91^0	14.	C
8.	∟X = 80	27.	a = 6 & b = 3	56.	43^0	15.	A
	∟Y = 100	28.	a = 4 & b = 10	57.	33^0	16.	A
9.	∟A = 160	29.	a = 6 & b = 2	58.	136^0	17.	A
	∟B = 160	30.	a = 10 & b = 6	59.	157^0	18.	C
10.	∟X = 131	31.	a = 8 & b = 9	60.	85^0	19.	A
	∟Y = 131	32.	a = 6 & b = 7	61.	95^0	20.	C
11.	∟A = 23	33.	a = 3 & b = 4	62.	159^0	21.	D
	∟B = 157	34.	a = 8 & b = 2	63.	152^0	22.	A
12.	∟X = 143	35.	a = 4 & b = 10	64.	137^0	23.	C
	∟Y = 143	36.	a = 9 & b = 2	65.	55^0	24.	A
13.	∟A = 43	37.	a = 6 & b = 3	66.	81^0	25.	B
	∟B = 137	38.	a = 5 & b = 6	67.	117^0	26.	C
14.	∟X = 147	39.	a = 9 & b = 2	68.	140^0	27.	A
	∟Y = 147	40.	a = 10 & b = 10	69.	107^0	28.	A
		41.	120^0	70.	103^0	29.	A

www.math-knots.com | www.a4ace.com

Week 30		Week 30		Week 30		Week 31		Week 31	
30.	B	59.	B	88.	A	1.	C	30.	C
31.	A	60.	D	89.	A	2.	D	31.	A
32.	C	61.	D	90.	B	3.	D	32.	C
33.	B	62.	A	91.	C	4.	C	33.	C
34.	B	63.	B	92.	A	5.	D	34.	A
35.	B	64.	D	93.	B	6.	A	35.	A
36.	A	65.	D	94.	D	7.	C	36.	B
37.	C	66.	D			8.	B	37.	C
38.	A	67.	A			9.	D	38.	D
39.	D	68.	A			10.	D	39.	B
40.	B	69.	B			11.	D	40.	D
41.	B	70.	A			12.	A	41.	A
42.	A	71.	A			13.	B	42.	C
43.	D	72.	C			14.	B	43.	A
44.	D	73.	B			15.	A	44.	C
45.	C	74.	B			16.	B	45.	B
46.	C	75.	D			17.	C	46.	B
47.	D	76.	A			18.	C	47.	B
48.	D	77.	C			19.	D	48.	B
49.	A	78.	D			20.	D	49.	C
50.	B	79.	B			21.	A	50.	D
51.	A	80.	B			22.	A	51.	D
52.	A	81.	B			23.	C	52.	C
53.	A	82.	B			24.	A	53.	A
54.	B	83.	D			25.	D	54.	A
55.	C	84.	D			26.	D	55.	D
56.	C	85.	D			27.	B	56.	D
57.	A	86.	A			28.	D	57.	A
58.	C	87.	A			29.	A	58.	A

www.math-knots.com | www.a4ace.com

Week 31		Week 31		Week 32		Week 32		Week 32	
59.	C	88.	D	1.	B	30.	C	59.	B
60.	C	89.	B	2.	B	31.	D	60.	B
61.	B	90.	D	3.	C	32.	C	61.	B
62.	B	91.	D	4.	C	33.	C	62.	D
63.	C	92.	D	5.	B	34.	B	63.	A
64.	C	93.	D	6.	A	35.	A	64.	D
65.	A	94.	C	7.	A	36.	D	65.	D
66.	D	95.	B	8.	A	37.	D	66.	A
67.	D	96.	C	9.	C	38.	B	67.	B
68.	C	97.	D	10.	D	39.	A	68.	B
69.	A	98.	B	11.	B	40.	B	69.	D
70.	A	99.	A	12.	A	41.	C	70.	B
71.	B	100.	B	13.	D	42.	B	71.	Yes
72.	C	101.	C	14.	C	43.	B	72.	No
73.	A			15.	C	44.	D	73.	No
74.	A			16.	C	45.	C	74.	No
75.	B			17.	D	46.	C	75.	Yes
76.	A			18.	A	47.	D	76.	D
77.	A			19.	C	48.	D	77.	A
78.	D			20.	C	49.	B	78.	B
79.	C			21.	A	50.	A	79.	A
80.	A			22.	C	51.	D	80.	D
81.	A			23.	C	52.	A	81.	D
82.	A			24.	D	53.	D	82.	B
83.	D			25.	A	54.	D	83.	A
84.	B			26.	A	55.	D	84.	D
85.	D			27.	A	56.	C	85.	589.3 sq.mi
86.	D			28.	A	57.	A	86.	C
87.	A			29.	B	58.	A	87.	A

www.math-knots.com | www.a4ace.com

Week 32		Week 32		Week 32		Week 33	
88.	D	117.	A	146.	A	1.	C
89.	113 sq.in	118.	C	147.	C	2.	C
		119.	A	148.	D	3.	C
90.	A	120.	B	149.	C	4.	D
91.	D	121.	D	150.	C		
92.	C	122.	D	151.	D	5.	B
93.	A	123.	B	152.	C	6.	D
94.	A	124.	B	153.	C	7.	D
95.	B	125.	B	154.	B	8.	D
96.	B	126.	B	155.	A	9.	D
97.	D	127.	B	156.	A		
98.	A	128.	D	157.	D	10.	C
99.	B	129.	D	158.	C	11.	B
100.	C	130.	C	159.	C	12.	A
101.	A	131.	A	160.	C		
102.	B	132.	A	161.	D		
103.	C	133.	D	162.	A		
104.	D	134.	B	163.	A		
105.	C	135.	A	164.	C		
106.	D	136.	A	165.	A		
107.	D	137.	A	166.	D		
108.	D	138.	C	167.	D		
109.	B	139.	C	168.	A		
110.	A	140.	C	169.	D		
111.	A	141.	A	170.	C		
112.	B	142.	D	171.	D		
113.	A	143.	A	172.	A		
114.	A	144.	B	173.	B		
115.	D	145.	C	174.	A		
116.	C						

13. Because of the very small discrepancy in the quantities it is unlikely any deduction can be made about the number of nails,screws or bolts in the bucket.

14. Based on the information presented he should keep more Brownies than cookies or cupcakes

15. Based on the information presented and the small samples gathered it is impossible to make any meaningful assumptions.

16. Based on the information presented he should keep more cupcakes than cookies or brownies.

17. Based on the information presented and the small samples gathered it is impossible to make any meaningful assumptions.

18. Based on the information presented

Week 33				Week 33		Week 33		Week 33	
18.	Based on the information presented more boys had cavities.			41.	D	66.	C	92.	C
				42.	B	67.	B	93.	A
19.	Based on the information presented there will be 27% more non-fiction books donated.			43.	C	68.	D	94.	D
				44.	B	69.	D	95.	C
20.	Based on the information presented Candidate A will have 14% more votes			45.	A	70.	D	96.	C
				46.	B	71.	D	97.	C
21.	Based on the information presented and the small samples gathered it is impossible to make any meaningfu assumptions.			47.	C	72.	B	98.	C
				48.	D	73.	A	99.	B
22.	A			49.	D	74.	D	100.	C
23.	D			50.	B	75.	A		
24.	D			51.	A	76.	D		
25.	B			52.	D	77.	D		
26.	A			53.	C	78.	A		
27.	C			54.	C	79.	C		
28.	B			55.	A	80.	B		
29.	A			56.	B	81.	D		
30.	B			57.	A	82.	A		
31.	B			58.	B	83.	B		
32.	A			59.	B	84.	D		
33.	B			60.	D	85.	C		
34.	C			61.	B	86.	B		
35.	C			62.	B	87.	C		
36.	B			63.	D	88.	C		
37.	C			64.	A	89.	A		
38.	A			65.	D	90.	C		
39.	D					91.	A		
40.	B								

Grade 7

Vol 2
Answer
Key

Week 34

1. $\frac{1}{6}$
2. $\frac{5}{12}$
3. $\frac{3}{4}$
4. $\frac{5}{12}$
5. $\frac{1}{12}$
6. $\frac{1}{2}$
7. $\frac{7}{12}$
8. $\frac{1}{3}$
9. $\frac{1}{3}$
10. 1
11. $\frac{3}{4}$
12. $\frac{2}{3}$
13. $\frac{2}{3}$
14. $\frac{5}{6}$
15. $\frac{1}{18}$
16. $\frac{5}{6}$
17. 1
18. $\frac{1}{2}$
19. $\frac{1}{12}$
20. $\frac{11}{12}$

Week 34

21. $\frac{5}{36}$
22. $\frac{1}{2}$
23. $\frac{8}{31}$
24. $\frac{9}{31}$
25. $\frac{29}{31}$
26. $\frac{22}{31}$
27. $\frac{23}{31}$
28. $\frac{29}{31}$
29. $\frac{1}{6}$
30. $\frac{1}{6}$
31. $\frac{1}{2}$
32. $\frac{5}{6}$
33. $\frac{1}{3}$
34. $\frac{2}{3}$
35. No. There is only one vowel (U)
36. $\frac{1}{12}$
37. $\frac{1}{9}$
38. $\frac{1}{36}$

Week 34

39. $\frac{1}{18}$
40. $\frac{1}{6}$
41. 1
42. $\frac{21}{25}$
43. $\frac{3}{64}$
44. $\frac{3}{64}$
45. $\frac{1}{16}$
46. $\frac{1}{64}$
47. $\frac{1}{16}$
48. $\frac{3}{24}$
49. $\frac{1}{16}$
50. $\frac{3}{128}$
51. $\frac{3}{56}$
52. $\frac{1}{14}$
53. $\frac{1}{28}$
54. $\frac{1}{28}$
55. $\frac{3}{56}$
56. $\frac{3}{28}$
57. 0
58. $\frac{1}{28}$

Week 34

59. Independent
60. Dependent
61. Independent
62. Independent
63. Independent
64. $\frac{9}{25}$
65. $\frac{1}{14}$
66. $\frac{1}{8}$
67. $\frac{1}{17}$
68. $\frac{1}{84}$
69. $\frac{1}{8}$
70. $\frac{5}{8}$
71. 0
72. $\frac{1}{64}$
73. $\frac{7}{552}$
74. $\frac{5}{46}$
75. $\frac{7}{92}$
76. $\frac{1}{92}$
77. $\frac{4}{25}$
78. $\frac{1}{10}$
79. $\frac{12}{19}$

www.math-knots.com | www.a4ace.com

Week 34		Week 35		Week 35		Week 35	
80.	$\frac{1}{4}$	1.	57	30.	25	59.	16
81.	$\frac{13}{400}$	2.	45	31.	23	60.	38
		3.	85	32.	8	61.	5.8
82.	$\frac{3}{26} \cdot \frac{16}{25}$	4.	22	33.	17	62.	C
		5.	33	34.	18	63.	B
83.	$\frac{1}{8}$	6.	68	35.	6	64.	C
84.	$\frac{25}{100} \cdot \frac{37}{100}$	7.	80	36.	42	65.	B
		8.	60	37.	44	66.	B
85.	$\frac{2}{9}$	9.	76	38.	5	67.	A
86.	$\frac{1}{169}$	10.	63	39.	12	68.	C
		11.	26	40.	12	69.	C
87.	$\frac{1}{169}$	12.	91	41.	5	70.	B
88.	$\frac{13}{51}$	13.	25	42.	17	71.	A
		14.	45	43.	15	72.	A
89.	$\frac{1}{4}$	15.	9	44.	8	73.	D
90.	$\frac{4}{15}$	16.	18	45.	11	74.	B
		17.	36	46.	9	75.	A
91.	$\frac{4}{25}$	18.	70	47.	9	76.	B
92.	$\frac{1}{2704}$	19.	24	48.	19	77.	D
		20.	24	49.	24	78.	D
93.	$\frac{1}{221}$	21.	16	50.	10	79.	B
94.	$\frac{1}{12}$	22.	28	51.	37	80.	B
		23.	11	52.	40	81.	B
95.	$\frac{1}{12}$	24.	15	53.	94	82.	B
		25.	12	54.	40	83.	B
96.	$\frac{2}{50}$	26.	5	55.	23	84.	C
		27.	21	56.	13	85.	A
		28.	19	57.	12	86.	A
		29.	12	58.	18	87.	C

www.math-knots.com | www.a4ace.com

Week 36		Week 36		Week 36	
1.	C	30.	8.35	59.	4
2.	C	31.	6	60.	3
3.	A	32.	7.5	61.	6
4.	D	33.	9.25	62.	3
5.	D	34.	1.75	63.	5
6.	B	35.	8	64.	5
7.	34.9	36.	7	65.	5
8.	32.55	37.	7.06	66.	6
9.	32.11	38.	4.5	67.	3.5
10.	27.9	39.	6.25	68.	6.5
11.	27.05	40.	8	69.	3
12.	35.95	41.	1.75		
13.	8.9	42.	6		
14.	17,900	43.	5.8		
15.	14,600	44.	4.56		
16.	17,616.67	45.	7		
17.	34,450	46.	4		
18.	9,950	47.	6.125		
19.	22,150	48.	2.125		
20.	12,200	49.	13		
21.	7	50.	17		
22.	6.5	51.	16.24		
23.	5.94	52.	9		
24.	3	53.	13		
25.	5	54.	19		
26.	7	55.	6		
27.	2	56.	5		
28.	8	57.	5		
29.	8	58.	4.88		

70.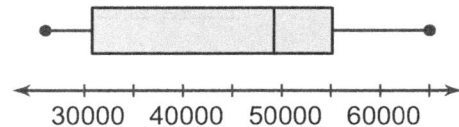

71.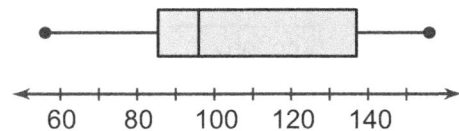

72.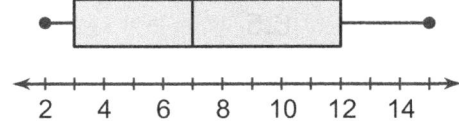

73.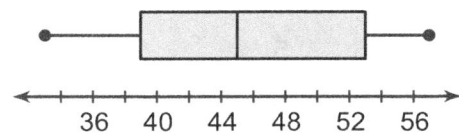

74.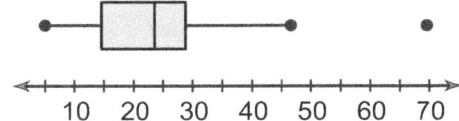

               www.math-knots.com | www.a4ace.com

Week 36

75.

76.

77.

78.

79.

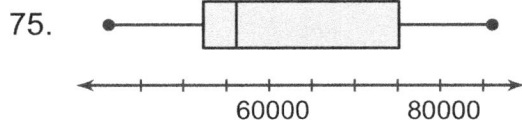

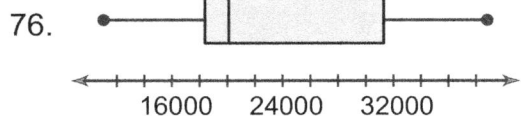

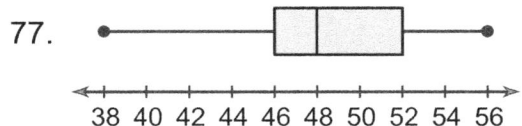

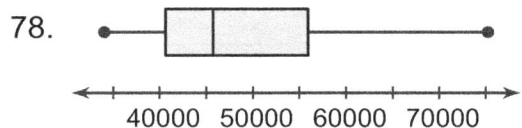

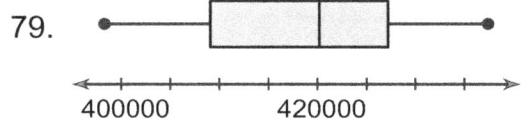

80.	3
81.	6
82.	6.5
83.	10
84.	3.5
85.	8.5
86.	5
87.	43
88.	46
89.	46.75
90.	12
91.	43

Week 36

92.	50.5
93.	7.5
94.	124
95.	94.5
96.	93.88
97.	114
98.	62
99.	124
100.	62
101.	8
102.	8
103.	8.94
104.	18
105.	5.5
106.	11.5
107.	6
108.	2
109.	3
110.	3.06
111.	5
112.	2
113.	4
114.	2
115.	2
116.	2
117.	2.5
118.	3
119.	2
120.	3.5

Week 36

121.	1.5
122.	17 & 18
123.	16
124.	16.2
125.	9
126.	14
127.	18
128.	4
129.	1,525
130.	1,492.5
131.	1,408.44
132.	830
133.	1,182.5
134.	1,637.5
135.	455
136.	3
137.	3
138.	2.88
139.	5
140.	2
141.	3
142.	1
143.	15
144.	16
145.	16.88
146.	9
147.	15
148.	20
149.	5

www.math-knots.com | www.a4ace.com

Week 36		Week 36		Week 36		Week 36	
150.	7	179.	70	208.	7.47	237.	20,550
151.	7	180.	70	209.	3.25	238.	8,750
152.	6.24	181.	19	210.	6.75	239.	20,075
153.	3	182.	66.5	211.	8.375	240.	11,325
154.	5.5	183.	74	212.	1.625	241.	5
155.	7	184.	7.5	213.	5	242.	5
156.	1.5	185.	6 & 7	214.	5	243.	5.41
157.	75	186.	6	215.	5.69	244.	9
158.	72.5	187.	5.94	216.	9	245.	3
159.	71.13	188.	3	217.	3.5	246.	7.5
160.	16	189.	5	218.	7.5	247.	4.5
161.	68.5	190.	7	219.	4	248.	7
162.	75	191.	2	220.	5	249.	7
163.	6.5	192.	179	221.	5	250.	5.73
164.	7.5	193.	177.5	222.	5.65	251.	6
165.	8	194.	176.88	223.	7	252.	4
166.	8.4	195.	13	224.	4	253.	7
167.	4.5	196.	175	225.	7	254.	3
168.	7.5	197.	179	226.	3	255.	5
169.	10	198.	4	227.	9	256.	6
170.	2.5	199.	7	228.	8	257.	6.25
171.	52	200.	6	229.	7.94	258.	8
172.	50	201.	6	230.	4.5	259.	5
173.	49.06	202.	3	231.	6.75	260.	7.5
174.	16	203.	5	232.	9	261.	2.5
175.	45	204.	7	233.	2.25	262.	7
176.	52	205.	2	234.	8,750	263.	6
177.	7	206.	6 & 7	235.	13,675	264.	5.75
178.	70	207.	7.25	236.	15,040.63	265.	3

www.math-knots.com | www.a4ace.com

Week 36		Week 36		Week 36		Week 36	
266.	5	295.	9	324.	1	353.	7
267.	7	296.	2	325.	2	354.	6.5
268.	2	297.	7	326.	3.5	355.	6
269.	6.5 & 7	298.	6	327.	4.94	356.	3
270.	6.75	299.	5.75	328.	16	357.	5
271.	6.7	300.	3	329.	2	358.	7
272.	2.25	301.	4.5	330.	8	359.	2
273.	6.25	302.	7	331.	6	360.	5
274.	7.25	303.	2.5	332.	7	361.	10.5
275.	1	304.	13	333.	6	362.	12.19
276.	7	305.	16	334.	6	363.	21
277.	8	306.	15.63	335.	10	364.	9
278.	8.25	307.	10	336.	3.5	365.	9
279.	7	308.	13	337.	8	366.	9.8
280.	7	309.	17.5	338.	4.5	367.	5
281.	9	310.	4.5	339.	16	368.	9
282.	2	311.	14 & 15	340.	16	369.	9
283.	46 & 50	312.	15	341.	15.88	370.	9.69
284.	46	313.	15.12	342.	7	371.	5
285.	47.73	314.	8	343.	14.5	372.	8 & 17
286.	21	315.	14	344.	17.5	373.	11.5
287.	43	316.	16.5	345.	3	374.	11.81
288.	53	317.	2.5	346.	2	375.	9
289.	10	318.	6	347.	2	376.	11 & 12
290.	9	319.	6	348.	2.94	377.	11
291.	8.5	320.	5.85	349.	4	378.	11.07
292.	8.18	321.	3	350.	2	379.	6
293.	4	322.	5.5	351.	3.5	380.	4
294.	7	323.	6.5	352.	1.5	381.	5

Week 36

382. 7.2

383. 20

384. 4

385. 5

386. 8.27

387. 20

388. 1.7

389. 1.4

390. 1.31

391. 1.4

392. 13 & 15

393. 14

394. 13.35

395. 14

396. 2

397. 2

398. 2.76

399. 4

427   www.math-knots.com | www.a4ace.com

428   www.math-knots.com | www.a4ace.com

Made in the USA
Las Vegas, NV
27 August 2024